Early Modern Prophecies in Transnational, National and Regional Contexts

Volume 1

Brill's Studies in Intellectual History

General Editor

Han van Ruler (*Erasmus University, Rotterdam*)

Founded by

Arjo Vanderjagt

Editorial Board

C.S. Celenza (*Johns Hopkins University, Baltimore*)
M. Colish (*Yale University, New Haven*) – J.I. Israel (*Institute for Advanced Study, Princeton*) – A. Koba (*University of Tokyo*) – M. Mugnai (*Scuola Normale Superiore, Pisa*) – W. Otten (*University of Chicago*)

VOLUME 324

Brill's Texts and Sources in Intellectual History

General Editor

Leen Spruit (*Radboud University, Nijmegen*)

Editorial Board

J. Lagrée (*Université de Rennes 1*)
U. Renz (*Universität Klagenfurt*)
A. Uhlmann (*University of Western Sydney*)

VOLUME 23/1

The titles published in this series are listed at *brill.com/btsi*

Early Modern Prophecies in Transnational, National and Regional Contexts

Volume 1: Continental Europe

Edited by

Lionel Laborie
Ariel Hessayon

BRILL

LEIDEN | BOSTON

Cover illustration: William Blake, 'Europe a Prophecy' (1794), plate 02

Library of Congress Cataloging-in-Publication Data

Names: Laborie, Lionel, editor. | Hessayon, Ariel, editor.
Title: Early modern prophecies in transnational, national and regional contexts / edited by Lionel Laborie, Ariel Hessayon.
Description: Leiden ; Boston : Brill, 2020. | Series: Brill's studies in intellectual history, 0920-8607 ; volume 324/1- | "This edited collection of primary sources originates from a major international conference on early modern prophecies, which we organised at Goldsmiths,University of London, in June 2014"–ECIP acknowledgements. | Includes bibliographical references and index. | Contents: v. 1. Continental Europe – v. 2. The Mediterranean world – v. 3. The British Isles.
Identifiers: LCCN 2020040926 (print) | LCCN 2020040927 (ebook) |
   ISBN 9789004442658 (v. 1 ; hardback) | ISBN 9789004442634 (v. 2 ; hardback) |
   ISBN 9789004442641 (v. 3 ; hardback) | ISBN 9789004342668 (hardback) |
   ISBN 9789004443631 (ebook)
Subjects: LCSH: Prophecy–Christianity–History–Sources.
Classification: LCC BR115.P8 E27 2020 (print) | LCC BR115.P8 (ebook) |
   DDC 231.7/4509015–dc23
LC record available at https://lccn.loc.gov/2020040926
LC ebook record available at https://lccn.loc.gov/2020040927

Typeface for the Latin, Greek, and Cyrillic scripts: "Brill". See and download: brill.com/brill-typeface.

ISSN 0920-8607
ISBN 978-90-04-34266-8 (hardback, set)
ISBN 978-90-04-44265-8 (hardback, vol. 1)
ISBN 978-90-04-44263-4 (hardback, vol. 2)
ISBN 978-90-04-44264-1 (hardback, vol. 3)
ISBN 978-90-04-44363-1 (e-book)

Copyright 2021 by Koninklijke Brill NV, Leiden, The Netherlands.
Koninklijke Brill NV incorporates the imprints Brill, Brill Hes & De Graaf, Brill Nijhoff, Brill Rodopi, Brill Sense, Hotei Publishing, mentis Verlag, Verlag Ferdinand Schöningh and Wilhelm Fink Verlag.
All rights reserved. No part of this publication may be reproduced, translated, stored in a retrieval system, or transmitted in any form or by any means, electronic, mechanical, photocopying, recording or otherwise, without prior written permission from the publisher. Requests for re-use and/or translations must be addressed to Koninklijke Brill NV via brill.com or copyright.com.

This book is printed on acid-free paper and produced in a sustainable manner.

Printed by Printforce, the Netherlands

Contents

Acknowledgements VII
Abbreviations VIII
Notes on Contributors IX

Introduction: Reformations, Prophecy and Eschatology 1
   Andreas Pečar and Damien Tricoire

1 Hussite Eschatological Texts (1412–1421): Introduction and Translations 23
   Martin Pjecha

2 Jacques Massard: Prophecy and the Harmony of Knowledge 84
   Kristine Wirts and Leslie Tuttle

3 Friedrich Breckling's *Paulus Redivivus* (1688) and *Catalogus Haereticorum* (c.1697–1703) 133
   Viktoria Franke

4 Huguenot Prophecies in Eighteenth-Century France 189
   Lionel Laborie

Bibliography 245
Index 264

Acknowledgements

This edited collection of primary sources originates from a major international conference on early modern prophecies, which we organised at Goldsmiths, University of London, in June 2014. The conference sought to reappraise the importance and impact of prophetic literature both across Europe and throughout the early modern period. It attracted nearly 100 speakers from 25 countries; an impressive achievement for what is usually regarded as a marginal subject.

The sheer diversity of the papers presented, together with their often transnational and interdisciplinary nature helped us demonstrate that prophets and prophecies have much to offer for the study of the early modern period. This collection therefore seeks to make rare prophetic and millenarian texts accessible to an international audience by presenting sources from all over Europe (broadly defined), and across the early modern period in English for the first time.

We are immensely grateful to our contributors who went through the trouble of transcribing and translating their primary source materials into modern, accessible English. This was no small task and we hope that the result is sufficient reward for their patience and effort. We are also greatly indebted to William Mitchell, currently PhD candidate in early modern history at the London School of Economics (LSE) for his assistance in checking and improving the quality of the English translations. Lastly, we would like to thank our publisher, Brill and especially our commissioning editor Arjan van Dijk, for believing in the value of such an unusual and indeed important project, as well as for supporting it since its inception.

Ariel Hessayon and Lionel Laborie

Abbreviations

ADH	Archives départementales de l'Hérault, Montpellier, France
AFSt	Archivs der Franckeschen Stiftungen, Halle, Germany
BPF	Bibliothèque du Protestantisme Français, Paris, France
FB Gotha	Forschungsbibliothek, Gotha, Germany
FRB	Josef Emler, Jan Gebauer, and Jaroslav Goll (eds), *Fontes Rerum Bohemicarum* 5 (Prague: 1893)
HK	Vavřinec z Březové, *Husitksá kronika; Píseň o vítězství u Domažlic*, trans. František Heřmanský and Jan Blahoslav Čapek (Prague: 1979)
Kaminsky, HR	Howard Kaminsky, *A History of the Hussite Revolution* (Berkeley: 1967)
LPL	Lambeth Palace Library, London, England
LSF	Library of the Society of Friends, London, England
ODNB	*Oxford Dictionary of National Biography*, online
Šmahel, HR	František Šmahel, *Husitská revoluce*, vols. 1–4 (Prague: 1995–1996)
StaBi Berlin	Staatsbibliothek, Berlin, Germany

Notes on Contributors

Viktoria Franke
is a researcher at the University of Halle-Wittenberg. She specialises in Dutch and European cultural history and her recent publications include *Dies- und jenseits der Grenze. Translokale Prozesse und ihre Einwirkung auf den deutsch-niederländischen Grenzraum* (2017). Her monograph on Friedrich Breckling (1629–1711) will appear in 2020. Her main areas of interest are Dutch-German cultural relations and the grey area between Pietism and the Enlightenment.

Lionel Laborie
is Assistant Professor of Early Modern History at Leiden University. His research concentrates on the cultural history of ideas and beliefs in early modern Europe, with a particular interest in religious dissenters, the Huguenot diaspora, radicalism and underground networks in the long eighteenth century. His monograph, *Enlightening Enthusiasm* (Manchester: 2015), explores the debate on prophecy and "religious madness" in early eighteenth-century English society and culture.

Andreas Pečar
is Professor of Early Modern History at the Martin-Luther-Universität Halle-Wittenberg. He has published on the court society of the imperial court of Vienna (*Die Ökonomie der Ehre*), on political Biblicism in Scotland and England in the 16th and 17th centuries (*Macht der Schrift*), on Frederick the Great as philosopher (*Die Masken des Königs*) and, together with Damien Tricoire, on our understanding of the Enlightenment (*Falsche Freunde*).

Martin Pjecha
is a doctoral candidate at the Central European University (Budapest) and a researcher at the Centre for Medieval Studies (Prague). He specialises on the radical Hussite movement, and questions relating to religio-political thought. His most recent publication is titled "Táborite apocalyptic violence and its intellectual inspirations (1410–1415)" *Bohemian Reformation and Religious Practice* 11 (2018). His main areas of interest include religious and political thought, revolutionary theory, terrorism and "New Religious Movements", religious persecution and violence, comparative religion, heresiology, and medieval/early-modern religion.

Damien Tricoire
is Professor of Early Modern History at the University of Trier. He specialises in early modern political, religious, intellectual and knowledge history, both in Europe and the colonial world. His recent publications include *Mit Gott rechnen* (2013; translated into French in 2018 as *La Vierge et le Roi*), *Falsche Freunde* (2014, with Andreas Pečar), and Der *koloniale Traum* (2018). His main areas of interest include the cultural and knowledge history of politics, the Catholic reformation, and the Enlightenment.

Leslie Tuttle
is Associate Professor of History at Louisiana State University in Baton Rouge. A specialist in the history of France in the seventeenth and eighteenth centuries, she is completing a book about changing explanations of dreaming during the Scientific Revolution and Enlightenment eras. Along with Ann Marie Plane, she edited *Dreams, Dreamers and Visions: The Early Modern Atlantic World* (Philadelphia: 2013).

Kristine Wirts
is Associate Professor of Early Modern European History at the University of Texas-Rio Grande Valley in Edinburg, TX. Wirts specialises in French religious culture during the seventeenth century and has authored a number of articles on early modern France. Her current book project covers the life of Jean Giraud, a Huguenot peddler, who fled his village of La Grave, France, for Vevey, Switzerland following the revocation of the Edict of Nantes.

Introduction: Reformations, Prophecy and Eschatology

Andreas Pečar and Damien Tricoire

Reformations and Eschatology

In 1419, thousands of people settled in a new city on a hill in southern Bohemia, which they named Tábor after the place where Jesus Christ not only showed his divinity to his disciples in the Bible, but where, according to tradition, he departed earth and ascended to Heaven. According to some commentators, Tábor would be the place where Christ would return to establish his thousand years kingdom and/or judge mankind. Taborites thought this event should be prepared. They sought to transform society in order to put into practice the biblical norms as they understood them. They established a theocracy where all differences between the estates were abolished, and even introduced initially community of goods, that is a form of proto-communism. Taborites devastated churches and monasteries in southern Bohemia and beyond, and had tremendous military success in the following years. They believed themselves to be the agents of God's wrath and endeavoured to create His kingdom with the sword. The established secular and clerical order was to be annihilated as part of the eschatological fight between Christ and the Antichrist.

How could such an eschatological, and even millenarian movement emerge in early fifteenth-century Europe? To be sure, eschatology was an integral part of Christianity for centuries. But that said, the forms and relevance of eschatological expectations had varied greatly across time and place, as well as between religious groups. In Western Christendom, between approximately 1100 and 1600, the idea that mankind was living in the last phase of its history may have become increasingly present. It was still forceful in the eighteenth century, especially in Protestantism. This had probably mainly to do with one central idea. A spectre was haunting Europe's clerical milieus: the spectre of church reform. In the view of ascetic-minded reformers, the visible church had become too worldly, and had barely anything left in common with the holy principles and the institutions that Jesus Christ had established.

Such a conviction was not necessarily heretical, and it was not linked from its inception with the belief that the end of times was near. In the 12th and 13th centuries, there was a widespread consciousness that a return to evangelical poverty was necessary. In the late 12th century, it led almost simultaneously to the creation of mendicant orders (of which the Franciscans and Dominicans were the most successful), that became major church institutions, to the foundation of beguinages, accepted by church authorities after some hesitations, and to the emergence of the so-called "Waldensianism", which was condemned as heretical. The "Waldensians", or rather, as they called themselves, the "paupers of Lyon" or "paupers of Christ" were a movement founded in Lyon around 1180. We know almost nothing about the founder Waldo (whose first name was perhaps Peter). He was a merchant in this thriving mercantile city at the confluence of the Rhône and Saône rivers, and gave up his wealth to imitate Jesus Christ. At first, the movement was not deemed heretical. But the "paupers of Christ" were not only laymen, but wished to remain so. Not only men, but also women preached the gospel, and they did so without any authorisation from church hierarchy. This led to the repression of the movement, which went gradually underground, especially around 1230, after the foundation of the inquisition. The teaching of the "paupers of Christ" departed more and more from those of the church. They held that sacraments administered by clerics living in sin were not valid (a position termed "donatism"), began to celebrate the Eucharist outside churches and without priests. The movement spread throughout France, Italy and the German-speaking world. Theologically speaking, it was diverse, but the "paupers of Christ" had some beliefs in common. They believed that the gospel was superior to any norm, that it was to be read in a literal manner, and that everyone was to imitate Christ and be poor. They rejected oaths and the belief in purgatory. They thought that church hierarchy was corrupted, and the sacraments it administered ineffective. Concerning the Eucharist, the "paupers of Lyon" had different teachings, but at least a significant part rejected the idea not only of transubstantiation (the transformation of the bread into the body of Christ by the priest), but also of the real presence of Christ in the Eucharist. They understood the Eucharist as a commemoration. As a consequence of persecution, the "paupers of Christ" developed more radical teachings. Furthermore, they ceased to try to convert the majority of the population. Rather they strove to maintain small communities persisting in the true faith despite all persecutions.[1]

From the late 12th century on, many reform-minded laymen and clerics were convinced that the church was corrupted. They created communities whose

---

[1] Gabriel Audisio, *Die Waldenser. Die Geschichte einer religiösen Bewegung* (Munich: 1996), 15–197.

members tried to imitate Christ. But they met with scepticism, or even with violent hostility. Hence the question they came to ask: how could such a moral decline in the church be explained? One possibility was eschatology (the teachings about the end of times). In the gospels and Saint Paul's letters, it is written that many will give up the true teaching in the period preceding the end of times. We know very little about eschatological teachings among the "paupers of Christ", but it seems that they understood themselves as the small flock of Israel keeping the true faith when all the rest had strayed from the true path, and this idea may have had eschatological undertones.[2] What is certain is that many reform-minded clerics of the 13th and 14th centuries who encountered strong resistance from the Church hierarchy, reached the conclusion that the end of times must be near. Something was rotten in the kingdom of Christ, and following the gospels and Saint Paul's letters, this could only be the work of the great deceiver of mankind, the Antichrist.

To be sure, before the beginning of the Bohemian Reformation in the fifteenth century, only a few medieval authors interpreted the book of Revelation as a key to events happening or to come. Since Augustine, the dominant interpretation of this book had been that it describes the establishment of the Church on earth. It was thus about past, not future. But we have to remember that in Christianity, the book of Revelation was one source among others of eschatological expectations. The Antichrist was known from the Gospels and Saint Paul's letters, and the prophecies of the Old Testament were also major sources of knowledge of what was to come in the period before the end of times. Thus, the interpretation of the book of Revelation as a description of past events did not preclude the flourishing of varied expectations that the Latter Days were coming and with them some kind of millennium. For example, according to Joachim of Fiore (around 1130/35–1202), there would soon come a new and final epoch in the history of the Church after the defeat of the Antichrist. This "third age of the Holy Spirit" would come after the reform of the Church. It was to be a period of peace and contemplation for the Church. Joachim propagated two ideas that would have an enormous influence on subsequent Christian apocalypticism. Before the 12th century, it was usually expected that the Antichrist would be a Jew and that the Jews would constitute his followers in the Latter Days, even though some authors expected that the Jews (or at least some of them) would convert to Christianity. By contrast, Joachim advanced the idea that the Antichrist would be a Christian (either a

---

2 Amedeo Molnár, *Die Waldenser. Geschichte und europäisches Ausmaß einer Ketzerbewegung* (Berlin: 1980), 76, 196, 389.

tyrannical secular ruler or a pope). Second, Joachim held that Jews would convert to Christianity in the end times. Following Saint Paul, he believed that everybody should be saved.[3]

Other popular prophecies about the Latter Days combined the Antichrist story with narratives about the Last Emperor or Last King, which were vaguely inspired by the prophetic books of the Old Testament announcing the coming of a messianic king in the Last Days. They originated in early-medieval Eastern Christianity, and quickly made their way into Western Europe.[4] From the 13th century into the seventeenth century, a great range of earthly rulers were presented as the Last Emperor who would establish a period of peace, justice and prosperity. Sometimes, the Last Emperor narrative was used by men claiming to be a "hidden" ruler who revealed himself in order to restore peace and justice. In the 13th century, this was the case of the many "false Frederics" who claimed to be Emperor Frederic II. Some of Joachim's followers, including the French Spiritual Franciscans Pierre de Jean Olivi (Peter John Olivi, 1247/48–1296/98) and Jean de Roquetaillade (John of Rupescissa; *fl.*1310–1366), as well as other mendicant monks, mixed such Last Emperor prophecies with Joachim's ideas about the coming Age of the Holy Spirit.[5] In the late 16th and 17th centuries, similar beliefs were present in the Iberian peninsula and the Iberian colonies of the new world. In Portugal and its colonies, especially, prophecies about the return of King Sebastian (1557–1578) circulated.[6]

---

3   Gian Luca Potestà, "Apocalittica e politica in Gioacchino da Fiore," in *Endzeiten. Eschatologie in den monotheistischen Weltreligionen*, ed. Felicitas Schmieder and Wolfram Brandes (Berlin: 2008), 231–248; Pavlína Cermanová, "Die Erzählung vom Antichrist und seine Funktion in der religiösen und politischen Imagination im luxemburgischen Böhmen," in *Antichrist—Konstruktionen von Feindbildern*, ed. Felicitas Schmieder and Wolfram Brandes (Berlin: 2010), 159–178.
4   Paul J. Alexander, "The Diffusion of Byzantine Apocalypses in the Medieval West and the Beginnings of Joachimism," in *Prophecy and Millenarianism*, ed. Ann Williams (Harlow: 1980), 53–106. For an English translation of one of these major prophecies see Pseudo-Methodius, *Apocalypse—An Alexandrian World Chronicle*, ed. and trans. Benjamin Garstadt (Cambridge, M.A.: 2012).
5   Hannes Möhring, *Der Weltkaiser der Endzeit. Entstehung, Wandel und Wirkung einer tausendjährigen Weissagung* (Stuttgart: 2000); Hannes Möhring, "Die Weissagungen über einen Kaiser Friedrich am Ende der Zeiten," in *Endzeiten*, 201–214; Felicitas Schmieder, "Prophetische Propaganda in der Politik des 14. Jahrhunderts: Johannes von Rupescissa," in *Endzeiten*, 249–260; Pavlína Cermanová, "Die Erzählung vom Antichrist und seine Funktion in der religiösen und politischen Imagination im luxemburgischen Böhmen," in *Antichrist*, 159–178; Rebekka Voß, *Umstrittene Erlöser. Politik, Ideologie und jüdisch-christlicher Messianismus in Deutschland, 1500–1600* (Göttingen: 2011), 153–166.
6   See Jacqueline Hermann and Luís Filipe Silvério Lima's chapters in volume 2 of this collection.

From the thirteenth century on, some clerics seeking for a radical Church reform—often mendicant friars—and facing resistance or even persecutions identified the pope with the Antichrist. This idea, which was developed by "spiritual" friars like Dominican Robert of Uzès (who wrote in the late 13th century) and the Franciscans Pierre de Jean Olivi (Peter John Olivi, 1247/48–1296/98) and Ubertino da Casale (1259–1328), became stronger from the mid-fourteenth century on, and especially by the latter part of the century as the Great Western Schism divided western Christianity.[7] Some of these reform-minded authors also believed in Christ's earthly kingdom in the Latter Days. In the Book of Revelation, this kingdom is said to last thousand years. This number was usually taken allegorically, but some authors took it literally. It inspired the idea of "millennium", and the concept of "millenarianism". They were different variants of this belief. Some held that there would be a phase of sorrow, which Christ would put to an end by coming back to earth (his "Second Coming"). He would then reign on earth (thousand years long or not) before the Last Judgement and the end of times. This scenario, which was attractive to reform-minded people thinking that there was already a general decadency of the church and the reign of the Antichrist, is called "pre-millenarianism". It is similar to the story told in the Book of Revelation. For the followers of "post-millenarianism", by contrast, the millennium was to take place before the Second Coming. The kingdom of Christ would be established by men under the guidance of the Holy Spirit. Christ was expected to come only in order to judge men.[8]

The ideas that the Antichrist was already deceiving men, and that some kind of millennium was near, contributed in a decisive way to the emergence of early reformation endeavours bearing many characteristics of later Protestantism. The Oxford professor John Wyclif (1330–1384) insisted that the invisible Church—that is the community of the predestined under the guidance of Christ—was the only true one. According to him, the visible Church was the kingdom of the Antichrist. Now the true Church was to become visible and destroy the false one. Wyclif developed ideas akin to the *sola gratia* and *sola scriptura*'s principles of reformation principles of the sixteenth century. Furthermore, like some "paupers of Christ" before him and like later Swiss and French reformers Huldrych Zwingli (1484–1531) and Jean Calvin (1509–1564), he challenged the idea of Christ's real presence in the Eucharist. But the move-

---

7 Nelly Ficzel, *Der Papst als Antichrist. Kirchenkritik und Apokalyptik im 13. und frühen 14. Jahrhundert* (Leiden: 2019).
8 Norman Cohn, *The Pursuit of the Millenium* (Fairlawn: 1957); Jürgen Moltmann, *The Coming of God. Christian Eschatology* (Minneapolis: 1996).

ment he created, the Lollards, did not manage to gain lasting support from the authorities, and thus went underground. They were persecuted in the fifteenth century and, like the "paupers of Christ", merged with other reformation movements in the following century.[9]

If the Hussite reformation was a turning point in European history, it was precisely because, unlike Wyclif's, it was a reformation that actually took place. It may appear unusual to call Hussitism a reformation, because we are used to beginning the story of reformation with Luther and Zwingli. But it is important to bear in mind that most major theological ideas of the German and French-Swiss reformations were not invented in the sixteenth century, but in the late fourteenth (in particular, the French-Swiss reformation theology is akin to Wyclif's). Nor were Luther, Zwingli and their followers the first to try to put them into practice: this was precisely what the so-called "Hussites" tried to do. The most remarkable thing about Jan Hus (1369–1415) was less his theology than the fact that his followers took power in a major city like Prague. Like Wyclif, Hus was a reform-minded university professor. Like his Oxford predecessor and his successors in the sixteenth century, he thought that only the invisible Church was the true one. For this reason, the orders from established ecclesiastical and secular hierarchy were only to be followed if they were consistent with the Bible. In his eyes, only some clerics belonged to the true Church, while the others were followers of the Antichrist. Like Wyclif and later Luther and Calvin, Hus identified the Papacy with the Antichrist. The struggle against the Antichrist was beginning, and the true Church was to be revealed in this process. Secular authorities should take over church property (which they did in Bohemia), and the true believers would imitate Jesus Christ. God's law was to be fully implemented on earth.[10]

Now, such a doctrine was certainly revolutionary, but it was not wholly new. What *was* surprising about Hus was that his condemnation to death and his execution in Constance (1415) did not end the Bohemian reform movement, on the contrary. Jacob of Mies (Jakoubek ze Stříbra, 1372–1429), who was even more radical than Hus, became the new leader of a movement that its enemies soon termed "Hussite". Jacob not only equated the papacy with the Antichrist much more unequivocally than Hus; he also introduced the communion under

---

9   Fiona Somerset, *Feeling like Saints: Lollard Writings after Wyclif* (Ithaca, N.Y.: 2014); Kantik Ghosh, *The Wycliffite Heresy: Authority and the Interpretation of Texts* (Cambridge: 2002); Curtis Bostick, *The Antichrist and the Lollards. Apocalypticism in Late Medieval and Reformation England* (Leiden: 1998).

10 See Martin Pjecha's chapter in this volume and Thomas Fudge, *Jan Hus. Religious Reform and Social Revolution in Bohemia* (London: 2010).

both kinds for all the believers ("utraquism"), which became a symbol of the reformation movement. In 1419, radical "Hussites" took power in Prague's New Town, and more moderate ones in the Old Town. Many churches and monasteries were looted, many images destroyed. Even the more moderate Hussites of the Old Town formulated a programme that comprised not only a radical reform of the Church, but also the reform of society following God's laws. In other words, they sought to establish a theocracy.[11]

The other peculiarity of the Bohemian reformation was that it gave birth to the first millenarian movement in Christian history since antiquity: the above-mentioned Taborites. Millenarianism is a term that is often used in English in a broad sense, to designate very different kinds of beliefs and practices related to the expectation that the Last Days are near. To avoid confusion, it appears to us better to define this term in a narrower way, that is as the belief, and corresponding actions, that men and women should change established social and political structures in order to create a wholly new society that introduces, or at least prefigures, Jesus Christ's kingdom on earth. Neither the Spiritual Franciscans nor the Lollards had such a sweeping project of total destruction of traditional structures and the rebuilding of a society where all inequalities, injustice, and violence would be eradicated. They did not undertake steps in order to destroy traditional order. By contrast, this is precisely what the Taborites did: instead of awaiting the reign of Christ, they tried to build God's kingdom of the Latter Days first by peaceful means and very quickly through violence. Taborites rejected all secular law; in their eyes, the Holy Scripture was a sufficient normative source. They suppressed Church hierarchy, theology (all learning was sinful for them), the cult of the saints, holy images and relics, liturgical utensils (among other liturgical books, apparel, and chalices), confession, the belief in purgatory and Lent. True Christians were expected to renounce luxury and all signs of rank, as well as dancing and gambling.

Many ideas of the Taborites were inspired by the Book of Revelation, which in their eyes described the eschatological fight, and some of the Old testament prophecies. According to them, Jesus Christ would come secretly in the Latter Days, and this coming would initiate a period a divine vengeance. Taborites thought this had already happened. They identified themselves with the angels of God's wrath who punish the followers of the Antichrist in the Latter Days. According to their interpretation, the priests who celebrated mass according to

---

11   On the theocratic programme of moderate Hussites, see the fourth of the famous Prague Articles in *Die Hussiten. Die Chronik des Laurentius von Březová 1414–1421. Aus dem Lateinischen und Alttschechischen übersetzt, eingeleitet und erklärt von Josef Bujnoch* (Graz: 1988), 113–114.

the established rite were the Great Whore of Babylon. The godly punishments described in the book of Revelation were coming for them, and indeed for all those who did not give up traditions. In this age of vengeance, every Christian was called to punish with the sword the enemies of Christ's law. All castles, villages, and towns (except five) were to be burned down, and the world wholly purified. At the end of this period of bloodshed and tears, Jesus Christ will descend in glory from heaven, and will invite all the righteous to the feast of the lamb, that is the wedding with His Church. Death and pain will disappear, as described in the prophetic books of the Old Testament.[12]

Although barely mentioned in many histories of the sixteenth-century German and Swiss-French reformations, Hussitism left two important legacies that would influence in a decisive way early modern Protestantism. First, Luther took over from Hussitism the equation between the Papacy and the Antichrist. This happened 1519 shortly after the famous Leipzig disputation, at which Luther disputed with Johannes Eck (1486–1543), a theology professor in Ingolstadt. Because Johannes Eck reproached him as "a patron of the Bohemian sect", Luther began to inform himself more closely about Hussite theology, and came to the conclusion that Hus and his followers were right. This conclusion convinced him that the Antichrist had already been active on earth for a long time. Hus had been condemned by a church council so that, in Luther's view, all the church hierarchy was corrupted by the great deceiver of men.[13] Subsequently, all early modern Reformation movements identified the papacy with the Antichrist. The idea that the Latter Days had come became a central feature of Protestantism.

The second legacy was millenarianism, although in this case the transmission channels are anything but evident. To be sure, the belief in an earthly kingdom of Christ was neither new nor necessarily "heretical". Indeed clerical milieus had long discussed whether the millennium would begin before, or only with Christ's Second Coming. But never had a Christian religious movement claimed to be building this eschatological kingdom since antiquity. In the sixteenth century, millenarianism was controversial. Neither the German (Luther, Melanchthon), nor even the more theocratic-oriented Swiss-French reformation (Zwingli, Bullinger and Calvin) believed man and women could erect such a millennial empire, as they held humans to be too corrupt for

---

12 Josef Bujnoch (ed. and trans.), *Die Hussiten. Die Chronik des Laurentius von Brezová 1414–1421* (Graz: 1988), 53–54, 116–151. See also Martin Pjecha's introduction in this volume.
13 Heiko A. Oberman, "Hus und Luther. Der Antichrist und die zweite reformatorische Entdeckung" in *Jan Hus zwischen Zeiten, Völkern, Konfessionen*, ed. Ferdinand Seibt (Munich: 1997), 319–346.

such a task. But some more radical movements like Thomas Müntzer's (1489–1525) and the sixteenth-century Anabaptists—as they were called by their enemies—clearly had a millenarian dimension.

Thomas Müntzer is often presented as a disciple of Luther who took his own, more radical path. But other theological influences might have played a more decisive role than Luther's. His ideas present striking similarities to the Taborites', even if we have no evidence of an influence of the radical Bohemian reformation on him. Müntzer did not study in Wittenberg, even if he stayed several times in this city. In the 1510s and 1520s, he was a cleric in Central Germany, and was forced to change regularly his position because of his unorthodox thinking: he lived among others in Aschersleben (1516), Brunswick (1517), Jüterborg (1519), Zwickau (1521), Prague (1521), Nordhausen (1522) and Halle (1523) before moving to Allstedt in Thuringia (1524). It is probable, though difficult to prove, that during his travels he came into contact with ideas of the Radical Reformation similar to the Taborites'. In Allstedt he became convinced that he had been chosen by God to introduce the reform of the Church and society in the Latter Days. The third and last age of the Church described by Joachim of Fiore was coming. All Christians would be enlightened by the Holy Spirit—an idea that he probably took over from the Spiritualists in Zwickau. For that process of spiritual renewal, Christians had to annihilate their self and achieve a mystical union with Christ. But this renewal of the Church was not only a mystical and personal matter. It was also to be achieved through a fight with the Antichrist, which Müntzer identified with the Holy Roman Empire. Like the Taborites, Müntzer was convinced that he was an instrument of divine vengeance. He thought that not only the ecclesiastical, but also the established political order was to be destroyed. In 1524, in a sermon on Daniel's vision of the colossus with feet of clay, he called prince elector Frederic the Wise to participate in this violent undertaking. One year later, the Peasant War broke out. Müntzer saw in the rebellious peasants the instrument of divine wrath. In late 1524 or in early 1525, he founded the Eternal League of God and took the lead of some peasant rebels. In May 1525, Müntzer was captured after the battle of Frankenhausen, in which the peasants were massacred by the troops of the princes of Saxony, Hassia and Brunswick-Lüneburg. He was executed some days later.[14]

The emergence of millenarian movements does not necessarily imply a central role of the Book of Revelation. Actually, it seems that millenarian movements had very different scriptural sources of inspiration. In some cases, the

---

14   Matthias Riedel, "Apocalyptical Violence: Thomas Müntzer," in *A Companion to the Premodern Apocalypse*, ed. Michael A. Ryan (Leiden: 2016), 260–296.

prophetic books of the Old Testament, which announce the creation of a New Israel in the Latter Days, seems to have been more important than the book of Revelation. This was the case of the Münster Anabaptists, who strove to turn their Westphalian city into the New Jerusalem of the Latter Days in the early 1530s. Anabaptists, who lived above all in the Rhineland region and in the Netherlands, shared many ideas with fifteenth-century Taborites. They deemed biblical laws superior to traditional ones. They wanted to abolish Church hierarchy, theology, all liturgical devices and rituals that are not described in the Bible, the cult of saints, images and relics, the auricular confession and fasting, distinctions of ranks and estates. They rejected oaths, dancing, gambling and luxury. The conversion of the faithful was equivalent to a rebirth in Christ that was to be marked with baptism. The book of Revelation was an important point of reference for Anabaptists. Their leaders usually equated true baptism with the sealing of the 144,000 righteous described in the book of Revelation. The reborn were to live separately from the followers of the Antichrist and the "lukewarm" Christians. They were to build the New Jerusalem of the Last Days.

This programme knew its strictest application in Münster in Westphalia. But the history of the "Münster Anabaptist kingdom" shows that we should be careful not to consider that Anabaptists thought they were building the Celestial Jerusalem described in the book of Revelation, as is asserted in some scholarly publications. The story of the takeover of the city by Anabaptists began with the arrival of Dutch prophet Jan Mathijs in Münster in 1533. In February 1534, his followers took power in the city council. Soon, Mathijs, who had prophesised that Jesus Christ would return on earth in Easter 1534, applied a programme similar to that of the Taborites. He closed churches, abolished the distinction between estates and even private property. But as Christ did not come back, the Anabaptists began to introduce political and social institutions inspired by the ancient Israelites of the Old Testament. The leader of this process was Jan van Leiden (Jan Mathijs had been killed as he rode unarmed out of Münster when the city was besieged by the troops of princes). First, Jan van Leiden, inspired by Moses, created a political order in which judges played a pivotal role, and then was anointed king in September 1534. Already a few months earlier, Anabaptist leaders introduced polygamy, following the example of Old Testament law.[15]

Millenarianism was especially strong in the Radical Reformation, but it was not a purely Protestant phenomenon. The Dominican friar Girolamo Savonarola (1452–1498) was able to gain an enormous political influence in Florence

---

15 Anselm Schubert, "Nova Israhelis republica. Das Täuferreich von Münster 1534/35 als wahres Israel," in *Peoples of the Apocalypse: Eschatological Beliefs and Political Scenarios*, ed. Rebekka Voß, Wolfram Brandes and Felicitas Schmieder (Berlin: 2016), 271–284.

in the mid-1490s with the announced goal of making it a New Jerusalem. Savonarola came to Florence in 1482 and soon became a famous preacher. In his sermons, he denounced the general decadency of mores and manners, the avarice of the rich, the oppression of the poor, and the corruption of clergy. He asserted that religion was not primarily about ceremonies, but about imitating Jesus Christ. For him, the government of the republic, the Signoria, was tyrannical as it levied unjust taxes and led unjust wars. Savonarola called upon the Florentines to do penance. He was influenced by Joachim of Fiore, and believed that the time of the renewal of the Church was near. Every Christian would be filled by the Holy Spirit, and become "drunken" of divine love. But if Florence refused to apply the divine law, it would be destroyed. In 1494, Savonarola became the de facto leader of a party that succeeded in changing the Florentine constitution by creating a Great Council. For Savonarola, Florence was now the city of God, the New Jerusalem. It was a republic in which Jesus Christ reigned. The friar interpreted political struggles as struggles between God and Satan. Everybody who was against the new government was against Jesus Christ. But unlike the Taborites or Thomas Müntzer, Savonarola did not think that his task was to punish the enemies of Jesus Christ with the sword. He did not call upon his followers to kill their opponents. He strove to abolish gambling, usury, avarice, immoral artworks, luxury and "sodomy", but not to suppress any differences between the estates or even private property. Savonarola was the most influential Florentine for a few years, but he never controlled the city government directly, and his influence was contested. In 1498, his adversaries attacked the Dominican cloister where he lived. He was arrested, tried and executed.[16]

In the early modern period, the idea that the Last Days were near was especially strong in Protestantism. The expectation of the Latter Days and even the expectation of a millennium were not specific to any particular Protestant confession. Luther himself was strongly convinced that he and his contemporaries were living in the Latter Days when the true believers had to struggle with the Antichrist in many ways. The same was true for the Lutheran ministers within the besieged city of Magdeburg during the mid-sixteenth century,[17] the

---

16 Bernard McGinn, "Forms of Catholic Millenarianism: A Brief Overview," in *Catholic Millenarianism: From Savonarola to the Abbé Grégoire*, ed. Karl Kottman (Dordrecht: 2001), 1–15; Richard Popkin, "Savonarola and Cardinal Ximines: Millenarian Thinkers and Actors at the Eve of the Reformation," in *Catholic Millenarianism*, 15–25; Lauro Martines, *Fire in the City: Savonarola and the Struggle for the Soul in Renaissance Florence* (Oxford: 2006).

17 Thomas Kaufmann, *Das Ende der Reformation. Magdeburgs „Hergotts Kanzlei" 1548–1551/2* (Tübingen: 2003).

Huguenots ministers during the French wars of religion and the reformed ministers in England at the time of the threat of the Spanish armada, as well as during the English Revolution of the 1640s and 1650s.

Within Protestantism, the rhetorical attacks against the Antichrist were particularly strong in the controversy against Roman Catholicism and the Catholic Church. But the idea that the Antichrist was committing evil on earth also had a huge impact on quarrels within Protestantism. This can be seen on the eve of, and during the English Revolution.[18] To legitimise the fight against the king, the supporters of Parliament claimed to be at war against Babylon. Parliament presented itself as a defender of true Protestant religion against Popery. Furthermore, it identified Popery not only with Rome or with Catholic monarchies like the Spanish and French, but also with the English church and monarchy as well—with the Bishops, with some canons of the convocation of the bishops, and with some ceremonies of the church. According to numerous members of both houses of Parliament, all these elements prevented the English Church from being a truly reformed church and brought England in danger. And as long as the king defended these church traditions instead of promoting a reformation of the church, he was dangerous for the salvation of England, too. The idea that true reformation and a life according to the rule of God were necessary, and thus that many traditions of the church and monarchy have to be suppressed, was propagated from the very beginning of the Long Parliament. The pulpit of St Margaret's church in Westminster was politically the most prominent place where the fight against Babylon was proclaimed again and again.[19] In St Margaret, all the members of the House of Commons came together every month to listen to the so-called Fast Sermons, preached by ministers chosen by a parliamentary committee. These sermons called for a true reformation of the English church, often described as a fight against Babylon.

---

18   Christopher Hill, *Puritanism and Revolution. Studies in Interpretation of the English Revolution of the 17th Century* (London: 1958); Christopher Hill, *Antichrist in Seventeenth-Century England*, 2nd ed. (London / New York: 1990); Bernard Capp, "The Political Dimension of Apocalyptic Thought", in *The Apocalypse in English Renaissance Thought and Literature. Patterns, Antecedents and Repercussions*, ed. Constantinos A. Patrides and Joseph A. Wittreich (Ithaca, N.Y.: 1984), 93–124. Paul Christianson, *Reformers and Babylon. English Apocalyptic Visions from the Reformation to the Eve of the Civil War* (Toronto / Buffalo / London: 1978).

19   Paul Christianson, "From Expectation to Militance. Reformers and Babylon in the First Two Years of the Long Parliament", *Journal of Ecclesiastical History* 24 (1973), 225–244; Hugh R. Trevor-Roper, "The Fast Sermons of the Long Parliament", *Essays in British History. Presented to Sir Keith Feiling*, ed. Hugh R. Trevor-Roper (London: 1964), 85–138. John F. Wilson, *Pulpit in Parliament. Puritanism During the English Civil Wars 1640–1648* (Princeton: 1969).

The ministers saw this fight as the main duty of Parliament. And they interpreted the civil war as part of the last struggle against the Antichrist, which would soon end with the final destruction of Babylon, that is of the episcopal and—later—monarchical authorities. In this narrative, the end of monarchy was only one of the last steps towards a truly reformed country and the first step towards Christ's second coming on earth.[20]

Although in the 1650s all groups like the Fifth Monarchy Men were disappointed in their hopes of Christ's return on earth, the rhetoric of a final struggle against the Antichrist and his supporters in church and monarchy remained popular. Indeed, after the Restauration of the Stuart Monarchy, it was revived in situations of political tension, during the Popish Plot, the Glorious Revolution and various plots and uprisings between both events.[21] Even during the eighteenth century, the verbal attacks on the Antichrist and Babylon had a mobilising effect. Their political impact and importance in the American Revolution, for instance, is an open question so far, and is a subject worthy of further consideration.

By comparison, the idea of the Latter Days had become more marginal in Catholicism in the late sixteenth century. To be sure, the idea of messianic kingdom had still some enthusiasts in the seventeenth-century Catholic world, but—with the exception, perhaps, of Portugal—these were individuals with rather limited influence. The new Jesuit-style dominant theology and devotional culture went hand in hand with a more positive view of society and man.[22] Even in times of crisis, like in the time of Swedish triumphs during Thirty Years War, Catholic writings and engravings only rarely presented the struggle for religion and the church in an eschatological manner.[23] Mil-

---

20 Blair Worden, "Oliver Cromwell and the Sinn of Achan", in *History, Society and the Churches. Essays in Honour of Owen Chadwick*, ed. Derek Beales and Geoffrey Best, (Cambridge: 1985), 125–145; Blair Worden, "Providence and Politics in Cromwellian England", *Past and Present* 109 (1985), 55–99; Bernard Capp, *The Fifth Monarchy Men: A Study in Seventeenth-Century English Millenarianism* (London, 1972); J.C. Davies, "Living with the Living God: Radical Religion and the English Revolution", in *Religion in Revolutionary England*, ed. Christopher Durston and Judith Maltby (Manchester: 2006), 19–41.

21 Warren Johnston, *Revelation Restored: The Apocalypse in Later Seventeenth-Century England* (Woodbridge: 2011); Richard Greaves, *Deliver Us from Evil. The Radical Underground in Britain, 1660–1663* (New York: 1986); Richard Greaves, *Enemies under his Feet: Radicals and Nonconformists in Britain, 1664–1677* (Stanford: 1990); Richard Greaves, *Secrets of the Kingdom: British Radicals from the Popish Plot to the Revolution of 1688–1689* (Stanford: 1992).

22 Damien Tricoire, "What Was the Catholic Reformation? Marian Piety and the Universalization of Divine love", *The Catholic Historical Review* 103 (2017), 20–49.

23 Matthias Pohlig, "Konfessionskulturelle Deutungsmuster internationaler Konflikte um

lenarianism and eschatological interpretations of present events was revived in eighteenth-century radical Jansenism, however, and this influenced some French revolutionaries like Abbé Henri Grégoire.[24]

The chapters in this volume bring further evidence of the importance of Latter-Days expectations in the history of Protestantism even in the second half of the early modern period, a time often associated with the birth of secularity. After the English Revolution, the seventeenth century saw the birth of more peaceful Protestant millenarian movements. This was the case in the British Great Evangelical Awakening, but also within Lutheran Germany, where a growing minority, soon called "Pietists" by their enemies, was convinced that men, after their "conversion" thanks to God's grace, were called to build up God's kingdom on earth. For churchmen and theologians like Jakob Spener (1635–1705), August-Hermann Francke (1663–1727), and Friedrich Breckling (1629–1711), Luther had established doctrinal truth, but then stopped his reform work halfway. After reforming the doctrine, it was now necessary to reform the temporal world (a process called the "reformation of life"). This included missionary work among all ranks of society, as well as among Jews, Muslims and "heathens" on other continents. Thanks to Francke and the patronage of the royal courts at Berlin, Copenhagen and London, the Halle Orphanage became a central node of the so-called Pietist movement. Far from being just an orphanage, it comprised eight schools for pupils from different ranks and gender; missionary institutes; and, among other institutes, one for the production of cheap Bibles. By the early eighteenth century, the Halle Orphanage coordinated missionary work from North America to South India.[25]

The orphanage in Halle is just one of many examples of the conviction, then common, that further reformation was needed and that the established confessional churches had failed to promote it. In the Netherlands, the idea that further reformation is necessary was widespread, particularly from the dissenters, who openly criticised the reformed church and who took inspiration from different traditions, both mystic (Schwenckfeld) and Lutheran ones. Not only outside but also within the reformed church, the demand for further reformation became more and more common during the second half of the

---

1600—Kreuzzug, Antichrist, Tausendjähriges Reich", *Archiv für Reformationsgeschichte*, 93 (2002), 278–316.

24 Jeremy D. Popkin and Richard H. Popkin (eds), *The Abbé Grégoire and His World* (Dordrecht: 2000); Caroline Chopelin, *L'Obscurantisme et les Lumières: Itinéraire de l'abbé Grégoire, évêque révolutionnaire* (Paris: 2013).

25 Holger Zaunstöck, Thomas Müller-Bahlke and Claus Veltmann (eds), *Die Welt verändern. August Hermann Francke—ein Lebenswerk um 1700* (Halle: 2013).

seventeenth century. Established and learned theologians like Gisbertus Voetius (1589–1676) promoted the idea of "Nadere Reformatie", the necessity of moral improvement both of each individual believer and of society, and the need of a rigid enforcement of moral and religious norms. They expected secular authorities to support this programme.[26]

In England, the idea of further reformation did not disappear after the Restoration of Monarchy and episcopal church in 1660. The struggle for a godly life and for a further reformation of the church remained powerful. Indeed, the Bishops struggled to defend their leading position in church and society, and tried to delegitimise all attempts for further reformation within the church as seditious and revolutionary.[27] The further reformation programme caused multiple conflicts within other denominations, too, because church authorities were mostly hostile to it. In German Lutheran territories, everybody who intended a reformation not only of doctrine, but also of society, had to face opposition from orthodox ministers who considered the supporters of a further reformation to be dangerous "enthusiasts" ("Schwärmer") intending to undermine any order in church and society.[28] The opposition of the established church hierarchies and of many ministers to further reformations, and the threat of punishment that faced everyone who was arguing for the need of it, confronted the reformers with the question whether they should promote the reformation inside or outside the established church. In England Nonconformists established their own communities that were at least tolerated after the Glorious Revolution.[29] In the Netherlands, dissenters built up their own networks outside established clerical structures, too.[30] In German Lutheran territories, most initiatives for further reformation took place within the established church, as was the case with Francke and his orphan-

---

26 Fred van Lieburg, "From Pure Church to Pious Culture. The Further Reformation in the Seventeenth-Century Dutch Republic", in *Later Calvinism. International Perspectives*, ed. W. Fred Graham (Kirksville: 1994); Johannes van den Berg, "Die Frömmigkeitsbestrebungen in den Niederlanden," in *Geschichte des Pietismus Bd. 2. Der Pietismus im achtzehnten Jahrhundert*, ed. Martin Brecht (Göttingen: 1995), 542–587.

27 John Spurr, *The Restauration Church in England, 1646–1689* (New Haven: 1991); Jacqueline Rose, *Godly Kingship in Restauration England: the Politics of Royal Supremacy, 1660–1688* (Cambridge: 2011).

28 Stefan Michel and Andres Straßberger (eds), *Eruditio—Confessio—Pietas: Kontinuität und Wandel in der lutherischen Konfessionskultur am Ende des 17. Jahrhunderts; das Beispiel Johann Benedikt Carpzovs (1639–1699)* (Leipzig: 2009).

29 Michael P. Winship, "Defining Puritanism in Restauration England: Richard Baxter and Others Respond to a 'Friendly Debate'", *Historical Journal* 54 (2011), 689–715; Tim Cooper, *John Owen, Richard Baxter and the Formation of Nonconformity* (Farnham: 2011).

30 Van den Berg, "Die Frömmigkeitsbestrebungen", 64–67.

age in Halle. But sometimes the plea for further reform came from individuals outside the church. In scholarship, the former movement is called moderate pietism, and the latter radical pietism.[31] Whether a further reformation should take place, remained an open and contested question within European Protestantism throughout the eighteenth century.

Reformations and Prophecy

The idea of reformation was closely connected to a fundamental concept (not only) of Christian religion: prophecy. To struggle for a reformation of church, state and society, was considered one of the most fundamental tasks of prophets. Martin Luther made his first step towards a final break with the established church by giving himself a new name when attacking indulgence on 31 October 1517: he signed as Lutherus instead of Luder. As a humanist, he turned his name into Greek: Luther sounded similar to "Eleutherios", meaning someone who becomes free.[32] Luther's freedom was the freedom from church hierarchy, from his membership within the order of the Augustinians. It was a freedom which, in his view, every Christian has in his faith to Jesus Christ and salvation. Within three years, the established church, particularly the papacy in Rome, became for him the seat of the Antichrist.[33] In the Lutheran-Protestant tradition, Luther was the last and most important prophet within a long-standing tradition of witnesses of the truth (*testes veritatis*) like Wyclif and Hus. Luther presented himself in his writings as a translator of God's will, as the very first authority to uncover the meaning of God's word in the Bible. And, following the example of the prophets of the Old Testament like Jeremiah, Luther confronted everyone, particularly the princes and even the Emperor of the Holy Roman Empire, with the alternative to follow him and his interpretation of true Christianity and pure gospel (*reines Evangelium*) or to be partaker of the Antichrist, and thus to live always in danger of being punished by God.[34] In the 1520s, Luther interpreted the military success of the Turks as God's immediate

---

31   See Hans Schneider, "Der radikale Pietismus im 17. Jahrhundert", in *Geschichte des Pietismus*, vol. 1, 391–437; Hans Schneider, "Der radikale Pietismus im 18. Jahrhundert", in *Geschichte des Pietismus*, vol. 2, 107–197.

32   Bernd Moeller and Karl Stackmann, *Luder, Luther, Eleutherius. Erwägungen zu Luthers Namen* (Göttingen: 1981).

33   William R. Russell, "Martin Luther's Understanding of the Pope as the Antichrist," *Archiv für Reformationsgeschichte* 85 (1994), 32–44.

34   Hans-Jürgen Goertz, *Ende der Welt und Beginn der Neuzeit. Modernes Zeitverständnis im „apokalyptischen Saeculum", Thomas Müntzer und Martin Luther* (Mühlhausen: 2002).

reaction to all those who were not willing to follow the Reformation, that is those who were not willing to break with the established church.³⁵

Within the Lutheran tradition, Luther was not only a prophet sent by God to bring Christianity back to its roots, back to true faith and salvation. He was the last prophet, too. From this perspective, after the reformation of faith and after the purification of doctrine, there was no need for any other prophet in Lutheran territories.³⁶ What was needed instead was a church of learned theologians which had to take care in keeping the doctrine true and pure. Luther himself drew a red line between himself and his followers who were fighting for a reformation of doctrine, on the one hand, and all the other reformers who propagated different conceptions of the true faith or who were engaged not only in a reformation of the doctrine but in the reformation of society as well, on the other. He called all these "prophets" "enthusiasts" ("Schwärmer"), although some of them—like Andreas Bugenhagen (better known as Karlstadt), Thomas Müntzer or the so called "Zwickau prophets"— had been Luther's collaborators at the very early stage of the Reformation.³⁷ Luther doubted that they were personally inspired by God. He criticised their support of local turmoil and their offensive attitude towards political authorities. This criticism became a central issue of Luther's concept of reformation during the Great Peasants' War in Germany (1524–1526). In Thomas Müntzer, Luther saw a false prophet leading himself and all his supporters into the misery of damnation. Müntzer propagated revolution in the name of the gospel: for Luther that was not only a crime within society, but also a sin against God, because every Christian has to be obedient to all political authorities (Romans 13), and even more because Müntzer suggested that disobedience and rebellion were what God expected.³⁸ In the middle of the 1520s, therefore, prophecy was in Luther's perspective a dangerous thing: for society and order, for the true faith, and for the ongoing process of reformation. If reformation came to be regarded just as another word for rebellion, Luther could lose

---

35   Gregory Miller, "Luther's Views of the Jews and Turks," in *The Oxford Handbook of Martin Luther's Theology*, ed. Robert Kolb, Irene Dingel and L'ubomir Batka (Oxford: 2014), 427–434; Thomas Kaufmann, *Geschichte der Reformation* (Frankfurt a.M. / Leipzig: 2009), 648–650; Thomas Kaufmann, *"Türckenbüchlein". Zur christlichen Wahrnehmung "türkischer Religion" in Spätmittelalter und Reformation* (Göttingen: 2008).
36   See Irene Dingel, "Luther's Authority in the Late Reformation and Protestant Orthodoxy," in *Oxford Handbook*, 525–539.
37   Amy Nelson Burnett, "Luther and the 'Schwärmer'", in *Oxford Handbook*, 511–524.
38   Harold S. Bender, "The Zwickau Prophets, Thomas Müntzer, and the Anabaptists," *Mennonite Quarterly Review* 27 (1953), 3–16; Hans Jürgen Goertz, *Thomas Müntzer. Mystiker, Apokalyptiker, Revolutionär* (Munich: 1989).

all support from princes and other authorities within the Holy Roman Empire sympathising with a reformation of doctrine and church. To avoid any further disruptions within the Reformation camp, the new Lutheran church had to be built on a strict control of doctrine by Luther himself and later by learned theologians within the church, in close collaboration with the political authorities.

The narrative of Luther as the last prophet closing a long tradition of witnesses of the true faith was, however, more than once contested within the Lutheran church in early modern history. Ministers as well as theologians could adopt the persona of a prophet, like Jeremiah, Paul or Luther had done. They could use that position to argue against whatever they found contradictory to God's word and the true faith within church and society. When they did so, they were always accused by other ministers of being "enthusiasts" and disturbers of peace and order within the church. That happened to the "Pietists" in Halle and elsewhere, and that happened indeed to Friedrich Breckling, as can be seen in chapter 3 of this volume.

To justify the ongoing tradition of prophecy even after Luther, those claiming prophetical authority continued the narrative according to which there was a tradition of witnesses of the truth leading from antiquity to their own lifetime, like Gottfried Arnold did in his *Unparteyische Kirchen- und Ketzer-Historie* (1699).[39] They all argue in the same way in the role model of a prophet, that the established church is in decay and shadowed the true faith so that reformation is needed—and this idea was used against the Lutheran church itself.

The role model of a prophet (which came originally from Judaism) was known in all different Christian denominations. And the same is true of the opposition between the established church and the idea that a reformation was needed in order to return to true faith and pure doctrine. In the Lutheran as well as in the Reformed churches, the established church authorities were highly skeptical towards any claim that someone was a prophet. And in both confessions this happened from time to time, sometimes even with remarkable success for the self-declared prophets. It is no coincidence that Thomas Hobbes, for instance, argued in his *Leviathan* that within Christianity no prophets could be expected after the life, death and resurrection of Jesus Christ.[40] He stressed

---

39   Katharina Greschat, "Gott Arnolds "Unparteyische Kirchen- und Ketzerhistorie" von 1699/1700 im Kontext seiner spiritualistischen Kirchenkritik," *Zeitschrift für Kirchengeschichte* 116 (2005), 46–62.
40   Thomas Hobbes, *Leviathan*, ed. Noel Malcolm (Oxford: 2012), vol. 2, 680–681.

this argument because, during the English Civil War, many godly ministers, and also laymen, had styled themselves as prophets in the public sphere, and had gained great authority and a wide audience.[41]

The most striking difference between the Lutheran and Reformed churches was probably the way in which the latter focused not only on the faith, but also on the life of the believers. Within the Lutheran churches, the ministers saw themselves responsible for keeping the doctrine pure, but they were much less engaged in the control of the lives of their members. That was quite different in Zurich, in Geneva, in Scotland, indeed in all the churches of the Reformed tradition. Within the Reformed churches, the law of God had to be kept not only in faith but also in daily life in order to avoid the wrath of God.[42] The discipline within church and society became a main issue for all the members of the church, clergymen as well as laymen. The more the Reformed ministers succeeded in their fight for the validity of the law of God and its importance for the everyday life of everyone, the political authorities included, the nearer they brought their communities to theocracy.

The Chapters of This Volume

The selection of sources in this volume reflects the fact that the belief according to which the Latter Days had come was largely a Protestant phenomenon after the sixteenth century, and millenarianism and prophetism features of the Radical Reformation. The first part of chapter one deals with the first reformation, the Hussite one, and the belief of its leading theologians that the Antichrist was already present on earth in the guise of church authority. Martin Pjecha then presents texts originating from the Taborite movement, or describing it, and thus gives insights in early millenarianism. The choice of sources of different genres is especially illuminating because it enables us to look at the Taborites from different points of view: a song enables us to grasp the *imaginaire* present in religious practice, whereas Taborite treatises as well as summaries of the

---

41   Andreas Pečar, *Macht der Schrift. Politischer Biblizismus in Schottland und England zwischen Reformation und Bürgerkrieg (1534–1642)* (Munich, 2011).

42   See Kai Trampedach and Andreas Pečar (eds), *Theokratie und theokratischer Diskurs. Die Rede von der Gottesherrschaft und ihre politisch-sozialen Auswirkungen im interkulturellen Vergleich* (Tübingen: 2013), particularly the contributions of Volker Reinhardt ("Mythos Theokratie? Politik und Reformation im Genf Calvins", 373–388) and Christoph Strohm ("Theokratisches Denken bei calvinistischen Theologen und Juristen am Beginn der Moderne?", 389–408).

Taborite ideas, or excerpts from their books by moderate (and thus hostile) Hussites, help to understand better their doctrine and its theological justifications.

The other three chapters of the volume introduce into the world of late seventeenth-century and early eighteenth-century radical authors and movements within the two major Protestant denominations: Lutheranism and Calvinism. The German Lutheran Friedrich Breckling and the French Calvinist Jacques Massard were productive and most original authors. Massard was hardly typical of Huguenots in general, but his writings do bear testimony of the experience and expectations of French Protestants in exile after Louis XIV's revocation of the Edict of Nantes in 1685. Like the famous Huguenot theologian Pierre Jurieu, he interpreted the persecution of what was in his view the true Church in an apocalyptic manner. Unlike Jurieu, though, Massard was not a theologian and distanced himself from Calvinist orthodoxy. As his book *The Harmony of Prophecies*—extracts of which Leslie Tuttle and Kristine Wirts have translated in this volume—shows, he searched intensively for prophecies explaining what was happening and what was to come, and selected them in an eclectic way, mixing among others modern Huguenot prophecies with medieval ones and Renaissance astrology. In his eyes, the prophetic age was not closed. On the contrary, his epoch, that of the witnesses preaching against the Antichrist, was intensively prophetic.

Like Massard, Breckling collected different modern prophecies ("testimonies") and thus believed prophecy to be a hallmark of his own times. Indeed, he presented himself as a prophet. But Breckling also condemned sharply many "enthusiastic" movements as heretical, as becomes clear from his *Catalogus Haereticorum* translated here by Viktoria Franke. This ambiguous position in the field of Protestant prophetic movements, oscillating between the acknowledgement and condemnation of contemporary prophets, had the consequence that Breckling lived rather at the margin of major religious groups. But while he was less influential than Spener and Francke, Breckling contributed to the re-emergence of millenarianism in Lutheranism. Like Francke, he saw in missionary work among Jews, Muslims and "heathens" a major task, as he explains in his book *Paulus Redivivus*, also translated by Victoria Franke in this volume.

The last chapter in this volume, by Lionel Laborie, presents prophecies mostly written by rather little-known lay prophets from the underground Huguenot movement in late seventeenth- and early eighteenth-century southern France. Unlike the treatises by Massard and Breckling, these texts are not *about* prophecies, but *are* prophecies. They are much less organised, and partly even rather obscure. They depart greatly from Calvinist orthodoxy, and indeed often reject any connection with established churches. In these regards, the last source presented in this chapter differs greatly from the others. Although also from a Protestant in southern France, it emanates from the still underground but orthodox mid eighteenth-century Calvinist church, indeed from one of its major figures, Paul Rabaut. It is not a prophecy, but a sermon on a fully authoritative prophecy, that is a biblical one. Rabaut saw in the rise of Protestant powers in eighteenth-century Europe a sign that the deliverance of the underground Huguenot church was near.

Conclusion

Our overview about reformation, eschatology and prophecy within Christianity in medieval and early modern times focussed mainly on the hot spots of conflict and turmoil in Europe caused or intensified by ideas about true religion and a godly society. Reformation meant questioning social and political traditions with regard to revelation and the will of God. These conflicts were often intensified by the idea that the Latter Days and the Last Judgment were to be expected soon. It has often been stated that the ideas of the millennium, the expectation of the kingdom of Christ on earth, of an end of history revealed in Scripture, became increasingly outdated in the course of the Eighteenth century.[43] This is probably true for a part of the European elites. But it is also true, however, that the idea of further reformation was very much present throughout the eighteenth century. The idea of divine providence, the concept of a covenant between God and his followers on Earth, individual believers as well as social groups or nations, and the expectation of a final judgment and divine justice remained powerful in the mind of a vast majority of people across all ranks. Even enlightened philosophers who criticised the clergy and its "superstitions", sometimes even as atheists, developed ideas that were in some respect deeply rooted in Christian traditions. They took over religious concepts, and secularised them: they replaced the idea of a trial by God by that of a trial by nature, and ideas about divine providence with concepts of a natural destiny of mankind. Nature took over the role of Scripture as the ultimate source

---

43 Arno Seifert, "Von der heiligen zur philosophischen Geschichte. Die Rationalisierung der Universalhistorischen Erkenntnis im Zeitalter der Aufklärung", *Archiv für Kulturgeschichte* 68 (1986), 81–117; Arno Seifert, *Der Rückzug der biblischen Prophetie von der neueren Geschichte. Studien zur Geschichte der Reichstheologie des frühneuzeitlichen deutschen Protestantismus* (Köln / Wien: 1990); Jacob Taubes, *Abendländische Eschatologie* (Bern: 1947).

of norms, but for most eighteenth-century authors, nature was of divine origin and ruled by the laws of God.[44]

More than half of the chapters in this three-volume collection focus on eighteenth-century sources. This can help to make a strong case for a revision of our narratives about this period, and for a reconsideration of the place of reformation and eschatological expectations in an era most often characterised as a time of secularisation and Enlightenment.

---

44 See Carl L. Becker, *The Heavenly City of the Eighteenth-Century Philosophers*, 2nd ed. (New Haven / London 2003); Pečar and Tricoire, *Falsche Freunde: War die Aufklärung wirklich die Geburtsstunde der Moderne?* (Frankfurt a. M.: 2015), 63–82.

CHAPTER 1

Hussite Eschatological Texts (1412–1421): Introduction and Translations

Martin Pjecha

Introduction

Before discussing the translated texts themselves, a brief overview of the Hussite movement, with special attention to the contexts surrounding these texts, may help orient the unfamiliar reader.¹ In the early 15th century, with the anxiety brought by the Papal schism in the background, the university-trained popular preacher, Jan Hus (c.1370–1415),² found himself at the head of a reform movement in Bohemia which drew some continuity both from earlier Bohemian reformers, and more recently from the works of the Oxford theologian and reformer, John Wycliffe.³ Drawing on these inspirations, Hus's reform movement stressed loyalty to the "law of God"—as expressed in the Bible—above "human laws" and authorities, including the Pope himself. Among other things, this meant the elimination of Church property, the subjugation of the Church to secular authority, and the abolition of certain abusive Church practices.⁴

---

1   Further literature will be provided below, but for some general overviews, see František Šmahel, *Die Hussitische Revolution*, vols. 1–3 [hereafter HR] (Hannover: 2002); Petr Čornej, *Velké Dějiny Zemí Koruny České*, vol. 5 (Prague: 2000); Howard Kaminsky, *A History of the Hussite Revolution* [hereafter HR] (Berkeley: 1967); Thomas A. Fudge, *The Magnificent Ride: The First Reformation in Hussite Bohemia* (Aldershot: 1998), 60–122.
2   Most recently, see Pavel Soukup, *Jan Hus: The Life and Death of a Preacher* (West Lafayette: 2019); František Šmahel and Ota Pavlíček (eds), *A Companion to Jan Hus* (Leiden: 2015).
3   For instance, see Vilém Herold, "The Spiritual Background of the Czech Reformation: Precursors of Jan Hus", in Šmahel and Pavlíček, *Jan Hus*, 69–95; also, Fudge, *Magnificent Ride*, 33–59; Šmahel, HR 2, 717–787.
4   František Šmahel, "The National Idea, Secular Power and Social Issues in the Political Theology of Jan Hus", in Šmahel and Pavlíček, *Jan Hus*, 214–253; Dušan Coufal, "Key issues in Hussite theology", in Michael Van Dussen and Pavel Soukup (eds), *A Companion to the Hussites* (Leiden: 2020), 261–296. The opposed practices and behaviours widely varied depending on individual authors and exact context, but broadly included lax clerical mores, obfuscation of scripture, those considered simoniacal and financially exploitative, and others that could apparently find no (strictly) scriptural basis.

Though Hus's followers won some significant victories in their early years—including the support of the Archbishop of Prague and the Bohemian King Václav IV (1361–1419), and significant control over the University of Prague in 1409—they soon encountered serious opposition from both secular and religious authorities. The Archbishop soon turned against the reformers, charges of heresy were brought against Hus and his followers, and in 1411 he was excommunicated for failure to appear before the curial court. Moreover, the alliance between the reformers and the King was shaken in 1412 over the issue of indulgences, and Hus was forced into exile later that year. Hus's absence, and growing pressure against the reformers from several directions, helped divisions emerge among the leading reformers, mostly university masters in Prague. In 1414, these divisions were exacerbated by the introduction of the practice of utraquism—the reception of the Eucharist in both the sacramental bread and wine for the laity—by a radical reformer, Jakoubek of Stříbro (c.1375–1429).[5] With the convocation of the Council of Constance that year, Hus accepted a summons to defend himself against charges of heresy, but was soon imprisoned by the Council. The following year, in 1415, it condemned the practice of utraquism and executed Hus as an unrepentant heretic.

The years following Hus's execution saw an eruption of the "Hussites" in Bohemia. Nobles immediately agreed to defend the reform movement, utraquism found adherents over large parts of the country, and inter-religious violence occasionally erupted.[6] The rapid and haphazard spread of Hussitism throughout Bohemia and Moravia, however, meant that doctrine and practice could not be easily centralised, and a rift emerged between the intellectuals of Prague and the more radical priests of the countryside.[7] In 1419 King Václav, facing pressure from several directions, finally took a firm stand against the Hussites, ordering them to return the churches they had captured to Catholics, and allowing utraquism only a very limited existence in the kingdom. Some

---

5   On Jakoubek of Stříbro, see Pavel Soukup, *Reformní kazatelství a Jakoubek ze Stříbra* (Prague: 2011); Paul de Vooght, *Jacobellus de Stříbro († 1429) premier théologien du hussitisme* (Louvain: 1972); Dušan Coufal, "*Sub utraque specie*: Die Theologie des Laienkelchs bei Jacobell von Mies († 1429) und den frühen Utraquisten", *Archa Verbi* 14 (2017), 157–201.

6   Reports complaining of violence against Catholics across Bohemia abounds at least from 1414 onwards: Kamil Krofta, "Zur Geschichte der husitischen Bewegung", *in Mittheilungen des Instituts für Oesterreichische Geschichtforschung* 23 (Innsbruck: 1902), 607–610; Josef Macek, "K počátkům táborství v Písku", *Jihočeský Sborník Historický* 22:4 (1953), 119–124; Johann Loserth, "Beiträge zur Geschichte der Husitischen Bewegung", in *Archiv für Oesterreichische Geschichte* 82 (Vienna: 1895), 386–391; František Palacký (ed.), *Documenta Mag. Joannis Hus* (Prague: 1869), 615–619; Bernard Pez, *Thesaurus anecdotorum novissimus* IV, ii (Augsburg: 1723), coll. 517.

7   Some of the radicals' doctrines—including Donatism, and the rejection of images and purgatory—are attested in Pez, *Thesaurus* IV, ii, coll. 539; Palacký, *Documenta*, 633–638.

Hussites reacted in the spring of that year by fleeing their towns, and instead congregating together outdoors on hilltops to attend the masses and sermons of their priests. This was the birth of the "Táborite movement",[8] perceiving itself in eschatological terms as a community of true Christians, imitating the primitive Church,[9] who would be saved by God from the wicked. In Prague, meanwhile, the king's measures were met with denunciation by radicals, who violently overthrew the New Town council in late July, with King Václav mysteriously dying shortly afterwards.[10] His half-brother Sigismund (1368–1437), King of Hungary and Holy Roman Emperor, became the new Bohemian king, and Hussites thereafter faced increasing violence and threats from Sigismund's supporters.[11] In October, violence erupted in Prague, and the Hussites captured positions around the city from Catholics, though they agreed to cede all but utraquism in a truce with Sigismund's forces in mid-November.[12] For the radicals in Prague and the countryside, the truce was understood as a "betrayal" of reform, and alienated them from the moderate Hussites. The Táborite priests simultaneously preached eschatology with a heightened sense of immanence, urging all the faithful to flee Prague and other cities for those which had not allied with the Antichrist, which would be refuges from the impending wrath of God.[13]

These exhortations of the eschatological—and then chiliastic[14]—Táborite prophets began a long polemic with the university masters of Prague, who rejected both their Biblical hermeneutics and the violence that they seemed to inspire.[15] Nor did the lapse of the eschaton seem to dampen the enthusiasm

---

8   In the Christian tradition, it is understood to be the location of Jesus's Transfiguration, as described in Mark 9:2–8 (and parallels). The name, along with that of others, is discussed in Čornej, *Velké Dějiny* 5, 205 f.

9   Josef Emler, Jan Gebauer, and Jaroslav Goll (eds), *Fontes Rerum Bohemicarum* 5 [hereafter *FRB* 5] (Prague: 1893), 401 f., trans. in Kaminsky, *HR*, 284 f.

10 Howard Kaminsky, "The Prague Insurrection of 30 July 1419", *Medievalia et Humanistica* 17 (1966), 106–126; David R. Holeton, "Revelation and Revolution in Late Medieval Bohemia", *Communio Viatorum* 36 (1994), 29–45.

11 For example, the extermination of Hussites at Kutná Hora, *FRB* 5, 351 f., trans. Kaminsky, *HR*, 310 f.; the attack on Hussite pilgrims František Palacký, *Scriptorum Rerum Bohemicarum* 3 (Prague: 1829), 29–33, trans. in Thomas A. Fudge, *The Crusades against Heretics in Bohemia, 1418–1437* (Aldershot: 2002), 29–32; for earlier threats from Sigismund, see Palacký, *Documenta*, 676 f., trans in Fudge, *The Crusades*, 20 f.

12 On these events, see Kaminsky, *HR*, 300–308; Šmahel, *HR* 2, 1042–1047.

13 The Hussite Chronicler Lawrence of Březová names the five cities, *FRB* 5, 356.

14 On the distinction, see Matthias Riedl, "Eschatology", in *New Dictionary of the History of Ideas* 2, ed. Maryanne Cline Horowitz (New York: 2005), 708–710.

15 Pavel Soukup, "The Masters and the End of the World: Exegesis in the Polemics with Chiliasm", *Bohemian Reformation and Religious Practice* 7 (2009), 91–114; idem, *Reformní kazatelství*, 314–354.

of the Táborites, who founded the new town of Tábor in southern Bohemia as the remaining Hussite towns weakened, and after Christ's advent failed to result. Moreover, their doctrines continued to develop, as one particularly eloquent prophet, Martin "Loquis" Húska (?–1421), appears to have gained a following behind "Pikartism", a rejection of Christ's real presence in the Eucharist.[16] Perhaps related to this, the Táborite prophets—either in mid-February or March[17]—apparently now exhorted the faithful toward purgative violence to prepare the world for Christ's pure kingdom.[18] Even as such currents within Tábor pushed away from the Prague moderates, some, like the Táborite general Jan Žižka (c.1360–1424), preferred unity with them. This was in fact soon demonstrated, by the agreement of joint defence against the first anti-Hussite crusade in July, and the simultaneous agreement on the joint Hussite platform of the so-called Four Articles of Prague.[19]

Eventually, the political and religious concerns of the rest of the Hussites, as well as the institutional growth within Tábor, proved incompatible with the goals of Húska's Pikarts.[20] In the beginning of 1421, Húska was imprisoned and his followers were expelled from Tábor. Thereafter, they expanded Húska's teachings into an even more heterodox direction, believing themselves to be perfected humans living in the promised paradise of God's kingdom like Adam and Eve. These "Adamites" apparently roamed the nearby countryside in the sinless nudity of the first couple, raiding villages and engaging in mass-orgies.

---

16 On Martin Húska (Loquis) and Pikartism, see Pavlína Cermanová, "The Apocalyptic background of Hussite radicalism", in Michael Van Dussen and Pavel Soukup (eds), *A Companion to the Hussites* (Leiden: 2020), 207–211; František Šmahel, *Dějiny Tábora* I (České Budějovice: 1988), 282–287; Howard Kaminsky, "The Free Spirit in the Hussite Revolution", in *Millennial Dreams in Action*, ed. Sylvia L. Thrupp (New York: 1970), 166–186; Jan of Příbram, *Život kněží táborských*, ed. Jaroslav Boubín (Příbram: 2000), 66–70; also see Vavřinec z Březové, *Husitská kronika: Píseň o vítězství u Domažlic* [Hereafter *HK*], trans. František Heřmanský and Jan Blahoslav Čapek (Prague: 1979), 351, nr. 59, note 2.

17 This is the period Kaminsky, *HR*, 340 f. associates with the birth of the "millenarian" stage. The turning-point of 10–14 February 1420 is known from Jakoubek's letter to a Táborite priest. See Kaminsky, *HR*, 540. Yet I believe this does not preclude the possibility that purgative violence was urged only the following month—when the crusade against Bohemia was announced—since we can allow for the reinterpretation of apocalyptic failure as postponement, as was common in this period (for instance, see Robert E. Lerner, "Refreshment of the Saints: the Time after the Antichrist as a Station for Earthly Progress in Medieval Thought", *Traditio* 32 (1976), 138 f.) and as the Táborites themselves later in fact did.

18 On the problems of apocalyptic violence, see Robert E. Lerner, "Medieval Millenarianism and Violence", in *Pace e Guerra nel Basso Medioevo* (Spoleto: 2004), 37–52.

19 On the Four Articles, see for instance Čornej, *Velké Dějiny* 5, 250–254; Kaminsky, *HR*, 369–375.

20 Petr Čornej, "Potíže s Adamity", *Marginalia historica* 2 (1997), 36–38.

Húska himself was executed in August, and the community of Adamites was exterminated by Jan Žižka only two months later.[21]

The later history of the Hussites is long and complex, as they survived one Church crusade after another until the agreement to cease hostilities with the Council of Basel in the mid-1430s. This period of intense prophetic speculation, however, would continue to mark the self-identification and goals of the Hussites, especially the radical parties, into the future.[22]

∴

The authorship and exact dates of the Hussite prophetic texts discussed below is a contentious matter, given that they often contain little information which could assist historians in dating them, and the authors do not commonly identify themselves or provide unambiguous information for their identification. When authors are identified, it is sometimes only by contemporary hostile copyists of the texts, a fact which must be critically considered by historians, as it introduces the copyist as a potential co-author of the surviving rendition, possibly distorting or abbreviating its content. Below, we shall attempt to provide a brief introduction of the texts which follow, including their possible authors and dates. For the sake of brevity, however, these cannot be considered comprehensive or conclusive results.

Text 1 is an anomaly amongst those presented, in that its authorship and dating can be definitively identified—to Jakoubek of Stříbro and January 1412, respectively[23]—though it has been shown that it drew heavily from a work of the earlier Bohemian reformer, Matthew of Janov, on the Antichrist.[24] It is a *Quaestio* presented at a quodlibet at Prague University, and was therefore meant for an educated audience familiar with Scripture.[25] As discussed above, 1412 would prove a dire year for the reform movement, but in January this was not yet the case. Instead, Jakoubek could identify the Pope as the

---

21 On the Adamites, see ibid., 33–63; Jakub Jiří Jukl, *Adamité: Historie a vyhubení husitských naháčů* (Prague: 2014); Kaminsky, "Free Spirit", 180 ff. For a more detailed summary of events, with reference to sources, see Cermanová, "The Apocalyptic".

22 For instance, see Martin Pjecha, "Spreading Faith and Vengeance: Human Agency and the 'Offensive Shift' in the Hussite Discourses on Warfare", *The Bohemian Reformation and Religious Practice* 10 (2015), 158–184.

23 Pavel Spunar, *Repertorium auctorum Bohemorum provectum ideam post Universitatem Pragensem conditam illustrans*, vol. 1 (Warsaw: 1985), 215 nr. 563.

24 Vlastimil Kybal, "M. Matěj z Janova a M. Jakoubek ze Stříbra: Srovnávací kapitola o Antikristu", *Český Časopis Historický* 11 (1905), 22–37.

25 Václav Novotný, *M. Jan Hus: Život a Učení* 1.2 (Prague: 1921), 43 ff.; Jan Sedlák, *M. Jan Hus* (Prague: 1915), 219 f.; Jitka Sedláčková, "Jakoubek ze Stříbra a jeho kvestie o Antikristu" (PhD thesis, Masaryk University: 2001), 19 f.

Antichrist in a context of relative confidence, when the battle-lines of the reform struggle were becoming increasingly clear. On the one hand, the reformers' alliances with the king and nobility were proving stronger than ever, and new supporters were sought and found abroad. The Bohemian king, queen, and prominent nobles had already been appealing to the curial court on behalf of the reformers long before, but starting in April 1411, King Václav IV actively opposed the Archbishop's accusations of heresy and ordered that his interdict be ignored, his ecclesiastic riches seized, and that he be forced to revoke his anathemas. The Archbishop was humiliated and mysteriously died shortly afterwards. Meanwhile, Hus received encouragement from the English Lollard Richard Wyche, and sought new ties with the Polish King Władysław II (c.1351–1434) after the latter's defeat of the Teutonic Knights at Grünwald. On the other hand, the enemies of reform were making their presence ever clearer. The message of Hus's excommunication was announced in Prague in March 1411, just as some in the Roman curia openly urged the most drastic measures—even crusade—to exterminate the "Wycliffites". In June, the Prague Archbishop Zbyněk had announced an (ill-fated) interdict on the city, and in December, (Anti-)Pope John XXIII (c.1365–1415) announced his intention of sending nuncios to announce indulgences in Bohemia, thus bringing the kingdom into his crusade against the Neapolitan king.[26]

The Hussite crowds already interpreted the conflict between the Archbishop and the king as having a wider significance, anticipating that between the Antichrist and God.[27] Moreover, at least since 1407, Hus himself had preached that "a true Antichrist" was anyone who confessed to know God but rejected him in his actions,[28] and later explicitly extended the definition to the Papacy.[29] Yet it was his colleague, Jakoubek of Stříbro, who produced the earliest and most systematic proof that not only linked the Papacy to the Antichrist, but explicitly argued that the final, greatest Antichrist (*summus Anticristus*) could only be identified with the Pope, and that he composed the head of a greater body of false Christians (*corpus Antichristi*). Although the text may not have drawn much attention from contemporaries,[30] it comprised an early part of an

---

26 Ota Pavlíček, "The Chronology of the Life and Work of Jan Hus", in Šmahel and Pavlíček, *Jan Hus*, 40–44; Šmahel, HR 2, 859–868; Kaminsky, HR, 73 f.; for early discussion of crusade, see Matthew Spinka, *John Hus: A Biography* (Princeton: 1968), 123.

27 The popular "song about Archbishop Zbyněk", in Fudge, *The Crusades*, 43 f.

28 Václav Flajšhans (ed.), *Mistra Jana Husi Sebrané spisy: Spisy latinské* 1 (Prague: 1904), 162; Ivana Dolejšová, "Eschatological Elements in Hus's Understanding of Orthopraxis", *Bohemian Reformation and Religious Practice* 4 (2002), 129.

29 See Pavlína Cermanová, *Čechy na Konci Věků: Apokalyptické Myšlení a Vise Husitské Doby* (Prague: 2013), 274, note 2; idem, "The Apocalyptic background", 188 f.

30 Novotný, *M. Jan Hus*, 47 f.

intensified Hussite discourse on the Antichrist which developed further, soon identifying the Church as this "body of the Antichrist".[31]

Text 2 is an anonymous song, probably sung by the hilltop congregations of the early Táborite movement, and may be dated to 1419,[32] perhaps to the spring or summer of that year.[33] As already noted, this was when like-minded congregants fled the persecution of their dwelling-places to attend solemn religious services—and especially to receive utraquist communion—on hilltops. Notable here is the tone of the text, which is completely quietist; it calls for sacrifice by the faithful, flight from evil, and divine salvation, as is echoed by another contemporary song.[34] Later texts, such as texts 6 and 7, as will be discussed, conversely place salvation and the eradication of evil in the hands of the faithful, in their willingness to enact violence.

Text 3 is an anonymous treatise that warned of the coming apocalypse, and urged the faithful to collect in several communities to avoid God's wrath. Historians have not been able to agree on a suitable dating, which ranges variously from November 1419 to April 1420,[35] and have also been divided on the possible author. On the latter issue, the Táborite priests Martin Húska[36] and Jan Jičín[37] have both been suggested, though I, like several others, am con-

---

31 S. Harrison Thomson (ed.), *Mistra Jana Husi Tractatus Responsivus* (Prague: 1927), 19, 25, 59, 138f., erroneously attributed to Hus by Thomson. Both Kaminsky, *HR*, 53 and Bernard McGinn, *Antichrist: Two Thousand Years of the Human Fascination with Evil* (San Francisco: 1994), 184, think Hus did not go this far himself. On other developments, see Miloslav Ransdorf, *Kapitoly z geneze husitské ideologie* (Prague: 1983), 105–110; Howard Kaminsky, "Nicholas of Pelhřimov's Tábor: an Adventure into the Eschaton" in *Eschatologie und Hussitismus*, ed. Alexander Patschovsky and František Šmahel (Prague: 1996); McGinn, *Antichrist*, 183–187; Cermanová, *Čechy*, 55–67; Lucie Mazalová, *Eschatologie v díle Jana Husa* (Brno: 2015).

32 Pavel Spunar, *Repertorium auctorum Bohemorum provectum idearum post Universitatem Pragensem conditam illustrans*, vol. II (Warsaw: 1995), 147 nr. 267; Zdeněk Nejedlý, *Dějiny husitského zpěvu* 4 (Prague: 1955), 263; Josef Macek, *Tábor v Husitském Revolučním Hnutí* I (Prague: 1952), 438.

33 Kaminsky, *HR*, 286, note 76.

34 Zdeněk Nejedlý, *Dějiny husitského zpěvu* 6 (Prague: 1956), 183–185. Partially translated by Kaminsky, *HR*, 316f., though he suggests a dating to 1420, ibid., 317, note 21.

35 See Macek, *Tábor* I, 437 f., nr. 4; František M. Bartoš, "Do čtyř pražských artykulů: Z myšlenkových i ústavních zápasů let 1415–1420", *Sborník příspěvků k dějinám města Prahy* 5 (1932), 568; Kaminsky, *HR*, 320 is not clear on the date, but seems to suggest early 1420. Spunar I, 259 f., nr. 719. suggests 1420. Bartoš's later dating is based on the assumption that the text was a response to a letter of Jakoubek from February 1420 (on which, see also Macek, *Tábor* I, 440, nr. 11; Kaminsky, *HR*, 518f., nr. 6), but it seems the text could also be a response to an earlier letter, see below.

36 Bartoš, "Do čtyř", 568.

37 See Macek, *Tábor* I, 437, nr. 4; Spunar I, 259 f., nr. 719. On Jičín, see *HK*, 352, nr. 59, note 3, 4, and Spunar I, 258.

tent with the text's anonymity.[38] Since the text seems to be responding to one of Jakoubek's refutations of Táborite prophecies—which itself is datable to between November 1419 and February 1420[39]—I suggest a dating in early 1420, and certainly before the shift to purgative violence, given the language of the text. Rather than exhort the faithful to violence, as would be done later in 1420 (texts 6 and 7), or to pacifism, as was done earlier (text 2), this text seems to be a transition from one to the other; flight to the mountains (now explained as fortified cities) is still urged to avoid God's wrath, but physical—apparently defensive—violence is a legitimate means of preserving the community. Indeed, self-preservation within the world is one of the purposes of flight, and this interest, rather than simple martyrdom, may be tied to the development of an inner-worldly understanding of Christ's kingdom, already fully-articulated in the later texts.[40]

Texts 4 and 5 are the only two known Latin apocalyptic treatises, both anonymous. The copyist of text 5 is unknown, while text 4 is contained in the so-called *Hussite Chronicle*[41] of the master of arts of the Prague University and Prague official, Lawrence of Březová (c.1370–1437).[42] In summary, Lawrence was a moderate Hussite himself, critical of the radicals both in Prague and Tábor, but likely increasingly disillusioned by the length and violence of the revolution. This may explain the dual purposes which Lawrence apparently ascribed to his *Chronicle*, which are preserved in the (at least) two recensions of the text; he began writing "for the future memory of events, which make known the hateful wickedness of the malice of those assailing and persecuting the bearers of the Law of God and its most sacred truth",[43] but apparently later changed his purpose, "so that the future offspring of the Bohemian nation shall not be deprived of knowledge of this horrendous, nay prodigious fall, and that it should not decay by mad idleness into the same or worse".[44] Lawrence's

---

38 Macek, *Tábor* I, 437; Kaminsky, HR, 320.
39 See Spunar I, 243, nr. 662, the text is in Kaminsky, HR, 519–522. For the dating of this text, see Macek, *Tábor* I, 439, nr. 8; Bartoš, "Do čtyř", 564; Ferdinand Siebt, *Hussitica: Zur Struktur einer Revolution* (Cologne: 1990), 202. I see a dating before February or March 1420 the most likely.
40 Cf. Příbram, *Život*, 41; František Palacký (ed.), *Archiv Česky Čili, Staré Písemné Památky České i Morawske* 3 (Prague: 1844), 220; Bartoš, "Do čtyř", 576 f., trans. Bernard McGinn, *Visions of the End: Apocalyptic Traditions in the Middle Ages* (New York: 1979), 268 f.; Bartoš, "Do čtyř", 591; text 6 below.
41 Spunar II, 82–84, nr. 115, text in *FRB* 5, 327–534.
42 I draw my discussion of Lawrence of Březová here from HK, 305–316.
43 Johann Peter von Ludewig, *Reliquiae Manuscriptorum Omnis Aevi Diplomatum ac Monumentorum*, 6 (Frankfurt: 1724), 124.
44 *FRB* 5, 329.

work covers about nine years of the early Hussite movement (1414–1422), but historians have long speculated about its own dating—ranging from 1419/20 to 1444—though most agree that it was completed years after the events it describes.[45]

Text 4 divides historians over its authorship, and especially its dating. Given its form as a scholastic *Quaestio*, the author was likely a university-educated priest.[46] According to the introduction by its copyist, the text may only represent an incomplete extract of a larger piece, while the relationship which he establishes between it and text 6 may give a hint as to its dating.[47] Indeed, one suggested date, supported by its scholastic form, was the summer of 1420 when the Táborite prophets were preparing, under the leadership of Martin Húska, to dispute with the masters of Prague.[48] Yet its placement in the chronicle need not be representative of its age, as another has suggested, and the text may have instead originated in the winter of 1419–1420.[49] This seems to be supported by several observations: the "collection" of the faithful is placed into the future, and a worldly age after the destruction of the wicked is clearly envisioned, but not yet counted (as in text 5), both of which were linked by other sources to earlier Táborite developments.[50]

Text 5 is also notoriously difficult to date and ascribe authorship to. For every proof of an early date, there seems to be another of a later one, supporting the suggestion of its modern publisher, that it actually represents various "layers" of eschatological thought.[51] On purely stylistic grounds, he suggests it may be linked to the works of the Táborite prophet Jan Čapek, though he admits that this is inconclusive. As for dating, he suggests the time immediately following the prophesied day of judgement in mid-February 1420, or perhaps after the fall of Plzeň to anti-Hussites in late March,[52] though others hypothesise an even later dating, from 1420–1421.[53] Indeed, a date after February/March 1420 may

---

45 *HK*, 387, note 76.
46 *HK*, 352, note 1. Based on this assumption, the possible authorship is very limited. See Šmahel, *Dějiny Tábora* 1, 314–322.
47 "pro veritate premissorum articulorum scripturas sacras ad sensum suum interpretantes adducebant, quarum parciunculam curavi pro posteris comportare", *FRB* 5, 416; cf. Bartoš, "Do čtyř", 573, note 70.
48 Bartoš, "Do čtyř", 573.
49 Howard Kaminsky, "Chiliasm and the Hussite Revolution", *Church History* 26.1 (March 1957), 56
50 František Palacký, *Archiv Český Čili Staré Písemné Památky České i Morawské* 6 (Prague: 1872), 43; Příbram, *Život*, 40, and 43 with the radical priest Václav Koranda's comments in Plzeň.
51 Bartoš, "Do čtyř", 574.
52 Ibid., 573f.
53 Macek, *Tábor* I, 442f.

be supported by the fact that the text seems to refer to Christ's "secret" coming as already transpired, as well as true chiliasm,[54] concepts that other sources link to the later development of Tábor.[55]

Yet similarities between texts 4 and 5, and their differences from texts 6, 7, and other later ones,[56] make possible the dating of text 5 to pre-February/March 1420. The matter of violence, it may be argued, is the crucial difference here; in the later texts, the brothers of Tábor are called upon to exterminate the wicked themselves, while in the earlier ones there is hardly any allusion to human violence at all, and certainly nothing as bombastic as later texts suggest. In earlier texts, however, the faithful will take flight, hide from the Lord's anger, and it seems the violence and destruction will be carried out by supernatural forces. Those instances of human violence are either taken for granted and given eschatological meaning *post facto*,[57] or envisioned in the future,[58] and text 5 appears conceptually much closer to these than the hortatory later texts. Nevertheless, it does contain passages that may be interpreted as violent exhortations.[59]

It is not exactly clear which historical moment of the Táborites text 6 refers to. According to its placement in the chronicle, following the entry of 5 August—when Táborites requested the Praguers agree with them on several issues[60]—it could be dated between August and September 1420.[61] The apocalyptic articles—along with another list that addresses mostly issues of practice[62]—may also be a later, abbreviated copy of another list of Táborite

---

54 Bartoš, "Do čtyř", 585 f., 591.
55 See note 40 above.
56 Bartoš, "Do čtyř", 576 f., trans. McGinn, *Visions*, 268 f.; Jakoubek ze Stříbra, *Výklad na Zjevenie Sv. Jana* 1, ed. František Šimek (Prague: 1932), 525–528; Ignaz von Döllinger (ed.), *Beiträge zur Sektengeschichte des Mittelalters* 2 (Munich: 1890), 691–700; Palacký, *Archiv Český* 3, 218–225; František M. Bartoš, "Španělský biskup proti Táboru a Praze", *Jihočeský sborník historický* 11 (1938), 69 f.; Příbram, *Život*, 42 ff.; FRB 5, 454–462, partially trans. McGinn, *Visions*, 266–268.
57 Palacký, *Archiv Český* 6, 41.
58 FRB 5, 423.
59 The widow of the Gospel begs to be avenged, removing the gown of peace for the "sackcloth of obstruction" (Bartoš, "Do čtyř", 583); there is a rhetorical question posed: "Who shall render death on this day, who will flee …?" (Ibid., 583); the day of destruction will come to the wicked "without any excuse" (Ibid., 583); the "adulterous generation" does not believe in Christ because of his perceived weakness (Ibid., 584); the Lord will descend to fight, perhaps with the saints (Ibid., 586 f.); the elect will rejoice in the punishment of sinners, washing their hands in their blood (Ibid., 591).
60 FRB 5, 397–399.
61 Kaminsky, HR, 344, note 88 supposes August 1420.
62 FRB 5, 403–405.

errors,[63] though this seems unlikely given the likely later date of that list.[64] Březová links text 6 with text 4, offering the latter as "proof" of the former,[65] though the stark dissimilarities between them, especially regarding the matter of violence, seems to preclude a close connection, chronologically or conceptually. As to their authorship, Březová states that they were "openly taught" by the Táborite priests Martin Húska, Jan Jičín, Markolt,[66] and Václav Koranda.[67]

The excerpts from the books of the Táborite prophet Jan Čapek, surviving as they do in the copies made by his ardent opponent Jan Příbram (text 7), are arguably suspect of embellishment or abbreviation by the copyist's hand.[68] Nevertheless, they are valuable as one of the few texts (ostensibly) of Táborite provenance from this period that explicitly urge violence. Příbram[69] was a Hussite university master of Prague who was dismayed much more than Březová by the direction the early revolution took. He quickly became a vocal opponent of the Táborites and longed for peace with Rome, a sentiment that earned him exile from Prague in 1426. The work which text 7 is preserved in, *The Life of the Táborite priests*, is a venomous diatribe against the Táborites from their beginnings, and was likely written in 1430 as part of a polemic against the Táborite synod of that year.[70] For all its bias, the work remains a valuable source of early Táborite history and belief, and collects excerpts from various texts that no longer survive elsewhere.[71] A precise dating of text 7 itself is nearly impossible; broadly speaking it has been dated to 1419–1421.[72] Yet its hortative violence, its placement by Příbram at the beginning of the wars, and other details suggest a more precise dating, perhaps right in the critical days of mid-February[73] and March 1420.

---

63 Published in Palacký, *Archiv Český* 3, 218–225.
64 Both Palacký, *Archiv Český* 3, 218, and Macek, "Táborské Chiliastické Články", *Historický Sborník* 1 (1953), 59–61, suggest a later date for this document than August 1420, either late 1420 or late 1420 to early 1421, respectively. If there is a relationship between the documents, then Palacký's would probably be dependent on Březová's, not vice-versa.
65 *FRB* 5, 416.
66 On Markolt, see *HK*, 336 f., nr. 30, note 4.
67 On Koranda, *HK*, 335, nr. 27, note 6. On other possible authors, ibid., 352, nr. 59, note 5.
68 Abbreviation is suspected by Bartoš, "Do čtyř", 568.
69 On the life and works of Jan Příbram, see Příbram, *Život*, 7–24; Petra Mutlová, "Major Hussite Theologians before the Compactata", in Van Dussen and Soukup, *A Companion to the Hussites*, 124–126.
70 Příbram, *Život*, 21–23.
71 For similar works, see Jana Zachová and Jaroslav Boubín, "Příbramova Excerpta z Táborských Traktátů z Kapitulního Sborníku D 49", *Mediaevalia Historica Bohemica* 8 (2001), 139–167.
72 Macek, *Tábor* I, 443.
73 Bartoš, "Do čtyř", 568 f.

Finally, the Adamite articles (text 8) survive in a letter copied by Březová into his *Hussite Chronicle*, authored by their persecutor, the Hussite general Jan Žižka, shortly after he exterminated the group on 21 October 1421. This source is not unproblematic, given that the information drawn from the surviving Adamite was likely done so by means of torture, and that the articles often seem to reflect common late-medieval stereotypes and clichés regarding heretics. These and other observations have led to scrutiny, sometimes to the extent that the very existence of the group is put into question,[74] though such extreme suspicion has been recently resisted convincingly.[75]

---

[74] Alexander Patschovsky, "Der taboritische Chiliasmus: Seine Idee, sein Bild bei den Zeitgenossen und die Interpretation der Geschichtswissenschaft", in *Häresie und vorzeitige Reformation im Spätmittelalter*, ed. Frantisek Šmahel (Munich: 1998), 169–195. For discussion on the sources and literature on the Adamites, see Jukl, *Adamité*, 14–25.

[75] Cermanová, "The Apocalyptic background", 208–211.

Hussite Eschatological Writings*

1   *Quaestio* "On the Antichrist"[76]

Whether, as is absolutely certain from Scripture, that Christ came personally in the abundance of time, it is clearly deducible from the same that the Antichrist will come in person at the completion of the age. [This] I cannot now fully decide at once [...] But it should first be noted for this investigation that the completion of the age is not understood here as a special delay, before which the Lord Jesus Christ will come to judge the living and the dead, or as any sudden or instantaneous cessation of the dominion of the age, but as the last time—from the writings of the prophets[77]—which is to endure the Antichrist himself, etc.

    I note secondly, that just as the name 'Christ' signifies through antonomasia and excellence—in the first manner—Christ, the son of God who lived, united in the unction of the Spirit with his kindred; in the second manner ['Christ' signifies] any faithful Christian not only by visible sacrament, but also in participation in spiritual unction with Jesus Christ, having the spirit of Jesus in him according to the unction—yet no one against that esteem, in mortal offence, is Christ. Thirdly, 'Christ' is understood, with his head Jesus Christ, as the whole Church of the saints connected in the unity of the Spirit. In the fourth, more degraded manner, it is understood as the man who may be anointed in the sacramental and perceptible chrism according to the rite of the Church, only retaining the resulting mark or name of 'Christian' from baptism or from another sacrament of rank. And because such is a false Christian, not holding to Christ according to faith, life, and love, he [and] every such [person] is

---

*   Like all translations, those presented here are also works of interpretation. The various semantic ambiguities in the texts have been consciously maintained. Difficult passages have been indicated, and my own interpretation is especially manifest there. For the translations and notes of Lawrence of Březová's Chronicle, I was helped by its modern Czech translation, Vavřinec z Březové, *Husitksá kronika; Píseň o vítězství u Domažlic* [Hereafter *HK*], trans. František Heřmanský and Jan Blahoslav Čapek (Prague: 1979).

76   Jitka Sedláčková, "Jakoubek ze Stříbra a jeho kvestie o Antikristu" (PhD thesis, Masaryk University: 2001), 28–64 *passim*, Vlastimil Kybal, "M. Matěj z Janova a M Jakoubek ze Stříbra: Srovnávací kapitola o Antikristu", *Český Časopis Historický* 11 (1905), 22–37 *passim*. Kybal and Sedláčková transcribe from different manuscripts, and Kybal's transcription is only partial. The translation alternates between both, and this is indicated by footnotes.

77   Sedláčková MS: *prophetatum*.

against Christ and therefore is the Antichrist according to the Gospel: "He who is not with me, is against me".[78] Thus Antichrist [is] etymologically contrary to Christ and is the one, who under the false name or guise of Christ, is opposed to Christ. Though Antichrist, just like Christ, is understood in a similar way—as any false individual Christian who is opposed to Christ under the guise of the sanctity of Christ—now the Antichrist may be [also] understood through antonomasia and superiority as one single person under the name and guise of Christian piety, the highest opponent to Jesus Christ in malice, who is the head of all his members.

Now, the third matter: the Antichrist [is], for the whole mass of all false Christians with him, their leader or head, the highest degree of malice in the current Church, and in that way the Antichrist is to be understood as [both] greater and worse than any of his members, as well as their head or leader. And in any part of holy scripture which speaks of the Antichrist, it shall speak of him according to the first and second and third manner of signifying, but particularly they [parts of scripture] seem to speak more principally of the Antichrist in the third said manner. [...] [here follow quotes from Augustine's *City of God*][79]

From this it seems that the greatest Antichrist is not, nor will he be, any foreign gentile, but [rather] the greatest domestic enemy under the name and appearance of Christ. Indeed, that Antichristianity—which is the greatest contradiction to the truth, life, and doctrine of Christ—is with this man, knowing evil and enacting it, and doing this covered in the likeness of good, and thus honoured as if he were good, though he promised not to do evil, and not wanting to confess the evil [he] has done or does lest he ruin his glory. And when he does evil—appearing personally great and worthy among the people, in the holy place and through a holy issue or affairs, though in the time full of grace and truth, and against God and the son of God, already sitting at the right hand of God the almighty father, and despising or taking lightly Jesus' crucifixion and his passions—then any such person is the greatest Antichrist himself. And when such a "sinning man and son of perdition"[80] shall attain the highest station or place, adapted to the only excellence and truth and justice of the Christian people, he without doubt is the greatest and notorious Antichrist, since he is then truly what the apostle said of the Antichrist, that son of perdition elevated above all, who is called or worshipped [as if] God, indeed he who

---

78   Matt. 12:30.
79   Sedláčková, 28 f.
80   John 17:12.

shall sit in the temple of God and exhibit himself as if he would be God in the heavens, but [rather he is] god among terrestrial men. [...]

Thus, this greatest Antichrist will not be any Saracen or any gentile or Jew, nor any other powerful tyrant, nor anyone outside of the Christian religion, because such [people], according to reason, have already arrived but are not elevated above all, called God, or worshipped above all rank of dignity and authority of the Church. Already many such tyrants have lived vigorously, and [yet] they are not deemed to be Antichrists themselves, but rather impious and manifest persecutors of the Church of saints, and because of the fact that the Antichrist, according to his own manner, is said to be the greatest evil, and yet such tyrants who have lived were not yet the highest grade of injustice and falsehood,[81] since he [the Antichrist] shall be more wretched in such tyranny and cruelty. Thus, if he [Antichrist] shall be any Christian [sic] prince or spiritual priest, bishop, or Pope, then he consequently shall not be the Antichrist himself, i.e. the greatest contradiction to Christ, because he shall not be ordained under the same type of religion, and according to logic, opposites should be under the same type. Thus, Christ and Antichrist, as the greatest opposites, are under the same type, according to the following analogy: if the Antichrist would be a Jew or a gentile or any infidel, he would not be accordingly the last [Antichrist], and the one instructed in everything by Satan toward all type of deception, invading every path of God's elect and deceiving them with every delusion, and thus his coming would not be for the seduction of all, which contradicts the apostle, but his own impiety and faithlessness in the Church of saints would be very evident.[82]

Yet the Antichrist will come—according to the words of Christ and his apostles—in a threefold manner to seduce the elect especially, namely, with tyranny or secular power usurped for him, secondly, with [his] acquaintance of the body and of this world, through arguments against Christ and scripture, just as was done among heretics, and thirdly, with a great deal of imitated justice and false sanctity, [so that he] externally appears to be excellent, but in reality is not. And the manifest persecutor of Jesus Christ will not be any powerful Christian tyrant, king, or emperor, because such [people] could not yet attain the fullness of injustice; more wretched would be he who, under the guise and the height of sanctity, would deceive the saints and lead [them] against the despised Church of the wisdom of God and the power[83] of Jesus Christ. Furthermore, such a superior position [i.e. the secular ruler] would not attain dignity, because the status of the Church of saints would be greatly superior to

---

81   Kybal: *felicitatis*, Sedláčková: *falsitatis*.
82   Kybal, 26–28; NKČR, XI D 5, fol. 169^{r-v}.
83   1 Cor. 1:24.

him—especially the status of the highest priest—and he could only do harm to Christians through tyranny and force, and through such acts he would accordingly be an unbelieving tyrant and manifest heathen enemy to the most holy Church. Therefore, he could not injure the elect and the greatest number of people by the subtlety of deception. Yet the greatest Antichrist neither is, nor will be, an ambivalent person—powerful yet falsely pious—since[84] he would not have authority, which is most powerful in convincing the simple, nor would such a superior be able to do harm, because he would himself be attacked by equal or greater authorities of the Church, and consequently be easily impeded. And there have been men like this, many of whom, like heretics, have sought to injure the saints with deception.

Likewise, no one covered in the Christian religion alone—however powerful in authority, power, and riches—is or will be the Antichrist, because he would be easily banished by the multitude of faithful, and he would be convicted as a machination of injustice, as is cherished by many who are heretics or other unjust people who have climbed to the highest seat of the Church, [an injustice] which could not persist without his assistance, because it could inflict no such injury anywhere against a part or the entire world of the Church, and it would not be able to damage anyone with its attempts. That is to say, he would keep his innumerable consenting members to himself, deceitfully introduced throughout every region and the governance of the Church.

Thus, the Antichrist is described as a false Christ or a Christian, deceitfully opposed to the truth of the life and teaching of Christ, overly-abundant in the highest degree of malice, yet covered either completely or mostly in malice, possessing the highest position in the Church and claiming the highest authority[85] over all clerics and laymen from the fullness of his power, and the highest patronages of the wealth and wisdom of the age throughout the entire Church, [yet] obtaining this not from his own activity, pursuits, and will, but [from] those agreeing with Satan, mighty in all the riches, authority, and honour of the world, yet particularly and especially abusing these good things of Jesus Christ—like those in scripture, the sacraments, and under the quality of sanctity—for his own glory and greed, misusing those spiritual matters [and] insincerely turning to the flesh, and by keenly and covertly confining[86] those things ordained and granted for salvation through Jesus Christ in order to seduce [people] away from the truth and virtue of Jesus Christ. Namely, just as [when] other Christians are diverted through this easier and clearer, yet more dangerous [path]—toward the love of the world, toward avarice, simony, lux-

---

84   Sedláčková: *quam*, Kybal: *quia*.
85   Sedláčková: *suamque*, Kybal: *summamque*.
86   Sedláčková: *opera coartando*, Kybal: *operte coaptando*.

ury, and vanity, toward riches and delights, and toward worldly fame—indeed, just as when people seem to compare themselves to the highest sanctity or the apex of virtue, they will finally know and suffer the highest injustice and hypocrisy to befall them. [...] [long quotations from *The City of God*]

[...] After this, I posit the first conclusion: Christ and Antichrist are, chiefly and certainly, the greatest opposites in purpose, will, and activity, but only in these things that come immediately and directly from will. This appears to be the conclusion: Because Antichrist is not opposed to Christ in his nature, [since] nothing of substance is opposed to him [Christ], nor is he [Christ's] opposite according to any foreign, certain and manifest law—as perhaps Mohammed would be—because, just as is said above, he would not be the highest degree of enemy, nor would he be the height of opposition [...] Thus only and especially according to will and intention will the Antichrist be opposed to Jesus Christ, and in acts immediately proceeding from intention and will ...[87] [the text follows with a discussion of passages from 1 John 2:10–11, 15–16, 18–19, and Matthew 7:16–17]

[...] For just as Christ was altogether truthful and came in truth, thus the Antichrist is altogether deceitful and came through lies into the place of Christ. Just as Jesus was altogether pious, thus this "man of perdition" is altogether cruel; this one, namely Christ, entirely humble, the other entirely cruel. This one fulfilled the will of the Father, even to the debasement of the shameful cross, the other does not fear to fulfil his own will even against the greatest enmity and contempt of God. Christ set forth for the salvation of all souls, Antichrist for the safety of his own unjust life, [meaning] the death of countless people. Christ decided it better that he himself should perish rather than all mankind, but Antichrist rather exposes the entire world of the Church to the danger of damnation than endure death or trouble. Christ humbled himself to the lowest of men, to such an extent that he would be regarded among the unjust, yet Antichrist elevates himself so greatly, even over everything, that he is called God, worshipped, and raised up. Also, in the mystical body of Christ, there was one heart and one soul among many believers, yet in the mystical body of the Antichrist you will not easily find even two mutually in accord with Christ among themselves.[88] The members of Christ [are] adorned in Christ, in the virtue of almighty God and the wisdom of God, walking in true charity, [while] the members of the Antichrist, or those defiled in the highest vices without fear of God, walk in every hypocrisy and disguise. And in the body of the Antichrist, that which is deemed [useful] for life by members of Christ [is] now concisely deemed unsuitable, [and] on the contrary that, which Christians

---

87   Sedláčková, 32–35.
88   Kybal, 30 f.; NKČR, XI D 5, fol. 172ʳ

in the mystical body of Christ would have spat out, is now deemed honesty and elegance in the body of the Antichrist. And you will find many similar things, if you faithfully compare, in greatest opposition, the primitive Church to the present heathen destruction among Christians. [...][89]

The second part of the conclusion: the first is proven, [namely] that all divinely inspired scripture which speaks of the mysteries and prophecies of Christ or his familiar enemy the Antichrist, thus hides his time with figures and conceals [it] with metaphorical words, so that no one could clearly reveal it in particular with certainty among themselves or others, unless inspired by the spirit—and particularly and most intimately taught [by it]—which inclined the first to write.[90] [...] Thus the prophetic hidden mysteries and signs of the Old and New Law, or of Christ or the Antichrist, cannot themselves be understood usefully and lucidly unless the readers or listeners would be remarkably instructed by the same Holy Spirit. [...]

It is first proven, that clearly he [the Antichrist] has already come and that this age will be particularly characteristic of him. For it is believed from faith and for the faithful, that just as it is characteristic of the crucified Jesus to congregate the Church into unity, so it is especially characteristic of the Antichrist to divide it. [...]

Thirdly, it is proven, namely that such a division[91] has already come,[92] as prophesised by the Apostle. For if this division is understood as in fact a division of obedience of the Roman empire and rule, and in spiritual matters [a division] of Papal obedience, then today that division is absolutely completed—whether permissible or not—to such an extent that it will not be necessary to demonstrate it except with an extended finger, [pointing] everywhere throughout the Church. [...]

Thus, because such a division already came a short time ago, from the cross of Jesus Christ and from justice—which is completed through the cross and in the cross through the Son of God for the vindication of many others—a division from the orders of God to the orders, inventions, and teachings of men, and a separation from the truth of the life and teaching of Christ and his apostles toward the fables and deceptions of the world, which are prophesised to occur in the time of Antichrist, it is not considered that another Antichrist shall come again, or is to be expected, since he has already come in the fullness of his being etc. [...][93]

---

89   Sedláčková, 37.
90   2 Pet. 1:21.
91   2 Thess. 2:3.
92   Kybal: *venit*, Sedláčková: *iam venit*.
93   Kybal, 31–33.

2 Adventist Song: "Let Us Rejoice, Having Finished Waiting"[94]

Let us rejoice, having finished waiting, now knowing the law of God, gathering to honour God.
To the feast of the renowned lamb, sacrificed for us, innocent of all sins.
Blessed, those who will be led to that approaching sacrifice, are removed from sins,
Obeying God in that which he spoke to his prophets and also to his apostles.
For God said to the prophet, [as] he revealed to Ezekiel,[95] that he made this sacrifice.
Saying: "Collect yourselves and come close, and convene all, and sacrifice to me the sacrifice,
which I sacrifice to all of you, the great sacrifice on the mountains. Do not pay attention to the detriment of the wicked.
Eat the sacrificed body and all together drink the blood, until you shall be satiated".[96]
Also Isaiah[97] asserts that God will prepare on the mountain feasts for all people.
Ezekiel, who had the revelation of God, again says, speaking about evil shepherds,
That God orders them to stop and to govern their sheep and not to feed on them.
Because he wants to free them and tear them out of their [the shepherds'] throats and graze them himself on the mountains.[98]
To find what died, to return what has gone, to solidify what is broken.
As the prophet says again, thus shown by Isaiah, that many will go to that mountain.
Saying: "let us step onto God's mountain, let him there teach us his ways". That is what those prophets tell us.[99]
We [are] shown an example of this, that the law and the new teaching of Christ is given on the mountain.
People [were] fed by bread on the mountain, when they were ready for it, [and they were] led by Christ into the desert.
Thus do not resist evil, but go up to the mountain, here you will learn truth.

---

94 Zdeněk Nejedlý, *Dějiny husitského zpěvu* 6 (Prague: 1956), 186 f.
95 Ezek. 39:17, 19.
96 A clear hortatory reference to utraquism, see introduction.
97 Isa. 25:6.
98 Ezek. 34:2, 10, 13.
99 Isa. 2:3.

Because Christ ordered thusly, when he prophesised on the mountain, preaching of the destruction of the temple.

Saying: "Whoever will be in Christendom, quickly flee to the mountains, because of the very heavy sorrow".[100]

Have mercy on us, Lord, because we await you in sorrow. May you be our strength in the morning![101]

For our life is very painful, it is stripped of goodness, deign to save us. Amen.

---

100   Matt. 24:16.
101   Isa. 33:2. Nejedlý, 187: *budiž naše v jitře rámé!*

3   Anonymous Apocalyptic Tractate[102]

May the Lord God be with you and enlighten and bring joy to your hearts during your sorrows and grief and sorrows [sic]. Most beloved brothers and sisters in God! According to this difficult and terrible and dangerous time, foreseen by Christ and the apostles and the holy prophets, which is the time of the greatest sorrow of the word, and very great daily retributions of God; and Christ lets that time be known especially by the many varied and hypocritical seductions, by wars, [and] by presumed wars. For already many are grieved against Christ's commands, assuming that battles should not be undertaken with the physical sword against malice and abomination, against error and heresy. But Christ said: Do not be grieved, when you hear wars and strife, those things must be, as the holy prophets prophesied.[103] And especially the holy Isaiah says: you will be victorious, especially [against][104] enemies, hypocrites, seducers and impeders of God's elect.[105] For holy John says in his revelation in the seventeenth chapter: They will make war against the Lamb, and the Lamb will conquer them, for he is Lord of lords and king of kings; and those with him are the chosen, the elect of God.[106] And also Christ lets that time be known by strife, by many scandals, by the spread of malice, by the oppression of many, by corruption, abominations in the holy place,[107] which are sins, idolatry, caves,[108] and other offences disgusting to God, by anguish, by the capturing and the murder first of God's elect.[109] And various[110] are the many signs and deeds, by which that time is made known, that is already close and is in the doorway; just as the summertime is known by the leaves and fruits, so Christ makes apparent that time of the greatest distress in his scriptures. In that time Christ gives a special command to his faithful, that they run not only from sins, but also from the midst of

---

102   František Palacký, *Archiv Český Čili Staré Písemné Památky České i Morawské* 6 (Prague: 1872), 41–43. Part 'a'. Part 'b' is translated in Thomas A. Fudge, *The Crusades against Heretics in Bohemia, 1418–1437* (Aldershot: 2002), 32 f.
103   Mark 13:7; Matt. 24:6; Luke 21:9.
104   The text is erroneous and difficult here: ... *w zwaštních wybojujete je* ...
105   Isa. 41:10–11.
106   Rev. 17:14.
107   Dan. 12:11; Matt. 24:15.
108   Palacký: *jeskyň*. The Biblical "den of robbers" (*spelunca latronum*, cf. Jer. 7:11) was a favourite of Hussite polemicists.
109   Though this could allude to any among a long list of anti-Hussite persecutions dating back to 1412, it may be a reference to the most recent, mass incarceration and murder of Hussites at Kutná Hora. See Josef Emler, Jan Gebauer, and Jaroslav Goll (eds), *Fontes Rerum Bohemicarum* 5 (Prague: 1893), 351 f., translated by Fudge, *The Crusades*, 40 f.
110   Or "different". Palacký MS: *jiná*.

the wicked, offensive and insincere people, and says: flee to the mountains,[111] namely to the faithful people, who have raised high their hopes, thoughts,[112] and prayers to God against all and above all powers. And again he says: pray, so that you will be runaways worthy of all things which will come.[113] And so the Lord God orders flight, first so that all may save their souls; second, so that [their] hearts do not become mollified among the wicked people; third, so that they do not fear the threats and commandments which will be heard on earth; fourth, so that they are not part of the wicked people; and fifth, so that they do not suffer blows with them [the wicked], as holy John and holy Jeremiah testify. Thus, knowing these things, hurry and hasten to flee from the midst of the wicked as if from fire, and neither doubt, nor let yourselves be deceived, that it is the will of Christ that you should congregate yourselves with God's elect in that time of great distress. For Christ says in the scriptures of holy Matthew in the 24th chapter: he will send his angels or messengers with a trumpet and with a great sound, and he will congregate his elect from the four winds.[114] And in the scriptures of holy Luke in chapter 17, when his disciples were asking him, saying, "where lord?", and he answered: where the body will be, here also eagles will gather. So do not say, "why should we flee before God[?]; wherever a good man dies, he dies well."[115] That is true sometimes, but not always. Just as it was good for Lot to be in Sodom for a long time among the wicked, in the time of vengeance, when God commanded him to go and flee from there, it was no longer good for him to die there, like his two sons-in-law, who fell with the wicked, not wanting to leave.[116] Also now honest people, though they may have lived and died well for a long time among the wicked, will not die well [among them] in the time of vengeance, because they will violate the special command of God issued in that time, which is the command to flee from the midst of the wicked. Thus Lord Christ orders, saying: remember Lot's wife; he who will desire to save his soul, namely among the wicked, will lose it, like Lot's wife lost her life, not only [for] remaining among the wicked, but [for] not heeding the pro-

---

111 Matt. 24:16; Luke 21:21.
112 Palacký MS: *masle*.
113 Luke 21:36.
114 Matt. 24:31.
115 A reference to Jakoubek's refutation of Táborite prophecies, see the introduction to this text. See especially Jakoubek's remarks, Howard Kaminsky, *A History of the Hussite Revolution* [hereafter *HR*] (Berkeley: 1967), 520: "Christi fideles viventes secundum ewangelica precepta [...] in quacumque civitate materiali, castro, opido, vel villa vel campo vel via vel silva [...] salvabuntur."; "Unde talis iustus nec in Praga nec alibi sic in iusticia perseverans debet timere dampnacionem ex hoc solo quod in Praga manet vel alibi ..."
116 Gen. 19:14.

hibition.[117] It is necessary to remember, because Christ also commands of us that one should not be concerned with houses, properties, [or] for any material things,[118] and should not believe the seducers, who say "wherever a righteous man falls, he falls well".[119] For Christ says: Then if they say to you: "Here or there is Christ", do not believe it,[120] namely if they say, "if a person would only run from sins, Christ is merciful to him in a village or in a city"; that is a great error. Because Christ says further: False prophets will arise and will produce signs and miracles, so that they [the faithful]—[and] if possible, even the elect—would be led into error.[121] And what are those great signs, which the false Christs and false prophets offer? They may be the renowned individuals [such as] masters and lords, and clearly [are], because they seemed to be something and they are nothing.[122] They seduce the elect of God, saying, "indeed neither masters nor lords support this [i.e. the prophecies], only some of those [people] who draw and interpret [scripture] from their own heads". And they lead the simple people to error from their own heads, where scripture and arguments are lacking, and they assert many other erroneous things against scripture, as when they say to people, "whoever the word of God propels to abandon and pay no attention to properties: do not go from your goods, they [the priests that urge this] lie to you!" They clearly say that against scripture, which says: "Whoever abandons his house, brothers, sisters, or father or mother, or lands or fields for my name, will receive a hundredfold more and will receive eternal life."[123] And again they say, in order to seduce people: "it is as if they would call a man from his wife, and wives from husbands, and thus cancel marriage, thus causing disorders to people and doubt", not honestly telling people scripture according to the time appointed by God. Because if they would recognise the current time of the days of vengeance, they would have to pronounce it themselves to the people, that in that darkened time Christ will divide the people of all estates, as holy Luke says in the 17th chapter: "On that night there will be two on the bed, one will be taken and the other will remain, two in one mill, one will be taken and the other will remain".[124] All the disciples asked him: "Where Lord?" And

---

117 Gen. 19:26.
118 Matt. 24:16–18.
119 See note 34.
120 Matt. 24:23.
121 Matt. 24:24.
122 Probably a reference to the truce of the university masters of Prague and their noble supporters with King Sigismund in November 1419. See introduction.
123 Matt. 19:29.
124 Luke 17:34–35.

he continued: "Where the body will be, here also the eagles will convene".[125] For that reason, brothers and sisters, you know where, indeed where the body of Christ is given with all the pieces of God's truth, collect yourselves here in the time of vengeance and of greatest sorrow. And those places in that time cannot be in villages or elsewhere, because of the strong and horrible Antichrist, but in fortified cities, of which the holy Isaiah names five,[126] namely on that day of the coming of the Lord Jesus Christ. And that is again ridiculed by many, and they say: "Indeed, there are more sins in cities than in villages". To which the answer is: "Indeed, also there were more sins in Egypt than in the land of the Jews, and yet Jesus with Joseph and Mary fled to Egypt from Herod, as the angel of God commanded him". And also now, God wants and commands that his faithful should congregate into the fortified cities in that time and run, and it is assured that he will cleanse the evil in his own time. Thus the Lord God commanded his priests to diligently call out and say: "Collect yourselves and go out to the fortified cities, for I am enacting a bad thing and I will bring a great affliction from midnight".[127] Thus it is necessary to congregate without delay, so that they may fast and wail over their own sins and those of others, so that they shall pray day and night to the Lord God, calling that he may deign to save [them] in the time of the greatest persecution. And also that they may align themselves with God's word, good examples and advice, and especially that they may fill themselves with the valuable feast and drink of the Lord Jesus Christ. Thus the Lord God says through the holy prophet Joel in the 2nd chapter: "Great and dreadful is the day of the Lord, and who will survive it?"[128] Thus, now the Lord God says: "turn yourself in your whole heart, in fasting, in weeping and wailing, and rend your hearts and not your clothing. Turn yourselves to your Lord God, for he is compassionate and gracious and patient, very merciful and forgiving of malice. Who knows whether he may hopefully turn and forgive and relent, and leave blessing behind him. A dry offering and a wet offering to our Lord God will be offered. Blow the horn in Zion, which is among the faithful, sanctify the fast, call a gathering, collect the people. Consecrate the gathering, collect the old and young, the children who are at the breast. May the bridegroom leave his bed and the bride her bed".[129] The grace

---

125   Luke 17:37; Matt. 24:28.
126   Isa. 19:18.
127   Jer. 4:6. Vulgate: *confortamini* [...] *quia malum ego adduco ab aquilone* [...]. The theme of night or midnight as an important time of change or action is a recurring theme in the apocalyptic literature. See also texts 4, 5, and 8 below.
128   Joel 2:11, 31.
129   Joel 2:12–16.

of God with you and may the Lord God grant you those things to turn to the beneficial and to salvation, and with them the understanding of God's will, and the fulfillment of God's commands. May the Lord God give us perseverance in all good things.

4   *Quaestio* "Proving" the Apocalyptic Articles (of Text 6)[130]

Further, for the truth of the abovementioned articles[131] they [the Táborite priests] cited holy scripture, interpreting it according to their own understanding; and from these I [Lawrence of Březová] have sought to convey a part for future people, so that it shall be clear to all what kind of insane heads led the simple people.

The first assumption: the authorities are right, from which the first is the writing in Revelation 10, namely that: "in the days of the seventh angel, who will begin to blow his horn, the mystery of God will be fulfilled, as he heralded through his servants the prophets",[132] and again in Daniel 22: "Once the power of the holy people is shattered, all these things will be fulfilled".[133]

The second assumption: once all the passions of Christ are fulfilled—predicted through the prophets by the Holy Spirit—then the subsequent prophesied glory will appear in all the house generally, and not before.

The third assumption: that the words of the Old and New laws and the words of the prophets and holy apostles, as they are laid down and as they sound, are true and can be adduced to be true.

The fourth assumption: that from the words of God nothing should be added nor taken.

And posing these assumptions in this way, I have formed the position, which is almost the entire foundation of my preaching.[134] Already now at the consummation of the age,[135] Christ will come, in the day which is called the day of the Lord, that he may subdue the rebellious house and cause the consummation in it, and that he may—restoring the Church—place that praise on the earth. He will come to receive the kingdom on this earth and to remove all scandals and all those "who make iniquity", and he will not allow "anything lying nor abominable".[136]

---

130   Josef Emler, Jan Gebauer, and Jaroslav Goll (eds), *Fontes Rerum Bohemicarum* 5 (Prague: 1893), 417–424.
131   Referring to Text 6. Indeed, the two texts are published in opposite order (Text 6 followed by Text 4), but I follow here a chronological ordering. See the discussion in the introduction.
132   Rev. 10:7.
133   Dan. 12:7. Kaminsky, *HR*, 351 note 119 suspects the influence of Joachim of Fiore here. See note 264 below.
134   The first-person voice now shifts to that the Táborite author.
135   "in consummacione seculi". The author distinguishes between the end of the age and the end of the world below.
136   Rev. 21:27.

I understand that consummation, which Christ predicted in Matthew 24,[137] and which he mentioned in Matthew 13,[138] and of which speaks Isaiah 10: "for the Lord God will consummate and shorten many";[139] which Jeremiah explains: "I will make a consummation in all the nations in which I have dispersed you, however I will not make a consummation in you, but I will punish you in the judgement, that I shall not seem innocent to you", Jeremiah 30.[140] "Because they abandoned God, they shall be destroyed"[141] Isaiah 1.[142] Yet the sins of some shall be consummated so greatly, and they shall become holy from among gentiles; and thus it is written: "His tongue devours like flame", Isaiah 3.[143] "He will crush the wicked and the sinners", Isaiah 1.[144] "I shall destroy all who afflict you", Zephaniah 3.[145]

I understand "age"[146] as the apostle receives it in Hebrews 9, saying: "but now in the consummation of the age";[147] where he marks that there is a plurality of ages, saying that some have already been consummated. And thusly Matthew 12 [also] understands, saying: "sin against the Holy Spirit shall not be forgiven in this age",[148] the consummation of which Matthew 12 predicts: "thus", it is said, "will be at the consummation of the age";[149] and foretelling that there will be another [age], he adds: "nor in the coming one". And again another, which is said in Luke 20: "But those, who are valued in that age".[150] He does not say the future one, but that one etc. And this also proves that there are more ages, making a distinction between age and world. For when there occurs a very notable change in people, then the age is consummated. Thus I address the consummation of the age as the change of the good to the better and the extermination of evil, because it is written: "I will make the consummation in all nations, but I will not make a consummation in you", Jeremiah 30.[151]

---

137 Matt. 24:1–31.
138 Matt. 13:49.
139 Isa. 28:22.
140 Jer. 30:11.
141 Literally "consummated" [*consumentur*].
142 Isa. 1:28.
143 Isa. 30:27.
144 Isa. 1:28.
145 Zeph. 3:19.
146 Here the author argues for a distinction in the understanding of age (*seculum*) and world (*mundum*). This is significant, because he argues that the end of the age does not mean the end of the world—as was the standard understanding—and thus not the end of humanity.
147 Heb. 9:26.
148 Matt. 12:32.
149 Matt. 13:40.
150 Luke 20:35.
151 Jer. 30:11.

The day of the Lord I call the day of vengeance, on which Isaiah 63: "The day of vengeance is in my heart and the year of my retribution has come."[152] And 61: "The Holy spirit[153] has sent me to proclaim the acceptable year and the day of retribution";[154] on which is written also in Luke 4.[155] "And that day will come like a thief in the night", 1 Thessalonians 5[156] and "it shall appear in fire", 1 Corinthians 3.[157] Indeed, the apostle predicted in 2 Thessalonians 2,[158] and also in Zechariah 14,[159] how the falling away will precede it.[160]

And on that day the coming Christ arrives, Habakkuk 2,[161] "and the eater and drinker comes and he is named the devourer and drinker of wine", Luke 7;[162] because he is coming on the immaculate road, the saints are singing psalms[163] and "the exaltations of God are in their throats", Psalm 100;[164] and they will sing, Psalm 150. "As the sacred sound of solemnity[165] and joy of heart, as he who goes forth with a flute", Isaiah 3[166] and Psalm 100. And they understand, because in the last days you will understand the plans of the Lord, Jeremiah 23[167] and 30.[168] Because now the book is sealed, Isaiah 29[169] and Daniel 12;[170] at the unfastening of the seven seals (1 John),[171] it is opened. For already Christ is coming in innocence and will walk in the middle of his house and will enact works of mercy. Nevertheless, he enacts just judgements, not knowing evil, to anybody who is agitating, because, not knowing evil, he says this: "I do not know

---

152 Isa. 63:4. Vulgate: *annus redemptionis*.
153 Vulgate: *spiritus Domini*. Isa. 61:1.
154 Isa. 61:2.
155 Luke 4:19.
156 1 Thess. 5:2.
157 1 Cor. 3:13.
158 2 Thess. 2:3.
159 Zech. 14:1–2.
160 Here again, Kaminsky, *HR*, 351 note 119 identifies the influence of Joachim of Fiore. See note 264 below.
161 Hab. 2:3: "For the vision is yet for an appointed time, but at the end it shall speak, and not lie: though it tarry, wait for it; because it will surely come, it will not tarry." (KJV).
162 Luke 7:34.
163 Psalm 100:2.
164 Psalm 149:6.
165 *FRB* 5: *Sicut vox sanctificate solempnitatis*, while the Vulgate reads *nox sanctificatae sollemnitatis*.
166 Isa. 30:29.
167 Jer. 23:20.
168 Jer. 30:24.
169 Isa. 29:11.
170 Dan. 12:4.
171 Rev. 5:5; 6:1; 8:1 ff.

you", Matthew 25.[172] Already he is persecuting the priests, who withdrew from their nearby hiding place. Already, with the proud eye of the master, he begins not to eat the bread of wisdom, and is returning it back, making his own foolish wisdom, Isaiah 44[173] and 1 Corinthians 1.[174] And the hearts of the avarous are unsatiated and reject their sacraments. The immaculate, namely the priests who are not possessors and who shook off all the dust of desire, already now sit with God serving Christ. Now he is setting out to chase out the proud from the house. Now, he who speaks the unjust words of his [own] iniquity, cannot direct [anyone] by the authorities of scripture, because "a vessel, which is made against you, does not prosper", Isaiah 44.[175] What yet remains is that in the morning he [Christ] destroy the sinners and "cut out all workers of iniquity from the city of God"[176] and "that they be confounded at night and not remain in the morning. This is the part of them that ravaged us, and the lot of them that plunder us", Isaiah 17;[177] in Psalm 100,[178] namely "I will sing of mercy and judgement to you, O Lord!" The signs of his advent are stated, when it is said: "I will sing the psalms and understand, when you shall come to me on the immaculate path".[179] Already even children sing the psalms and some understand the hidden secrets. "For the name of the Lord is coming from afar with ardent fury and grave severity, his lips are full of indignation and his tongue devouring like fire, his spirit overflowing and scorching, reaching up to the neck, to crush the nations to nothing and to curb the error, i.e. heretical decrees, which were in the jaws of the people", Isaiah 30.[180] "For the rage of the Lord is upon all nations and his fury is upon all their malice,[181] he destroyed them and delivered them to slaughter", Isaiah 38.[182] "Because now I shall arise, says the Lord, now I shall be praised, now I shall be elevated. Take the flame, bring forth the straw; your spirit will devour you like fire and the people will be like ashes of the flame, the thorns will be collected and burned by fire. And thus

---

172 Matt. 25:12.
173 Isa. 44:25.
174 1 Cor. 1:19. The sentence is ambiguous but seems to refer to the priests of the previous sentence, and likely also to the university masters of Prague who were seen as traitors to God's law.
175 Isa. 44:17.
176 Psalm 100:8.
177 Isa. 17:14.
178 Psalm 100:1.
179 Psalm 100:1–2.
180 Isa. 30:27–28.
181 Goll MS: *maliciam*. In Vulgate, *militiam* (army).
182 Isa. 34:2.

the sinners were crushed[183] on Zion, and shaking took hold of the hypocrites", Isaiah 33,[184] "they are a rebellious house", Ezekiel 3.[185] Because "there will come a strong warrior and he will leap in the midst of the land of destruction", and in a moment a magnificent nation will perish, i.e. the heavenly status of priests will be destroyed quickly and suddenly, Wisdom 18,[186] "and the sky will pass away in a great assault", 2 Peter 3,[187] and "the heavens and the earth will be shaken" Joel 3.[188]

By the praise of the Church I mean, firstly, that it will be collected, secondly that it will be cleansed, thirdly, that it will be multiplied, fourthly, [that] it will be pacified, fifthly [that] it will be established in equal glory with the primitive Church, sixthly, that it will be more glorious than ever. It is urged through Isaiah, so that all the saints implore this of the Church from the Lord God in prayer: "when you think of God, do not be silent and do not give the silence of God [sic][189] until he establishes and enacts Jerusalem [and its] glory in the world", Isaiah 62.[190] Zephaniah explains this world, saying: "I will give them glory and honour in every land of their shame", Zephaniah 3.[191]

On the collection and unity of the Church. "I have other sheep, Christ says, which are not from this sheepfold, and they need to come to me and they will hear my voice", John 10.[192] "For he will send his angels and they will collect the elect from the four winds", Matthew 24.[193] "Because I will congregate them from all lands to which I expelled them in my rage and anger and great disdain, and I will lead them again to this place, and will make it so they live safely, and they will be my people, and I will be their God, and I will give to them one heart and one path, that they may fear me every day, and that they will live well and their sons after them, and I will make with them an eternal covenant." This is to be read and well-noted: "And I will not cease doing good to them, and I will give my dread into their hearts, that they do not step away from me, and I will rejoice in doing them good, and I will plant them in this land in truth." Jeremiah 32.[194]

---

183 Goll MS: *contriti*. In Vulgate, *conterriti* (terrified).
184 Isa. 33:10–12, 14.
185 Ezek. 3:9; 26–27.
186 Wis. 18:15.
187 2 Pet. 3:10.
188 Joel 3:16.
189 Goll MS: *dei*, instead of Vulgate *ei*.
190 Isa. 62:6–7.
191 Zeph. 3:19.
192 John 10:16.
193 Matt. 24:31.
194 Jer. 32:37–41.

And "they will see eye to eye, when the Lord reverses the captivity of Zion", Isaiah 22.[195] Because "Lo, the days are coming, and they do not say:[196] the Lord lives, who led [the sons of Israel][197] from the land of Egypt, but the Lord lives, who led [the sons of Israel] from [all] the lands", Jeremiah 16 and 23 and 31.[198] "Because when I will be consecrated in you, I will indeed raise you from all lands", Ezekiel 36.[199] This congregation and collection most certainly will come, because Christ also predicted it. And in those collected, all things according to the good sense of the Holy Spirit will be fulfilled, which are touched upon by the authority of Jeremiah, which in truth is to be fulfilled, which shows that the sons will yet enter secretly with the departing fathers,[200] but always to be understood according to intent of the Holy Spirit. "God will congregate his own, even if they shall be dispersed to the boundaries of heaven" Deuteronomy 20.[201]

On the purification and cleansing of the Church. "Christ will clean out his threshing-floor", Matthew 3,[202] and "the father will clean every vine-branch which produces fruit in Christ, and which is poorly cut, so that it may offer more fruit", John 15.[203] Lo, this relates to merit, because when the evil will miserably perish at the Lord's coming, the vine will be committed to those restoring the fruit. Indeed, "clean water will be poured over the elect and they will be cleansed from all filth", Ezekiel 36.[204] And tried in faith, just as fire tries gold, they will appear clean "on the day of revelation", 1 Peter 1.[205] Because "the sons of Levi will be cleansed, and he will cleanse them like gold and silver" and thus they will be clean, "offering the sacrifice in justice, and then the sacrifice of Judah and Jerusalem will please God, just as in the days of the age and just as in the days of old".[206] And again he presents the work of merit. Again it is said: "I am turning my hand to you until I burn your slag pure and I remove all your alloy, and restore your judges like in the beginning, and your advisers like in days of old. After this you will be called the just city, Zion, the city of faith.[207] It

---

195   Isa. 52:8.
196   Goll, 421: *et non dicent*, instead of Vulgate: *et non dicetur ultra*.
197   Goll, 421: "who led us" (*eduxit nos*).
198   Jer. 16:14–15; 23:7–8.
199   Ezek. 36:23–24.
200   4 Bar. 8:9–10.
201   Deut. 30:4.
202   Matt. 3:12.
203   John 15:2.
204   Ezek. 36:25.
205   1 Pet. 1:7.
206   Mal. 3:3–4.
207   Goll, 421: *Post hec vocaberis civitas iusta, urbs fidelis Sion. In iudicio redimetur* […], but in the Vulgate: *Post hec vocaberis civitas iusta, urbs fidelis. Sion in iudicio redimetur* …

will be redeemed in judgement and they will restore it in justice. It will crush the wicked and the sinners alike, and those who forsook him, the Lord, will perish", Isaiah 1.[208] "And lo, I will destroy all those who afflicted you", Zephaniah 3.[209]

On the spread of the Church. For "the clean will bring more fruit", John 15.[210] "And the wedding will be filled with guests", Matthew 22,[211] because the lame and the deaf will be congregated, and will hear the voice of the Lord on that day. Thence Jeremiah 31: "Lo, I will lead them from the land of the north wind and I will congregate them from all ends of the earth, among whom will be the blind and the lame, pregnant and birthing, a great collection returning here, they will come with tears and with prayers, I will lead them through to the liquid waters in a straight path", Jeremiah 31.[212] "For the sons of barrenness will say: The place is too narrow for me, make space for me, where I shall live". The mother speaks of them in her heart: "Who begot them to me, I am sterile and not [capable of] giving birth, transmigrated and captive, who will nurture them? I, who am destitute and desolate? And where will they be?", Isaiah 49[213] and 50. Because "when he will lead the children into the land which their fathers possess, blessing them, he will make their number greater than that of their fathers." Deuteronomy 30.[214]

On the peace of the Church. The arising Jesus will rule the winds and the sea, "and there will be a great peace on that day", Matthew 8.[215] The elect will have peace with God, because he will not be angry with them anymore. Just as it is written: "In a moment of anger I briefly hid my face from you, but I had everlasting mercy for you, said your God the redeemer. It is for me just like in the days of Noah, to whom I vowed I will not conduct the waters of the downpour onto the lands, thus I vowed I will not be angry and I shall not rebuke you".[216] And below: "my mercy will not recede from you, and the treaty of my peace will not be moved", they will have peace with the people.[217] "For kings will serve them, and the nation that will not serve them will perish", Isaiah

---

208 Isa. 1:25–28.
209 Zeph. 3:19.
210 John 15:2.
211 Matt. 22:10.
212 Jer. 31:8–9.
213 Isa. 49:20–21.
214 Deut. 30:5.
215 Matt. 8:26.
216 Isa. 54:8–9.
217 Isa. 54:10.

60.²¹⁸ "The enforcer will cease, the tribute will stop", Isaiah 14.²¹⁹ They will not be impeded by the wise of this world just as now, because they will not be "the worst vessels of the deceitful, which he devised for the destruction of the meek with false speech, when the poor man speaks judgement", on which things Isaiah 32.²²⁰ Now, finally "they will judge every tongue opposing them", Isaiah 54.²²¹ "Because they will be magnificently withdrawn from their midst of haughty pride²²² and the poor people will be abandoned among them", Zephaniah 3.²²³ "I will ordain, says the Lord, peace as your officers", Isaiah 60.²²⁴ Because the last holy ones are the feet, "who are leading into the way of peace", Luke 1.²²⁵ "God will place peace in the borders", Psalm 147.²²⁶ Nothing will stand against these feet, which will be covered by shoes—[as] it was denied to the predecessors to extend over Edom—²²⁷ and with which the prodigal son was shoed when he came to the father.²²⁸ Thus it is said: "I will establish the multitude of peace for your children", Isaiah 54.²²⁹

On the equality of glory with the primitive [Christians]. "For the days of the saints will be restored, as in the beginning", in the last [chapter] of Lamentations.²³⁰ "And the saints will inherit, just as from the beginning", Ecclesiastes 36.²³¹ "And they will be, as they were, as if they were not scattered", Zechariah 10.²³² "They will be turned to their country", Jeremiah 23.²³³ "They will be planted and they will thrive and live in the mountains, just as in the beginning", Ezekiel 36.²³⁴ "Again they will be established and adorned with drums and they will ascend in a playing chorus", Jeremiah 31²³⁵ and Zechariah 10.²³⁶ "Because

---

218   Isa. 60:11–12.
219   Isa. 14:4.
220   Isa. 32:7.
221   Isa. 54:7.
222   Goll, 422: *superbie*; Vulgate: *superbiae tuae*.
223   Zeph. 3:11–12.
224   Isa. 60:17.
225   Luke 1:79.
226   Psalm 147:3.
227   Psalm 59:10.
228   Luke 15:22.
229   Isa. 54:13.
230   Lam. 5:21.
231   Sir. 36:13.
232   Zech. 10:6.
233   Jer. 23:3.
234   Ezek. 36:11.
235   Jer. 31:4.
236   Zech. 10:6.

these last ones were working one hour and were made equal to those carrying the weight in the heat of the day", Matthew 20.[237]

On the greater glory of the last house. With the expulsion of all offences and "workers of injustice"[238] from the kingdom of Christ, "the following days will begin to dawn and the morning star will appear in hearts",[239] "then the just will shine like the sun", Matthew 13.[240] Furthermore, "the sun of human intelligence will not shine for them", Isaiah 60,[241] but they will be "the light of the gentiles", Isaiah 44.[242] Already those seeing the vengeance will rejoice, and indeed those enacting the revenge, Luke 19.[243] Now they, who trampled the Church for 42 months, Revelation 11,[244] will be a stumbling block[245] to the feet, that is to the last saints. To whom the apostles were like despised filth, as if bound to death, whose "children will come bowed to worship the soles of [your] feet", Isaiah 60.[246] Because already "they will be established and they will be praised in the land", Isaiah 62.[247] And this "in the land of their confounding", Zephaniah 3.[248] Already "their sadness will be turned to joy", John 16.[249] These things combined with the preceding show the "greater glory of the last house above the first", Haggai 2,[250] and they note that they [the saints] will be given greater gifts[251] than they had at the beginning, Ezekiel 36.[252] And this will truly be done after all the passions of Christ will be completed. Indeed, the apostle declared this, for example, saying in 1 Corinthians 13:[253] "the head cannot say to the feet" etc., to here: "if one member [of the body] boasts, the others shall also rejoice".[254] I do not deny that the comparison also means that he understands it to relate to the body, in which there are ranks of status, in which the very disparaged are to

---

237 Matt. 20:12.
238 Matt. 13:41.
239 2 Pet. 1:19.
240 Matt. 13:43.
241 Isa. 60:19.
242 Isa. 49:6.
243 Luke 19:27, though *HK*, 137 suggests 18:7.
244 Rev. 11:2.
245 Goll, 423: *in scandalum*.
246 Isa. 60:14.
247 Isa. 62:7.
248 Zeph. 3:19.
249 John 16:20.
250 Hag. 2:9.
251 Goll, 423: *donis*, in Vulgate: *bonis*.
252 Ezek. 36:11.
253 1 Cor. 12:21.
254 1 Cor. 12:26.

be established at the judgement.²⁵⁵ And to whomever is owed honour in such a body, honour shall be given. This [comparison], however, also concerns these new saints, addressed [as] the feet, which furthermore shall receive this land as an inheritance, whence it is written: "and I will give to you and to your offspring all the land of Canaan in which you sojourn to possess eternally, and I will be their Lord", Genesis 27²⁵⁶ and also Daniel 7: "the kingdom, which is below all of heaven, shall be given to the holy people".²⁵⁷

---

255 1 Cor. 6:4.
256 Gen. 17:8.
257 Dan. 7:27.

5 Chiliast Tractate of an Unknown Author[258]

Since "there is a path for the remnant of the people—which is left behind from the Assyrians"—who are referred to as elevating vigils of the Lord,[259] i.e. from the enemies of the Church, "just as there was on the day when he climbed out from the land of Egypt",[260] it seems necessary that on the day of the Lord's works, when he led the children back onto such a path, we shall recall the Mosaic law, where this way is written.[261] But lest we seem to deceive the faithful of Christ's angels in religion, "walking in error puffed up by the perception of the flesh", we shall have a head above all things,[262] i.e. the gospel of Jesus Christ and the whole body of prophecy through the connection and associations of the law and the prophets,[263] we shall furnish [this] so that it may increase into the growth of divine association.[264] Thus, remembering the escape from Egypt by the Israelites, we shall begin in this manner.

For when the children of Israel, dismayed by awful labor [and] lamenting in Egypt, cried out to God, then "the Lord heard their lamentation and remembered his covenant which he had pledged" with their fathers[265] and he felt pity: he sent his wisdom in the spirit of his faithful servant, directing her to "stand in sign and omen against dreadful kings", and to "render the reward to the just, she led them in the marvellous way, giving to them cover by day and the

---

258 František M. Bartoš, "Do čtyř pražských artykulů: Z myšlenkových i ústavních zápasů let 1415–1420", *Sborník příspěvků k dějinám města Prahy* 5 (1932), 582–591.

259 Probably a reference from the popular medieval Biblical glossary *Interpretationes nominum Hebraicorum*. Its entry for *Asyrii* reads: "facture vigilantes domino, vel sustollentes vigilias domini" (Cambridge, Corpus Christi College, MS 484: Bible, fol. 636ᵛ).

260 Isa. 11:16. The Vulgate retains a future tense: "Et erit via residuo populo meo qui relinquetur ab Assyriis".

261 Mal. 4:4.

262 Col. 2:18–19.

263 The gospel and the body of prophecy; the law and the prophets: the Old and New Testaments.

264 Kaminsky, *HR*, 351 note 119 again identifies the influence of the controversial twelfth-century theologian, Joachim of Fiore. The apparent source of this was Václav the innkeeper in Prague (see note 404). See his discussion, *HR*, 336–360, esp. 351f. On another Táborite prophecy, Bernard McGinn, *Visions of the End: Apocalyptic Traditions in the Middle Ages* (New York: 1979), 267 note 29, notes that it displays "extreme Joachitism". Though knowledge of the Joachite tradition is certainly not impossible, and the later Adamite sect perhaps shows signs of living in the "Age of the Spirit" (see text 8)—the last age according to Joachim's tripartite view of history—the passages noted by Kaminsky here do not clearly display Joachim's historical theology. On the possible links of Joachim to the Hussites, see Martin Pjecha, "Táborite Revolutionary Apocalypticism: Mapping Influences and Divergences", in *Apocalypse now!*, ed. Damien Tricoire (Routledge: forthcoming).

265 Exod. 2:23–24.

light of fire by night".²⁶⁶ And they were carried across the sea and their Egyptian pursuers were wholly exterminated.²⁶⁷ She fed them with miraculous bread and they were lifted before the face of all their enemies in the world, from which he [the Lord] had sworn she would lead them.

We, who ought to be spiritual, shall "compare these spiritual things with the spiritual" of the New Law.²⁶⁸ Certainly we know that the widow of the gospel— staying in the city, enduring the burden of her adversary, collecting the chaff and baking the bricks for the rebellious house of the Pharaoh to be built— repeatedly comes to the judge (on which Luke 18),²⁶⁹ begging to be avenged. For this reason, she takes off the gown of peace and, covered in the sackcloth of obstruction,²⁷⁰ she cried out to her final days, but also urged her children to cry out: "Be courageous", she said, and "cry out, children, to the Lord, and he will take you away from the hand" of the men of the Pharaoh, i.e. the unjust leaders.²⁷¹ But what appears to those, who see this desertion with Judaised eyes?²⁷² Do you think he will not hear her, exclaiming to him with her children day and night? Surely, he heard her and endured with his children,²⁷³ and he sent not a servant but his son, who began to liberate her from her great misery. But because he is coming from a distance, not finding any faith,²⁷⁴ once he found it sleeping among the children, which was against the command, he thus burned with his anger²⁷⁵ against it [i.e. the faith] and with his anguish rages against it, yet by these [means] it will be cleansed and well-disposed.²⁷⁶ But his enemies are destroyed with his rival in turn,²⁷⁷ because the place of repentance is given to them, and they are struck with the seven last plagues,²⁷⁸ with which they are afflicted unless they will be corrected, all will be exterminated together in one moment.²⁷⁹ And terrible things will come to those on that day from their doubt in this day, because "he appeared in fire",²⁸⁰ cleans-

---

266   Psalm 105:45.
267   Wis. 10:16–19.
268   1 Cor. 2:13.
269   Luke 18:2–5.
270   Vulgate: *obsecracionis*.
271   Bar. 4:20–21.
272   Bartoš, 583. *iudaisantibus oculis*
273   Luke 18:7.
274   Luke 18:8.
275   Isa. 30:27.
276   Wis. 16:1–2.
277   Wis. 16:4.
278   Rev. 21:9.
279   Wis. 18:12.
280   Exod. 3:2.

ing the elect like gold,²⁸¹ and with the judgement from the house of God begun, he does not allow the rebellious house to remain unharmed.

And for these reasons the saints said terrible things of this day. Firstly, a great tribulation of that day which is about to come was predicted, to which no other can or will be compared; another says it is revealed in flame;²⁸² by another designation, [it is] the day of wrath, calamity, and misery, because on this day no one is spared, but the anger of God will rage against all by diverse means, and they will abound in anguish. By these things they will be set in order, as is said of the properly elected, but this destruction will come to the wicked without any excuse, i.e. to the house of the Antichrist, to those exercising tyranny. Who shall render death on this day, who will flee, where will we hide or to whose help will we flee when now the unjust of the world will finally be punished? Oh if only we could enter the tabernacles and be comforted in the closed doors for a little while with the people, until his anger has passed.²⁸³ And although his anger falls upon the elect with the biting of evil beasts and snakes, they [i.e. the beasts and snakes] are destroyed, and that anger will not remain forever, but soon the troubled [will] have the sign of salvation when they are examined before the declaration of God, who restores all things. And this is the marvellous way of those things, which the great and many are having difficulty [accepting], with which all the Egyptian abominations²⁸⁴ which clung to them shall be burned just as by fire, and they will find them [i.e. the abominations] displeasing in the promised land. And although they thus shall suffer in this glorious path, they are not abandoned without mercy, because in every place of mount Zion and wherever God is invoked, they have created a cover above themselves in the cover of the day,²⁸⁵ i.e. the body of Christ, and according to his will the sun does not burn them by the heat of the day, but he guards the furnace in works of love and ignited speech,²⁸⁶ burning in the night, just as it was predicted.²⁸⁷ Wherefore the just are led through fire and water with the awaited silver, and when the destruction of the unjust will have come, they will be liberated and, entering the land in which they will boldly reside, it will be well-established for them and their children after them, and they will not recede from the Lord, and they will be planted in that land in truth.²⁸⁸

---

281   Mal. 3:3.
282   Exod. 3:2.
283   Isa. 26:20.
284   i.e. superstitious or offensive practices or beliefs.
285   Wis. 10:17.
286   Psalm 118:140.
287   Isa. 4:5–6.
288   Jer. 32:37, 39–41.

Already Christ is coming on this great day to restore his church and to end the adulterous generation. When the apostles wanted to know about this coming through signs, saying: "tell us, what will be the sign of your coming and the consummation of the age", Christ said to them [of] the proposed signs: "thus raise your heads to these things beginning, because your redemption will approach",[289] but [then] they desired to know the time and the exact hour, as if seized by impertinence[290]—thus he shall satisfy you with signs to investigate this coming. And because God revealed his secret to his servants the prophets, giving them understanding, we shall not require more abundant signs [than] these. But it is an amazing wonder that the wise of this world can know with certainty the shape of the land through signs and [yet] cannot discern this time. How else should they be understood, except as those of the adulterous generation, who are unworthy, although understanding of the signs is given to them? But the solitary sign of the prophet Jonah shall be shunned by them,[291] declaring that Christ is weak and feeble, a conclusion they draw from those things, from [his] burial and death, and therefore they do not believe in such an impotent, considering impossible whatever he said himself. But what is to be judged of them? This, because they are slower than the prostitute in recognising the coming of Christ. Indeed, the prostitute not only recognised the appearance long before, but is also foretold in the proverbs, thus saying: "my husband has gone off on a far off journey, he took with him a sack of riches, he returns on the day of the full moon".[292] What is the moon? A showing of time and a sign of eternity. What else, then, is the full moon if not the complete sacrament of the body of Christ? That body of Christ, because it utterly proceeded from David, is called in another place the "root" of David, which is opening the sealed book, and will make it known.[293] And therefore it shines on this day, just like the full moon on its days, when it shall also be coming, because he is about to return. Behold how aptly the prostitute is waiting, already perceiving long ago, and [yet] now the wise do not recognise the fact! Thus, just like the prophecy, the prostitutes surpassed them.[294]

---

289 Bartoš, 584: *hiis sic incipientibus levate capita vestra, quoniam appropinquabit redempcio vestra*; Vulgate: *his autem fieri incipientibus respicite et levate capita vestra quoniam adpropinquat redemptio vestra*.

290 Luke 21:7–28.

291 Matt. 12:39: "But he answered and said unto them, An evil and adulterous generation seeketh after a sign; and there shall no sign be given to it, but the sign of the prophet Jonas." (KJV).

292 Prov. 7:10–20.

293 Rev. 5:1, 5.

294 Matt. 21:31.

If only, like the blind groping at a wall,[295] to whom the sun falls at midday,[296] this knowledge would be rationed out to them. For seeing that Christ is coming, they denounce the certain fact of his arrival. What signs are beginning? He came on his day, which he entered secretly like a thief,[297] finding us all sleeping, just as was predicted by Isaiah: he said, "As soon as they were sleeping",[298] and again: "They were all sleepy and sleeping".[299] When, therefore, we had been sleeping a deadly sleep in this way, the whirlwind of the Lord's anger secretly entered, preceded by the separation, the revelation of the Antichrist which was predicted by the apostle,[300] the appearance of Christ's sign, every kind of initial destruction of the idols, and the abduction of the little Israelites;[301] the leading of the beasts of burden to be sacrificed to God, and the singing of the infants before the victory of Christ, draws nigh. Egypt is being struck by the seven last plagues; the people of Babylon are evoked through Jeremiah, whose king eats hay like an ox.[302] Truly the people are the hay, and [will remain] this until the seven ages will be transformed. The waters of the Egyptians are changed into blood, for they burned the children and threw them into the waters, [those children] through whom the light of the world was beginning to shine, their first-born children—i.e. that noblest offspring—are destroyed[303] partially by the angel of the priests and the rest by the striking angel, and all other signs contained together in the Gospel, in the apostles and the prophets, which preceded and followed the day of the Lord, are fulfilled. Who then shall not believe this day has come unless from an apparent lack of faith?

The following concerns the reformation and liberation of the Church

Christ is coming to renew his Church, because the elect will be turned toward the stone from whence they fell, and to the cavern of the place from which they fell.[304] For the tested cornerstone will be placed at the foundations of

---

295   Deut. 28:29.
296   Amos 8:9.
297   1 Thess. 5:2.
298   Isa. 43:17.
299   Matt. 25:5.
300   2 Thess. 2:3.
301   Bartoš, 585: *signi Christi apparicio et ydolorum inicialis omnimoda intericio et Israeliticorum parvulorum.*
302   Dan. 4:29.
303   Exod. 11:5; Wis. 18:12.
304   Isa. 51:1.

Zion,³⁰⁵ and then the stones will be laid over it in order, and will be founded with sapphires. And the stone will be set into the ramparts and sculpted stones into its gate,³⁰⁶ and the House of the Lord will be restored. And indeed the stone is set at the foundations of Zion, above which many, like living stones, are built upon into spiritual houses,³⁰⁷ and they will again be set. And therefore the writings of Peter pertain to this end: "I shall set",³⁰⁸ and Isaiah: "I shall send" and likewise: "I shall place the stone in the foundations of Zion, tried in the foundation".³⁰⁹ For the house of God is deserted³¹⁰ and it is made as it could not be. Therefore the stone, Jesus Christ, will be set for the foundations so that the tabernacle of David, which fell, shall be lifted, and the holes in his walls, which collapsed, shall be rebuilt, which surely must be rebuilt, just as in ancient times.³¹¹ And therefore the prophet states in that very place: I will rebuild it, because the former which was built is collapsing. Likewise he is coming to liberate the Church and to lead it into one sheepfold. For he will send his angels, and congregate the elect from all lands to which he expelled them in his anger and grave disdain,³¹² because he had brought upon them four winds from four plagues of heaven,³¹³ i.e. from the spiritual place, and exposed them to all the winds, and there is not a people to whom they did not come, like detested exiles;³¹⁴ and through this they had squandered their liberty. But already he has come to congregate them and to lead them back to that place. He has suffered so that he may congregate the dispersed children into one. And then truly they will be free, when they will be liberated by Christ. And that congregation and liberation of the children of God will be at the destruction of the damned, whence it is written: "I will gather all the congregating from the face of the earth, said the Lord, the gathering men and livestock, the birds of the sky and the fish of the sea and the impious will be destroyed."³¹⁵

---

305   Isa. 28:16.
306   Isa. 54:11–12; Rev. 21:19–21.
307   1 Pet. 2:5.
308   Vulgate: *pono* (1 Pet. 2:6).
309   Isa. 28:16.
310   Hag. 1:4.
311   Amos 9:11.
312   Jer. 32:37.
313   Bartoš, 586: *a quatuor plagis celi*.
314   Jer. 49:36. Bartoš: *quasi profugi ... imitando eos in abhominacione*.
315   Zeph. 1:2–3: "I will utterly consume all things from off the land, saith the Lord. I will consume man and beast; I will consume the fowls of the heaven, and the fishes of the sea, and the stumbling blocks with the wicked". (KJV).

On the method

I raise the question, what is the method of this coming? The angels have sufficiently expressed it to the apostles when they said: "men of Galilee, why do you look in the sky? This Jesus (who has been taken from you into heaven) will come thusly, in the manner you saw him proceeding into heaven".[316] Because he was taken in a cloud, he will thus return in a cloud. And therefore Christ says: "and they will see the son of man coming in the clouds of heaven with great virtue and majesty".[317] But is it possible that you knew the paths of the great clouds and the perfect wisdoms?[318] To this method even the apostle Paul declared: "For by order of the Lord himself"[319]—just as David asked: "stand in the Lord's command"[320]—and in the voice of the archangel,[321] which Mark said in a great voice,[322] and he will descend from the sky with the trumpet of God,[323] with which he sent the angels. And already those speaking of this coming, in the word of their new wisdom, say that Christ is coming upon everyone. Whence it is written: "for when all things were tranquil and silent, and the night was in the middle of its course, your almighty speech, Lord, came from the royal thrones of heaven, a stern conqueror[324] lept into the midst of the land's borders."[325] Also Isaiah: "As the lion and the cub of the lion shall roar over their prey, when a multitude of shepherds attack him, he will not fear their voice and he will not be terrified by their number: thus the Lord of hosts will descend, so that he shall fight on mount Zion."[326] And Deuteronomy: "The Lord appeared from Mount Paran and with him a thousand saints, the burning law in his right hand".[327] Also Isaiah: "Behold, because the Lord will come in fire",[328] and again: "Behold the name of the Lord is coming from afar",[329] and the Psalm: "the Lord will send forth the staff of your power from Zion to dominate in the midst of his

---

316 Acts 1:11.
317 Matt. 24:30.
318 Job 37:16.
319 1 Thess. 4:15.
320 Psalm 7:7.
321 1 Thess. 4:15.
322 Mark 5:7.
323 1 Thess. 4:16.
324 Bartoš, 586: *duris debellator* Vulgate: *durus debellator*.
325 Wis. 18:14–15.
326 Isa. 31:4.
327 Deut. 33:2.
328 Isa. 66:15.
329 Isa. 30:27.

enemies".³³⁰ What then is the staff? Say what you see, Jeremiah! "I see a vigilant branch. You see well, because I will be watchful of my word".³³¹ From all these things, it seems that he will come in a word. But just as the flesh of Christ was covered by garments by the Virgin Mary, so that few recognised him, thus also it is today for those dying [i.e. for mortal men], that the words of Christ are covered, and therefore, like the worst mockers, walking according to their own sentiments, they say jeeringly: "where is the coming of Christ?"³³²

Likewise, on how long that coming will last, the angel of Daniel seems to have responded, "until the time and times and the half of time".³³³ This time means the time of vision,³³⁴ in which all signs should be fulfilled, marking the advent of Christ. There are seven ages, which will be changed in the king of Babylon, i.e. the seven last plagues. The half of time is the time which will be shortened for the elect, that the impious will not be halved. "And when these things will have been completed, [along with] the scattering of the power of the holy people, all these things will be fulfilled",³³⁵ and the end of this most cruel advent visiting the iniquity of the world, will arrive.

On the kingdom

The Lord Christ, who said before Pilate: "but now my kingdom is not here",³³⁶ will reign from faith, in the way it is written: "and the Lord will be king above all the world",³³⁷ and also: "and the kingdom will be for the Lord".³³⁸ Whence also John: "and the kingdom of this world is made the kingdom of our Lord Jesus Christ",³³⁹ for which we pray in Matthew,³⁴⁰ and generally, before he comes. The apostles also were asking about it after the resurrection.³⁴¹ This [kingdom] the father deigned to give to a small flock here on earth after the restoration of the elect, the manner of which is written: "and the time came and the saints acquired the kingdom", and below: "and the judgement will

---

330 Psalm 109:2.
331 Jer. 1:11–12.
332 Isa. 44:18–19. Possibly a reference to the critiques of the Prague masters.
333 Dan. 7:25.
334 Joel 2:28.
335 Dan. 12:7.
336 John 18:36
337 Zech. 14:9.
338 Obad. 1:21.
339 Rev. 11:15.
340 Matt. 6:10.
341 Acts 1:6.

remain, so that the power shall be removed and crushed and shall disappear until the end, but the kingdom and the power and the greatness of the kingdom, which is the heaven over all, shall be given to the people of the saints of the most high".[342] And whence the apostle says: "it is necessary he reign",[343] etc. In order that we frequently pray for this, Isaiah advises us: "You who remember the Lord", he says "do not be silent and give him quiet, until he establishes, and until he places Jerusalem a glory in the land."[344] But how long will this kingdom last, which is asked when it is said in the Gospel: "and he will reign in the house of Jacob for eternity"?[345] And Isaiah: "he will sit on the throne of David and over his kingdom, so that he may strengthen it and reinforce it in judgement and justice from now until forever."[346] And Daniel: "whose kingdom is an eternal kingdom, and all kings will serve him and obey him."[347] For now it [the kingdom of God] will come observably, which had previously come unnoticeably, without beginning or warning,[348] because Christ said: "the kingdom of God is within you",[349] which, however, came unnoticeably.

On the removal of offences

Now Christ has appeared to us in his sacrifice in the consummation of the age, the consummation which he himself addressed as the harvest,[350] in which the angels will be sent to destroy all offences and thus to forget none of those things to be destroyed, because they neither forget anyone who is polluted nor anyone enacting abomination,[351] because in that kingdom they will have become—and will be—just. They will shine like the sun and they will roam like the sparks in the reeds,[352] and they will shine like the brightness of the sky,[353] from which those rejected will be banished like impudent and poisonous dogs. I do not think that anyone who is evil and offensive shall remain in this kingdom, but

---

342 Dan. 7:22, 26–27.
343 1 Cor. 15:25.
344 Isa. 62:6–7.
345 Luke 1:33.
346 Isa. 9:7.
347 Dan. 7:27.
348 Bartoš, 588: *sine* [...] *iniciative et orabter*.
349 Luke 17:20–21.
350 Matt. 13:30.
351 Rev. 21:27.
352 Wis. 3:7.
353 Dan. 12:3.

it is clear that five foolish virgins will remain outside this kingdom,[354] and thus those standing outside the kingdom will say to Christ: "we ate and drank with you and you taught us in the streets."[355] But also other innumerable people, who are also running and lamenting, say to the Lord: "come, we shall climb up the mountain of the Lord, and the Lord will teach us his ways."[356] None of these will be able to enter the kingdom, unless first purified of all filth. And thus it is said in Revelation, that the gates of this city will not be shut either by day or by night.[357] Therefore it seems that only the good will remain in this kingdom, [and] the wicked [will be] expelled from it. Whence it is also read in an allusion of the apostles in the acts of apostles: "No one else dared to join them".[358]

Will the inhabitants of this kingdom be led back to the state of innocence of the first man?[359] If we find honey, let us eat so much as is enough, lest it should cause us to vomit. It shall be enough for us to believe these things, but the greatest teacher, who is coming, will produce other things after the days of vision. Yet it seems to us, if it is not given to other generations, like to the holy apostles of God, that the apostles themselves were delivered to a miraculous condition of a new paradise, in which Christ was the tree of life, and beyond doubt they were here more perfect than the first man. Yet they were expecting a future miraculous glory for themselves, furnished in the last age, revealed in us, to which the present sufferings cannot be worthily compared, in which all creation will be liberated from the servitude of corruption, and only to the liberated sons [of the sowing][360] will it be said: when you shall arrive to [this glory], holy ones, I wholly do not know to whom they will be comparable. Does that glory seem small, which they will be given in the light of the peoples, "in name and praise among all the people of the world"?[361] And then their arriving children, who humiliated the holy, will all worship the soles of the feet of those who they now disparage, and they will call them "the city of the Lord (Zion) of the holy Israel".[362] Because they will not be a second house, but the last, [and] of greater glory than the first.[363] Their days will be restored as it was in the

---

354   Matt. 25:1–2.
355   Luke 13:26.
356   Isa. 2:3. Note the similarity with text 2.
357   Rev. 21:25.
358   Acts 5:13.
359   It seems the answer to this question is interrupted by a warning.
360   Bartoš, 589: *sermentis*. I assume *sementis* is meant.
361   Zeph. 3:20.
362   Isa. 60:14.
363   Hag. 2:9.

beginning,[364] and they will be inherited as it was in the beginning,[365] and they will be as they were when they were not scattered, and they will be rewarded with greater goods than those they had in the beginning. Thus it appears from these things that they shall be led to such or such kind of state of holiness in the kingdom of Christ and in this glory that will be revealed.

In this kingdom, one will be soothed from the existing sins and will not anymore remember the iniquities,[366] because when they will have been collected from various lands, clean water will be poured over them and their stony heart [will be] taken, [and] a new heart of flesh will be given to them. And those walking in the commandments and those keeping the judgements will dwell in the land of their fathers, and will recall the worst of the ways, and their own injustices will displease them.[367] Thus it appears that in this kingdom, from which all offences will be expelled and into which nothing polluted will enter, there will not be any sin. If, however, there will be original or actual sin in any little one or adult, he will not be of this kingdom, in which there will be peace, [and] injustice will no longer be heard in the land, [nor] ruin and grief within its borders.[368] Whence also Jeremiah says to the congregated: "I will give them one heart and one soul,[369] so that they fear me every day, and it will be good to them and their children after them; and I shall strike an eternal pact with them, and I will not cease doing good to them and I will give my fear into their heart, so that they shall not withdraw from me; and I will rejoice upon them, and I will have done well with them and I will plant them truly in that land."[370]

When these things are [to be] fulfilled, or in which manner they are expected to be fulfilled after the resurrection.

They will beget in [this] kingdom without disturbance.[371] For now the crying Church is in pain and has few daughters, but afterwards many will be born without grief. Of this the mother will say: I am the sterile Church. "Who birthed them?"[372] And also: "the place is too narrow for me, make me a place [to dwell

---

364 Lam. 5:21.
365 Sir. 36:13.
366 Jer. 31.
367 Ezek. 36:25–28, 31.
368 Isa. 60:18.
369 Vulgate: *una via*.
370 Jer. 32:39–41.
371 Isa. 65:23.
372 Isa. 49:21.

in]".³⁷³ But it seems to me regarding the carnal children, who most certainly shall be born in that kingdom by the sound will of the holy spirit, that the children born and baptised after the baptism from mortal sin will never die if they will be in the kingdom, because there will no longer be death, [so] when "a child will die a hundred years old" in a good old age, full of days, it will be as now if an infant of one year dies.³⁷⁴

Of the physical miseries

For along with the banished sins, he will dismiss the penalties for sin; for grain will be brought forth and multiplied with the fruit of the tree and the sprout of the field, and they will no longer bear disgrace of the spirit nor of bodily hunger among the people,³⁷⁵ now the grieving will be comforted,³⁷⁶ now [that] the tabernacle will be in the shade of God from the heat, and in safety and shelter from the storm—i.e. from the blast of the mighty, striking the rampart—and from the rain.³⁷⁷ And they will be delivered from all of the misfortunes that occur now, whence it is written: "Thus when all these things shall come upon you, whether blessing or curse, which I have set in your presence, and lead your heart to repentance among all the peoples to whom the Lord your God scattered you, you will be turned to him and you will obey his orders, as I command today, with your children, with all your heart and all your soul: the Lord will return you from your captivity, and he will pity you, and return and congregate you from all the people among whom he scattered you before. If you were scattered to the borders of heaven, your Lord God will draw you back from there, because he sends the son of man to gather the angels and he will take [them] from the height of the heavens and lead them into the land which your fathers possessed, and you will possess it. Blessing you, he will grow you to a number greater than your fathers. And the Lord God will circumcise your heart, and the heart of your offspring, so that you esteem your Lord God with all your heart and with all your soul, so you can live. Moreover, the Lord will turn all these curses upon your enemies, and all who hate and persecute you. Also, now that you are returned, you will hear the voice of your Lord God and will follow all the things com-

---

373 Isa. 49:20; *angustus mihi est locus fac spatium mihi ut habitem* (Vulgate) Bartoš, 590: *Augustinus: est michi locus fac michi locum michi.*
374 Isa. 65:20.
375 Ezek. 36:29–30.
376 Matt. 5:5.
377 Isa. 4:6 and 25:4.

manded, which I command to you today. And your Lord God will make you abound in all the works of your hands, in the progeny of your womb, and in the fruit of your cattle, in the abundance of your land, and in the bounty of all things. For the Lord will return, to rejoice over you in all good things, just as he rejoiced over your fathers."[378] What, therefore, can physically or spiritually be absent from those good conditions for the just, or what can trouble him, when it is written: "whatever will befall the just will not disturb him"?[379]

On the endurance of the sacraments[380]

Yet all the sacraments necessary to salvation will endure, but they will no longer be subject to falsity, because in his time he will liberate his wheat and his wine and he will not give it to the enemies of the children to eat, just as he vowed in Isaiah, but only those who collect it will eat, and they will praise the Lord. And those who carried it will drink in his holy halls,[381] because no men who are called and refused to come will taste the dinner; nor will the foolish virgins be admitted to it,[382] nor those who are unworthy[383] of Christ's renown. They will eat and drink the one so great [Christ] in a new way, in joy, unmindful of those that came before, which will recede, nor will they remember them anymore—for: "you will not remember the previous ones, and you will not regard the ancient things."[384]—but they will rejoice and revel for eternity in these new things which are created.[385] For they will not do this anymore in the memory of Christ's passion, as they had been accustomed [to do], but for the memory of Christ's victory, because until he comes, the apostle said, those eat-

---

378 Deut. 30:1–9.
379 Prov. 12:21.
380 The following passage seems to speak against the Joachite influence on the Táborites which Kaminsky, *HR*, 351f. assumes, since most Joachites actually rejected the continuity of the sacraments into the third *status*. I thank Matthias Riedl for this observation. See Brett Edward Whalen, "Joachim the Theorist of History and Society", and Sven Grosse, "Thomas Aquinas, Bonaventure, and the critiques of Joachimist Topics from the Fourth Lateran Council to Dante", in *A Companion to Joachim of Fiore*, ed. Matthias Riedl (Leiden: 2018). A better case for Joachism could be made for the Adamites (see text 8, and also my "Táborite Revolutionary").
381 Isa. 62:8–9.
382 Matt. 25:1–2.
383 Bartoš, 591: *indigui*.
384 Isa. 43:18.
385 Isa. 65:18.

ing and drinking will announce Christ's death,[386] but after these things [they will announce] his joyous victory, because for this whole time the just were grieving. But now they will rejoice, seeing the punishment and washing their hands in the blood of the sinners. Wherefore Christ said: "I will drink that new wine, when the kingdom of God comes,[387] and I walk with you to arrange that you shall eat and drink upon my table in my kingdom".[388] With such things foreseen, the man sitting at the dinner with Christ said: "blessed is he, who eats the bread in the kingdom of God".[389] And marriages will be holy and the wedding-bed will be unstained;[390] all will be an acquired people and a royal priesthood,[391] because all will be clothed doubly, in wool and linen.[392] Behold the royalty and dignity of the priests. How, therefore, can someone say that there will not be sacraments? And if after so great a resurrection all shall be kings and shall understand, then it shall be [only] for a thousand years and not more. Yet they will not be priests by office, but by dignity etc. Yet whether all seven sacraments will remain, I do not know, because even now some already are not attended to.

On the doctrines

All the children of the Church will be taught by the Lord and they will all be disciples of God. "All will know me, from the great to the small", and a man will no longer teach his neighbour.[393] For he will destroy the wisdom of the wise, and he will condemn the knowledge of the knowing,[394] because he will destroy the wise of Edom.[395] And the learned will not be prepared, nor the one pondering the words of the Law,[396] [and] the eloquence of his tongue, in which there is no wisdom, cannot be understood. Everything is the flower of the grass,

---

386 1 Cor. 11:26.
387 Mark 14:25.
388 Luke 22:29–30.
389 Luke 14:15.
390 Heb. 13:4.
391 1 Pet. 2:9.
392 Deut. 22:11; Lev. 19:19.
393 Jer. 31:34. A similar sentiment was attributed to the radical priest Václav Koranda, who repeatedly rejected the necessity of books and Bibles after the destruction of the wicked: "those of God's elect who remain [...] will not have need for any written books because they will all be taught by God". See Příbram, Život, 53.
394 1 Cor. 1:19; Isa. 29:14.
395 Obad. 1:8.
396 Isa. 33:18.

drying up,[397] because Christ is coming to dry up the waters. For eloquence [is] ignited,[398] [and] he is coming to melt these elements; just as wax flows from the face of fire, thus this wisdom will perish in the face of the fiery wisdom of God, etc.[399]

---

[397] 1 Pet. 1:24.
[398] Psalm 118:140.
[399] Probably again a reference to the Prague masters.

6 Apocalyptic Articles[400]

[...] Also, not content with these evil things, with which they marred the once renowned name of the Bohemian Kingdom, they even added to the previous worst evils,[401] twisting the scriptures of the prophets and the gospels with their own foolish understanding, announcing that the kingdom of Christ is now in our days renewed, posing many and diverse articles, some heretical, others erroneous and many offensive. The principal author, announcer, and defender of these was one young priest from Moravia, of fine intelligence and great memory, Martin, called Loquis[402] because of his eloquence, because he fearlessly spoke [the opinions] not of the doctors, but his own. His principal helpers were Master Jan Jičín, Markolt, a bachelor of arts, Koranda,[403] and other aforementioned priests of Tábor. And all these respected a certain Vaclav, an innkeeper in Prague, who was more familiar with the Bible than all of them, explaining the New Testament through the Old and vice-versa.[404] But it was the following [articles] which they openly taught:

First, that already at the consummation of the current age, Christ will come secretly as a thief, in a new advent to renew his kingdom, for which we pray: "May your kingdom come!"[405] And this coming will not be in the time of grace, but of vengeance and retribution with fire and the sword, indeed that all enemies of the law of Christ must perish by the seven last blows,[406] which the faithful are to be provoked to execute.

Item, in that time of vengeance, Christ should not be imitated in his meekness and compassion to those sinners, but in zeal and rage and just retribution.

Item, in this time of vengeance, any of the faithful—including the priest, [and] however spiritual a person—is damned, who holds back his physical sword from the blood[407] of the enemies of the law of Christ, but [rather] he should wash and sanctify his hands in their blood.

---

400 Josef Emler, Jan Gebauer, and Jaroslav Goll (eds), *Fontes Rerum Bohemicarum* 5 [hereafter *FRB* 5] (Prague: 1893), 413–416.
401 Referring to certain teachings, see *FRB* 5, 410–413.
402 Martin Húska.
403 Václav Koranda.
404 On this Václav, see Václav Vladivoj Tomek, *Dějepis města Prahy*, IV, 2nd ed. (1899), 91. Kaminsky, *HR*, 351f. considers this influenced by Joachism. See also id., "The Free Spirit in the Hussite Revolution", in *Millennial Dreams in Action*, ed. Sylvia L. Thrupp (New York, 1970), 166–186.
405 i.e. the *Pater noster*. Matt. 6:10.
406 Rev. 15.
407 Jer. 48:10.

Item, in that time of vengeance, whoever hears the preached word of Christ—in which he said: "then those who are in Judea, shall flee to the mountains"[408]—and does not leave the cities, villages, and castles for the physical mountains, where presently the Táborites or their brothers are congregated, sins mortally against the order of Christ and will perish in his sin, because now no one can be saved from the blows of the Lord, unless he will come to the faithful on the mountains.

Item, in this time of vengeance, all cities, villages, and castles should be abandoned, destroyed, and burned, because neither the Lord God nor anyone [else] will enter them anymore.

Item, that the brothers of Tábor are, in that time of vengeance, the angels sent to lead the faithful from all cities, villages, and castles to the mountains, just as Lot [was led] from Sodom, and that the brothers, with their adherents, are that body to which, wherever it will be, "also the eagles will be congregated",[409] of which is said: "every place, on which your foot will step, is and will be yours".[410] For they are the army sent from God through the whole world, to destroy all scandals from Christ's kingdom, which is the Church militant, and to expel the wicked from the midst of the just, and to enact vengeance and [inflict] blows onto the nations of the enemies of the law of Christ and their cities, villages, and castles.

Item, that in this time of vengeance, there will remain only five physical cities in all Christianity [i.e. Christendom] to which the faithful should flee and there be saved,[411] [after which] all others will perish and be destroyed like Sodom.

Item, one or another married spouse may and should, if the other spouse is unwilling, abandon the other, along with their children, and everything else, and flee to the aforementioned mountains or to the five said cities.

Item, that all temporal goods of the enemies of the law of Christ should be eliminated, plundered and devastated, destroyed, or burned by the aforesaid faithful.

Item, at the end of that consummation of the age, Christ will descend out of the sky and will come in his own person manifestly, and will be seen by physical eyes to receive the kingdom in this world, and will make a great banquet and

---

408   Mark 13:14.
409   Matt. 24:28; Luke 17:37.
410   Deut. 11:24.
411   Isa. 19:18. The five cities appear as Plzeň, Žatec, Klatovy, Louny, and Slaný or Písek, see FRB 5, 356. Yet, if Kaminsky is correct, the naming of the five cities was restricted to the short period between late-January and mid-March 1420. See his HR, 325, 332 f., note 57.

supper of the lamb, just as the wedding of his spouse the Church, here on the corporeal mountains. And Christ the king will enter to see the dinner guests, and all which will not have a wedding garment he will send out "into the darkness".[412] And just as it was in the time of Noah, when all outside the ark were swallowed up in the water of the flood,[413] so in one moment all the wicked will be swallowed up who are not on the mountains, and thus he will cast out all scandals from his kingdom.

Item, at that second coming of Christ before the day of judgement, kings, princes, and Church prelates will be invalidated, so that there will not be in this renewed kingdom any fees or tax-collectors (Is. 14:3–4),[414] because the sons of God will tread upon the throats of kings, and all royal authority under the sky will be given to them, as the book of Wisdom [chapter] 7.[415] And thus the elect will not suffer further persecution, but will return retribution.

Item, in this renewed kingdom there will be no sin, no scandal, no abomination, [and] no lies, but all will be the elect sons of God, [and] all passions of Christ and his members will cease.

Item, in the Church or the renewed kingdom women will give birth to their babies without pain and without original sin, Isaiah 66: "they will give birth without disturbance".[416] And 1John 5. Item the children born in this kingdom, if they will be of this kingdom, will never die, because there will be no more death, Revelation 21.[417]

Item, the glory of this kingdom, renewed in this way,[418] will be greater than the primitive Church before the resurrection of the dead.

Item, the sun of human understanding will not shine for mankind in the renewed kingdom, because one will not teach his neighbours, but "all will be disciples of God".[419]

Item, they said most faithlessly, that the most perfect law of grace,[420] after which there will be no other guide for man, will be emptied and will cease as a deed and an accomplishment in this life and in the renewed kingdom.

---

412 Matt. 22:12–13.
413 Gen. 7:21–23.
414 Isa. 14:3–4. The Latin *exactor* may be variously translated as oppressor, enforcer, or expeller. I do not use the Czech translation, accepted by HK, 353, nr. 60, note 20, "oppressor of the poor" (*dráč chudiny*), which has a slightly different meaning.
415 Wis. 5:16–17, and perhaps Josh. 10:24; 2 Esdr. 9:22.
416 Isa. 65:23.
417 Rev. 21:4.
418 In some manuscripts, *via* is replaced with *vita*, thus "in this life". See FRB 5, 415 note 'g'.
419 John 6:45.
420 i.e. the New Testament.

Item, Paul's custom of assembling at church will not be followed after the transformation, nor should it be enforced, because temples will no longer exist, Revelation 21: "for the Lord almighty is its temple".[421] For just as faith and hope will be destroyed, so will temples.

Item, at this manifest arrival, Christ will come in the clouds of heaven and in great majesty with his angels, and all who died in Christ will rise corporally and will come first with him to judge the living and the dead. Then all the elect who still remain alive, from the end of the earth will bodily "be carried along with them in the clouds, to meet Christ in the air", as says the apostle.[422] And they said that it will happen soon, in a few years, [and] some of us who will still be alive will see the saints of God rise from death, and among them Master Jan Hus, because the Lord will shorten that time of vengeance and accelerate the consummation of the age for his elect.

Item, those elect who will thusly remain alive will be returned to the state of innocence of Adam himself in paradise, like Enoch and Elijah, and will be without any hunger and thirst and any other pain, either spiritual or bodily. Also, those in holy marriage and in the immaculate bed will bodily beget sons and grandsons without any pain and disturbance, and without any original sin, here on earth and on the mountains. Nor will there be baptism by water then, because they will be baptised in the Holy Spirit, nor will there be the visible sacrament of the holy Eucharist,[423] because they will be nourished in the new angelic way, not in memory of the passion of Christ, but in his victory.

---

421 Rev. 21:22.
422 1 Thess. 4:17.
423 Note the difference with the "anti-Joachite" opinion of text 5, note 287.

7 Excerpts from the Books of Jan Čapek

About the books of Čapek, murderous from the beginning of the world.[424]

Item, although all these things are known all over the Czech lands,[425] for a better and easier testimony of all those things, I will here introduce the books of one of the main and greatest of the first seducers, the priest named Jan Čapek, in which he adduces many false and erroneous writings of the Old Law, by which he supports all those cruelties, commanding and directing everyone to commit them without hesitation. On these books he and other priests founded those unjust, un-Christian, and cruel wars, and they used them to defend and excuse themselves. I will touch upon certain short pieces from them, from which all can understand the inexcusable cruelties and errors of that Čapek and all his companions.

How Čapek writes most cruel and murderous pieces in those books.

First he states and says: "The present time is called the day of vengeance and castigation to those who would not want to make true penance."[426]

Item, with three castigations the sinful will be castigated. First they will be flogged as with a scourge and then with clubs and other blows. Then he releases fire and sword. Inferring from the letters of Isaiah 28, he says: "First God commands to whip the scourge like millet, second to beat it with clubs, third to destroy it".[427]

Item, he says that that castigation is from the will of the Holy Spirit. He infers [this] from the letters of Proverbs 27.[428] Item, the writing of the prophet Amos in the third chapter, where he says: "Announce and say to the people and congregate on the mountains of Samaria."[429] Item, these things the Lord God says: "The world will mourn, because it will be circumvented around. And your strength will be torn from you and the height of your structure will be destroyed."[430] "The horns of the altar will be cut off and will fall on

---

424 Příbram, *Život*, 44–47.
425 A reference to Táborite calls to violence, which Příbram previously documents.
426 Luke 13:3; Rev. 2:16.
427 Isa. 28:27–28.
428 Proverbs 27:5–6: "Open rebuke is better than secret love. Faithful are the wounds of a friend; but the kisses of an enemy are deceitful." (KJV).
429 Amos 3:9.
430 Amos 3:11.

the ground. And the houses built expensively will perish, and the great houses will be destroyed."[431]

Item, of the Proverbs 14: "These houses will be destroyed, but the tents of the righteous will flourish."[432] But if something should befall the righteous, it will not harm him. Because Christ stands for damages.[433]

Item, Revelation 18: "My people, come out of the people of Babylon, so that you do not receive their blows.[434] For their sins reach even unto heaven."[435] Item, for this, Amos the prophet calls and convenes the people to the mountains. Because of this, the people of Babylon are boiling over, as everyone will be able to understand from the writing of Revelation 18: "his great blows, death, wailing and hunger and burning fire will come upon Babylon."[436] And he says to him: "Woe, woe, that great city of Babylon, that in one hour came your damnation! And there will be no more buyers of the world's merchandise: merchandise of gold and of silver and of precious stones, of pearls, of fine linen, purple, silk, of figures and of all kinds of expensive wood, nor diverse containers (neither copper, iron and marble), nor cinnamon, nor licorice, nor anything perfumed, nor expensive oils, nor incense, of wine and of oil and of white flour and of wheat and of livestock and of horses, carriages, servants, souls, and people."[437]

Item, Isaiah 2: "The height of all people will be bowed, and the height of all men lowered. And in that day the Lord God himself will be lifted up, and idols will be destroyed totally."[438]

Item, if there is one who does not want to believe these sayings, then believe in deeds.[439]

Item, that the Lord God will introduce the greatest castigation by miraculously leading the leaders and his people against the enemy. Of those leaders and hetmans[440] the prophet Zachariah testifies in the twelfth chapter, saying: "On that day I will establish leaders like a fiery furnace among the wood and like a fiery scythe among the hay. And you will burn all people in their midst, on the

---

431   Amos 3.14–15.
432   Proverbs 14:11.
433   i.e. Christ repays these damages.
434   i.e. the blows which are directed at the people of Babylon.
435   Rev. 18:4–5.
436   Rev. 18:8.
437   Rev. 18:10–13.
438   Isa. 2:17–18.
439   John 10:25, 38.
440   *Hetman* or *hejtman*, a political title traditionally assigned to military commanders.

right and left."[441] But the fact that this address is only aimed at the evil themselves is founded on the address of Malachi in the last chapter: "Lo, there will certainly come such a day, and it will be like a fiery furnace. And all the proud and those who cause cruelty will be a stubble-field, and they will burn when that day comes, says the Lord God of hosts. And he will leave them neither root nor stem."[442]

The leaders and hetmans have already been spoken of; now also hear about those people who will be with them. The prophet Joel in the second chapter writes of those people and thusly speaks of the people and of the hetmans: "Together, a people great and strong, with whom there was no equal from the beginning, nor will there be unto the years of generations and generations. Before the face of those people, destructive fire, and behind them, the burning flame. The land in front of those people [is] like a delightful garden, and behind them deserts and wastelands. And no one will escape them. As one should watch a horse, thusly you will gaze upon those people. And how one rides a horse, thusly they will run."[443] "They will run like the strong and like warrior men, thusly they will scale walls. And they will invade through windows, and they will not injure themselves. They will attack cities and they will run up walls, entering through windows like thieves, and the whole world will fear their faces."[444]

Item, of these peoples' manner of fighting.

Through these aforementioned people, the Lord God wants to fight in a new way. Isaiah 12th chapter. On what will it depend? In singing and drumming, he will fight.[445] And if you want to know who and how, listen to the prophet Jeremiah in chapter 51: "The Lord God of hosts says these things: Daughter Babylon is as the threshing floor, and the time of her threshing will come. And also in a little while will come the time to harvest."[446] "They did not know the thoughts of God and did not comprehend his counsels. And thus he took them in a heap and lay them on the threshing floor like hay. Stand and thresh, daughter Zion."[447] "And feed your enemies with their own meat and drink, [and] they

---

441 Zach. 12:6
442 Mal. 4:1.
443 Joel 2:2–4.
444 Joel 2:7–10.
445 Isa. 12:2; 5–6.
446 Jer. 51:33.
447 Mic. 4:12–13.

will [be drunk] on their blood like sweet wine. And every person will know, that I am he who saves you."⁴⁴⁸

For confirmation of these sayings, hear the command of the Holy Spirit in Ecclesiasticus in the fortieth chapter: "Death, blood and strife, weapons sharp on both sides, and oppression and famine and flogging, those creations are prepared for hypocrites."⁴⁴⁹ "Fire, hailstorms, death and hunger"⁴⁵⁰ in Ecclesiasticus in the thirty-ninth chapter, "all these things are created for vengeance; cruelly-toothed animals, scorpions and snakes, and weapons sharp from both sides, for vengeance and for the despoliation of tyrants, etc."⁴⁵¹

Item, of fire and of killing.

To the Hebrews in the tenth chapter: "Very horrible is the certain waiting for the judgement and the burning of the fire, which will burn all enemies. He who despised the law of God, had no mercy. But when two or three testified against him, they caused his death without any mercy. He would be worthy of a greater penalty than anyone, [he] who would suppress the Son of God and would befoul the blood of the covenant, in which man is sanctified, and caused the disgrace of the Holy Spirit."⁴⁵²

In the letter to the Thessalonians in the first chapter: "But it is righteous to repay payment to him who torments you in front of God, and to you who are tormented, may you have rest with us in the revelation of our Lord Jesus Christ from heaven, with the messengers of his power. In the burning fire he will repay those, who did not know God and were not obedient to the gospels of our Lord Jesus Christ."⁴⁵³

As proof of all these sayings, hear the speech of the gospel of St. Luke in the nineteenth chapter: Christ himself says thusly: "The enemies, who did not want me to rule over them, bring them before me and kill them."⁴⁵⁴ And in the gospel of St. Matthew in the twenty-second chapter "The king, having heard this, was angered, and sent his army, and killed the murderers and burned their city."⁴⁵⁵

All those things Čapek [said] with his helpers, the other priests.

---

448 Isa. 49:26.
449 Sir. 40:9–10.
450 Sir. 39:29.
451 Sir. 39:30.
452 Heb. 10:27–29.
453 2 Thess. 1:6–8.
454 Luke 19:27.
455 Matt. 22:7.

8   Adamite Articles[456]

Item, in that year [1421], when many were seduced by Martin,[457] a priest of Tábor, falsely perceiving the sacrament of the altar and falling into the heresy of certain Pikarts, of which was mentioned above, some people of both sexes, brothers and sisters, expelled from cohabitation in Tábor by the brothers, captured an island situated between Veselí and Jindřichův Hradec.[458] And once they had inflicted many damages to the surrounding parts, they assumed a bestial nature, [and] seduced by a certain peasant who called himself Moses, they fell into errors and heresies previously unheard of, inspired by their father the devil, as will be made evident from the articles below, which Žižka—the blind captain of Tábor—sent in writing to the Praguers after their slaughter. And these are laid down in the Bohemian language thusly:

Firstly, that they are deceived by the priest Martin Loquis[459] regarding the communion of the body and blood of the Lord Jesus, calling any ordinary bread and every meal the body of God. They have no books, nor do they have regard for them, because they have the law of God written in their hearts, so they say. When they sing the *Pater*,[460] they say thusly: "Our Father, who art in us, illuminate us, let your will [be done], give us all bread", etc.

Item, they do not say [the confession of] faith, because they hold our faith to be an error.

Item, they do not have regard for any holidays, but rather hold every day to be a[n ordinary] day, and they interpret the seventh day as the seventh age.

Item, they hold no fasts, always eating whatever they have.

Item, they call the sky above them the roof, and they say that there is no God in heaven nor devil in hell, but only [the devil] in wicked people and God in good [people].

Item, they already witnessed the renewal of the holy Church, and they believed and held it would remain here eternally.

Item, they called Peter[461] Jesus, the son of God, and Nicholas[462] they called Moses, and held this to be a message for the whole world.

---

456 *FRB* 5, 517–519.
457 Martin Húska.
458 The location of the Adamite settlement was probably the island at the mouth of the stream Řečice flowing into the Nežárka, *HK*, 374, nr. 111, note 1; For a more recent discussion of the theories and their uncertainties, see Čornej, "Potíže s Adamity", 40–42.
459 i.e. Martin Húska. See introduction.
460 i.e. *Pater noster* prayer.
461 The former Táborite priest, Peter Kániš.
462 Nicholas, a simple peasant, was their leader, and thus they were called by some "mikulášenci" ("Nicholasists"). *HK*, 374, nr. 111, note 5.

Item, they called the Lord Jesus Christ a brother of theirs, but a mistrustful one because he died, and they say that the Holy Spirit can never die, and the son of God should be of the Holy Spirit.

Item, they founded their law on adultery, for the Gospel says: "adulterers and harlots will go before you into the heavenly kingdom".[463] Therefore, they would not welcome anyone into their law who is not an adulterer or a whore, not even the smallest little girl, who would have to be violated and fornicate with them if they were to accept her. And they conducted their law thusly: everyone, men and women, undressed and danced around a fire, singing God's Ten Commandments while dancing. Then, standing around the fire, they stared at each other and, if any man had any undergarment on, the women ripped it off him, saying: "let your spirit out of prison and give it to me, and receive my spirit!" Every man ran with any woman, and every woman with any man, in order to sin. But first they incited or inflamed themselves in Sodomite desires, calling these acts the love and will of God, [and] they enacted [the will of] the devil and then bathed in the river. And after a time they indulged with Moses and were never ashamed by one another in that act, because they all lay together in one shack.

Item, they said that they opened the graves of the saints.

Item, saying [on] the time of the spilling of the bowls of the seventh angel in the Revelation of holy John, that blood will [flow] over the whole world up to the mouths of horses,[464] they said that the scythe was already sent upon the whole world and called themselves God's angels, sent to get revenge on the whole world and to sweep out all scandals from God's kingdom; they did not forgive anyone but rather murdered all men, women, and children without exception, burning villages, cities, and people at night, saying that scripture says: "at midnight there was a cry", etc.[465]

Item, they engaged in murders by night and lechery by day.

Item, they called their battle and their murders holy, but held the battle for God's law to be accursed.

Item, they called our priests the devil incarnate, and for that reason they killed the priest John[466] amongst themselves.

Item, they called and named the communion of the body of God "bread bins".

---

463 Matt. 21:31: "Jesus saith unto them, Verily I say unto you, That the publicans and the harlots go into the kingdom of God before you." (KJV).
464 Rev. 16:17–20.
465 Matt. 25:6.
466 Perhaps John Bydlinský. *HK*, 374, nr. 111, note 10.

Item, one woman among them calling herself Mary lost her head, spending a night with one man, for which they beheaded her themselves.

Item, they said of Zdena that she was drawing some of them away from the true faith, for which she and others were burned at Příběnice.

Item, they call Sigismund of Řepan[467] a faithful journeyman, except for his being in wedlock.

Item, they said to their faithful that when their enemies strike against them, that they [the enemies] will all be blinded and will not be able to do anything to them, if only they [the Adamites] will stand with their father.

Item, they feared neither cold nor heat, rather roaming the world naked, endowed like Adam and Eve in paradise. But that all failed, and thus they suffered a shameful death that Tuesday after St. Luke's in the year of our Lord 1421.[468]

---

467 A nobleman who defended the Pikart teachings, but later recanted, FRB 5, 430 f. He was still living in 1428. See HK, 354, nr. 63, note 1, and František Šmahel, Dějiny Tábora I (Jihočeské Nakladatelství: České Budějovice: 1988), 322. On Pikartism, see introduction.

468 21 October 1421.

CHAPTER 2

Jacques Massard: Prophecy and the Harmony of Knowledge

Kristine Wirts and Leslie Tuttle

Introduction

In the late 1670s, a physician in the French city of Grenoble began to establish a reputation as an iatrochemist, or specialist in the new chemical model of physiology and healing. Working in the tradition of Paracelsus and Jan Baptiste Van Helmont, Jacques Massard (*fl.*1679–1693) formulated remedies for common illnesses and published blistering critiques of the traditional Galenic regime of bleeding and purges. But Massard was also a Protestant—a Huguenot—, and the deepening persecution of French Calvinists in the early 1680s both sent him into exile and catalysed a remarkable intellectual transformation. As it was for so many others, the Revocation was a major turning point for Massard. By 1686, he was living in the French refugee community in Amsterdam and publishing—at first anonymously—a serial work of apocalyptic interpretation, *L'Harmonie des Prophéties anciennes avec les modernes*.[1] Over the next five years, in the wake of the ferment and mass migration caused by the 1685 revocation of the Edict of Nantes, the tenor of Massard's work evolved in notable ways. While his career as prophetic interpreter began from the traditional goal of deciphering the biblical book of *Revelation*, it later turned on a far more controversial agenda: claims for the authenticity of contemporary prophecies voiced through members of his own exiled Huguenot community. Massard's short but intense career, concentrated in the years 1686–1693, illustrates the confrontation between the continuing intellectual authority of prophecy and the millenarian revival among French Huguenots in a period of social and political crisis.

Contemporary scholars have shown Massard scant attention. His contribution to French Protestant millenarianism has been overshadowed by that of his more famous contemporary, the pastor Pierre Jurieu (1637–1713). Jurieu's

---

[1] *Harmonie des Propheties anciennes avec les modernes, sur la durée de l'Antechrist et la souffrance de l'Eglise* ([Cologne]: 1686). The work appeared in five instalments between 1686 and 1688.

Accomplissement des Propheties appeared in 1686, the very same year as Massard's *Harmonie des Prophéties*. Both works subscribed to a view, common among Protestants, that the sixteenth-century Protestant Reformation was a central event in the divinely conceived historical framework, representing a definitive turn toward the end times in the struggle of the faithful against the Papal Antichrist.[2] Similarly, both works attest to a revived interest in the book of *Revelation* as a resource to understand the crises of Europe in the age of Louis XIV; both Massard and Jurieu associated the revocation of the Edict of Nantes and the resulting tribulations of French Protestants with events in *Revelation* chapter 11. This chapter speaks of two witnesses, who carry on their ministry of truth despite persecution during a period of 1260 days.[3] They become martyrs when the beast of the Apocalypse rises to slay them, leaving their unburied corpses to rot in the street; but they are resurrected after three and one half days. The grim image of persecution followed by triumph attributed eschatological significance to contemporary European politics, and to the suffering of the French Protestant community.

Yet while Massard and Jurieu shared similar assumptions about the role of French Protestants in eschatological history, Jurieu's prophetic work enjoyed a more organic relationship to Calvinist tradition. Not only was Jurieu a pastor, and indeed professor of theology at the famed Academy of Sedan, he was the grandson by marriage of the famous theologian Pierre du Moulin, author of the most authoritative apocalyptic interpretation in a French Reformed church that was officially circumspect in its approach to apocalyptic speculation.[4] It is worth noting that even Jurieu's impressive pedigree did not shield him from criticism when he sought to associate French Protestantism's recent history with specific events in *Revelation*. Not long after Jurieu's *Accomplissement* rolled off the presses, Dutch ministers complained to their French-speaking brethren about the apocalyptic prophecies that circulated within Huguenot exile communities in the Netherlands, worrying that they

---

2 On the apocalyptic tradition in Protestantism, see Jean Delumeau, *La Peur en Occident (XIVe–XVIIIe siècles), Une Cité assiegée* (Paris: 1978). For the seventeenth-century French Protestant context, specifically, see Jacques Solé, *Les Origines intellectuelles de la Revocation de l'Edit de Nantes* (Saint-Etienne: 1997).

3 Like most millenarians, Massard and Jurieu interpreted these 1260 prophetic days as analogous to 1260 calendar years by calculating the total number of years between the date of the establishment of the Roman Catholic Church, sometime in the 4th and 5th centuries, and the year of the expected second coming of Christ, sometime during the late seventeenth or eighteenth centuries.

4 Pierre Du Moulin, *Accomplissement des Propheties: ou est monstré que les Propheties de S. Paul, et de l'Apocalypse, et de Daniel, touchant les combats de L'Eglise sont accomplies* (Sedan: 1624). Notice that Jurieu's book adopted the same title.

might "give new rise among some to dashed hopes of a territorial kingdom of Jesus Christ and the Apostles."[5]

Massard entered this delicate theological terrain as a layperson whose background did not seem, at first, to lead toward an interest in apocalypticism. Born in the late 1630s, he grew up a Calvinist in Grenoble, France, the son of a master apothecary. Virtually everything we know about him is gleaned from his publications, which named him as a member of the medical faculty of Grenoble, and reveal an initial focus on chemical medicine in the Paracelsian tradition.[6] By 1679, he had ventured into print as the author of a work entitled *Panacée*, touting the virtues of chemically based "universal remedy" for many health complaints.[7] When precisely Massard fled France for the Netherlands is unknown, but by 1686 new editions of his medical works in both French and Dutch appeared under his own name in Amsterdam, suggesting attempts to rebuild a medical practice there. At the same time, the first parts of his apocalyptic work, *Harmonie des Prophéties* appeared anonymously, perhaps because he lacked the clerical training that would licence such a venture into biblical interpretation.[8]

Yet it is precisely Massard's lay status and scientific background that make his prophetic works particularly worthy of scholarly attention. As the translated excerpts that follow show, Massard developed an eclectic method of apocalyptic interpretation that drew inspiration from his Paracelsianism and related forms of Renaissance-era hermeticism. As historians of science have made clear, these ideas remained important well into the seventeenth century, especially among natural philosophers. Like his predecessors Paracelsus and Van Helmont, Massard believed that knowledge concerning God's providential plan was transmitted through multiple channels. It was visible in the so-called book of nature, preserved in the Bible, and also might come via direct

---

5   See the complaints about apocalyptic writing, and Jurieu specifically, among synodal leaders at Balk in 1686 in *Livre Synodal contenant les articles résolus dans les synodes des eglises wallonnes des Pays-Bas* (The Hague: 1896), 20–21. The Netherlands had itself been the site of a number of apocalyptic movements that alerted authorities. See E.G.E. Van de Wall, "'Antichrist Stormed': The Glorious Revolution and the Dutch Prophetic Tradition", in *The Worlds of William and Mary*, ed. Dale Hoak and Mordechai Feingold (Stanford: 1996), 152–164.

6   Allen Debus, *The French Paracelsians: The Chemical Challenge to Medical and Scientific Tradition in Early Modern France* (Cambridge: 2002).

7   *Panacée, ou Discours sur les effets singuliers d'un Remede experimenté, & commode pour la guerison de la pluspart des longues maladies* ... (Grenoble: 1679).

8   For a bibliography of Massard's works, see C., "Notes bibliographiques sur Massard", *Petite Revue des bibliophiles dauphinois* 6 (April 1908), 9–21.

revelation. Accordingly, astrological signs and visions might be as illuminating as knowledge derived empirically or from the Scriptures. Furthermore, the correct interpretation of dreams, natural disasters, and prodigies might shed light on the eschatological timeline outlined in the Bible. All roads of knowledge led, ideally, to the same transcendent and providential truth, such that all knowledge, and all valid foreknowledge, would ultimately prove to be in harmony. Practitioners in this field denied rigid distinctions between Scriptural prophecy and other forms and sources of knowledge. Indeed, to know the divine plan, it was imperative to collect, sift and compare all forms of evidence to reveal their hidden patterns and overlapping themes. Massard joined his famous contemporaries Robert Boyle and Isaac Newton in their simultaneous devotion to deciphering Biblical prophecy and identifying the laws of nature.[9]

Massard's distinctive method of prophetic interpretation came to focus around two basic claims. First, his conviction that a common spirit of truth [*Esprit de vérité*] spoke through all inspired persons translated into an ecumenical embrace of the remarkably diverse array of prophecies circulating in early modern Europe.[10] This included conventional biblical sources like *Revelation* and the *Book of Daniel* but also the works of medieval Catholic visionaries like Catherine of Siena, Hildegard of Bingen and St. Brigid of Sweden. More controversially still, it led him to reclaim as prophecies works that his contemporaries categorised as natural magic rather than religious visions, such as the work of the 14th century alchemist Jean de Roquetaillade.

Most important of all these unconventional sources was Massard's unquenchable fascination with the sixteenth-century French physician-astrologer Michel de Nostredame (1503–1566), who hailed from the same region as Massard, and with whose works, for this reason, Massard was likely most familiar. Massard rechristened Nostradamus, "the French prophet", and argued that Nostradamus had been divinely inspired. He was not unique in this view. Seventeenth-century readers credited Nostradamus with predicting many of their era's violent political reversals and tended to consider such talent more

---

9 Charles Webster, *From Paracelsus to Newton: Magic and the Making of Modern Science* (New York: 1982); idem, *Paracelsus: Medicine, Magic and Mission at the End of Time* (New Haven and London: 2008); Bruce T. Moran, *Distilling Knowledge: Alchemy, Chemistry, and the Scientific Revolution* (Cambridge, Mass.: 2015). On the ties between natural philosophy, prophetic science and apocalypticism, see Margaret C. Jacob, "Millenarianism and Science in the Late Seventeenth Century", *Journal of the History of Ideas* 37:2 (April–June 1976), 335–341 and Richard H. Popkin, "Predicting, Prophecying, Divining and Foretelling from Nostradamus to Hume", *History of European Ideas* 5/2 (1984), 117–135.

10 *Harmonie des Prophéties*, ch. 1. See below, p. 115.

likely a reflection of divine inspiration than astrological prowess. Their faith that once his enigmatic verses were properly understood, they could reveal the future fuelled a never-ending stream of new editions of Nostradamus's works. Massard, like many of his contemporaries, was particularly taken with the so-called "sixains", supposedly a lost addendum to Nostradamus's *Centuries* that appeared to speak directly and accurately to seventeenth-century political reversals; modern scholars consider the text to be a forgery.[11] For Massard, the authority of the sixains was demonstrated by virtue of their having come true. When later editions of Nostradamus left out the sixains, presumably having discovered they were spuriously attributed to the sixteenth-century doctor, Massard interpreted this editorial decision as a Catholic, and specifically Jesuit plot. Catholic authorities had censored the sixains, he claimed, because they revealed too many secrets about the French monarchy and its plan to persecute the Protestant minority.[12]

By validating the prophecies of Catholics as well as Protestants and incorporating visionary evidence from divinatory techniques associated with natural magic, Massard's method underscored the continuity of prophetic experience across disciplines, confessional divides and also across time. Indeed, Massard's ecumenical pursuit of diverse paths to knowledge cannot be overemphasised, and arguably provides the bridge between his work as a medical practitioner and as a prophetic interpreter. Much as he rejected the Galenic orthodoxy in medicine, he definitively rejected the orthodox cessationist view of most Protestant theologians that the age of miracles and prophecy had ended at the time of the apostles, marking *Revelation* as the last revelation. Although he had been taught this idea by pastors during his youth, he reported, he considered it unsubstantiated by Biblical authority, and, happily, God had prevented him from ever accepting it as truth.[13] In other words, Massard asserted that both the exercise of reason and his inner sentiment compelled him to dispute what had long counted as authoritative knowledge.

In sharp contrast to the cessationist claim, Massard argued, God had raised a veritable flood of visionaries since the Protestant Reformation, precisely to clarify the obscurities of *Revelation*. This greater clarity would constitute use-

---

11 On Nostradamus, see Popkin, "Predicting", and Stéphane Gerson, *Nostradamus: How an Obscure Renaissance Astrologer Became the Modern Prophet of Doom* (New York: 2012), esp. 93.

12 See the "suite de l'apologie pour Nostradamus" in *Harmonie des prophéties anciennes avec les modernes, sur la durée de l'Antechrist et les souffrances de l'eglise. Seconde partie* (1687), 275–282.

13 See below, "Remarks on the gift of prophecy, visions, prodigies and miracles", p. 125–126.

ful information for the Protestant chosen people, guiding them in their quest to avoid apostasy and to separate themselves from the mystical Babylon as the age of Antichrist reached its end. Nostradamus, despite being Catholic, was among this chosen group of prophets. For the same reason, Massard attached special credit to Jan Amos Comenius's 1657 *Lux in Tenebris*, a collection of the prophetic writings of three Central European Protestants, Mikulás Drábik (Drabicius), Christoph Kotter (Kotterus) and Krystyna Poniatowska. Massard reported that he read in Louis XIV's royal library the copy of this rare work specially delivered to Louis XIV at Comenius's behest, and he cited the prophecies it contained extensively throughout his prophetic career.

Nostradamus, Drabicius, and Kotterus were important touchstones of Massard's prophetic science, but they constitute only a fraction of the voices that Massard sought to harmonise in his symphony of prophecies. As we might expect, the French Protestant's writing is filled with stories and quotations from both the Hebrew and Christian scriptures. But it also attests to eclectic reading habits. For example, Massard read the serial *Lettres pastorales* of his fellow Huguenot apocalypticist and prophetic rival, Pierre Jurieu. But Massard also cites Pierre Bayle's *Nouvelles de la République des Lettres* and the popular (and anti-Huguenot) French periodical the *Mercure Galant*. In his diatribe against the corruption and cruelty of the Papal Antichrist, Massard incorporated the (spurious) "prophecy of the popes" attributed to the 12th century Irish Archbishop Malachy, as well as the authoritative and influential works of the reform-minded St. Catherine of Siena. He mentions prophecies incorporated in early works of scholarly history by Philippe de Commines and those of the French royal historiographer, François Eudes de Mézeray. The variety and range of Massard's sources is evidence that late seventeenth-century European print culture was suffused by prophetic claims aimed at learned and mass audiences of both Catholic and Protestant sympathies.

The eschatological prediction that Massard derived from this multiplicity of sources proposed that the defeat of the Papal Antichrist was approaching—but not as imminently as was predicted by Jurieu. Both Jurieu and Massard interpreted the 1260 days of *Revelation* 11:3 as years and added 1260 to a time ca. 400–500 CE when the reign of Antichrist was thought to have begun. This led them to understand their own era ($1260 + 400$–$500 = 1660$–1760) as a time of heightened apocalyptic significance. In his reading of Revelation 11, Jurieu had originally identified French Protestants with the biblical witnesses who are resurrected after three and a half days (Rev. 11:9–12), leading Jurieu to suggest that his coreligionists could expect relief for their sufferings approximately three and one half years after the Revocation—a claim that led many of Jurieu's readers to interpret the tumult of European politics in the late 1680s, in particular the Glorious Revolution, in eschatological terms.[14] Far from sharing Jurieu's optimistic expectations of deliverance, Massard believed the sources predicted a period of tribulations for the beleaguered Huguenots, at least until around 1710, when Papal authority would begin to wane. Indeed, by juxtaposing the persecution of the two witnesses of *Revelation* 11 with Nostradamus's sixains using his signature prophetic method, Massard in 1686 darkly forecast that French Protestants could expect, in 1691, to be the victim of another wave of massacres on par with those of St. Bartholomew's Day.[15]

Huguenot thinkers understood French Protestants to be living through important events of the end times foretold in Scripture; a significant corollary of this view was an expectation that signs and prophecies would intensify as the end times drew nearer. Works by French Protestants of this era frequently allude to the promise of Joel 2:28, repeated with an emphasis on its apocalyptic context in Acts 2:17: "In the last days, God says, I will pour out my Spirit on all people. Your sons and daughters will prophesy, your young men will see visions, your old men will dream dreams." These expectations were answered soon after the Revocation, most famously in the person of Isabeau Vincent, a young Protestant woman from a small town in Dauphiné who began to prophesy in her sleep in early February 1688. Massard's rival, Pierre Jurieu, made Vincent famous by defending her experiences and the possibility of continuing prophetic inspiration in his *Lettres Pastorales* of that same year.[16] Massard, for his part, claimed to have written a pamphlet about Vincent even before Jurieu took note of her case, a claim that seems reasonable given Massard's origin and family ties in Dauphiné.[17] More telling, however, was Massard's own shift to integrating contemporary prophecies into his serial *Harmonie des Prophéties*. He took this step he took even before Vincent came on the scene, in spring 1687, with the publication of the first three of the dreams of the unnamed "young refugee lady" in the fourth instalment of the *Harmonie des Prophéties*.[18] While Massard did not herald this shift with any extensive explanation, it neverthe-

---

14 On this tendency, see Warren Johnston, *Revelation Restored: The Apocalypse in Later Seventeenth-Century England* (Woodbridge: 2011).
15 See below, preface to *Harmonie des propheties* (1686), p. 106.
16 Pierre Jurieu, *Lettres pastorales addressées aux fidèles de France qui gémissent sous la captivité de Babylon*, 1 and 15 October 1688.
17 Exactly which publication related to Vincent is Massard's is unknown, although in all likelihood, Massard is referring to the anonymous *Abrégé de l'histoire de la bergère de Saou prèrs de le Crest en Daufiné* (Amsterdam: 1688); for a convincing theory see Jason Charbonneau, "Huguenot Prophetism, Clerical Authority, and the Disenchantment of the World", (M.A. Thesis, Carleton University: 2012), 37–42.
18 See below, page 119.

less signalled an important evolution in Massard's prophetic method, as he began from that point forward to incorporate the dreams and visions of his contemporaries into his ongoing work of apocalyptic interpretation. Massard's previous focus on delineating the "harmony" of well-known prophetic texts from the past—works that arguably enjoyed greater credit by virtue of their age and circulation through the medium of print—shifted to focus on contemporary prophetic texts. This was, in one sense, the logical culmination of Massard's assumption that all inspired persons had access to the same transcendent truth, as Massard argued when he wrote that the visions of the young refugee woman "conform[ed] entirely to other predictions", adding merely "marvellous precision" to an outline of events already signalled in other works. But it served to mark Massard clearly as an "enthusiast" to the critics against whom he made scalding remarks in subsequent works. These tensions were heightened by Massard's strident claims that his project of prophetic interpretation was, itself, divinely inspired and that he too had received sacred insight via dreams.[19]

Over the next six years, between 1687 and 1693, Massard's published works incorporated around two dozen dreams or visions collected from fellow Protestant exiles, which arrived to him as handwritten accounts and even by mail, as readers in other cities entrusted their own visions to his interpretive project. Massard also embraced the (likely fraudulent) prophetic dreams of famous people with some connection to the political turmoil of the age that circulated in Protestant news sheets. These included purported dreams of Louis XIV's former mistress Louise de la Vallière (1644–1710), the deposed James II of England's wife Mary of Modena (1658–1718), and even a dream attributed to Louis XIV himself.[20] All of these night-time visions, he suggested, contained important information that could help his French Protestant community better endure the hardships that were coming.

---

19 Lionel Laborie, *Enlightening Enthusiasm: Prophecy and Religious Experience in Early Eighteenth-century England* (Manchester: 2015); Michael Heyd, *"Be Sober and Reasonable": The Critique of Enthusiasm in the Seventeenth and Eighteenth Centuries* (Leiden: 1995).

20 These dream interpretations are collected in several of Massard's works, including *Recueil des prophéties et songes prophetiques concernans les temps presens & servant pour un eclaircissement de les Propheties de Nostradamus* (Amsterdam: 1691) and *Explication de quelques songes prophetiques et theologiques qu'il a plu à Dieu d'envoier à quelques dames refugiées pour nôtre instruction, & pour nôtre consolation dans ces tems de deuil, d'iniquité et d'ignorance ...* (Amsterdam: 1691). The so-called dream of Louis XIV received multiple interpretations from Protestant writers. See Marianne Carbonnier Burkard, "Le Prédicant et le songe du roi", *Etudes théologiques et religieuses* 62/1 (1987), 19–40 and eadem, "Propagande et prophéties protestantes autour d'un rêve de Louis XIV", *Bulletin de l'Association Suisse pour l'histoire du Refuge huguenot* 27 (2006), 2–15.

Massard's tendency to quote extensively from other sources gave even his early prophetic works like the *Harmonie des Prophéties* an anthological and multivocal quality. This only deepened as he incorporated contemporary prophecy into his writing. Massard usually presented the integral text of the dream or vision in question, followed by his own interpretation, in which he made frequent allusions to his previous work, or to a specific text from the Bible, or Kotterus or Nostradamus. As in the case of the dreams of the young refugee included here, this results in sharp differences in tone. The dreams (Massard terms them "revelations" but they occur in sleep) present recognisable versions of Huguenot life experiences, such as going to services at the temple or, understandably, witnessing violence and persecution, mixed with symbolic visions that have clear Biblical antecedents. Massard's interpretations, in turn, process these visions into data for his rapidly unfolding eschatological narrative, transforming them—sometimes awkwardly—into evidence for the "harmony" of all revealed knowledge.

By 1689, Massard had revealed his name and claimed authorship over his prophetic works. He believed that his prophetic interpretation had proved more accurate than those of other interpreters of *Revelation* including Jurieu, but complained bitterly about the lack of credit he had received for his work and the great peril of ignoring the prophetic insight that God was providing in modern times. He warned that his contemporaries' mockery and indifference would increase the righteous anger of the divine and result in terrible punishments. Although he promised more instalments of his series, his prophetic works ceased after 1693 and indeed he disappears from the historical record after 1696.[21]

Massard attached his contemporaries' prophetic experiences to a tradition of prophecy and its interpretation that remained vibrant and intellectually persuasive to many readers at the end of the seventeenth century. He harnessed the extraordinary wealth and variety of prophetic sources that a burgeoning print culture made available and used it to illuminate the eschatological meaning and context of the struggle of his own Huguenot community. Massard's work is remarkable for the way that it united a learned tradition of apocalyptic interpretation with the phenomenon of popular prophecy among French Protestant populations that surged in the aftermath of the revocation of the Edict of Nantes. His work complicates any effort to make sense of millenarian prophesying as the last resort of illiterate Huguenot men and invites us to reconsider simplistic narratives of "disenchantment."

---

21   Massard's last work to appear in print was the medical treatise, *Divers traitez sur les panacées, ou remèdes universel* (Amsterdam: 1696).

1   [Jacques Massard] *The Harmony of Prophecies and Predictions, Ancient and Modern, Regarding the Duration of the Suffering of the Church* (1686)

Preface [1686][22]

The name of *revelation* suits all the books of Holy Scripture, since they are all revealed by God. However, it has pleased God above all others to call *Revelation* the inspired visions of St. John, in order to mark the greatness and majesty of this divine book. It is for this same reason that the Holy Spirit has joined some special promises to the reading he orders us to make of *Revelation*. For he has reiterated this twice in it: *Blessed are those who read the words of this prophecy*.[23] Jesus Christ raised in the Heavens, and seated at the right hand of the Divine Majesty, often speaks in *Revelation*. This is why some have called *Revelation* the gospel of Jesus Christ glorified, to distinguish it from the words collected by the four Evangelists at the time of Jesus's crucifixion.

    Yet the obscurity of this book has hindered several of the faithful from examining it, and perhaps even from reading it. It is necessary to aver, however, that the truths that we must know are marked there so clearly, that one can say that there is no book in Holy Scripture in this respect more clear than this one. The goal that God proposes via this book is to teach men, especially the faithful, that there must be two Antichrists in the world, one of the East (Orient), and one of the West (Occident), both in order to test the faith of his children, and in order to prevent them for moving with the rest of the world toward the abandon of perdition. He sought above all to identify the great Antichrist, that is to say that of the Occident, namely the Pope, because his seduction is much more dangerous, his corruption infinitely greater, and his persecutions without comparison more violent and more cruel that those of the Antichrist of the Orient.[24] Now, there are in the entire book of *Revelation* only four or five truths that each of us must know to avoid apostasy and the persecution of the Antichrist. This book teaches them in a very clear way, as we shall see in the rest of this discussion.

    The first thing that we must know, and that *Revelation* reveals clearly to us, is that the Pope is the Antichrist, that his seat is the city of Rome, that his religion is an apostasy, and a revolt against the faith. St. John teaches this dogma so

---

22   The preface is irregularly paginated. Page numbers have not been reproduced here for this reason.
23   Rev. 1:3.
24   Though later distancing themselves from such claims, the Huguenots first formally identified the Pope as the Antichrist at the Synod of Gap in 1603.

obviously that even the doctors of the Roman Communion are forced to admit that the Antichrist will rise in the city of Rome, and that he will reign there three and one-half years over the ten kings his vassals.

The second truth that we must know, and that this book teaches us with clarity is that in order to be saved, it is necessary to separate oneself from this confusion and Babylonian mystique, which does not stop at corrupting the entire Christian religion, but indeed transforms it to *absinthium*,[25] that is a poisonous and bitter doctrine. It goes even further, forcing men to make a public profession of its heresies and abominations. Everyone knows that the Roman Catholic church compels people to embrace its religion in two ways; firstly by promises similar to those that the Devil made to Jesus Christ in the desert.[26] And then, secondly, by the prisons and the torments that it inflicts on those who do not wish to embrace its communion.

The third important truth that *Revelation* clearly teaches us is that God gave a fixed time to the Antichrist, beyond which he will not endure. After that time elapses, God will destroy him, in order to establish his kingdom, that is, the authentic religion, throughout the entire world.

The fourth point that St. John clearly expresses, and whose clarity is of paramount importance to the faithful, is that during the time of the Antichrist there will continue to be in the confines of his Empire two witnesses, or Martyrs, and a certain small number of faithful, clad in sackcloth. These people will testify to the truth during 1260 years, or 42 prophetic months. Nevertheless, after this time St. John tells us that *the Beast will rise from the abyss and make fierce war against two witnesses of Jesus Christ, and will defeat them and kill them: but they will rise again after three and one-half days.*[27] I will show that this war of the Antichrist against the faithful began in the year 1684, and that it must last thirty years. For these thirty years will complete the three and one-half years of the Pope. (Daniel 12:11)[28] I will also show that at the end of this time the two witnesses will be resurrected, that is to say that the great reforma-

---

25 *Artemisia absinthium*, wormwood, is a bitter herb that was used for medicinal and flavouring purposes in medieval and early modern Europe; it is a traditional ingredient in the distilled liquor *absinthe*. At high doses it is toxic.
26 The Temptation of Christ is repeated in all the synoptic gospels. For example, Matt. 4:8–9: "Then the devil took him up to a very high mountain, and showed him all the kingdoms of the world in their magnificence, and he said to him, 'All these I shall give to you, if you will prostrate yourself and worship me.'"
27 Rev. 11:7–11.
28 "From the time that the daily sacrifice is abolished and the abomination that causes desolation is set up, there will be 1,290 days."—ed.

tion of the entire Roman Church will arrive in the year 1714, after the three and one-half days that God has given the Antichrist.²⁹

This reformation began in the year 1508,³⁰ which was the first year of the sound of the seventh trumpet, and which will be perfectly completed the last year of the sound of the same trumpet, which will arrive in the year 1753. At that time, all the people of the world, both Jews and Gentiles, will embrace Christianity. *Then God's temple in heaven was opened, and within his temple was seen the ark of his covenant* ... (Revelation 11:19)

To gain a general sense of the [meaning of the] great events of the world, of the time of the Antichrist, and of the sufferings of the Church, it will be necessary throughout this work to keep in mind the idea, drawn from the revelations of Kotterus,³¹ as well as those of Saint John, that the Pope has [already] received four wounds from which he has healed, because they were not fatal.

The final three wounds of the Pope will be mortal wounds. The first began in the year 1684 with the war the Great Sultan³² made against the Empire of the Antichrist, and by the solemn edicts that the King of France made against the infallibility of the Pope, and against the other extremely arrogant prerogatives he claimed. It is by these two factors that the authority of the Pope will be entirely exhausted in 28 years, in the year 1714.

The second mortal wound of the Pope will begin in the year 1714 and finish in the year 1753,³³ which is the last year of the seventh trumpet.

The third mortal wound begins the year 1753 and ends in the year 1759, which will complete the age of the Antichrist, and lead us to that blessed time that

---

29   Pierre Jurieu, by contrast, calculated 1685 as the date for the death of the two witnesses and thus the starting time for the fall of Rome, the final collapse of which Jurieu determined to occur in 1715. See Warren Johnston, "Revelation and the Revolution of 1688–1689", *The Historical Journal* 48/2 (2005), 364–366.

30   In 1508, King Vladislav II of Hungary issued an edict that initiated persecution against the Bohemian Brethren, the sect associated with one of Massard's cherished prophetic forebears, Jan Amos Comenius. On the origin of the Bohemian Brethren, see Martin Pjecha's chapter in this volume.

31   Christoph Kotter (1585–1647) was one of the three Central European visionaries whose work was collected in Jan Amos Comenius's *Lux in tenebris* (Amsterdam: 1657). This work constituted one of Massard's key sources.

32   Mehmed IV, Sultan of the Ottomans (r.1648–1687).

33   Massard's date for the last year of the seventh trumpet interestingly coincides with the Hanoverian succession and the Jew Bill of 1753, which was debated in millenarian terms. See Andrew Crome, "The 1753 'Jew Bill' Controversy: Jewish Restoration to Palestine, Biblical Prophecy, and English National Identity", *English Historical Review* 130/547 (2015), 1449–1478.

Daniel predicted after 1290 years of the Pope: *Blessed*, he says, *is he who will see the 4th year after the 1290*. (Daniel 12:12)

Malachy Archbishop of Ireland[34] names for us in a wonderful way the Pope who is supposed to begin the war against the faithful, and also he who will be the last of the Popes. He names the reigning Pontiff Innocent XI *Bellua insatiabilis*,[35] or Insatiable Beast, making an obvious allusion to this *Beast [who] will rise from the abyss and make fierce war against two Witnesses of Jesus Christ, and will defeat them and kill them*.[36] Because Innocent XI, insatiable in his vast designs, is not satisfied with his jurisdiction over the papists, he is trying to cause perdition for the faithful by arresting them in his dominions and making them embrace his cursed religion, and even in killing by torture those who refuse to worship his execrable idols and the great abomination of papism, a little God of dough.

Malachy named the very last Pope, who will be the 25th after this one, *Gloria Oliva*, because only the extinction of the Pope and of Papism will bring the olive branch to the Church, that is to say, peace, and will mark the *end of the Papist flood*, of which the olive branch is a symbol (Kotterus).

Nostradamus in his emblems, which one can find referenced in an English book entitled *Catastrophe mundi*,[37] tells of four doves, each carrying an olive branch, [which will come] after the destruction of the Pope. He makes this prediction in Century 6, quatrain 6:

There shall die at Rome a great man, the night being past.[38]

This means that after the extinction of the Pope there will be no more false religions in the world, nor affliction for the faithful. God will then bless all the peoples of the earth with his most precious blessings, spiritual as well as temporal. All the ancient and modern prophecies foretell the same thing; I shall speak more about this elsewhere. I shall, however, speak in this preface about the prodigious and terrible catastrophe which is beginning to be

---

34 The *Prophecy of the Popes*, attributed to the 12th century Irish Archbishop Malachy of Armagh, was published in 1595 within a history of the Benedictine order compiled by Arnold Wion. It purports to predict the identity of the pontiffs until the Apocalypse.

35 The pontificate of Pope Innocent XI, born Benedetto Odescalchi, lasted from 1676 until his death in 1689.

36 Rev. 11:7.

37 Probably [John Holwell] *Catastrophe mundi, or, Europe's many mutations until the year 1701* ... (London: 1682). Holwell was an English mathematician and astrologer.

38 All English translations of Nostradamus are from Theophilus de Garencieres, trans., *The True Prophecies or Prognostications of Michael Nostradamus, Physician to Henry II, Francis II and Charles IX Kings of France and one of the best Astronomers that ever were* (London: 1672).

seen in the world, and which will last from the year 1684 to the year 1714. It includes the time of the death of the two witnesses, and of their resurrection, as well as the first mortal wound of the Antichrist. After this fifth wound of the Pope, which is the first of his incurable wounds, he will be completely stripped of his authority while awaiting the eternal flames to which the Holy Spirit condemns him. He will creep along in this world for 45 years, both he and his clergy living an unhappy and miserable life, from the year 1714 until the year 1759. The revelation of Drabicius[39] which I have cited on page 253, offers two portraits of the Pope, one of his first, and the other of his second old age.[40]

We read in the third book of the life of St. Catherine of Siena, and in several places in her works themselves, that the *reformation of the Church will only occur by flames and by torments*,[41] that this is how God will purify the Church, and correct its errors and mistakes. In this fashion he will make the church so pure and so holy that Catherine wished to suffer several martyrdoms, if it were possible, to enjoy the happiness of seeing this great and marvellous reformation.

Nostradamus foretells the same thing; as the knowledge of his prophecies may enable the [Protestant] Powers to prevent the evils from which Europe is threatened, I will endeavour to give an understanding of it in just a few words. *He who has ears to hear, let him hear.*

> Century I quatrain 16
> *Plague, famine, death by a military hand*
> *The age groweth near to its renovation*

This is to say, when the time of the great reformation of the Church approaches there will have been plague and famine in the world. And war will be so cruel that the soldiers will commit terrible butchery of men.

---

39   Mikulás Drábik (1588–1671), Czech visionary whose work was published by Comenius in *Lux in tenebris*. See introduction above.

40   "I then saw a specific person whose face was terrible to look at, so covered with sores, scales, pustules and filth; and when this person had passed, I saw coming another sorry person, dying, so very bent over, and on the verge of falling." Massard cites Drabicius's Revelation 98 v. 5 from 1652.

41   Several versions of the life of Saint Catherine of Siena, and of her letters and spiritual works were published in French in the seventeenth century. The precise source of this quotation is unknown.

Century I quatrain 67
What a great famine do I see drawing near
To turn one way, then another, and then become universal,
So great and long, that they shall come to pluck
The root from the wood, and the child from the breast.

Nostradamus teaches us that before this terrible famine that must precede the great reformation, there will be several smaller famines. He predicts one in France, principally in the Provinces of Languedoc, Dauphiné, and Provence, after the cruel mission of the Dragoons, and the torments which the Protestants now suffer so cruelly, [which he mentioned in] sixains 32 and 33. The prophecy of Nostradamus was fulfilled by the famine suffered in the southern provinces of France.[42]

In sixain 50, Nostradamus threatens England with famine and extreme sickness in the aftermath of those that France must endure. The prophecy of Usserius printed with permission in London in the year 1678 likewise predicts great misfortunes.[43] The [Protestant] Powers could prevent this great famine by prudence similar to that of Joseph. They could also avoid some of the terrible tribulations which are to happen to them, if they only knew the time they were to arrive, and if their hearts were not hardened, and enchanted by magicians worse than those of Pharaoh, by whom I mean the Pope, the clergy, and the monks, above all the Jesuits. [I say this] because the Roman Antichrist and his clergy do not want to recognise the finger of God in the darkness into which they have descended, and in the evils which are on the verge of overwhelming them and plunging them in the burning lake of fire and sulfur, as it is written in the *Revelation* of St. John and those of St. Brigid, in revelation 41 of book one.[44]

---

42   Louis XIV's dragonnades had commenced their campaign against the southern French provinces and Huguenot strongholds of Languedoc, Dauphiné, and Provence in the early 1680s.

43   *Strange and Remarkable Prophesies and Predictions of the Holy, Learned, and Excellent James Usher, Late L. Arch-Bishop of Armagh, and Lord Primate of Ireland: Giving an Account of his Foretelling* ... (London: 1678). James Ussher (1581–1656) is perhaps best known as a contributor to scholarly debates attempting to establish the date of the world's creation based on Biblical sources. He never claimed to have prophetic insights; however, his biographer, Nicholas Bernard, introduced this notion and the predictions written in Bernard's biography were then extracted as a pamphlet for a ready market. See Ute Lotz-Heumann, "'The Spirit of Prophecy Has Not Entirely Wholly Left the World': The Stylisation of Archbishop James Ussher as a Prophet", in *Religion and superstition in Reformation Europe*, ed. Helen Parish and William G. Naphy (Manchester: 2002), 119–132.

44   The *Revelations of Saint Brigid of Sweden*, given approbation by the Council of Constance in 1436, circulated widely in early modern Europe; at least four Latin and four French

Scripture teaches us that Balak King of Moab sent Balaam from far away to curse the people of God, but this false prophet, nevertheless inspired by the Holy Spirit, blessed these people expressly, in saying, *how would I curse them, whom God has blessed?*[45] In some ways the same thing happened to the Pope as to the King of Moab. He has canonised several ecstatic persons, as Comenius[46] puts it, such as St. Hildegard, St. Elizabeth, St. Bridget and St. Catherine of Siena, so that their reputation gives some odour of holiness to his confession. However, since these people are animated by divine enthusiasm and holy fury, they have forthrightly described the abominations of the Pope, of Papism, and of the Roman clergy, and they have predicted their temporal and earthly destruction if they do not repent. They have also prophesied the reformation of the Roman church. They have said that after the destruction of the Pope, and his clergy, God will call the Jews and the Nations to knowledge of God. The visions of Robert the Dominican[47] that I have cited in this book, also predict the same thing.

God never leaves himself without witnesses, even among the enemies of his name, so that that they are without an excuse before his Majesty. The Prophet [Isaiah] teaches us that he has pruned his vine, which is his Church, with all the preparations that could be made,[48] as God once sent his prophets to the ten tribes of Israel, who revolted by their idolatry not only against their legitimate king, but also against God. This great God has aroused the same way, in the very breast of the Roman Church certain holy persons, who are animated by his Spirit and have preached the truth, such as John de Roquetaillade and Peter [sic] Savonarola, Dominicans, that the Popes have put to the fire, as I shall observe in this book, because they taught that the Pope is the Antichrist.[49] It

---

editions appeared in the seventeenth century alone. See, for example, Jacques Ferraige (trans.), *Les Revelations celestes et divines de Saint Brigitte de Suede* (Paris: 1624). Chapter 41 speaks of divine retribution against unbelievers and the protection and multiplication of a small number of faithful.

45 Num. 23:8.
46 Jan Amos Comenius (1592–1670), pansophist philosopher and apocalyptic interpreter who compiled *Lux in Tenebris* (1657). See introduction and note 52 below.
47 Robert d'Uzès (1263–1296), originally from the Cévennes, was active in Avignon most of his life. By the early sixteenth century, his visionary works appeared in printed Latin editions alongside those of other more famous figures whom Massard also cites, like Hildegard of Bingen.
48 "For afore the harvest, when the bud is perfect, and the sour grape is ripening in the flower, he shall both cut off the sprigs with pruning hooks, and take away *and* cut down the branches." (Isa. 18:5).
49 Girolamo Savonarola (1452–1498) was a Dominican reformer who was executed by hanging and fire for defiance against the papacy. Jean de Roquetaillade (c.1310–1370),

is for this same reason that the Pope condemned the doctrine of the Abbott Joachim [of Fiore]. Savonarola powerfully exhorted Charles VIII to reform the Roman Church; he even threatened [the Emperor] with severe punishment, if he did not acquit the commandment he made to him on behalf of God, as Philippe de Commines[50] reports. This celebrated historian, speaking of the prompt and unhappy death of the Prince, and of his heir, notes that these deaths were the fulfilment of the prophecy of Savonarola, caused by the disobedience of Charles VIII.

Drabicius in his revelations similarly orders the King of France to work on the Reformation of the Roman Church. He has made him hope for all the glorious successes which God has favoured him from the year 1665 until now. He promises him the Empire of the West (Occident), and all the delights of Heaven and of Earth, if he executes the great work God has prescribed for him. God commanded Drabicius to send his revelations to this King. Comenius, whom God has given to Drabicius for Secretary, fulfilled this commission around the year 1665. He went expressly to Paris for this subject.[51] He gave the revelations of Drabicius to his Majesty, or to his Ministers. I have seen and read the copy that he left in the King's Library.[52]

Nostradamus promises the Empire to the King of France under the same conditions as Drabicius. His prophecies teach us that the King of France who becomes Emperor will be a Protestant, and a capital enemy of the Pope and his Clergy. I will cite on this subject several quatrains which predict with abundant clarity this great and marvellous event, and which give us word that the domination of France will be a happy occasion for the world and for the Church, which is at present unhappy under the Empire of the Antichrist.

---

however, was a Franciscan best known for his works of alchemy and for prophetic commentaries. He did denounce ecclesiastical abuses and was imprisoned for a time, but there is no evidence he was executed.

50   Philippe de Commines (1447–1511), late medieval historian and author of a work titled *Mémoires* that chronicled European politics in the late fifteenth century. For his interaction with Savonarola, see Book VIII, chapter 3.

51   Johannes Jacob Redinger served as Jan Amos Comenius's envoy to Paris as this time.

52   Comenius compiled the visions of Czech visionaries Mikuláš Drábik (Drabicius) Christoph Kotter (Kotterus), and Krystyna Poniatowska (Christine Poniatovie) in the Latin collection *Lux in Tenebris* (1657). This collection of seventeenth-century apocalyptic writings, quite rare at the time, was one of Massard's chief influences. Comenius apparently did send a copy of this work to France, with a political memo intended for King Louis XIV, under the care of his secretary. See R.-J. Vonka, "Les Évangéliques tchèques et les protestants français aux XVIe et XVIIe siècles", *Bulletin de la Société de l'Histoire du Protestantisme Français* 76/4 (Oct-Dec. 1927), 488.

> Century 2 quatrain 69
> *The French King, by the Low Countreys right hand,*
> *Seeing the discord of the great monarchy*
> *Upon three parts of it, will make his sceptre to flourish,*
> *Against the cap of the great Hierarchy.*

That is to say, that the King of France, seeing Germany's divisions, will profit through force of arms. And that later he will reign happily over three quarters of the Empire, against the Pope, and against all the Roman clergy.

> Century 3 quatrain 49
> *French Kingdom thou shalt be much changed,*
> *The Empire is translated in another place,*
> *Thou shalt be put into other manners and Laws,*
> *Rouan and Chartres shall do the worse they can to thee.*

That is to say, great changes will happen in the kingdom of France. The Empire of Germany will move to a different place. And at the same time there will be change in religion and customs there. Rouen and Chartres[53] will do all they can in order to oppose this blessed reformation.

> Century 5 quatrain 74
> *Of Trojan blood shall be born a German heart.*
> *Who shall attain to so high a power,*
> *That he shall drive away the strenge Arrabian Nation,*
> *Restoring the Church to her former splendor.*

By Trojan blood Nostradamus means the French. He is thus saying that from the royal blood of France a German Emperor will be born, who will become so powerful, that he will repulse the Turks, and restore the Church to its first purity.

> Century 5 quatrain 77
> *All the degrees of Ecclesiastical honour*
> *Shall be changed into a Dial Quirinal,*
> *Into Martial, Quirinal, Fluminick,*
> *After that, a King of France shall make it Vulcanal.*

---

53   Rouen and Chartres were Catholic strongholds in the seventeenth century.

The Pope, who has made himself master of all the dignities of the clergy, and who disposes of them as absolute ruler, will render his clergy *Martial*, by the wars which this Pontiff will undertake against the faithful; he will also make the clergy *Quirinal*, for it will devote itself more and more to the service of the Roman Church. He will also make it *Flaminick*, for he will cause it to receive and adopt day by day all the superstitions of pagan Rome. And when this abominable clergy shall have filled the measure of its iniquities and its execrable idolatry, then the King of France punishing his crimes will burn it, and make of it a worthy sacrifice to God.

> Century 10 quatrain 86
> *As a Griffon shall come the King of Europe,*
> *Accompanied with those of the North,*
> *Of red and white shall conduct a great troop,*
> *And they shall go against the King of Babylon.*

We know that the King of Babylon is the Pope. Drabicius and Nostradamus name the King of France the great Monarch, and the great King of Europe during the time that he destroys the Pope and his Clergy. This is how Nostradamus named him in Century 2 quatrain 12:

> *Eyes shut, shall be open by an antick fancy,*
> *The cloths of the alone shall be brought to nothing.*
> *The great Monarck shall punish their frenzy,*
> *For being ravished the treasure of the temple before.*

The princes will open their eyes one day, and recognise how much they are abused. They will then annihilate the Ecclesiastical Roman State, the Monks, who take vows not to marry, and thus are always named "the alone" by Nostradamus. The King of France will be distinguished among from all the other princes by the revenge he will exact on the Pope and his clergy. For having become the great Monarch of Europe, he will chastise their furor, and their cruelty, and he will openly seize all their possessions. Quatrain 93 from Century 4 promises to Monsieur the Duc de Bourgogne a reign so holy and merry, that all the princes of the world will bless God for the ascension of this prince to the throne of France.

Yet if the benefits that Nostradamus promises the King of France for the reformation of the Roman Church and for the destruction of the Pope and his clergy, are extremely glorious, it is necessary to acknowledge that the misfortunes which he predicts to befall all his Kingdom after the persecution of the

Protestants are worthy of our tears. It is quite difficult to read in sixain 32 about the desolation of the French state after the Dragoon mission and what follows without being touched by compassion.

Nostradamus in his sixains describes all the events of the last war of the Antichrist against the faithful. He describes there the death and resurrection of the two witnesses and prophets of Jesus, who must suffer martyrdom for the testimony that they offer to truth in all of the states of the Antichrist. This is why I will give a brief explanation here:

> Sixain 32
> *Plenty of wine, very good for troopers*
> *Tears, and sighs, complaints, cries, and alarms,*
> *Heaven shall cause its thunder to rain,*
> *Fire, water and blood, all mixed together,*
> *The sun heavens quaketh and shaketh for it,*
> *No living man hath seen what he may see then.*

Nostradamus predicts here the Dragoon Mission, *the tears, the sighs, the complaints, the cries, and the alarms* of the Protestants of France, and the horror that the Christian princes will suffer from Antichristian conduct.

> Sixain 33
> *A little after shall be a great misery,*
> *Of the scarcity of corn that shall be upon the ground,*
> *Of Dauphiné, Provence and Vivarois,*
> *In Vivarois*[54] *is a poor presage,*
> *Father of Son shall be Anthropophage.*

After the cruelties which are done to the Protestants, Nostradamus predicted that France would be punished by very great misery, and first of all a famine, which would be extreme in her southern provinces; and we know that there has hardly been a harvest of wheat in these provinces.

---

54 While in Amsterdam, Massard was the first to publish on Isabeau Vincent and the *petits prophètes*, whose movement began in Dauphiné and spread to Vivarais. See the corresponding historical introduction to this text.

Sixain 34
Princes and Lords shall war one against another,
[First cousin],[55] *the brother against brother*
The Arby finished of the happy Bourbon
The Prince of Hierusalem so lovely
Of the enormous and execrable fact committed.
Shall ressent upon the bottomless purse.

Nostradamus predicted here that the government of the House of Bourbon would cease to be happy after the revocation of the Edict of Nantes, and that in following years France will be afflicted not only with famine, but also civil and foreign war.[56] The Christian princes and the faithful will avenge themselves against the Roman clergy for the cruelties they committed against the Protestants of France.

Sixain 35
A lady by death great afflicted
Mother and tutor to the blood that hath left her
Ladies and Lords made orphans
By asps and by crocodiles
Shall strong holds, castles and towns be surprised
God almighty keep them from the wicked.

This sixain predicts the extreme affliction of the Reformed Church of France, and the barbarity of the Roman Clergy, who here are called *asps and crocodiles*. And, in the following lines, Nostradamus warns the Protestant powers to be on guard to defend themselves against the violence, and the artifices of these Scoundrels. He joins finally his prayers to theirs, in hopes that *God almighty keep them from the wicked*.

Sixain 36
The great rumour that shall be through France,
The powerless would fain have power,
Honey Tongues, and true chameleons,
Blasters and lighters of candles,

---

55 Garancières translates *Cousin germain* as "German cousin".—ed.
56 Nine Years' War (1688–1697) and War of Spanish Succession (1701–1714). The revocation of Edict of Nantes was followed by the Camisard Rebellion (1702–1710).

> *Magpies and Jays, carriers of news,*
> *Whose biting shall be like that of scorpions.*

This sixain predicts the rumours, and the news of war that now exists in France. It is said that the *powerless would fain have power*, that is to say that the faithful will wish from the bottom of their heart to recover the precious liberty which they once enjoyed. In the four last lines he decries the monks and the clergy of France, treating them as scoundrels who have stolen liberty of conscience from the kingdom. And so that we cannot fail to recognise them, he describes them by the character that St. John gives them, in saying *whose biting shall be like that of scorpions*, Revelation 9:3,5, and 10.

> Sixain 37
> *The weak and powerful shall be at great variance,*
> *Many shall die before they agree,*
> *The weak shall cause the powerful to call him victor,*
> *The most potent shall yield to the younger*
> *And the older of the two shall die,*
> *When one of the two shall invade the Empire.*

This sixain continues to observe the conflicts surrounding religion in France, the oppression of Protestants and their weakness, in saying *weak and powerful will be in great discord*. Nostradamus predicts that the conflicts will endure rather a long time.[57] Because, he says, *many will die before they agree*. He then records all the details of the fight of the faithful against the Papists. He assures that the Papists, having abused their tyrannical power and having languished in ignorance, will finally recognise their errors, and will admit the wrong they have committed in persecuting the witnesses of Jesus Christ. He calls them young because in calling themselves Reformed, they in fact presuppose an older Religion. He also calls them young because they must grow in force; and for contrast, he calls it the ancient Roman Religion. Because, he says, it must be extinguished when *the King of France shall invade the Empire*.

The ascension of the King of France to the Empire is supposed to end all the misfortunes of Europe, as Nostradamus says, if one compares the last line of this sixain with sixain 48. Because, he says, in that place, *that the older Religion will die*. That means the Papacy. He calls it the older for three reasons, first

---

57 Nostradamus, born Michel de Nostredame (1503–1566), was active during the French Wars of Religion (1562–1598).

in comparison to the Reformed faith; in the second place because the Papacy began in the year 424, as we have proved elsewhere;[58] in the third place because that which is old is near its end, as St. Paul said. This is why [the verb] *antiquare* means in the Latin Language "to abolish."

Sixains 52 and 53, which I explained on page 8 of this book, teach us that this blessed time will not arrive until 1710. Until that year the misfortunes of the Protestants of France will only get worse.[59] Indeed, [Nostradamus] teaches us in these two sixains that in the year 1691 there shall be a second massacre in France similar to that of Saint Bartholomew.

> Sixain 52
> *The great city that hath not bread half enough*
> *Shall once more engrave*
> *In the bottom of her soul St. Bartholomew's day ...*[60]

Oh Alas! Though Nostradamus would not say it, the partisans of France tell us already. The author of *Letters on the siege of Bude, and on the League of Augsburg*,[61] does not permit us to doubt this enterprise worthy of the Antichrist and the great destroyer. The author of these letters calls himself Bourgeois of Cologne. He speaks to the League of Augsburg, in the same way that Rabshakeh, cup-bearer of Sennacherib, spoke to the forces of King Hezekiah.[62]

The sixains that Nostradamus cites for us show us that France should have no other hopes in reward for her conduct than similar underhanded tricks, and that her misfortunes will be no less great than those of the neighbours whom she threatens with such pride.

Nostradamus predicts in many places great misfortune for those princes who have persecuted the faithful. This quatrain is worth consideration.

---

58 Massard claimed that, in the year 424, popes began referring to themselves as "vicars of Jesus Christ" which he associates with the Greek for "Antichrist." By adding 1260 to 424, Massard arrived at 1684 as a date for the end of the age of Antichrist. See *Harmonie des Propheties* (1686), 138.

59 The year 1710 corresponds to the end of the Camisard Rebellion (1702–1710).

60 Massard truncates this sixain here.—ed.

61 [Anon.], *Lettre d'un Bourgeois de Cologne, a un ami, sur la prise de Bude, et sur les autres affaires presentes* (Cologne: 1686). The first letter, dated 14 September 1686, was followed by a second dated 30 September 1686. Several responses were published.

62 2 Kings 18:13–19:37. The cup-bearer advises the people of Jerusalem to submit to the Assyrian king rather than fight a war they will lose.

Century 6 quatrain 9
To the holy temples shall be done great scandals,
That shall be accounted for honours and praises,
By one, whose medals are graven in gold and silver,
The end of it shall be in very strange torments.

Nostradamus speaks in this quatrain of a prince who will count it an honour to persecute the faithful, to tear down their holy temples, and who will derive vanity from it. In the last line he predicts a terrible punishment for this prince. This is what we have already seen happen to most of the Princes who have afflicted the Church. But this vengeance of heaven will still appear in our days for those who imitate their conduct, if God does not grant them the grace to be converted by a prompt and serious repentance.

In order to reply in a few words to the threats of the Bourgeois of Cologne, partisan of France, it suffices to add this epigram:

De Turcis a Caesare profligatis Epigramma ad Gallos
Cognatas Turcarum acies gens Celtica luget,
Que fladio, Cesar, interiere tuo.
Deserit ergo meas inquit victoria partes!
Hostibus audebit forte favore meis!
Scilicet ipsa tuas horret victoria vires,
Quis ipsum credis vincere posse Deum.

This so-called Bourgeois of Cologne maintained that, although the Great Sultan had suffered considerable losses, nevertheless the Empire could not resist the efforts of France and the Turk. But as God is able to derive the greatest benefits from the most extreme evils, both for his glory and for the salvation of his Church, it so happens that this strange mixture of wars and massacres, which is to arrive in a short time throughout Europe, will in the end provide for the establishment of the Kingdom of Jesus Christ. This will be accomplished by means of the complete destruction of the Pope, the Papacy and the Antichristian Empire. All of the ancient and modern prophecies predict it. Nostradamus says it clearly in this quatrain:

Century 2 quatrain 30
One that shall cause the infernal Gods of Hannibal
To live again, the terror of Mankind,
There was never more horror, not to say ill dayes,
Did happen, er shall, to the Romans by Babel.

Nostradamus tells us that there will be a prince so powerful that he will be the terror of nations, and that the conduct of this prince will engender in the spirit of the people as much hatred against Rome and against the Romans as Hannibal had in the past. This prince will also create a confusion of war without parallel, which will finally produce such terrible misfortune for Rome and for the Romans, that its like has never been seen since the creation of the world. Drabicius, to express the confusion and the horror of great wars that are to occur in Europe, uses the same expression as Nostradamus, by calling them Babel, which means confusion.

The two letters of the Bourgeois of Cologne, about the Fort, and the Huningen Bridge, and the pole which was raised next to the door of Namur with the arms of France, and indeed all the prophets teach us that we will soon see this confusion of wars that Nostradamus and Drabicius predict in Europe. If we compare this quatrain with the quatrain 54 of Century 4, which I shall explain shortly, we will see that the prince of whom Nostradamus speaks in this place is Louis XIV, who has begun without knowing it the destruction of the Pope and the Papacy, much as Henry VIII did in England. The printed letters of Queen Christina [of Sweden] in the *Nouvelles de la République des Lettres*, and a letter in response to Monsieur de Meaux, allow us to see the opinion of this Queen, who judges that the [French] King's actions are very disadvantageous to the Pope and Papism.[63]

The interests of the King of France and that of the Great Sultan being identical, it is impossible that these two powers would not unite perfectly for the destruction of the Antichristian Empire. For if kings command peoples, [national] interest commands kings. This conformity of interests will now make Europe the theatre of a sad tragedy. Yet, after the destruction of the Pope, the union of these two great princes will produce the happiness of the entire world. It is thus what Nostradamus predicts in the Quatrain 89 of Century 2.

> *One day the two great masters will be friends,*
> *Their great power shall be increased*

---

63 Pierre Bayle inserted a letter from Queen Christina of Sweden, a Catholic, to the Chevalier de Terlon, French ambassador to Sweden, into the May 1686 issue of his *Nouvelles de la République des lettres*, pages 529–532. The letter expressed criticism of the French crown's religious policy in the aftermath of the revocation of the Edict of Nantes. On the controversy about this letter between Bayle and the Queen, see Samy Ben Massaoud, "Bayle et Christine de Suède", *Bulletin de la Société de l'Histoire du Protestantisme Français*, 155 (2009), 626–655.

The new land shall be in a flourishing condition,
The number shall be told to the bloody person.

By the bloody person Nostradamus means the one which St. John in *Revelation* calls Abaddon, and Angel of Death. He foretold its destruction by the union of these two powers. I explained this quatrain on page 293.

The author of the *Mercure Galant*, a little before the Dragoon Mission, reported a prediction of Monsieur de la Riviere which is found in the Memoirs of Monsieur de Béthune [The Duc de Sully].[64] That prediction explains in three words the prophecies of Nostradamus on the present state of France. Here's how.

Henri IV ordered Monsieur de la Rivière his doctor in the year 1600, to make a horoscope of Louis XIII. Sometime afterwards he asked him why it was that he did not complete the commission he had given him. Monsieur de la Rivière responded to the King, that he had recognised the vanity of astrology, and that he no longer studied it. The King replied to him that he had commanded him to read the stars on the birth of Monsieur the Dauphin. He thus said, *Sire, Monsieur le Dauphin will have inclinations in opposition to yours. He will live to grow up and be a man, he will have male children, he will do great things, he will make matters worse, his son will ruin everything.* The King responded to his Doctor: *I can see, Monsieur de la Rivière, that it is the Huguenots of whom you speak. That may be, Sire, if you say so*, responded the astrologer, *but you will not know more about it from me.*

Allard, who writes in the *Mercure Galant*, concludes that since Louis XIII made the affairs of the Huguenots worse,[65] and that the present King has continued on this path, he could not fail to ruin and destroy entirely the Protestant religion in France. It is certain that this term *to worsen* and *to spoil*, always mean bad things. Monsieur de la Rivière having said that the affairs of Louis XIII would *worsen*, that his son will *spoil all*, he predicted in three words all this that the King presently does in France.

---

64 "Lettre sur la pronostic du Sr. de la Riviere, Medecin du roy Henry IV touchant la religion protestante en France", in *Mercure Galant* (May 1685), 38–48. The letter purports to be a story that Allard found in the memoirs of the Duc de Sully.

65 Armand-Jean du Plessis, cardinal and Duc de Richelieu (1585–1642), was chief minister to Louis XIII of France. Richelieu crushed the Huguenot "state within the state", in authorising a royal campaign into southern France to suppress a Huguenot uprising. Richelieu's final assault ended with the siege and then collapse in 1629 of the Huguenot stronghold of La Rochelle. Henceforth, the Huguenots were denied their political and military rights (right to maintain fortifications) but permitted freedom of worship until Louis's XIV's revocation of the Edict of Nantes in 1685.

Nostradamus predicted in a way more flattering to the King the prodigious events that are happening during his reign, for example, in Century 4 quatrain 54. I shall reprint it here:

> *Of the name that a French King never was,*
> *There was never a lightning so much feared,*
> *Italy shall tremble, Spain and the English,*
> *He shall be much taken with women strangers.*

There will be in France a great king who will distinguish himself no less by his heroic virtues, than by his glorious name *Louis the Great, God-given*. There has never been in the world a prince so terrible, nor so dreadful as he shall be. He will cause Italy, Spain, and England to tremble before his power. Nevertheless, the warlike occupations of this monarch will not prevent him from loving the beautiful sex.

Nostradamus predicts in this quatrain the glorious actions of the king, but the name *lightning* which he attributes to him means, I think, that he will *spoil all*. We all know that that lightning never improves anything. Nostradamus predicted the same thing in several different places.

Since the author of the *Mercure Galant* has given me a chance to include the prediction of Monsieur de la Rivière, I am obliged to examine here what the Devil knew of this business, by which I mean the misfortune of the Protestants of France.

Mézeray reports that Henri IV knew the year of his death by means of a diabolic vision which a celebrated magician had shown to Catherine de Medici.[66] This Queen was very curious about the future, as everyone knows, and often consulted magicians to satisfy her curiosity. She hoped to see all the Kings who had reigned in France as well as all who would reign. The magician who showed her this enchantment drew a circle. All the Kings entered and made as many turns as they reigned in years. Catherine's spouse came in his turn, which terrified her, as did her children, François II, Charles IX and Henri III in succession. Then Henri IV entered the circle, helmet on his head, and having made a few turns, he removed it. Catherine, having recognised him, asked the Magician whether the man from Béarn would reign despite the Duc

---

66   Appears to reference François Eudes de Mézeray's *Abrégé chronologique de l'histoire de France* (Paris: 1667); Mézeray mentions that Henri IV knew the length of his reign as a result of this prophecy, but does not relate the full story, whose precise source is unknown.

d'Alençon. He replied that this Duke would not be King. Afterwards two persons with red hats came in to the circle, representing the Cardinals Richelieu and Mazarin. Afterwards wolves, tigers, bears, lions, and indeed all sorts of man-eating beasts entered the circle.

If the King put credence in the prediction of Monsieur de la Rivière, and in prophecies, he would see that his faith has been abused, and he would say, like Catherine, after the Colloquy of Poissy, *these Jesuits deceive us*: but he might also add, they are the reason why I *spoil all*.

The following sixains confirm only too well this sad prediction, and as the King after the Revocation of the Edict of Nantes gave troops to crush the Waldensians of the Valleys of Piedmont, we shall see also in these sixains that the massacre of the Protestants of France will follow a general massacre in all the states of the Papist Princes. Still, what consoles us in this extreme affliction, is that Nostradamus and the other Prophets put their *soul in heaven*, when their bodies fall under the sword of the executioners.

> Sixain 55
> *A little before or after a very great lady*
> *Her soul in Heaven and her body in the Grave*
> *Shall be lamented by many,*
> *All her kindred shall be in great mourning*
> *Tears and sighs of a lady in her youth*
> *And shall leave the mourning to two great ones.*

Haman in past times was not content to crush Mordecai alone, but wished at the same time to destroy the whole of the Jewish nation by a general massacre.[67] Likewise, now it is not enough for the Roman Antichrist, this fierce insatiable Beast, Innocent XI, to put to death the two witnesses of truth in all his states; he wishes also to crush the Protestant powers. But Nostradamus teaches us in sixains 5 and 38 that Monsieur the Prince of Orange will arrest the progress of the Papal League, and that he will triumph so gloriously, that his name will be immortal, and that the whole Church will bless forever the memory of this great hero.[68]

---

67 Esther 3:5–6.
68 Two years following publication of Massard's *Harmonie des prophéties anciennes avec les modernes* (1686), William III overthrew James II in the Glorious Revolution of 1688.

Sixain 38
By water, by fire, and by great sickness
The Purveyor to the hazard of his life
Shall know how much is worth the quintal of wood
Six hundred and fifteen, or the nineteen
There shall be graven of a great Prince the fifth
The immortal name upon the foot of the Cross.

It calls Monsieur the Prince of Orange the fifth, in the quatrain placed below his Portrait in these terms,

Here is the Fifth Prince of the great Sun of Orange ...

By the term Purveyor, Nostradamus means the Archbishop of Cologne, who is the Chancellor of the Italian Empire. He contrasts in this Sixain the evils which this prelate has committed, and which he will inflict on Christianity, and the punishments which are due to him, to the great and marvellous benefits that Monseigneur the Prince will bring to the whole Church, and to the immortal praises which this hero will receive from all the peoples of the world, until the end of time.

Nostradamus predicts that this great prince will triumph against the Papal League; that history will *engrave his name at the foot of the Cross of Jesus and Christ, and render him immortal*, and that the Church will preserve his memory forever, as its liberator.

Nostradamus records the years when these great events are to begin. He predicts that this will be from the year 1685 up to the year 1689.[69] Because he implies seventy, just as does sixain 54, which we shall explain in its turn. This prophecy is beginning to be fulfilled by the protection that the Messeigneurs of the States General [of the Netherlands] and Monseigneur the Prince [of Orange] have given to the refugees after the revocation of the Edict of Nantes.[70] The ambitions of the *insatiable Beast* of Malachy will soon give opportunity to

---

69 The dates 1685 and 1689 correspond to the revocation of the Edict of Nantes and the coronation of William III, respectively. Concerning William III's rise to power and his rivalry with Louis XIV see Charles-Édouard Levillain, *Vaincre Louis XIV: Angleterre-Hollance-France-Histoire d'une relation triangulaire 1665–1688* (Seyssel: 2010).

70 Following the revocation of the Edict of Nantes, approximately 35,000 Huguenot refugees settled in the Dutch Republic. For the Huguenot experience of exile in the Dutch Republic, see David Van der Linden, *Experiencing Exile: Huguenot Refugees in the Dutch Republic, 1680–1700* (Farnham: 2015).

this great hero to fulfil the glorious promises that God made about him in this sixain from the mouth of the French prophet.

Sixain 5 explains this one, and records for us the date when Monseigneur the Prince will stand up to the arms of France and will triumph, that is why I shall explain it briefly at this point.

> Sixain 5
> *He that the Principality*
> *Shall keep by great cruelty*
> *At last shall see a great army*
> *By a fire blow most dangerous*
> *He should do better by agreement*
> *Otherwise he shall drink juice of Orange*

The term *juice of Orange* which Nostradamus uses in the last line of this sixain, makes it clear that by the Principality he means Orange, by *he that shall keep it by great cruelty*, he means the King of France, and by the Prince who will make him drink *juice of Orange*, he refers to the legitimate prince of that city.

In the first two lines Nostradamus speaks of the Principality of Orange, where at present the greatest cruelties in the world take place;[71] but in the following he confuses the interest of the Estates with those of Monseigneur le Prince. He predicts thus that after the capture of the city of Orange, the King of France will be make war against the United Provinces. He says that the Monseigneur the Prince will be victorious over the arms of France, and that this monarch would be much better off to lend his hands to a sincere peace than to violate it, both with regard to Messeigneurs of the States General, and to Monseigneur the Prince. *Otherwise he will drink the juice of Orange.* Everyone knows that to make someone drink the Chalice means in the language of Scripture and of several nations to give great affliction and great cause for chagrin to someone. Kotterus predicts the same thing as Nostradamus in chapter 6 verse 20 of his Revelations. He says *that the successors of King Frederick of Bohemia will give the Pope and his Protectors a bitter chalice, which will be very unhealthy for them to drink.* By the successors of Frederick, Kotterus, Christine Poniatovie, and Drabicius always mean the Protestant Powers.

---

71 The armies of Louis XIV seized the southern French principality of Orange, a Huguenot stronghold in 1682. The territory was part of the feudal lands of the house of Orange, belonging to William of Orange, Stadtholder of Holland and later William III of England.

Nostradamus in Quatrain 100 of Century 6 predicts for the city of Orange the misfortunes with which it is currently afflicted, and says *thou shalt be taken captive above four times.*

There are a great number of Protestants in favour of the Dutch, and of other Protestant Powers, which I will discuss elsewhere.

All these things show us that God never abandons his church; if he strikes it down on one side, he raises it on the other; he holds it as dear as the apple of his eye, and he loves it with an eternal love. Just as the people of Israel were not delivered from their servitude in Egypt until Pharaoh had pushed his tyranny to the extreme, and murdered all the male children of the Israelites, so too the deliverance of the Christian Church, can take place only after the extreme tyranny of the Antichristian Princes, after the death of the two witnesses of truth, and after the massacre of the Protestants in the states of the Papal Princes. *But after the three and a half days the breath of life from God entered them, and they stood on their feet, and terror struck those who saw them. Then they heard a loud voice from heaven saying to them, "Come up here." And they went up to heaven in a cloud, while their enemies looked on. At that very hour there was a severe earthquake and a tenth of the city collapsed. Seven thousand people were killed in the earthquake, and the survivors were terrified and gave glory to the God of heaven.* Revelation 11:11–13.

St. John describes for us in verses 11 and 12 the glorious resurrection of two witnesses of truth, and in the end he predicts the destruction of the Antichristian Empire, and of the Roman clergy. I explain these three verses on page 278. This is what will lead to this terrible Catastrophe which is about to happen in Europe ...

Chapter 1: Of the necessity of knowing the Prophecies, to avoid the evils of God, and to enjoy the goods which He promises us.

1 *The secret things belong to the* LORD *our God, but the things revealed belong to*
2 *us and to our children.*[72] And as it is temerity to desire to penetrate things that the wisdom of God has sought to conceal from us, and that we do not probe his Majesty with impunity, it is, on the other hand, a criminal neglect to despise the Prophecies. II Thessalonians 5:19:20.[73]

Blessed are those who read the words of this Prophecy, says St. Jean the Theologian. Although this oracle is true in all the ages of the Church, it is nevertheless

---

72 Deut. 29:29.
73 *Sic.* I Thess. 5:19–20: *Quench not the spirit; despise not prophesyings.*—ed.

very certain that the knowledge of the prophecies is much more necessary before the time of their fulfilment than after they have been fulfilled. Before they are accomplished, the knowledge we have of them makes us avoid the evils with which God threatens us, and enjoy the benefits that He promises us. It is on this subject that God cries to use us in *Revelation, leave Babylon my People, lest you partake in its sins, lest you receive its plagues.*[74] This oracle should at this moment be ringing in our ears, so that we may avoid the extreme evils which will happen to the faithful in the states of the Mystical Babylon, which are due to last until the year 1714.

The name *Revelation* is not only appropriate to the book of the revelations of St. John, it is also appropriate to all the revelations that God has provided us in the centuries that followed; and this because not only do they conform to the revelation of this Apostle, but also because they proceed from the same Spirit, which is the Spirit of Truth. As a result, it is quite right that Comenius named the revelations of Kotterus, of Christine Poniatovie, and of Drabicius, *the Revelation of Revelations*. Prophecies are more or less clear by virtue of whether they are more or less distant. Balaam who saw the Saviour of the World from afar saw him as a star, while Malachy who sees him nearest of all saw him as a Sun. When God revealed to the Prophet Daniel and to St. John things which were to happen long afterwards, he commanded them to hide them and to seal them, to let them know that these prophecies being distant would be understood only in the time of their fulfilment. At that time, God would raise up prophets or interpreters to unveil | these mysteries, knowledge of which is so important to the glory of God and to the good of the Church.

It is for this reason that God has raised in this last century a horde of witnesses, both prophets and interpreters, who have broken the mysterious seals under which several prophecies of Holy Scripture were hidden.

God once sent an angel to the Lord Jesus to console him in his agony. It is likewise necessary that in the agony of the Mystical Body of Jesus Christ, *in whom is fulfilled the measure of his sufferings*,[75] God would send prophets to console and comfort it, even in the sad state to which the enemies of God, and his truth have reduced it. And as the Lord Jesus was gloriously resurrected after his battles and entered his Triumph, so the Church after this last and cruel persecution of the Roman Antichrist will enjoy the rest which it is promised. Satan, being bound for a thousand years, will no longer have the power to afflict the faithful in any way, and he will no longer worry the world, tempting the faithful or accusing them before God.

---

74 Rev. 18:4.
75 Col. 1:24.

5   The Jews knew the time when their deliverance was to arrive when they were captives in Babylon. But beyond this, God wished to provide a greater consolation to them by revealing, through the ministry of the Prophet Isaiah, the name of Cyrus their liberator, long before this Prince was born. God takes care of the Christian Church just as he did the Church of the Jews. Even when the Christian Church had scarcely formed, he warned it to retire from Jerusalem to Pella, in order to prevent it from perishing along with the Jews in the sacking of that unhappy city. The same thing is happening today. The revelations of Drabicius are explicit on this subject: *Behold, I that am the Lord of the earth, send trial upon trial, and I will smite the wicked with the rod with my mouth, according to my ancient words, and according to those which thou hast spoken of me. 3. I repeat these words to you, who are children of light, who know me and my name. 4 That ye may be as simple as doves, and prudent as serpents, and that ye shall seek each*

6   *early morning a Pella, a refuge, a place of safety, to preserve your life | until the tempests of my anger are past.* Revelation 104 in the year 1661. God takes care of His Church at all times. *He holds it engraved on the palm of his hands, and dear as the apple of his eye.*[76] That is why in this century, when the plagues of God on the Church multiply in order to punish it, and when we see them about to fall on the Antichrist to destroy him, God has raised up a great number of prophets to encourage repentance, and to give his children the means to avoid the evils with which he threatens them, and to enjoy the great benefits which he promises them after this era of affliction and mourning. There will be, says Usserius in his prophecy, *a great difference between this last persecution and the preceding ones; For in the former the most eminent and spiritual ministers and Christians did generally suffer most, and were most violently fallen upon. But, in this last, these shall be preserved by God as a seed to partake in that glory which shall immediately follow, and which will come upon the Church as soon as ever*

7   *this storm shall be over; For, said he, as it shall be the sharpest, | so it shall be the shortest persecution of them all, and shall only take away the gross hypocrites, and formal professors; but the true spiritual believers shall be preserved till the calamity be over-past.*[77]

This prophecy is already fulfilled by virtue of the persecution against the faithful and their Ministers that arose in France. Those who had faith in their heart fled the cursed kingdom, some with the permission of the king, and others licenced only by their zealous ardour. Jesus Christ tells us, that *the children*

---

76   Isa. 49:16.
77   *Strange and Remarkable Prophesies and Predictions of the Holy, Learned, and Excellent James Usher, Late L. Arch-Bishop of Armagh, and Lord Primate of Ireland: Giving an Account of His Foretelling* ... (London: 1678), 2–3.

of this age are more prudent in their ways than the children of light.[78] If the Protestants of France would have had as much knowledge of the prophecies and of the misfortunes which were about to happen to them as the Papists their countrymen, they might have prevented them, both by leaving the Kingdom of France, and by following the practice of the Jews, who keep all their wealth in movables.

The Papists have long understood the fulfilment of the prophecies of Nostradamus, which predict the desolation, the massacre, | and the destruction of the Protestants of France, year by year, date by date. This is why the last printing of this author, in Paris about the year 1680, left out the sixains which contain all the details of the misfortunes which have happened, which are happening, and which will continue without fail to happen, not only to the Protestants of France, but also to the inhabitants of the other states of the mystical Babylon. Sixains 52 and 53 speak thusly:

> *The great city that hath not bread half enough*
> *Shall once more engrave*
> *In the bottom of her soul St. Bartholomew's day*
> *Nîmes, Rochelle, Geneva, and Montpellier*
> *Castres, Lion; Mars coming into Aries*
> *Shall fight one against another, and all for a lady.*
>
> *Many shall die before the Phoenix dieth.*
> *Till six hundred and seventy he shall remain,*
> *Above fifteen years, one and twenty, thirty nine,*
> *The first shall be subject to sickness*
> *And the second to iron, a danger of life,*
> *Thirty nine shall be subject to fire and water,*

Nostradamus predicted in these sixains that a massacre would take place in Paris on the day of St. Bartholomew. This massacre happened on the very day that he predicted it six years after his death. He predicted that there would be another massacre in the year 1691, again in Paris. He predicted that these two massacres would begin in the city of Paris, and that they would be continued in the provinces of France, even in the towns where the Protestants were in the majority. In the following sixain Nostradamus tells the history of the reformed population of France over the past century. He says they will remain peaceably

---

78   Luke 16:8.

in France, and that they will enjoy the advantages of the Edict of Nantes until the year 1670, up to the year 1685. It took all that stretch of time to deprive them of their privileges by means of repeated edicts. He then predicts their illness, which is the revocation of the Edict of Nantes in the year 1685. He warns the Protestants of this Kingdom that there they will be massacred in the year 1691 in a general massacre similar to that of St. Bartholomew; finally, in the last line he tells them that this cruel butchery will | continue in France until the year 1709.[79]

So, he says, that those of the [Protestant] Religion will be treated as criminals against the state and rebels, prohibited use of fire and water. He alludes in this place to the ancient Romans who used this form of torture to put to death those who had conspired against their republic. Finally, he predicts the deliverance of the Church, which like another Phoenix will rise from its ashes. Everyone knows that the ashes of the martyrs have always been the seed of the Church. Nostradamus also speaks here of the resurrection of the two witnesses of *Revelation*, that is to say, of the faithful, of whom he predicts death in the two following sixains.

The years that Nostradamus designates for us in these sixains, both for the last sufferings and for the deliverance of the Church are precisely the same as the Prophet Daniel, Saint John, Kotterus, Christine Poniatovie and Drabicius tell us in their revelations. This is what I shall show in the following chapters. *God does nothing that he does not reveal unto his servants the Prophets*, saith the Lord.[80] As | we are now in the time of the fulfilment of all the prophecies, God has raised by his infinite compassion many prophets who, following the very texts of Scripture, mark for us year by year all the evils and all the good which shall arrive in the world, and in the Church.

Knowledge of all these great events and circumstances is extremely necessary for us, in order to bring us to repentance and avoid the cruel persecutions and massacres which will happen to the faithful in all the States of Antichrist. We shall also be able to avail ourselves of the deliverance of the Church, which must arrive immediately after this great tribulation. We see by the same scripture that all that is necessary for salvation is clearly taught, and that *if the Gospel is obscure, it is obscure to those who perish, and to those whom the God of this age has blinded the eyes of understanding.*[81] We can say the same thing of the prophecies. These that are necessary for our salvation are written in a manner very clear, so | that the faithful may profit by them.

---

79 This prediction coincides with the defeat of the Camisards.
80 Amos 3:7.
81 II Cor. 4:3–4.

The prophecies are more or less obscure according to our changing needs. In fact, God commanded Daniel and St. John to seal the revelations he sent them, the knowledge of which was not then necessary to the Church. And in the course of this discussion we shall see that all those prophecies which we must know to regulate our actions and customs are clear, and that the little understanding we have of them comes only from the contempt in which we hold them. The ignorant, however, perishes with his ignorance, and it is this defect that makes several fall victim to various temptations, which propel them to revolt, and to many other misfortunes. All of this proves clearly how important the knowledge of prophecies is, especially in the terrible conjuncture in which we find ourselves, here in the last war of the Antichrist, who seeks to overcome the faithful and make them die in all the states of the Great City ...

2   *Notice (From the Harmonie des prophéties anciennes avec les modernes, pt. 4, March/April 1687)*

For the clarification of the eleventh chapter of *Revelation* and of the other modern prophecies that I have cited, I will here report three revelations of a young woman who is a refugee in Amsterdam. | They conform entirely to other predictions, and mark with a marvellous precision the details of the prodigious events that are happening and will happen during our lifetimes, both in the world and in the Church. One could say of this young girl what Jesus Christ said of Nathaniel, namely that *she is a true Israelite, in whom there is neither deceit nor guile*.[82] She is a person incapable of vanity of the body or spirit. Although she is very well educated in her faith, she nevertheless has a true Christian simplicity. For an entire month, she continually experienced revelations of the tongue, the spirit, and the heart (though mostly the last of these) in such fashion that during that time she could think of nothing but these marvellous things that had ravished her spirit with the contemplation of things to come.

The day after the last revelation, two younger sisters of this young lady who sleep alongside her told their mother they had been afraid during the night, | because their sister had been extremely agitated, had sat up in bed as if she meant to get up, had spoken loudly for a long time, then had cried bitterly, and then been taken by laughter several times, and that although they had done all they could to awaken her, she had gone directly back to sleep and been angry they woke her. I report all these facts because I heard them myself firsthand from the accounts given to me by the mother and the young woman's sisters.

---

82   John 1:47.

Several days ago, the young lady and I were discussing the treatises I have written on the harmony of prophecies, and she happened to show me the three revelations that follow, pretending as if they had happened to some other person. After having read them, I recognised by virtue of certain details that it was she herself who had seen these marvellous things, which obliged her to admit it to me, and to grant me the account she had written in her own hand, but only by virtue of the promise that I made to her never to reveal her name.

209 **First Revelation**

During the month of March 1685, I dreamed of being at the Temple, and hearing a very touching sermon on the afflictions of the Church, which made me cry very hard.[83] And then I saw a venerable old man, completely white with age, who carried a baton in his hand, and struck me on the shoulder, and turned me toward him, and asked *why are you crying*? I responded by asking if he knew the misfortunes that befell us, that our Temple was condemned to be demolished, and our pastors sent into exile. *He told me, that was only the beginning of our sorrows. Just as when quicksilver is contaminated with tin, you can no longer use it, so you pass it through a skin*[84] *and it comes out as pure as it ever was; so also the Church, by being filtered by afflictions, will emerge as pure as it ever has been.*

Second Revelation

210 In the month of July 1685,[85] having | fallen asleep at Temple, I dreamed I saw a sick man at whom all the people were looking. He was becoming so thin that little by little it seemed that one could see daylight through the skin of his neck and his hands. His body started to dissolve as had his neck; he no longer had arms, nor thighs, and in fact no longer had human form, because his entire body was no bigger around than his neck. Nevertheless, his head was completely healthy, robust, and beautiful to see. And as I was watching this sickly man, lo and behold, I saw his body start to come back little by little, and in just a little space of time he regained his natural form, and his figure, in fact he became more handsome and more robust than he had been before. And then he walked away from me. As I was watching him take leave of me, here again came that whitened old man from the previous vision, who asked me, *if I knew well what this meant*. I told him no. *He said that it was the Church, and just as*

---

83 James II's coronation occurred one month later on 23 April 1685 in the city of Westminster.
84 "un cuir"—a reference to a filter of some sort—ed.
85 The Monmouth Rebellion in England commenced just a few months earlier in May 1685.

this good fellow had become completely deformed in his body, so too the Church had become deformed, without resemblance to the | Reformed Religion, but as the head had remained healthy, so also healthy doctrine still dwelled in the heart of the truly faithful. Just as I had seen this sick man regain his health in short order, one would soon see the Church flourish like never before.

Third Revelation

In September 1685, I had a dream. I saw a large field where there were an infinity of men women, and children naked from the waist up. The right sides of the adults bled profusely, but the children only bled in drops. Then I turned away, and saw a woman who had been beaten and thrown to the ground. After that, I saw another woman, magnificently dressed. She was seated on a royal throne; but her face was so red and blemished that I was astonished by her extreme ugliness. I also saw | a large crowd that admired and adored her. She commanded these people that each one take a club, and go break the head of the woman lying on the ground. These people armed with clubs came in a band to crush her skull, and beat her, but they were unable to break her head open. Thus they turned to their queen. She then commanded that they gather dirt and mud in order to bury the woman's head alive, leaving her body unharmed. So they came to bury her head, but it was instead the body that they buried, up to her throat. But her head remained still healthy, and she spoke continually against those who treated her so ill, saying that they would never prevail over her. Then, behold, there came six moons which on their front were of blood, and on their reverse of fire. And these six moons turned three times around this woman, and around all those | with bleeding sides. Then I saw a sun coming in the midst of a dark and thick fog.

    The sun came with incredible speed: it chased away the six moons, and then took its place on the woman lying on the ground, lifted the veil that covered her face above her mouth, and gave her little by little the strength to lift herself. When she was standing on her feet, there fell like a ray of light from above a white cloak to clothe the woman. After that the woman took by the hand all that poor afflicted people, placing them within her cape to console them every one. Then the six moons came to rest above the queen, shaking her throne so violently that she fell off it with a great cry. All her people, seeing her extreme desolation, ran away with great fear to throw themselves at the feet of the other woman, begging her pardon for the injuries they had caused her. She also took these people by the hand, and placed them under her cape. They came and went freely. The queen, seeing herself abandoned | by all her followers, let loose a loud scream. There came from under the earth a cry in a language I did not know, and then six serpents came, the largest entwining itself around her head, and the others around her body, in such a way that she was unable to free herself. She screamed, and then her flesh crumbled. After that, behold six fire-breathing lions arrived to afflict her in all her limbs. They turned three circles around her, and then burned her up, so that she disappeared not leaving even any ashes. After that, I turned to gaze on the other woman, who was victorious, and she was brighter than the sun; then it all disappeared before my eyes. I then saw a beautiful young man who asked what I had seen. I told him the story, and he asked if I know what it meant I told him that I couldn't understand a thing. He told me that the large number of people that I had seen whose sides bled profusely, who were in a great field, these people, he said, those are

215 the people who have been forced to abandon the [Protestant] Religion. | Their consciences are wounded and bleeding from the affliction and regret of having abandoned God and the faith. The children who lose only drops of blood are those who begin to know God and faith. The woman stretched out on the ground, that's the Church. We see her abandoned by all her children without a single one to protect her. The queen seated on the royal throne is the Papist Church, which will be victorious for a time. She has commanded her people to kill the woman with clubs, and to focus on the head, signifying that the Papists target only the conscience, which they destroy and crush with sorrows, nevertheless they will never demolish the heart of the truly faithful. These six moons that you have seen, those are six times that the Church will suffer with blood and fire. But the sun that comes after the moons, which crosses the thick clouds, signifies that the faithful will receive help and succour from an unexpected and unknown source. It will come from a place that they did not anticipate, coming to rest on the church of God. This great God will lift up His church by the

216 force of | his pure truth, even clothing it with a cloak of truth. All the children of the church will return to its communion. Even those who were its enemies come to beg its pardon for the injuries they had caused. This indicates that the church's persecutors will repent, they will enter the communion of the [true] Church, abandoning their queen. Then I asked what was the meaning of those six moons that came to rest above the queen. He told me when the era of the afflictions of the Church has passed, God's vengeance will chase that queen to her ruin. The six serpents you saw are the six schisms that will cause her to perish. I asked him what she had screamed, and he told me that she had called the devil to her aid, but he had responded that she was doomed to perish. The six lions that you saw are the sovereign powers that will destroy her and burn her up entirely, reducing her to ashes.

Reflections on the first prophecy of the young lady refugee from the month of March 1685

The first revelation is extremely clear, and its fulfilment makes its meaning even more obvious. I will note only that prophecies are more or less obscure according to whether they refer to things more or less distant; I proved this on page 3 of the first volume. The young refugee's three prophecies are explained quite clearly because it pleased God to reveal them in the very time of their execution.

When God communicates to humans through visions, it is with the help of angels, or through one of the persons of the very holy and venerable Trinity. Both the Old and New Testaments, and modern prophecies—all these books, I submit—are full of similar examples. In terms of the first and second visions of this young lady, it can only be the first person of the holy Trinity who explains them. | Daniel saw the first and second persons of the blessed Trinity in vision, when he said: *In my vision at night I looked, and there before me was one like a son of man, coming with the clouds of heaven. He approached the Ancient of Days and was led into his presence.*[86] The explanation that God gave to this girl is entirely in keeping with His wisdom and His providence. He alerted her that the present misfortunes of the Church are only the beginning of troubles. Then he taught her the end he has in mind for the afflictions he has visited upon his Church: to purify it, and to rid it of every sort of impurity and filth. He used, for this purpose, a comparison that has a relationship to those in Scripture and also to the occupations of this young girl.[87]

Reflections on the second prophecy

The explanation that God provided the girl about the second prophecy is so clear that it doesn't need greater exposition. I wish only to point out the vision that Robert the Dominican[88] had | of the Pope, because two contrasting things placed in opposition each illuminate the other. I cited the vision of this Jacobin on page 25 of the first volume, but as it is short I shall repeat it here: *I was praying on my knees, he says, my face lifted to the heavens, and I saw in the air before me the body of a Pope clothed with a sheet of white silk, and his head was not visible. Looking carefully to see if he was actually headless, I saw his head was*

---

86 Dan. 7:13.
87 Here, Massard suggests that the young girl's occupation involved chemical processes of refinement and filtration; was she a family member or alchemical apprentice?
88 Robert d'Uzès. See above, note 47.

dry and thin as if was made of wood, and the Spirit of the Lord told me, this vision signifies the current state of the Roman Church, in which there is no longer life.

The vision of this Dominican represents the Pope and the Roman Church with a head dried out and thin, as if it were made of wood, because this sect is not a religion, but a worldly, earthly monarchy. By contrast, the vision of this young refugee represents the head of the [Protestant] Church healthy, robust and beautiful to see, while the rest of the body is deformed and almost withered away. And in the following vision we see that the enemies of the Church can never | destroy this head, nor can they bury it. The pope in the Chronological Tables of the Church, which I wrote about on page 88 of the second volume nevertheless prides himself on breaking heads; still, according to this revelation God will not permit him to achieve this: he will never extinguish the light of religion in the spirit of the faithful, no matter how enormous his tyranny and cruelty.

Reflections on the third prophecy

God showed this third vision to the young lady refugee six weeks before the revocation of the Edict of Nantes. As the time of the fulfilment of this revelation was very near, it teaches us with great precision all the details of the suffering of the Church and of its deliverance.

In order to have a clearer understanding of this revelation we must compare it with Nostradamus's 53rd sixain. I explained this on page 8 of the first volume, and on page 165 of the previous volume; I will nevertheless repeat it yet again in this place:

> *Many shall die before the Phoenix dieth.*
> *Till six hundred and seventy he shall remain,*
> *Above fifteen years, one and twenty, thirty nine,*
> *The first shall be subject to sickness*
> *And the second to iron, a danger of life,*
> *Thirty nine shall be subject to fire and water.*

The first three lines of this sixain mark the three different statuses of the Protestants of France from the year 1685 until the end of 1709. And as this refugee's revelation speaks about the same era of the Church's suffering and deliverance as does Nostradamus, it is important to explain these prophecies together, in order to show their relationship to one another, and their harmony. In the fourth line, Nostradamus notes the malady of the [Protestant] Church of

France in 1685. That indeed happened in that year by virtue of the revocation of the Edict of Nantes and the elevation of a papist king to the English throne.[89] The revelation of this refugee teaches us that the misfortunes of the Church will begin by the efforts | that the ministers of the Antichrist make to crush or bury his head. In other words, according to the explanation of the oracle, that the enemies of the faithful take aim at their consciences which they will strive to destroy and crush by force of afflictions, nevertheless, it said, they will never remove faith from their hearts. The prophecy of this girl makes us understand clearly what is this malady of the Phoenix that Nostradamus speaks of, which is to say, the Church from the year 1685 until the year 1691. And, it foresees with great precision the criminal actions being taken against those who profess the truth.

The fifth line of the sixain tells us that the malady of the Phoenix will end by the sword in the year 1691, by a general massacre like that of St. Bartholomew's Day, while the final line predicts that they will not stop at slaughtering the faithful by the sword, but will also martyr them by fire and by water, for 18 years until the end of 1709. The prophecy of this refugee girl foretells to the French Church the same | misfortune as Nostradamus, because it teaches us that as the ministers of the Antichrist were not able to succeed in the manner they hoped to destroy the conscience of the faithful and make them abandon God, they will then turn to the sword and the fire in order to achieve their wretched undertaking …

3 REMARKS *on the gift of prophecy, visions, prodigies, and miracles* (1690)[90]

I was raised in the so-called Reformed Religion, and taught by ministers who claim that God no longer conveys to humans the gift of prophecy, that he no

---

89 With respect to the year 1685, Gilbert Burnett (1643–1715), Bishop of Salisbury and confidant to William III, wrote: "This year, of which I am now writing, must ever be remembered as the most fatal to the Protestant religion. In February, a king of England declared himself a papist. In June, Charles the Elector of Palatine dying without issue, the electoral dignity went to the House of Newburgh, a most bigoted Popish family. In October, the King of France recalled and vacated the Edict of Nantes. And in December, the Duke of Savoy, being brought to it, not only by the persuasions, but even by the threatening of the Court of France, recalled the edict that his father had granted to the Vaudois. So it must be confessed that this was a very critical year." See Gilbert Burnet, *Bishop Burnet's History of His Own Time*, vol. III (London: 1725), 1088.

90 From Jacques Massard, *Songes Prophetiques & Theologiques Qu'il a plû à Dieu d'envoier à quelques dames refugiées pour nôtre instruction & pour nôtre consolation, dan ces tems de deuil, d'iniquité & d'ignorance* (Amsterdam: 1691).

longer sends them visions, and that he no longer makes prodigies or miracles. But as God has destined me to be a witness to his holy truth, and to correct such a crude error among Protestants, he never permitted me to be infected with this false belief. Since my early youth, I have seen and understood that this doctrine of Protestants has absolutely no grounding in | Holy Scripture nor even in right reason. I saw that the sole motivation that led Protestants to such a pitiable extremity was the error of Papists who made them believe in false prophets and lying miracles. In their effort to separate themselves from one criminal extreme, Protestants fell into another, hardly less dangerous than the first. It has now been three years since I published a vindication for modern prophets, in the preface to the second part. I cited in that section the famous text of Joel that Saint Peter restates in Acts 2:17 and gave it a clear and true explanation. In that oracle, Joel uses the same expressions as those of St. John of Patmos, in his story of the sixth seal of the Apocalypse.[91] The current war being waged by the Sultan and the king of France against the Emperor mark the opening of the sixth seal, as was proven in the preface to the second part [of the *Harmonie des Prophéties*]; and also my explanation of the sixth seal on page 315, in the fifth part of the Harmonie,[92] and also in my explanation of the King's dream, and of the first dream of the Gentleman from The Hague.[93] It is thus that I have proved that the oracle of Joel, cited by St. Peter promises in the present to the Church of God and to the | world *an extraordinary effusion of gifts and graces from the Holy Spirit, the gift of prophecy, visions and divine dreams*. God promises moreover *that he will make prodigies in the heavens, and extraordinary signs on the earth, of blood, fire, and smoky vapours*.[94] Since that time God has fulfilled his promise, and has done the things I predicted in my explanation of the oracle of Joel and of St. Peter. It has also pleased this mighty God to have me know by means of divine dreams what would happen to me, and what would happen to those who oppose the doctrine I am advancing by his holy command. Beyond that, God has continued to give divine revelations to the young lady refugee, as much for the public, as for her, and me. God has also continued sometimes to give her sleeping ecstasies much like those of the

---

91 Rev. 6:12.
92 [Jacques Massard], *Harmonie et accomplissement des propheties, sur la durée de l'Antechrist et des souffrances de l'Eglise, quatrieme et cinquieme parties* ([Cologne]: 1687).
93 Jacques Massard, *Explication d'un Songe Divin de Louis XIV. Et de deux autres Songes Divins d'une personne de qualité, & de merite de La Haye. Avec sept Revelations de la Dem. Refugiée à Amsterdam, Qui éclaircissent le Songe du Roi, & prouvent l'Esprit de Prophetie* (Amsterdam: 1690).
94 Joel 2:28–31 and Acts 2:16–21.

petits prophètes of Dauphiné.⁹⁵ When she sleeps, it rather often happens that she prays out loud for a half hour or hour. Sometimes she will provide a very fine explanation of a scriptural passage, and then offer a beautiful prayer. Nevertheless, she remembers none of it the next day. I will speak elsewhere of her first waking ecstasy, which happened as she was walking to the temple. Her sisters, who hear her marvellous and miraculous prayers while she sleeps, have also experienced diverse revelations, which I shall publish very soon. The mother of the young lady refugee also had diverse revelations, which we will publish along with those of her daughters. God revealed to the youngest sister of the refugee her eternal election, and the year of her death, along with the special protection with which it has pleased God to favour me. He caused her to see her deceased sisters received into heavenly glory. Soon I will publish the details, completely marvellous or better yet miraculous, of what happened to the two eldest sisters.

If one accepts these things as true, which in fact they are, then we have less reason to be surprised by the large number of revelations that it has pleased God to address to us in this century, by means of holy persons that we cited in the harmony treatises. But above all, we will have less reason to be astonished at the large number of inspired people, who are called *petits prophètes*, that God has raised up in Dauphiné and Languedoc. I published a pamphlet account of the Bergère de Crest even before Monsieur Jurieu did.⁹⁶

In the next book I publish, I will add a brief report about the Bergère de Crest and about the *petits prophètes*, which she predicted. I will examine and explain their prophecies, because there is no one who understands them, and as a result, there is no one who could have suggested these prophecies to them, because they surpass the understanding of all the ministers joined together. That is why there is no reason to be astonished that three of these *petits prophètes* who sought refuge in Geneva were ignominiously chased out of town, because the ministers of Geneva are no more capable in discernment of spirits than those of this country, and also because the ministers of Geneva are no more well intentioned towards modern prophets than other Protestant ministers.

---

95 The *petits prophètes* refers to the mass visionary phenomena that arose in southern France in the aftermath of the revocation of the Edict of Nantes. Sometimes translated as "minor prophets" we have chosen to retain *petits* because so many of the visionaries were children. The teenage prophetess of Dauphiné, Isabeau Vincent, whose revelations Massard was the first to publicise, was part of this movement. See Lionel Laborie's chapter in this volume.

96 Massard is likely referring to the anonymous *Abrégé de l'histoire de la bergère de Saou prèrs de le Crest en Daufiné* (Amsterdam: 1688).

The effusion of the Holy Spirit that God spilled over the Apostles on the day of the Pentecost was only a sample of that which God shall spread now over all flesh. That is also why this mighty God will no longer allow to be taught in his church the false doctrine that He no longer communicates directly with man as he used to.

As I have already mentioned, it pleased God to make me know by means of two divine dreams that he will punish with a great confusion | those who teach in the future this pernicious doctrine and who thereby oppose with all their forces both the plan and the counsel of his Divine Majesty.

An anonymous minister, on the 30th of May, 1689, wrote a letter against Monsieur Jurieu, on the subject of the *petits prophètes*, a letter that is filled entirely with impiety and ridiculous reasoning.[97] This minister cites some passage by some other minister in order to show that it is the opinion of Protestants that God no longer performs miracles, and that the gift of prophecy has ceased. But if this preacher seeks to embrace such a doctrine, and have others believe it, it would be his duty to cite a passage of Holy Scripture that supports this interpretation. But neither he nor any other person could cite a single text of scripture that supported this claim. Nevertheless, on this false supposition and false pretext, Protestants reject not only the *petits prophètes*, but beyond them an infinity of revelations that it has pleased God to manifest to his holy servants during the century in which we are living.

In the year 1659, the famous Amyraut had printed at Saumur by Isaac Des Bordes a *Discourse on Divine Dreams*.[98] This author, like other ministers, denied without any proof that there are presently these sorts | of dreams, but admitted angelic dreams. He then reports several dreams, which he calls angelic, which are quite interesting, and which prove incontestably that there are now, as there used to be, divine dreams. Monsieur Amyraut argues that angelic dreams are uncertain, and [as a result] they are not divine, as if the pure intelligences of angels were capable of misleading us, or revealing anything to us, without an explicit commandment from God. The ridiculous arguments of the minister I mentioned above are a clear example of how ingeniously men fool themselves when they are biased toward some false opinion. On page 105 the minister similarly distinguishes miracles performed by angels from those performed by God himself, as if God were not the author of both. Monsieur Amyraut, in his treatise on divine dreams used much the same sort of arguments as the anonymous

---

97 [Anon.], *Réponse de M. ***, Ministre, à une lettre écrite par un Catholique Romain, sur le sujet de P. Prophetes du Dauphiné et du Vivarets. De Hollande le 30 May 1689* (S.l.: 1689).
98 Moyse Amyraut, *Discours sur les Songes Divins dont il est parlé dans l'escriture* (Saumur: 1659).

minister who wrote against Monsieur Jurieu on the subject of miracles and the *petits prophètes*. Neither one provides a single reason to justify the claim that there should no longer be prophets nor that God no longer performs miracles. Nevertheless on the basis of their faulty and indeed criminal misinterpretations they both determine to deny true miracles and to reject persons claiming to have had | revelations or divine dreams. I wrote about this subject in the preface to the second part [of the *Harmonie des Prophéties*] where I proved clearly that God promised to *show wonders in the Heavens and on the Earth* and *to pour our his spirit over all flesh* at the end of this century.[99] God has started to fulfil His promise and the prediction that I made about it by virtue of a large number of astonishing prodigies that He has produced in the last two or three years. I have spoken of them above, but I will expand upon this point in more detail in what follows. However, it is important to note that the criminal bias of these men prevents chroniclers of history from speaking of the prodigies that are [now] happening, and forces them to excuse themselves before the reader if the unfolding of their story should even mention these things in passing. Most men are even more impertinent when it comes to the subject of revelations and divine dreams. For although God has continued to fulfil the promise made by the prophet Joel and predicted by me some three years ago in the preface to the second part and in my explanation of the sixth seal, they persist in their same error. If the Protestant ministers have some valid reason that supports their stance against miracles and modern prophecy, then they are bound | by their honour and duty to edify the public to make it known. Although I am 52 years old, I can assure that I have never heard nor read a single argument that supports such an error, except in Spinoza.[100] Monsieur Jurieu has written quite correctly on this subject in his Pastoral Letters,[101] defending true miracles and modern prophets. The ministers and most Protestants have mocked him, as they have also mocked me, but they have not responded to the questions Monsieur Jurieu and I have posed on this subject. In so doing, they followed the

---

99   Joel 2:30 and 2:28.
100 Here, Massard is likely referring to the common view regarding Spinoza's *Tractatus Theologico-Politicus*, published anonymously in 1670. While Spinoza's position on prophecy and miracles is actually complex, the common view of his contemporaries was that Spinoza denied divine revelation and prophecy *tout court*. In other words, Massard is attempting to associate his opponents with the philosopher of the age most notorious for questioning Christian dogma.
101 Pierre Jurieu, *Lettres Pastorales adressées aux fidèles de France qui gémissent sous la captivité de Babylon*. The letters, an early periodical, appeared every two weeks from 1686 until 1689 and were also printed as collections. For defences of miracles and modern prophecy, see the letters dated 1 and 15 October 1688.

maxims of the orators who teach that it is possible to elude through ridicule those subjects for which one has no ready response. As a result, most of them have mocked Monsieur Jurieu for the fact that his predictions on the deliverance of the Church have not come true. They ought to consider that they have fallen into the same trap as their colleague, and that they are no more intelligent than he when it comes to understanding prophecies. They have had nothing better than raillery to counter the arguments of Monsieur Jurieu. They have not responded in any manner to the evidence that I have offered. It seems to me that they should at minimum condemn, or at least respond somehow to a matter as important as this one.

Hans Engelbrecht of Brunswick, sent from the Most High, | explained it in these terms in the revelation he had of the Three States:[102]

> I would never have believed that it was possible to find such terrible people among Christians, and especially among the Doctors, if I had not experienced it myself, and even if they had assured me it was true, I would have found it impossible to believe. Because it was not only the people, but it was principally the Doctors and even the ministers who opposed me in this divine work. It is a great impiety that those who have the reputation among the people to be those who work toward the advancement of God's honour and His work, are in fact that work's greatest enemies, down deep in their hearts. It seems that they seek God in word only; they preach admirable sermons, and yet their hearts are so distant from God and so opposed to Him. It is now that it is becoming apparent how much evil is in their souls, it is now, I say, that I make the divine light so obvious, shining in a way that has not been true for a long time. Because for several centuries, we have not seen God choose simple people, and idiots, to announce his message, as He does now in the present through my ministry.
>
> 104. Before the coming of Christ the Pharisees were considered honourable people, but after that Divine light had come, and had illuminated the shadows, it became apparent | that those Doctors of the Law and those Pharisees were ungodly people, except for a few among them. The same

---

102   Hans Engelbrecht (1599–1642)—A German Lutheran mystic visionary. A French version of his visions was published in Amsterdam in 1680: *Divine Vision et révélation des trois états: l'ecclésiastique, le politique et l'oeconomique, laquelle moy Jean Engelbert, ... ay vue de mes yeux et veillant, étant à Winsem, au païs de Lunebourg, l'an 1625, écrite pour une seconde fois à Embden, l'an 1640, par l'autheur mesme, en allemand et traduite en françois* (Amsterdam: 1680).

is happening now that the light of God through me shines again in this world, in the middle of the shadows. By virtue of that light it is clear that the Doctors of the Law are ungodly in their hearts, except for a very few among them. For all those who rise against the work of God that I do, who oppose me, or who refuse to help me advance it in any way they can, I take those people to be evildoers no matter what reputation for sanctity they hold before the world. Although they know how to write beautiful sermons drawn from the word of God, they are nonetheless evil and ungodly in their souls before God. This is because their hearts are filled with falseness, hypocrisy, pride, hate, envy, avarice, and love of the world. All of this I can easily show them if need be.

105. And just as the learned, and those who have studied are generally speaking ungodly and evil in their hearts, except for a few among them, the same is true in the civil and economic state. There are few people in this status who love in their hearts the Divine light that I bring, because they cannot believe that this work is God's work. They must not believe it, because if they did believe it, they would love it as well. If these people were living in the love of Jesus Christ, they would readily believe that the work | that I do is God's work. And besides, they can see nothing evil in me, but only good. That is why they ought to believe that what is happening is a Divine operation; the charity of Jesus Christ believes all that is good, and raises no suspicion about that which is good.

Up to now God has spoken to Christians by a number of prodigies and miracles that he has performed before them, and by a large number of true prophets that he has raised for them. The time has come, and will no longer be delayed, that God will come to humans in his righteous anger, and that he will visit upon them punishments more terrible than any seen since the universal flood.

Divine Dreams of the Author

Since this last writing, printed last March,[103] I have had six divine dreams. Three of these concerned the most important affair in Europe. The other three concerned the mission and commission that God gives me to make known among men some of his mysteries, and the terrible events that are set to take place in this world. Of these last three dreams, two were about the ecclesiastical estate. In previous years, I had four divine dreams, two of which predicted the

---

103 March 1689.—ed.

extraordinary misfortunes of French Protestants, and indeed their apparent extinction. The two other | dreams had to do with me, but also with the public. I shall have these ten dreams printed in the future. I have also had several other divine dreams that are relevant only to me, and those I shall not have printed.

Finished and printed the first day of the month of January 1690. May God grant to men the grace to make good use of the Holy New Year's gift I give them on this first day of the year, that they may prepare themselves by means of a holy life for the three terrible and glorious comings of the Lord Jesus, terrible for the evildoers, but advantageous for the righteous. They will be advantageous to the faithful, even as they may be obliged to sign with their blood the truth of the Holy Word of God. Because God will wipe away every tear from their eye, and receive them into the bundle of life where they will rejoice forever in the infallible joys that God has promised to his children.

FIN

The entire universe is in the hands of the Eternal, our God, as if it were a mote of dust.

Translation by Kristine Wirts and Leslie Tuttle

CHAPTER 3

Friedrich Breckling's *Paulus Redivivus* (1688) and *Catalogus Haereticorum* (c.1697–1703)

Viktoria Franke

Breckling's Life and Network

Friedrich Breckling (1629–1711) came from the northern German town Handewitt, near Flensburg. He was born in the middle of the Thirty Years' War into a renowned family, whose male members had been Lutheran theologians since the Reformation. Breckling followed the path of his ancestors and studied theology between 1647 and 1652 in Rostock, Königsberg, Helmstedt, Leipzig and Gießen. In 1653, still a student, he travelled for the first time to the Netherlands and met a merchant in the public library in Hamburg the following year, who criticised with kindness his wordly dress and asked him what he wanted to be and to become and what he wanted to preach? This made Breckling recognise the unpretentious truth and led to his conversion to—supposedly—"true Christianity". In 1656 he travelled to the Netherlands for the second time, where he spent the summer building a network of religious dissenters.[1] When he returned home, he was completely changed. He predicted doom and disaster and was willing to reform society where it was needed.[2] A year later, in 1657, after several unpaid jobs and a stint as a military chaplain, Breckling became an assistant to his father, who was pastor in Handewitt. The rural population in Breckling's home region had suffered horribly from the Danish-Swedish war (1657–1660). Additionally, the church forced the farmers to pay taxes, draining them financially. This caused Breckling to protest publicly in his *Speculum Pas-*

---

1 For biographical information on Breckling, see Peter Meinhold, "Breckling, Friedrich", in *Neue Deutsche Biographie*, ed. Historische Kommission bei der Bayerischen Akademie der Wissenschaften, vol. 2 (1955; repr. Berlin: 1971), 566; John Bruckner, "Breckling, Friedrich", in *Biographisches Lexikon für Schleswig-Holstein und Lübeck*, vol. 7 (Neumünster: 1985), 33–38; Friedrich Wilhelm Bautz, "Breckling, Friedrich", in *Biographisch Bibliographisches Kirchenlexikon*, ed. Friedrich Wilhelm Bautz, vol. 1 (1975; repr. Herzberg: 1990), 736–737; Dietrich Blaufuß, "Breckling, Friedrich", in *Theologische Realenzyklopädie*, ed. G. Krause and G. Müller, vol. 7 (Berlin/New York: 1993), 150–153.
2 Friedrich Nielsen, "Breckling, Friedrich", in *Realencyklopädie für protestantische Theologie und Kirche*, ed. Albert Hauck, 3rd ed. (Leipzig: 1897), 367–369, here 368.

torum (1660), which led to his conviction and arrest. He was able to flee and arrived in Amsterdam, where he was welcomed by Johann Amos Comenius (1592–1670).[3] From December 1660 onwards, Breckling worked as a pastor of the Lutheran congregation in Zwolle, where he succeeded Johann Jakob Fabricius (1618/20–1673), whom Christian August von Pfalz-Sulzbach (1622–1708) had recruited to the newly founded "Simultaneum" in Sulzbach, a church which was shared by Lutherans and Catholics. Breckling's parish became a meeting point for people of all sorts of denominations, including Lutherans, Reformed, Catholics, and Mennonites.[4] Different religious groups asked him to join them, such as the Quakers and the supporters of Antoinette Bourignon (1616–1680), Jean de Labadie (1610–1674) and Johannes Rothe (1628–1702), but he turned them all down, as he was too individualistic and firm in his convictions to join forces with anybody else.[5] It was during this period that Breckling published most of his tracts, approximately 28 titles.

After his dismissal, Breckling stayed in Zwolle until spring 1672, when he moved with his family to the Egelantiersgracht in Amsterdam, where he rented a living space in the house of the printer and publisher Christoffel Cunradus (c.1615–1684) and probably earned a living as a corrector and translator. In that year, he also made a journey which took him through the Netherlands and the lower Rhine area to Düsseldorf during which he tried to erect Christ's apostlate among the Jews, Socinians, Collegiants and other "sects". A series of short tracts, such as *Leo Rugiens* (1681), *Christus Mysticus* (1682) and *Paulus Redivivus* (1688), as well as a larger work, *Anticalovius* (1688) appeared among a total of seventeen titles between 1681 and 1690. Apart from these titles, there is not much known about his activities.

In March 1690, Breckling and his wife moved to The Hague. That same year, he undertook a second journey, which led him across the Netherlands, to Utrecht, Woerden, Arnhem, Dieren, Deventer, Zwolle, Kampen, Katwijk, Monster, Honselerdijk, Loosduinen, Delft and Rotterdam to search for "witnesses of truth". He then spent the rest of his life in The Hague until his death in 1711, helping to build the Pietist kingdom of God. Breckling believed that his lifelong activities in the Dutch Republic gave an important impulse to the formation of Halle pietism. He noticed that his ideas about the improvement of the human heart and mind with the help of ancient knowledge, the reform of the Lutheran church, worldwide missionary activities and care for the poor,

---

3 On Comenius, see also Kristine Wirts and Leslie Tuttle's chapter in this volume.
4 Gotha, Forschungsbibliothek (hereafter FB Gotha), Chart. A 297, fols 289–290 (untitled manuscript).
5 FB Gotha, fols 290–291.

were realised in development of the "Glauchasche Anstalten". For Halle Pietists, not only were the diplomatic circles in The Hague interesting, but the town also offered a stopover between Halle and London, where they tried to spread their reform project. He was an advisor to August Hermann Francke (1663–1727), with whom he corresponded between circa 1695 and his death in 1711, and even met when Francke visited the Dutch Republic in 1705. He advised Francke in 1698 to look for donators among Collegiants and Mennonites in the Dutch Republic for the construction of his orphanage in Halle.[6] Breckling not only transferred manuscripts to Halle, but also over nine hundred books on various subjects from his extensive library, thus laying the ground stone for the Halle orphanage library which was the first public library in the German lands. The costs for the transport of books were willingly paid by Francke. Breckling's motivation to donate his books to Halle stemmed from his social commitment. Thus, he did not want his books to be sold for money, but rather to serve everyone for free in a godly manner.[7]

From 1690 onwards, he received a yearly allowance from the wife of William III, Mary II, which continued to be paid by her husband after her death in 1694. After William's death in 1702, the English parliament froze several granted allowances, but Philipp Jakob Spener (1635–1705), one of the founding fathers of Halle pietism and provost at St. Nicolai church in Berlin at that time, helped Breckling out financially and even secured an allowance for him from Anna Sophie of Denmark (1647–1717), the elector of Saxony. August Hermann Francke and Carl Hildebrand von Canstein (1667–1719), a German nobleman and important supporter of Halle pietism, also donated money to him during that time and even Breckling's funeral was apparently paid for by the Halle Pietists.[8]

---

6   Friedrich Breckling to August Hermann Francke ([The Hague?], c.07.01.1698–26.09.1698). Halle, Archivs der Franckeschen Stiftungen (hereafter AFSt), H D 93, fols 62–64, here fol. 62.
7   Breckling to Francke ([The Hague?], after March 1702). Berlin, Staatsbibliothek (hereafter StaBi Berlin), Francke-Nachlass, 7/7:40.
8   Breckling to Francke (The Hague, [?].03.1703), StaBi Berlin, Francke-Nachlass, 7/7:32. Peter Schicketanz (ed.), *Der Briefwechsel Carl Hildebrand von Cansteins mit August Hermann Francke* (Berlin/New York: 1972), 437.

Sources

I have translated two of Breckling's writings: a sixteen-page religious tract entitled *Paulus Redivivus* (1688)[9] and a manuscript, the *Catalogus Haereticorum*,[10] which is likely to have been written around 1697. *Paulus Redivivus* gives a good impression of Breckling's publication activities and of his main motivation to present himself as a "witness of truth" and to call for conversion. The *Catalogus Haeriticorum* is to be seen in relation to Breckling's better known *Catalogus Testium Veritatis*, a collection of biographies of true Christians after Luther.[11] At the same time, the *Catalogus Haereticorum* demonstrates Breckling's immense disappointment about his position on the religious marketplace in later years.

---

9   Friedrich Breckling, *Paulus Redivivus Cum suo Vale Mundo, sive Separatismus Verus â falso Syncretismo ac Mixtura Harisæorum & Pseudo apostolorum cum Satana carne & mundo vindicatus, ut nos â communione amicatia & interitu hujus Mundi ejusque Sectarum educat, & ad unionem cum Deo ac Sabbathismum Christi reducat: atque sic causam Dei ejusque Ecclesiæ & verbi contra tot homicidas ac infanticidas Gentium & animarum defendat ad solius Dei ejusque Christi Ecclesiae & Regni triumphantis gloriosam exaltationem, Babelis & omnium Mundi Sectarum perpetuam Confusionem, & Universalis Gratiae ac Theosophiæ ac Divinæ æternam prædicationem. Letzter Abschied und Außgang. Von allen heutigen Phariseern Secten/ falschen Propheten und Aposteln mit allen ihren eigen Gemeinschafften/ falschen Gottesdienst/ Babelkirchen/ zusam[m]enrottungen und eusserlichen tempelwesen/ darinnen sie wie die Fledermäuse/ Nacheulen/ Kirchenteuffel/ Irrwische/ Poltergeister/ Gespenster und Nachtthiere in und ausser ihren Stein-Kirchen umb ihre Guldene Kälber und Thierische Menschen Bilder herumb lauffen/ heulen/ singen/ tantzen/ und mit ihren Cantzelgötzen Menschen und Creaturen/ denen sie mehr als Gott selbst nachlauffen/ lauter Abgötterey treiben/ dafür daß sie mit dem klugen Jungfrauen von der Welt und ihrem Babelwesen außgehen/ und mit dem Brautigamb durch recht Christliche absonderung zu seiner Ruhe eingehen sollten; ja auch keinen falschen Geistern Lehrern Secten und Propheten mehr Glauben zustellen/ all sagten sie auch hier oder dar ist Christus selbst/ weil uns der rechter Christus einmahl so hoch für solche gewarnet/ und auch die klugen Jungfrauen mit Daniel das alles von sich bekennen und sich dessen alles schuldig geben/ was Gottes Wort an sie straffet/ ja daß sie noch dazu eingeschlaffen sind/ da nun im Finstern alle Katzen und Brodtratzen nach Gold und Brodt/ Geld und Welt herumb laufen und viele gutmeinende Seelen mit ihrem falschen Engelschein und vorgewandten Glaubens leben verführen und betriegen. Der Welt zum Zeugniß Bezeuget durch Fridrich Breckling, unwürdigen Diener Christi* (Amsterdam: 1688).

10 Friedrich Breckling, *Catalogus Haereticorum Ketzer-Historia dieser Zeiten* (c.1697–1703), FB Gotha, Chart. A 306, fols 215–237.

11 Friedrich Breckling, "Catalogus Testium Veritatis post Lutherum continuatus huc usque", in Gottfried Arnold, *Unparteyische Kirchen- und Ketzer-Historie: vom Anfang des Neuen Testaments biß auff das Jahr 1688*, vol. 3/4 (Frankfurt/Main: 1729), 1008–1110. Published for the first time in 1700. A preliminary version of the catalogue survived in manuscript in the Gotha Archive, FB Gotha A 306, 111–203.

1. Paulus Redivivus

Paulus Redivivus was printed by the widow of Christoffel Cunradus in Amsterdam, whose maiden name is unknown. Cunradus came from Saxony and was, according to the German poet and writer Philipp von Zesen (1619–1689), one the main printers of German books in Amsterdam.[12] He worked in Amsterdam from 1649 until his death in 1684.[13] He printed a wide variety of religious works and translations, including works of religious nonconformists and dissenters like Jacob Boehme [Böhme] (1575–1624), Johan Amos Comenius (1592–1670), Paul Felgenhauer (1593–1677), Joachim Betke (1601–1663), Christian Hoburg (1607–1675), George Fox (1624–1691), Edward Burrough (1634–1663), Benjamin Furly (1636–1714), Tanneke Denys (1637/38–1702?) and William Penn (1644–1718). After his death, his widow continued the business. She died in 1688, the year in which *Paulus Redivivus* was published. Cunradus himself had printed tracts for Breckling in his early years: *Ankündigung des Rach-Tages* (1660), *Das Ewige Evangelium* (1660), *Catalogus Catechizandi* (1662) and *Majestas & Potentia* (1663). Moreover, there existed a long relationship between Breckling and Cunradus, since Breckling, his wife and two children had moved in 1672 from Zwolle to Amsterdam, where he rented a living space in Cunradus's house on the Egelantiersgracht. *Paulus Redivivus* was published for a second time in 1700,[14] in Gottfied Arnold's *Kirchen- und Ketzerhistorie*, where it follows the

---

12   Philipp von Zesen, *Beschreibung der Stadt Amsterdam: Darinnen von Derselben ersten ursprunge bis auf gegenwärrtigen zustand/ ihr unterschiedlicher anwachs/ herliche Vorrechte/ und in mehr als 70 Kupfer-Stükken entworfene führnehmste Gebeue/ zusamt ihrem Stahts-wesen/ Kauf-handel/ und ansehlicher macht zur see/ wie auch was sich in und mit Derselben märkwürdiges zugetragen/ vor augen gestellet werden* (Amsterdam: 1664), 370–371.

13   Isabella Henriette van Van Eeghen, *De Amsterdamse boekhandel 1680–1725*, vol. v¹ (Amsterdam: 1978) 39–40. Cunradus is often wrongly identified as the printer of Spinoza's *Tractatus theologico-politicus*, which was actually printed by the little-known Amsterdam printer Israël de Paul (1630–1680). For more information about Cunradus' biography, Noel Malcom, *Aspects of Hobbes* (Oxford: 2002), 374.

14   Breckling, "Letzter Abschied und Außgang. Von allen heutigen Phariseern/ Secten/ falschen Propheten und Aposteln mit allen ihren eigen-gemeinschafften/ falschen Gottesdienst/ Babelkirchen/ zusammen-rottungen/ und äusserlichen Tempel-wesen/ darinnen sie wie die Fleder-mäuse [...] in und ausser ihren Stein-Kirchen/ um ihre güldene Kälber/ und thierische Menschen-bilder herumb lauffen [...] und mit ihren Cantzel-götzen/ Menschen und Creaturen [...] lauter abgötterey treiben: Dafür daß sie mit den klugen Jungfrauen/ von der welt und ihrem Babel-wesen/ ausgehen/ und mit dem Bräutigam durch recht Christliche absonderung zu seiner ruhe eingehen sollten [...] ja auch keinen falschen Geistern/ Lehrern/ Seelen und Propheten mehr glauben zustellen [...]", in Arnold, *Unparteyische Kirchen- und Ketzer-Historie*, vol. 3/4, 1116–1127 (= *Paulus Redivivus*, 1688).

tract "Vom Zustand und Beschreibung der Kirchen" (1700).[15] My translation is based on the first edition from 1688.

Breckling presented himself in his writings as a prophet and a "witness of truth". He believed that everyone had the individual right and freedom to prophesy and that only freedom of the press enables the word of God to flourish under the people. In *Religio libera* (1663), he described a religious marketplace where opinions could range freely.[16] If liars and imposters could spread their teachings without restrictions, why not those who profess the word of God? On the religious marketplace Breckling challenged the established churches on the one hand, yet fought with competitors for influence on the other. The actual places of which the marketplace consisted were not only books and letters, but also pulpits, streets, open fields, annual fairs and ships. The religious marketplace was a communicational sphere complementary to the republic of letters. It was not a sphere of learned communication, but of communication by "simple" believers. For Breckling, the free press was a means to give the persecuted and suppressed a voice, as well as an effective instrument to restore the lost concord in Christianity, by giving people the opportunity to embrace the truth on a voluntary basis. Thus, although he was a promoter of a free marketplace of opinions, Breckling did not think that its pluralism was a positive element. As a result, he thought that his competitors were preventing the restoration of Christian concord but did not believe that he was part of the "problem". After 1680 he saw his influence on the marketplace waning and complained that although he undertook so many efforts and made so many sacrifices, nobody listened to him.[17] His writings were not intended to provoke open discussion but possess elements of advertising and political communication.

---

15   Breckling, "Zustand und Beschreibung der Kirchen", in Arnold, *Unparteyische Kirchen- und Ketzer-Historie*, vol. 3/4, 1110–1115.
16   Breckling, *Religio libera Persecutio relegata, Tyrannis Exul & Justitia Redux. Hochnötige Erinnerung an die hohe Obrigkeiten in Deutschland/ Engeland/ Dennemarck/ Schweden/ und andern Fürstenthümern/ Ländern und Statten Europæ über einige Gewissens Fragen Von der Gewissens Freyheit/ und andern hochnötigen Sachen der Obrigkeit Ampt und Persohn anbelangend: Daß sie sich nicht durch ihre Phariseer/ Hoffteufel und Bauchdiener zur Verfolgung und Außrottung deß Unkrauts/ vielweniger der rechten Nachfolger Christi anreitzen lassen: sondern in Religions Sachen einem jeden seine Gewissens-Freyheit/ nach Gottes Wort/ lassen/ wenn sie nur in eusserlichen Dingen der Obrigkeit gehorsam seyn/ damit sich die Obrigkeit nicht weiter versündige/ und Gottes Gericht über sich und ihre Unterthanen bringe. Zur Rettung derer bißher unter dem Nahmen des Unkrauts unschuldig verfolgeten Kinder Gottes/ an die hohe Origkeiten in Europa geschrieben und bezeuget/ durch Fridericum Breckling, aus Holstein/ Evangelischer Prediger in Zwoll* (Freystat [Amsterdam]: 1663).
17   Friedrich Breckling, *Verbum abbreviatum ad victoriam verbi & Regni Divini, interitum verbi humani & excidium mundi Diabolici* (s.l.: c.1682), 15–16.

All these elements can be found in *Paulus Redivivus*. The main theme of the tract is the conversion of the Jews, Turks and heathens. He accuses false teachers and sect masters of not spreading true Christianity to non-Christians and regarding them as lost from the start. Moreover the discord among Christians and their misbehaviour gave God and Christ, in Breckling's view, a bad name in the world. Accordingly, he criticised them for believing that they believed that they alone were chosen for eternal life and excluding the heathens forever from eternity. He thought that it was the duty of the true church to spread its light all over the world. He even went as far as to think that the heathens themselves should complain about such ungrateful Christians, who did not provide them with essential spiritual needs, but stole their natural recources and goods, slaughtered them like cattle and wanted to enslave them forever.[18] In his eyes, true Christians should turn to the heathens, Jews and Turks and others who need help and preach Christ's gospel.[19]

To be clear, this did not mean that Breckling thought that only Christians could reach salvation. Breckling believed that most people, Christians and non-Christians alike, possess an internal light, which enables them to act morally. Knowledge of Christ and the Holy Spirit would give the heathens an impression of heaven and motivate them even more to do good.

His missionary views were certainly inspired by the Jesuits, but also by the Quakers, who wanted to convert the Jews.[20] To underline his words, he refers to authorities like Martin Luther (1483–1546), Jacob Boehme (1575–1624), Ludwig Friedrich Gifftheil (1595–1661), Bartholomäus Sclei (c.1600), Joachim Betke (1601–1663), Justianian Ernst von Welz (1621–c.1664), Heinrich Ammersbach (1632–1691) and Philipp Jacob Spener (1635–1705) and others who according to him represent the "truth".[21] Boehme in particular seems to be an important reference in *Paulus Redivivus* because he gives heathens, in contrast to Lutheran orthodoxy, some hope of salvation.[22] Boehme believed that non-Christians could receive salvation, even if they had not heard of Christ, because he acknowledged free will and the freedom of conscience.[23] Breckling seems also to have been attracted to Boehme's writings because Boehme was critical of the existence of different "church parties" and, according to Breckling, had been given a great inner light of wisdom and truth for the benefit of all.[24]

---

18   Breckling, *Paulus Redivivus*, 2.
19   Ibid., 3.
20   Ibid., 3.
21   Ibid., 7, 9–10.
22   Ibid., 2.
23   Margaret Lewis Bailey, *Milton and Jakob Boehme. A study of German Mysticism in Seventeenth-century England* (1914; repr. New York: 1964), 82.
24   Breckling, *Paulus Redivivus*, 7.

In *Paulus Redivivus* Breckling mentions two controversies with representatives of Lutheran orthodoxy. Abraham Calov (1612–1686) and Samuel Pomarius (1624–1683) called Breckling a separatist and banned him from the church.[25] In the same year as *Paulus Redivivus*, Breckling published an attack on Calov, who had accused Breckling in his *Antiböhmius* (1684) of publishing "Quakerish", as in Quaker-like, and heretical tracts. In his *Anticalovius* Breckling defended Boehme and other "witnesses of truth".[26] Breckling's other opponents in *Paulus Redivivus* were dissenters with whom he competed in the religious marketplace to reach a wider audience. He mentions Quirinus Kuhlmann (1651–1689), Eva Margaretha Frölich (*d*.1692), Peter Moritz (*c*.1670) and "other false sects, supporters of Boehme, Lutherans, Quietists, separatists, free and erratic spirits."[27]

2. Catalogus Haereticorum

The *Catalogus Haereticorum* seems to be the opposite of the *Catalogus Testium Veritatis*: The catalogue of heretics displays the worst of contemporary religious nonconformists and the catalogue of witnesses of truth the best. The two catalogues are not the same in character. The catalogue of witnesses of truth contains one hundred and sixty-three male biographies and an additional catalogue of pious female persons, which contains approximately sixty-five names, of which only sixteen have biographies. The catalogue of heretics contains no biographies, but an introduction in which Breckling warns against "false sects" and offers an extensive explanation of why various dissenters such as the Quakers, the Labadists, the Philadelphians, Antoinette Bourignon (1616–1680)

---

25   Ibid., 3, 9, 13.
26   Friedrich Breckling, *Anticalovius sive Calovius cum Assectis suis prostratus et Jacob Böhmium Cum aliis testibus veritatis defensus. Darin gelehret wird was von D. Abraham Calovii, Pomarii Francisci und anderer falschgelehrten Büchern/ Apologien und Schriften wider Jac. Böhmen/ Hermannum Jungium, I.C. Charias M. Henricum Amerßbach/ mich und andere Zeugen der Wahrheit zu halten sey. Und ob ein recht Christlicher Lehrer oder Zuhörer Darin mit D. Calovio, Pomarius und andern Feinden der Warheit übereinstimmen. Und des Iacob Böhmens/ Jungii/ Seidenbechers/ Grosgebawers unserer und anderer Zeugen der Warheit Personen und Schrifften ohne verletzung seines gewissens und übertretung des Wortes Gottes also richten und verdammen könne wie D. Calov, Pomarius, Artus, Francisci der unverständige gerrard Antognossius und andere so unGöttlich gethan haben […]. Dabey zugleich des sel. J. Böhmen und vieler anderer Zeugen der Warheit Unschuld gerettet und verthädiget wird/ und angewiesen/ was doch von Jacob Böhmen Person und Schrifften nach dem Grunde der Warheit zu halten seye/ und wie solche mißbrauchet/ theils recht gebrauchet werden können? Und Ob ein rechter Christ mit gutem Gewissen in solcher falschen Lehrer Richter und Verfolger Kirchen oder Gemeinschafft sich begeben bleiben und beharren könne/ welche also die Warheit und dessen Zeugen von sich außstossen lästern und verfolgen?* ([Wesel]: 1688).
27   Breckling, *Paulus Redivivus*, 10.

and her supporter Pierre Poiret (1646–1719), were allegedly evil. The manuscript of the *Catalogus Haereticorum* must have been written after March 1697 and before June 1703, when a period of silence[28] was ordered by Jane Lead (1623–1704), the leader of the Philadelphian Society, because Breckling writes about the first volume of the *Theosophical transactions* or "Acta philadelphica", a series of five small memoirs published between March and November 1697 in England by the Philadelphian Society.[29] The *Catalogus Testium Veritatis*, on the other hand, was probably written largely before 1678, because in 1678 Breckling was already looking actively for publishers for a manuscript with that title.[30] The manuscript of the catalogue of witnesses of truth was not published until 1700 in Gottfried Arnold's *Kirchen- und Ketzerhistorie*. Both documents have an autobiographical character, as Breckling draws on his experience to determine why someone was a "witness of truth" or a heretic.

Why the *Catalogus Haereticorum* was written and whether it was intended for publication is unclear. As a church historian, Breckling thought it was his task to describe who was good, better, best, evil, more evil and most evil in church history. To be hated and persecuted or to be loved and cherished by the world seems to have been an important distinguishing feature to discern between true Christians and heretics.[31] Apart from the prophet Antoinette Bourignon, there is not much overlap between the two documents. Bourignon is mentioned in the "Catalogue of pious women", which was part of the *Catalogus Testium Veritatis*, though Breckling did not give her an individual biography.[32] In the *Catalogus Haereticorum*, the supposed vices of Bourignon, Pierre Poiret, Quirinus Kuhlmann and others are described in detail. Breckling asserts for instance that the supporters of Antoinette Bourignon consisted of men who left their wives to join her and that the supporters of the Labadists were mostly women who were willing to leave their husbands. Fur-

---

28 Cf. Lionel Laborie, "Philadelphia Resurrected: Celebrating the Union Act (1707) from Irenic to Scatological Eschatology", in *Jane Lead and her Transnational Legacy*, ed. Ariel Hessayon (London: 2016), 213–239, here 216.

29 *Theosophical Transactions by the Philadelphian Society, Consisting of Memoirs, Conferences, Letters, Dissertations, Inquiries, &c. For the Advancement of Piety and Divine Philosophy* (London: 1697). On Jane Lead and the Philadelphian Society, see Ariel Hessayon's chapter in vol. 3 of this collection.

30 Cf. Breckling, "Catalogus einiger Tractaten, welche noch bey mir theils entworffen/theils außgearbeitet zum Gemeinen Nutzen und Dienst der Christenheit/ ob Gott dazu Verlag geben/ oder Verleger erwecken wolle", in Friedrich Breckling, *Compendium Apocalypseos Reseratæ* (s.l.: 1678), 8–16.

31 Breckling, "Zustand und Beschreibung der Kirchen", 1112.

32 Breckling, "Catalogus Testium Veritatis", 1110.

ther, in the *Catalogus Haereticorum* Breckling accuses Jane Lead of spreading a "new gospel". The document appears to be directed especially against the increasing influence of the Philadelphian movement on the European continent.[33] Breckling received information about Lead and others who would later become known as "Philadelphians" from the prophet Tanneke Denys (1637/1638–1702?), who travelled to England in 1679, 1689 and 1690.[34] Denys did not just provide Breckling with oral information, but appearently also with publications, though Breckling does not mention any titles. Breckling's role in the success of the emergence of the Philadelphians on the continent was mixed, as he writes in the *Catalogus Haereticorum* that he supplied readers in the Dutch Republic with writings, thanks to which they had become popular in the first place.

---

33   On Jane Lead and the Philadelphians, see Ariel Hessayon's chapter in volume 3 of this collection.
34   Mirjam de Baar, "Denijs, Tanneke", in *Digitaal Vrouwenlexicon van Nederland* (http://resources.huygens.knaw.nl/vrouwenlexicon/lemmata/data/Denijs, accessed 13 January 2020).

1. Paul revived with his farewell from the world or true separatism against false syncretism and pharisaic intermingling and fake apostles with their diabolical flesh and punished world, about the way our friendly community shows to get away from the sects and the decline of this world and to lead back to unity with God, to Christ's Sabbath and to His only godly church of Christ, triumphant reign, glorious exaltation, eternal sermon of universal grace and godly theosophy and about the defence of God's church and word against so many humans, human and beastly child murderers, against Babylon and the entire sectarian world and its eternal confusion.

Last farewell and outcome. About all latter-day sects of the Pharisees, false prophets and apostles with their own communities, false religion, churches of Babylon, gatherings and outwarded false churches, in which they, like bats, night owls, church devils, little rascals, poltergeists, ghosts and animals of the night in and outside of their churches of stone, walk, cry, sing, dance around their golden calves and beastly human images, and about their false gods of the pulpit, humans and creatures, which they follow more than God. Because they are up to nothing, but idolatrousness, it should be made sure that they leave, together with the wise virgins and the evil world and enter with the groom through true Christian isolation into His peace. Also so that nobody believes false spirits, teachers, sects and prophets, even if they say here or there is Christ himself, because the true Christ has warned us against such people. Even the wise virgins, together with Daniel, admit this and plead guilty to everything, for which God punishes them. Because they fell asleep all the cats and rats are now craving for gold, bread and money and walk around in the world in the dark and seduce and betray many well-meaning souls with their false angelous appearance and fake religious life. To the world as a testimony, witnessed by Friedrich Breckling, unworthy servant of Christ. Printed in Amsterdam by the widow of Christoffel Cunradus,[35] 1688.

The contemporary false teachers and sect masters imagine themselves alone to be the chosen generation, people and church of God and that all other sects, Jews, Turks and heathens together, with their children must be lost to them, because these neither know Christ after the flesh, nor have His baptism, word and Last Supper among them. At which no one is more guilty than us Christians who let this matter lie unfertile among us and do not propagate it further among the heathens. | Because today the contemporary preachers

1

2

---

35   Christoffel Cunradus (c.1615–1684), printer and publisher of German books in Amsterdam from 1649 onwards.

and teachers, especially under the Lutherans, imagine themselves to be—as they openly write—the only medium for enlightenment or only instrument and way through which God wants to enlighten the blind humans in the world and that God, apart from them, could not invent any other instrument or way to enlighten the people and to bless them as through such academic teachings and preachers. And therefore, they have to confess to themselves that they bear thereby the only and chief blame and are the cause of all blindness and ignorance among the remaining sects, because they are ordered by God as the only instrument to enlighten everyone and to preach everyone the gospel. Unfortunately, they did not preach the gospel, which God has bequeathed upon them, to the farthest corners of the world. Therefore, the remaining Turks, Jews and heathens are, by nobody else's blame than these Lutheran preachers who believe they are alone the true church, stuck in their blindness and stay deprived of such light, together with their children who are also rejected and condemned as blind heathens.

The Lutheran preachers also banned Jacob Böhme[36] for this reason who gave the heathens some hope of salvation. Therefore, God cannot rightfully accuse anyone else for the cause and blame of all blindness and wrongness under the remaining Jews, heathens and Turks, but those Christians who deny them their proprietary light and give them major offence and reason to doubt the truth of the Christian religion, because the Christians themselves do not agree with each other and do not practice their religion and faith properly. Yes, through their unchristian life, they even blaspheme the nature of God and the name of Christ[37] and imagine that they alone are destined for and summoned to the eternal life and that the heathens, Jews and Turks must be excluded and lost forever. Because the Lutheran teachers pride themselves and dream to be the true Christian church and demonstrate this the least of all by actions and do not worry how the gospel according to Christ's order should be preached to all creatures to the farthest corners of the world. After all, it is the nature and characteristic of the true church to shine its light for every human being as an example and as a wake-up call for others and to propagate the seed of the word of God everywhere in the world. If they do not, but bury their money nearby,[38] they lose the name and the privilege of the churches and moreover should be accused before all other sects to bear the main blame of all blindness and wrongness of the world. Yes, the heathens with their children should shout

---

36   Jacob Boehme (1575–1624), German mystic, philosopher and theosopher.
37   In the original text: "ja durch ihre Unchristliches Leben und Wesen Gottes und Christi Nahmen in aller Welt verlästern machen".
38   In the original text "sie ihr Pfund bey sich begraben". Cf. Matt. 25:18.

their grievance about such ungrateful Christians who deprive them of the light and word of God, which they received in their place, and who do not supply them like faithful housekeepers on time with necessary dishes of the soul and who further rob the heathens of their bodily goods, treasures and gifts on the land and in the water and enrich, grace and heighten themselves at their costs, and even slaughter and sell the poor blind heathens like inane cattle and plan to keep them forever as slaves.

And because we, Jacob Böhme and other witnesses of truth punish the contemporary false teachers and churches, they expel us together with God's word, light and truth, separate themselves from us, cast us out of our office and service, like Saul did David, and scold us as separatists, Quakers and Quietists and persecute us with words and works as much as they can, or, if they do not do this all themselves, they agree with the persecutors. Therefore, we share neither part nor | fate with them, like with pastor Pomarius,[39] inhabitant of Hamburg, pastor Calovius[40] and others. What can we do, but leave such false teachers and Babylonian sects after the word and order of Christ, Our Lord, help them to wipe the dust from their heads as a testimony, flee from such blind leaders, persecutors of truth and enemies of Christ's cross and turn, like the apostles in Jerusalem, to the remaining heathens, Jews, Turks and other poor lame and blind, who are sitting in the dark in the alleys of the town and the roads of the world, preach to them the gospel of Christ and invite them to the great Lords Supper of the almighty God, in order that the heathens become entirely part of the church and that His house becomes full.

Finally, the whole of Israel will wake the world through the rise of the general light and will be brought with us to Christ's kingdom [and] blessedness, in order that the richness of God's mercifulness, which floats over everyone of us and which can be acquired through Christ, may be known to everyone of them, because God, as a father of mercifulness of all spirits, even today still does not want that someone becomes lost. He wants all humans to receive help to recognise the truth, in order that they repent and inherit the eternal life through faith, to which God invites us and bears us through the affluence of His kindness. He orders us to be merciful, forbearing and patient and to spread our light, rain and blessing among all human beings, for the purpose of their persuasion and enlightenment, like God does daily to all of us, and not to act without, but with the help of humans to reveal and to preach His grace and truth.

---

39 Samuel Pomarius (1624–1683), also known as Samuel Baumgart, was an orthodox Lutheran theologian and superintendent in the northern German town Lübeck.
40 Abraham Calov (1612–1686) was a professor of theology in Wittenberg. He became publicly known through his defence of Lutheran orthodoxy against inner and outer opponents.

Who does not want to wake up and convince himself of this and let himself be called to the vineyards of His Lord to service Him this last hour with earnings[41] of the Christian faith, to advance His kingdom and combat His enemies like a loyal worker, servant, soldier and worker in His Lords work and service, does neither want to confess to nor spread His faith, nor wants to help to extinguish this general misery and fire. He only thinks of his peace and quietness, even though Christ has called the workers to lead them to peace. He will have to account for his wrongness before God and will be judged by Him in His court if he is guilty to be the cause of evil, blindness and downfall of the entire human race. God has warned you faithfully for that and has reminded you of this with the help of many witnesses of truth, so you cannot apologise to Him that you did not know, because you yourselves write whole books about God's word and testimony on earth. You are very blind and wrong and neither want to know nor hear about things that concern you. On the contrary, you reject all good writings and witnesses. The old Pharisees did this too, but they, to their defence, travelled around, unlike you, to make a Jew their companion and to build the prophet's graves.

What should God do to such false teachers and obdurate Pharisees who condemn Jacob Böhme and other witnesses of truth to the abyss of hell and want to defend their false nature against God, but make an end to them and save the poor sheep from their mouths, in order that they are not devoured, after Ezek. 34, Psalm 13, 14, Jer. 6, 7, 8, 23, Matt. 23, 24. How keen the papists and other sects are to convert the remaining heathens in the East- and West Indies everyone can read in their Indian histories and letters and in the very learned book by Thomas à Jesu[42] and other writings, in the biography of Caspar Barzeus[43] and others. We do not condemn them, but where are our Christ-shaped fruits with which we prove that we are the right grapevine and oil tree of Christ and that we are doing it better?

The Quakers, by whose name Lutheran teachers call every witness of truth nowadays, | treat the heathens a thousand times better than the Lutherans, the papists and all other sects have done. Should they not judge and condemn us? What have the Lutheran teachers done up to now in this particular case?

---

41   Original: "Pfunde", Breckling meant probably "Pfründe".
42   Thomas à Jesu (1564–1627) was a Spanish Carmelite who wrote an introduction to a Catholic mission to the indigenous peoples of the Americas, *On procuring the salvation of All Men* (1613).
43   Caspar Barzaeus (1515–1553), from the Dutch Republic, was a Jesuit missionary in Goa and on Hormuz Island in the Persian Gulf. Nicolas Trigault published in 1610 at Antwerp a biography of Barzaeus' life, *Vita Gasparis Barzaei Belgae Societate Iesu, B. Xaverii in India socii*.

Should they not be silent and ashamed before God, the angels and all humans, because they do not act properly and only look for their own advantage, honour, pleasure and progression with the help of Christ's gospel? What can they expect, other than to be thrown into the darkness of hell, together with Capernaum[44] and the useless servant? What else could they have possibly earned with their pharisaic nature than that the kingdom of God will be taken from them and given to the remaining heathens and Jews who, with the help of Christ, will be able to find peace and sit at His table during the Last Supper? Because they imagine they are the true children of the kingdom and neither want to hear about nor accept God's testimony about the future Sabbath rest and victorious Kingdom of Christ, they have excluded themselves from the Lords Last supper and have even, by contradicting us, denied such grace and new Jerusalem to their audience. My and baron Justinian von Welz's writings attest to this and have become known in the entire Lutheran world.[45]

Among Lutheran teachers and communities, as among other sects there are still a few who reject and despise the apparent wrongness of their false fellow believers. They should demonstrate before the eye of the world through actions and public confessions that they defend Christ's word, truth, kingdom, peace, cordiality and church against Satan's false enemies of the world, like Paul did against the Pharisees. We would like to accept those very much who have shown to be true soldiers and servants of Christ by leaving Babylon, the false Babylonian nature of the world and their sectarian servants of the flesh. If they dissemble, are silent, agree and run along with the crowd, with sects, money and worldly priests God will not spare them, but judge them with and because of their silence and hypocrisy, make them guilty of every sin in the world, they will receive every "reward" which the world, Babylon and their false

---

44   Town in the New Testament in which Jesus preached. In Luke 10:15 the destruction of Capernaum is predicted.

45   Justinian Ernst von Welz (c.1621–1664) was blessed by Breckling to convert heathens to Christianity. He travelled to the region of Surinam/Guyana after which never was heard of him again. Around the supposed time of his death, he published several writings concerning the conversion of the heathens: Justinian von Welz, *Einladungs-Trieb zum herannahenden Grossen Abendmahl und Vorschlag zu einer Christ-erbaulichen Jesus-Gesellschaft. Behandlend die Besserung des Christentums und Bekehrung des Heidentums.* Nürnberg: 1664; Idem, *Eine Christliche und treuhertzige Vermahnung An alle rechtgläubige Christen/ der Auyspuryischen Confession. Betreffend eine sonderbahre Gesellschafft/ Durch welche/ nechst Göttlicher Hülffe/ unsere Evangelische Religion möchte außgebreitet werden* (s.l.: 1664); Idem, *Ein kurtzer Bericht/ Wie eine Newe Gesellschafft auffzurichten wäre/ unter den rechtglaubigen Christen der Augspurgischen Confession. Mit einer Christlichen Vermahnung an die Herren Reformirte, nur mit wenigen Zeilen angezeiget/ und in Druck verfertiget* (s.l.: c.1665).

teachers "earn". For being a friend to the world means to be an enemy to God and to those who want to be the world's friend forever, we deny friendship and community and ignore them after the order and example of Christ and His apostles, after 2 Cor. 6, 1 Cor. 5, 2 Tim. 2, 3, 4, 1 Tim. 4:6, 2 Pet., 2 Titus 1, Rev. 18.

He who wants to believe the false teachers of Christ and sects and follows them into their false Jerusalem any further to their own demise and detoriation is free to do so and to experience this himself. God has ordered me to listen to Christ and His spirit in His servants and members of the cross and to flee and avoid all false prophets and apostles, strange shepherds, false Christs, sect masters, rascals, blind leaders, servants of the flesh who are hostile to the cross, heretics and human Satans, even if they are disguised as angels of light and preachers of justice. He has ordered me to do this not without important reasons, because those who greet or house them become part of their evil works, after 2 John 1:10–11. This I will obey, believe and follow after so many important sayings of the scripture. Matt. 7, 15, 23, 24, John 10, Rom. 16, Eccles. 2, Phil. 1, 2, 3, Gal. 1, 5, 2 Cor. 6, 11, 2 Thess. 2, 2 Titus 1, 2 Pet. 2, Rev. 18. He who does not want to leave Babylon together with me will experience where his disbelief and disobedience will take him.

If the authorities and listeners obey false teachers, Pharisees and sect masters, in spite of Christ's specific word and order, if they follow such false gods of the pulpit more than the true existing God in Christ they are free to do so, but the authorities should know that they will have to account for their subjects' souls when they force such false teachers and church devils upon them, like Jeroboam forced upon the Israelites, and through their word and example keep them away from the imitation of Christ. The consequence will be that they will be destroyed together with those false teachers and sects as certain as the authorities of the Israelites and the Jews and their Pharisees and high priests in Jerusalem will be. | As long as they do not leave their sects and blind leaders and return to Christ, listen to Him and follow Him and His apostles, like Nicodemus, Joseph of Arimathea and thousands of Jews did, they are not attached to the church of Christ and its community of the servants of the cross, which is persecuted and banned by the Pharisees in the temporary and eternal life. The suffering of the true Christians will save the world. They will be saved with them in their pella,[46] because they have accepted Christ's members of the cross wholeheartedly.

---

46   By tradition Pella is the city to which the Christians were warned miraculously to flee after the destruction of Jerusalem AD 70. Pella means here something like a safe haven.

I instruct them to investigate their conscience to find out why Christ often warns us for false teachers and why God's word often persistingly and without a reason insists on fleeing them? Have the entire world and all their sects not been seduced by their false teachers to reject the true cross of Christ? Are the worst animals and hostile birds, thieves, murderers and robbers today not more evil and do they do not more damage than these false teachers in churches and schools have done in the past in the world and in their kingdoms? If they do not leave them, should they not also necessarily perish together with them and be corrupted in the same way as the old Pharisees and sects in Jerusalem were? How and in what way are people today better than their predecessors? Has God not warned us enough for this?

In the end, who is guilty that the entire world and all sects have been seduced to such corruption, disunion, war, agitation, rebellion and every other disaster? Would we like to be saved from that or not? If they do not want to improve themselves and reject Christ's truth, like they have done up to now, what advice and means of rescue from their corruption does God's word give us? Should we accept the godly advice how to leave their Babylon or should we stay among those who want to follow the false teachers in their immoral sects until they are damned too? 2 Pet. 2:1 ff. Who does not break with them and with the world cannot be in an alliance with God. Those parents, teachers and schoolmasters in churches, homes and schools and their children, pupils and students who have been separated together with the world from God and would like to stay on the broad road of the world will be lost. God still addresses you through all of His prophets and speaks. You shall not live after your fathers commands and not accept them as legal and not impurify yourselves with the false gods which they, to God's grievance, have erected in their temples, on their pulpits, in their churches, schools and hearts and which they love more than they love God and which they follow more than they follow God. After which they have all been separated from God and have pursued the idols of their hearts, they drag you along and therefore want to sacrifice Beelzebub and Moloch to the world. God testifies this himself and who can say that this is not true. Ezek. 8, 14, 20, Jer. 2 ff. Because God, our Lord, has ordered you to listen to and follow Christ and not the antichristian teachers and sects so that you may be taught by Him, wish for His wisdom and be punished and taught by the spirit and salvation of Christ, abide by what Christ has commended you, according to the covenant of the New Testament, to which you have attached yourselves through holy baptism. Heb. 8, 10, 1 John 2, Matt. 3, 15, 16, 17, 23, 24, 28, James 1, John 6, 10. Therefore, you have to leave the broad road of the world and walk the narrow way of the cross and ask for the previous roads of the apostolic churches and walk them, then you will find peace for your sects, according to Jer. 6:16.

Speak to those who return, on behalf of God, to the children of Israel. The work of our fathers, which we have to deal with all our lives, should perish disgracefully, because we have sinned against God, our Lord, from an early age on. As long as you leave their pharisaic worldly and Babylonian existence, God will accept you like a lost son and be your father. Then, you will be truly His sons and daughters says God to you in Jer. 3, 4, 2 Cor. 6 vers 17, Psalm 45. | What you lose in the world for His sake God will reward you a hundred times, but as long as you prefer your father and mother, your pharisaic teachers and Babylonian wine more than Christ and you say, "we do not want to do it", Jer. 6:17, Jer. 44:16–17, it will happen to you like it happened to the disobedient children of Israel. Ezek. 20:21 ff.

6

God himself threatens us still today like he threatened the disobedient children of Israel. Therefore, we linger in our disbelief and disobedience after the example of our fathers. He would like to hit us seven times and more for that, four times after another, as he does daily to us and shows us in the Revelation of John such fourfold and sevenfold penalisation and punishment. If we do not obey His fatherly reprimand and chastity to us in the words of the seven epistles, he will open His seven seals over us and defeat us with all kinds of persecution, war, hunger and pestilence. If this does not help, he will let His seven trumpets sound over us and punish us with heretical sects, destabilising spirits, false teachers and seducers to injustice. If this does not help either, he does not want to scare us with His seven thunderous voices any longer, but will pour His seven bowls of God's anger and, by doing so he will finally show us His entire anger and put an end to Babylon's game-playing. In the end, the cities of the heathens will be torn down etc. Rev. 2, 6, 8, 16. Ezek. 20, 21, 22, 23, 24. They are all lost, because they do not want the name of the Lord to be remembered in truth and justice among them. Isa. 48, 59, Amos 6.

Through the word of God, we now know how this worldly Babylon and their false teachers and sects will end, after Josh. 13, 14, 34, 47, 48. Therefore, we flee from Babylon and turn to Zion, climb on the lamb to His holy community at the mountain of Zion, because only under His wings are we able to seek and find our salvation and protection, after Isa. 48, 49, 50, 51, 55 ff., Jer. 50, 51, Joel 2, Rev. 14. And because, with Adam's help, God has made an eternal covenant with all humans and has re-erected and reconfirmed them with Noah's and his descendants' help all over the world and also has redeemed everyone in Christ, has reconciled, appointed, invited, tolerated, carried, preserved, protected, supported, convinced, dragged and called them and therefore has awakened all humans on the face of the earth, we invite everyone, every Jew, Turk and heathen to this last supper, peace, refreshment, kingdom of heaven and wedding of the lamb and lion from the house of Judah, in order that the large house of the great God becomes full.

We ask all people and Christians to work towards this goal, in order that every word of God addressed to us becomes true and will be made public to every heathen, Jew and Turk in the entire world and they will be united in one faith and knowledge of the son of God and become a perfect man, to the degree in which Christ is perfect, after Eph. 3, 4, Col. 1, 2. God reminds us over and over again of his first covenant, so that His word, which the false Christians despise, reaches all humans anew and brings them to acknowledge the truth, after 1 Tim. 2. Who does not want to bury his money and be found guilty of the downfall, blindness and detoriation of the remaining Turks, Jews and heathens should strive like a common member of the true church, with all of his power and talents which he has received from God for the common benefit and service of man, to reveal the light in the darkness to the remaining blind humans in the entire world. Or else, he will be found negligent in the service of the Lord and work in His vineyard and because of his ingratitude lose his light, money and gifts, as it happened previously to the Jews, because God has put his trust in him for the common benefit at his own expense as His housekeeper to propagate and increase them.

What I think of the remaining Turks, Jews and heathens, their innocent children and their condition in life and death, I do not find anywhere put better into words and described than in the holy Bible and | in Jacob Böhme's blessed writings, especially in his excellent preface about the *Aurora*.[47] To whom God will give eyes and wisdom to acknowledge this properly, is for Him to decide, like everything else is too. What the blessed Jacob Böhme has written very thoroughly and truthfully about the contemporary ungrateful Christians and their sects, about the papists, Lutherans, Calvinists and their articles of faith, about which they disagree, everyone can read in his writings. In him, God has lit a big candle for us to see all hidden wisdom and truth and has put it on a candleholder for the common benefit. Who does not recognise and accept this from God and wants to separate the good seed from the chaff may keep his blindness. These ungrateful despisers may bestow upon themselves everything they believe is evil and wrong in Jacob Böhme, Sley[48] and others and argue, dispute,

---

47 *Aurora oder Morgenröthe im Aufgang* (1612) was Boehme's first work. We do not know which edition of the *Aurora* Breckling consulted. Perhaps it could have been the second volume of the critical edition, published 1682 in Amsterdam by Johann Georg Gichtel: *Morgenröte im Aufgang/ Das ist. Die Wurtzel oder Mutter Der Philosophiæ, Astrologiæ und Theologiæ, Aus rechtem Grunde. Oder Beschreibung der Natur/ wie alles gewesen* [...].

48 Bartolomaeus Sclei (Scleus) (c.1600), from Lesser Poland, is mentioned as the 39th witness of truth in Breckling's "Catalogus Testium Veritatis". There are two writings by his hand: *Pater Noster. Das ist Eine geheime allgemeine Außlegung Des Heiligen Unsers/ Darinnen gehandelt wird/ Was Bethen seye? Was man Anbeten solle? Neben einem Anhange etlicher*

preach, write, quarrel and speak until they become tired to search for the key of the door to Lot's house among them. They are just as less able to distinguish the spirit, light and mercy of Christ among them as among the old Pharisees were.

You want to deprive yourselves and everyone else too of this general light, mercy, knowledge of God, spirit, life, insight and gifts and persist in your darkness and blindness. You want to put us to death, exhaust, run into, destroy, entrap and disgrace us and other witnesses of truth, as long as God chooses the foolish and disgraces the wise and the bright, after 1 Cor. 1, because the godly foolishness and weakness are more clever and powerful than your human wisdom, power and fortune is. When the sun rises, how and in what way do you want to withstand the godly power, truth and light of God which darkens every human fake light and every heavenly star! Josh. 1, 11, 60. God has sent His wise prophets and scribes to you in your Jerusalem which I have sought with hard work, great pain and journeys. God has let me find many of them or has sent me their writings, among which I count the blessed Jacob Böhme, Gifftheil[49] and other witnesses of truth which I have mentioned in my *Fridericus Resurgens*.[50]

Notwändiger Puncten zum Verstande des Wahren Christenthumbs gehörig (s.l.: 1639); and Idem, *Theosophische Schrifften: Oder Eine Allgemeine und Geheime/ jedoch Einfältige und Teutsche Theologia; Anweisend/ wie ein jeder Mensch durch das Geheimnuß Jesu Christi in uns/ zu dem wahren und lebendigen Glauben und Erkäntnuß des Drey-Einigen Gottes/ seiner selbst und aller Creaturen wesentlich gelangen/ und also das Reich Gottes in der Seele wieder finden/ eröffnen/ und im rechten Gebrauch aller Dinge/ empfindlich geniessen solle. Gegründet und angewiesen In dem Dreyfachen Göttlichen Offenbahrungs-Buche/ Der H. Schrifft/ der grossen und kleinen Welt. Geschrieben aus Göttlichem Liecht und Liebe zur Warheit vor alle Menschen Anno 1556 in Klein-Pohlen, Anjetzo aber wegen seiner Vortrefflichkeit und hohen Nutzen in dieser Zeit/ zum gemeinen Besten ans Liecht befördert/ und mit einem Register versehen* (s.l.: 1686).

49   Breckling met the prophet Ludwig Friedrich Gifftheil (1595–1661) in 1656, during his second stay in the Dutch Republic. In his writings Breckling frequently mentions Gifftheil as an inspiring example.

50   *Fridericus Resurgens* is a compilation of Breckling's own writings and those of Gifftheil. Friedrich Breckling; Ludwig Friedrich Gifftheil, *Fridericus Resurgens. Anfang und Aufgang des Wortes und Zeugnissen Gottes/ Welches der tewrer in Gott ruhender Mysteriarch/ Zeuge/ Knecht und Kriegsman Gottes Ludwig Friderich Gifftheil/ im Geist und Glauben/ Davids/ Josua/ Elias und der Alten Propheten dieser gegenwertigen Welt und allen ihren Secten/ Königreichen/ Fürstenthumern/Regenten/ Priestern/ Ländern und Städten in gantz Europa und Deutschland bey 40. Jahr lang an allen Ortern biß in den Todt bezeuget hat. Wie solches alles heut in der That anbrennet und erfüllet wird/ und an dem Heiligthumb oder Hause Gottes und dessen falschen Lehrern und Priestern den Anfang nehmen muß. Samt einem Bann und Fluch/ damit Er die Erde geschlagen/ und die Ungehorsame und Ungläubige Welt-Menschen nach Gottes Wort verfluchet. Dabey ein Extract und Abschrifft der Wunderbahren Vision Käysers Sigismundi von dem Priester Friderico Langenaugio. Und wie viel andere Zeugen mit der Wahrheit des Wortes Gottes von diesen letzten Zeiten übereinstim-*

Because you do not want to respect, recognise or hear and accept them, but expel and persecute them as ungrateful as the old Jerusalem, we turn together with Christ and the apostles to the remaining Jews, heathens and Turks, in order that the unspeakable richness of the benevolence and patience of God, through which God carries all humans and brings them to repentance may be known to them. The entire greatness of the love, charity and mercy of God will be revealed to them, because it will help them to convert and to become blessed. In the end, the infinite wise, hidden and wonderful government and provision of God over every human being for their preservation and blessedness will be revealed to everyone, to honour, praise and heighten His very holy name, powerful mercy and truth about everything, so that no one can accuse Him of being guilty of someone's destruction and failure and He will be found innocent of all human detoriation.

At the same time, it will be disclosed, why, until this day, so many millions of Jewish, Turkish, Christian and pagan souls have dwelled on their blindness and have perished. If these causes will be removed among us, the light that has been given to us to enlighten them may shine again on them. At the same time, God will take vengeance upon so many murderers of souls, thieves of His honour and desecraters of His holy name for the sake of the infinite glorious salvation and heightening of the imprisoned and pestered children of God who reside in the darkness of the night and shadow of death. He will heighten His holy name in a glorious way any time very soon, by destroying His revengeful enemies with the help of the mouths of young children and infants everywhere in the world. | 8 Amen Hallelujah.

And because we all seceded from God and have made ourselves guilty of spiritual whoredom and idolatry, fornicated with ourselves, with human creatures, with money, with the world, with books, priests, absolution, churches, baptism, the Lord's supper and with the best gifts and means God has given us, it is the right thing to recognise and admit, with Daniel, that we are very guilty and should apologise for this, abase ourselves willingly before the eye of God, convert ourselves joyfully to Him and seek His mercy for absolution, improvement and recovery, because he concedes this even to the greatest sinners and rebels.

---

men. Durch ein Mitt Glied der Jesus-Liebenden Früchtbringenden Apostolischen Gesellschaft von dem Orden des gecreutzigten/ einen Königlichen Priester und Frey-Herrn In Christo/ den Brechenden. Auff daß durch das Geistliche Schwerd und Hammer des Wortes Gottes alle Gewalt/ Heucheley/ Lügen/ Abgötterey/ Thorheit und Eigenheit der Gottlosen Phariseer und falschen Apostel in der Welt zu erst zerbrochen und außgerottet/ und also Gottes Nahmen/ Ehre/ Gewalt/ Wort/ Reich/ Ampt und Kinder wieder erhöhet werden in Gerechtigkeit. Amen/ Halleluja (s.l.: 1683).

He swears that he does not want the death of godless sinners, but that he would like them to convert and be alive. After Ezek. 18, 33. If not, we testify especially for those unremorseful Pharisees among the Lutherans, to everything God's word, Jeremiah, Christ, Paul, Luther and all prophets, wise men and scribes which were sent to them, have testified in court and have written down in their books as a testimony. Luther left them shortly before his death to set an example and show them that their judgment is coming soon. Their future will be that they will have to hide themselves and be quiet. Yet, we continue to be in debt to everyone who is truly searching and listening and are pledged to serve them as much as possible.

Hereupon should be revealed who believes to be an enemy or a friend of Christ's word, truth and of His servants of the cross and who is, with his heart, mouth, hand, teaching and life, in favour of the world and its false, hypocrite churches, servants of the flesh, sects, antichrists and worldly priests and who is not? Does he want to crush the world and its kings, who constitute together Satan's head, or does he want to serve Satan for worldly glory? Does he want to idolise the beast and his image in man or listen to, honour and capture Christ and His image in us? Does he want to deny his own being and the being of the world or does he also want to deny, reject, judge and destroy Christ and His heavenly kingdom? Does he want to crush and overpower Satan's worldly kingdom or does he want to be crushed and overpowered by Satan, the world and his own glory, lust and love? Does he want to hate, lose and murder or love, keep and lose his own life, piety, will and wisdom forever? Does he want to reside on the side of the world, its sects, churches and priests and be the enemy of Christ, His church of the cross and its servants? In this particular case, nobody can be neutral nor position himself in the middle between good and evil, because Christ will spit out the half-hearted, Rev. 3. Is it not better for us to be despised, blasphemed, separated, persecuted, crucified, hated and murdered with Christ than to be loved, praised, honoured, heard, called and heightened by the world and its priests? Woe betide us if this troubled world notices, loves, respects, honours and prefers us! The world loves what belongs to her and there should be a difference between the church and the world as there should be between Christ and Antichrist, light and darkness, spirit and flesh, God and Lucifer, life and death, heaven and hell, sheep and wolves, doves and raptors. Do you want to follow money-loving and worldly priests and their victims? We do not want to! Do you want to search for the best and juiciest services of the church and choose voluntarily to marry the wealthiest daughters of this world? Does this not reveal whose spiritual children you are? Gen. 6. Do you want to bless all unremorseful people, hirelings, followers and buyers and strengthen and deepen them in their evilness? We absolutely do not want this!

If you want to exclude Jacob Böhme and other witnesses of truth from you and from eternal bliss, you should be excluded instead! Do you want to separate yourselves from Christ and us for the sake of truth? You should be separated instead! Do you want to leave Christ's church of the cross, its members and servants? You should be expelled instead! Do you want to besiege and famish us with the help of Bethulia and cut us off from all consolation and support?[51] Then the same should happen to you like it happened to Haman, pharaoh, Holofernes, Assur and their followers![52] Do you want to hate, judge and | condemn us? You convict and condemn thereby yourselves! Do you want to persecute us? You should be persecuted! Do you want that also the weed is considered to be tares and extirpated too early?[53] Then you should be extirpated! Do you want the heathens to stay blind? You should become blind again! Everything should be done to you like you have done to us and others and you have in mind to do like the Pharisees did in Jerusalem, because they wanted to destroy Christ's kingdom, church of the cross and His followers among them. Would you like to rob God's office, honour, godliness, church service and everything else and increase yourselves eternally with their help? Then you should be pushed down with Lucifer and convicted like thieves, murderers and robbers of God's honour! Do you want to follow D. Calov and Pomario, Pharisees in Hamburg, and the rest of the crowd on their worldly road?[54] Then, you should fall down and collapse with them! Do you want to justify yourselves with them and condemn all witnesses of truth? Then you should be disgraced with them! Make your choice!

Should it be in vain that we and so many pious and legitimate sad witnesses of truth from Luther onwards have complained so long and often about your spiritless teachings, lives and acts, and about which God himself has grieved, cried, shouted and lamented, with the help of the holy scripture, the prophets and the apostles? Would you like to improve yourselves and reject all godless creatures, leaven,[55] false teachers, money-loving, voracious and worldly priests or not? Do you want to cast out your antichristian nature and spiritless teachings, messengers and buyers from God's temple or preserve these and other things which are of eternal ungodly pharisaic nature? What you teach and how you act, will turn against you! We had to lose, hate, deny, leave and neglect our

---

51   Jdt. 7:6–12.
52   Esth. 7:10, Ex. 12:29, Jdt. 13:7–8 and Ezek. 32:22–23.
53   Matt. 13:25–40.
54   Abraham Calov (1612–1686) and Samuel Pomarius (1624–1683). See chapter introduction, p. 140.
55   Cf. Matt. 16:6: "Then Jesus said unto them, Take heed and beware of the leaven of the Pharisees and of the Sadducees".

lives, well-being and everything that you seek in the world, in order to serve God, to follow Christ, to speak for His poor, to testify to His truth which opposes entirely your word, preaching, service, false church and fake gods of the pulpit. And you have persecuted, blasphemed and expelled it in us and other witnesses of truth like ungrateful Jews, until it turned like fire, hammer and sword against you. The more you want to suppress and exterminate it in us like the papists wanted to do in Luther and the Jews in Paul, the more it will reveal, devour, annihilate and devastate you. You will not have rain or blessing from heaven over you until you give back to God what you have taken from him and search, capture, hear and follow once again His banned word, witnesses and servants of the cross. You will have to act like Elias, David, Joseph, Job and Christ who also had to search Ahab, Zedekiah and Belshazzar and had to neglect all of their wise men, priests and prophets to hear and find God's true word and testimony in Micah, Daniel and Jeremiah. Josiah had to act like this to find it in Huldah.

To seek and hear God's testimony on earth among you, when you and D. Arcularius[56] shout God's word from your pulpits, is like seeking life among the death, like seeking figs among the thorns. You neither know the spirit of the new Adam in Christ nor in God's word, church, kingdom and servants. You have discarded it a long time ago and banned it from you from the time of Luther onwards. How do you think you can find God's word, church and testimony, if you just follow the flesh? That you do not want to know, hear or accept, because you are only interested in yourselves. You judge us, Jacob Böhme and all witnesses of truth as wrongly as the Pharisees and papists judge, hate and persecute Christ and Luther.

The most important witnesses of truth from the times of Luther onwards everybody can search and read in Johann Micraelius's *Historia Ecclesiastica*[57]

---

56   Probably Johann Daniel Arcularius (1650–1710), pastor from 1686 at the Katharinenkirche and senior at the Lutheran ministerium in Frankfurt/Main. He wrote a polemical work against Bartolomaeus Sclei: Johann Daniel Arcularius, *Das Zeugnüß Gottes auff Erden. Wie solchs nach Anweisung Göttl. Worts auf Erden zu finden/ und heylsam zu gebrauchen stehet. Sam[m]t kurtzen Anmerckungen über des so genanten Bartholomaei Sclei, Theosophische Schrifften/ Die Er nennet: Allgemeine und geheime/ doch einfältige Teutsche Theologie, gegründet in dem dreyfachen Göttlichen Offenbahrungs-Buch/ der H. Schrifft/ der grossen und kleinen Welt. Deren Grund und Warheit hiessigen Christlichen Gemeinde/ und allen rechtglaubigen Christen zum Unterricht und Warnung kürtzlich auff die Prob gestellet* (Frankfurt [Main]: 1688).

57   Johannes Micraelius, *Historia Ecclesiastica, Qua Ab Adamo Judaicae, & à Salvatore nostro Christianae Ecclesiae, ritus, persecutiones, Concilia, Doctores, Haereses & Schismata proponuntur, edita cura Danielis Hartnacci, Pomerani* (Leipzig/Frankfurt [Main]: 1699).

and Petrus Glaserius's *Prophesies of Luther*,[58] Amersbach,[59] Spitzel, Saubert, Winckler, Kortholt, Meyfahrt, Heinrich Müller[60] and in my Speculum *Pastorum*[61] and other tracts, in *Excidium Germaniae* by Joachim Betke,[62] in the writings of Potinius and his book about the great affliction,[63] in Ratthmanius's | 10

---

58 Martin Luther, *Hundert und zwanzig Propheceyunge/ oder Weissagung/ des Ehrwirdigen Vaters Herrn Doctoris Martini Luthers/ von allerley straffen/ so nach seinem tod über Deutschland von wegen desselbigen grossen/ und vielfaltigen Sünden kommen solten. Aus seinen Büchern zusammen gezogen/ und welche Lateinisch geschrieben verdeutscht Durch M. Petrum Glaser/ Kirchendiener zu Dresden* (Eisleben: 1557).

59 Probably Heinrich Ammersbach, *Rettung der reinen Lehre Dd. Lutheri, Meisneri, Speneri, und andrer/ welche lehren: Daß aus einem Christen und Christo gleich als eine Person wärde/ daher ein gläubiger Christ wol sagen könne: Ich bin Christus/ Gott zu Ehren und frommen Christen zum Trost/ Satan aber zum Trotz/ und sonderlich dem so genandten Balthasar Rebhan, als einem Erz-Lästrer das Maul zustopffen/ Und dann nicht weniger Hn. Johann Conrad Schneidern/ Predigern im Dom zu Halberstadt/ Seine hiebevor von diesem Punct herauβgegebne Theses zu examiniren / Auffgesetzet und in den Druck gegeben Von Henrico Hansen/ M. I.U.D.* (Frankfurt [Main]: 1678).

60 Probably Heinrich Müller, *Himmlischer Liebes-Kuß/ Oder Ubung deß wahren Christenthumbs/ fliessend auß der Erfahrung Göttlicher Liebe / Vorgestellet von M. Henrico Müllern/ Predigern der Gemeind zu S. Marien in Rostock* (Frankfurt [Main]/Rostock: 1659).

61 Friedrich Breckling, *Speculum Seu Lapis Lydius Pastorum: Darinnen alle Prediger und Lehrer dieser letzten Welt sich beschawen/ und nach dem Gewissen/ als für Gottes alles sehenden und richtenden Augen/ ohne Heucheley ihrer selbst/ ernstlich prüfen und examiniren sollen/ Ob sie rechte/ von Gott erkandte und gesandte Prediger/ Lehrer/ Bisschöffe und Superintendenten seyn/ oder nicht; Ob sie den rechten oder falschen Propheten gleich; Ob sie Christi oder deß Antichrists Bild an sich haben; Ob sie mit der rechten oder falschen Apostel Ken[n]zeichen und Eigenschaften bezeichnet. Denen Frommen/ und die sich von dem Geist Gottes lehren und straffen lassen/ zu Christ-brüderlicher Erinnerung/ Aufweckung/ Prüfung und Besserung; den Gottlosen/ Heuchlern/ Halßstarrigen und Wiedersprechern aber zum Zeugniß auffgesetzet/ und auff ihr Gewissen/ nach der Regel deß Wortes Gottes/ vor Augen gestellet/ durch M. Fridericum Brecklingium, Pastorem zu Handewitt/ in dem verwüsteten Holstein* (Amsterdam: 1660).

62 Joachim Betke, *Excidium Germaniæ. h.e. Gründlicher und warhafftiger Bericht/ wer daran Ursach/ daß zur Zeit des Alten Testaments/ das Judenthumb/ und zur Zeit des Newen Testaments/ Deutschland/ zum zehenfachen Sodom worden/ und Gott deßwegen mit Schwerdt/ Krieg/ Hunger und Pest/ als seines Zorns-Plagen/ dasselbe verderben/ außbrennen/ schleiffen/ zur Wusten machen/ und Menschen und Vieh darin ohne Barmhertzigkeit außrotten lassen; und vollends wie das Alte Israel/ nach der Drewung Pauli, Rom. II. v. 20. von seinem Angesicht verstossen muß. Sampt einer kurtzen Delineation des Decreti Stultiæ, oder dem Geheimnüß der Göttlichen Thorheit. Durch Joachim Betkium, Weyland trewen Zeugen und Dienern Jesu Christi, des Königs über alle Könige/ zu Linumb verfertiget/ und nun durch Christliche Hertzen zum Druck befordert; mit einer Vorrede des Editoris von dem Inhalt und Zweck dieses Buchs* (Amsterdam: 1666).

63 Conrad Potinius, *Deß Ehrwürdigen hochbegabten Herren Conradi Potinii Pastoris zu Wittmund/ Sehr heylsahme Erinnerung/ Von der letzten grossen Trübsal/ Welche der gerechte*

Glaubens-Posaune Lutheri,[64] in the *Apologia Praetorii*[65] and other writings by Hoburg, in Derschau's *Hodosophia*,[66] in the "Piis desiderii", D. Speners *Theosophia*[67] and *12 complaints about the annoying Christendom*[68] and in my *Fredericus Resurgens*[69] and *Anticalovius*.[70] A preacher in Holstein, my blood brother[71] Fredericus Petri, has compiled a lot of such witnesses and published

---

Gott/ über den gantzen Erdenkräyß [...] Fürnehmblich über Teutschlandt/ und gantz Europam, zwar Zur Läuterung und Reinigung der Frommen und Bußfertigen/ Aber gäntzlicher vertilgung und schändlichem untergang der Gottlosen in kurtzem ergehen lassen wird. Zwar ohn vorwissen deß Authoris, doch auß guter Wolmeinung/ und vielen irrigen Sündern zur warnung/ und Rettung Ihrer Seelen/ kürtzlich ans Liecht gegeben/ Von Christophero Roselio, Predigern zu Schwarne (Bremen: 1636).

64   Hermann Rathmann (1585–1628). Breckling mentions the work in his "Catalogus Testium Veritatis", nr. 26, but a copy of it could not be located.

65   Elias Praetorius [Christian Hoburg], *Apologia Praetoriana. Das ist: Spiegels derer Mißbräuche beym heutigen Predig-ampt/ Gründliche Verthedigung: Wider die Lutherische Prediger in Lübeck/ Hamburg und Lüneburg. Darinnen Dero gedruckte Warnung von Wort zu Wort ordentlich und gründlich wiederleget/ auch dero Crimina falsi, in verfälschung der Allegaten, zerstümelung und verkehrung der Worte/ fein deutsch vor augen gestellet werden. Ihnen Zur nottürfftigen Uberweisung ihrer Verführung/ Heucheley und Falschheit/ auch zu besserer Prüffung/ und da es beliebet zur redlichen Beantwortung/ fein deutsch vorgehalten. Vor dem nunmehr hereinbrechenden grossen Gerichtstage des Herrn/ Herrn Zebaoth* (s.l.: 1653).

66   Reinhold von Derschau, *Hodosophia Viatoris Christiani. Das ist: Die Christliche Wanderschafft Des Christlichen Wandersmanns/ auff dem Wege deß Lebens/ denselben zu finden und zu gehen; hingegen den Weg des Verderbens/ zu fliehen und zu meyden. In einer Tafel Bildnüßweise vorgestellet/ und mit heylsamer Erklärung außgeleget. Darin unser gantzes Christenthumb practice gezeiget/ auch eines jeden Menschen/ insonderheit Christen/ Ursprung und Anfang/ Leben und Wandel/ Mittel und Ende/ mit lebendigen Farben abgemahlet wird. Zuförderst aus Heil. Göttl. Schrifft/ hernach aus vieler vortrefflicher Theologen und anderer vornehmer und berühmten Männer Schrifften/ methodicè zusammen getragen/ mit lieblichen Rosen und Lilien/ Christlicher Freundlichkeit und Bescheidenheit/ auch bittern durchdringenden/ doch heilsamen Wermuth der nöthigen Redlichkeit und Warheit angefüllet/ und zur treuen Nachfolge und Warnung/ und vätterlicher Schuldigkeit/ Kindern und Kindes-Kindern hinterlassen* (Frankfurt [Main]: 1675).

67   Probably Philipp Jakob Spener, *Die allgemeine Gottesgelehrtheit aller glaubigen Christen und rechtschaffenen Theologen. Auß Gottes wort erwiesen/ mit den zeugnüssen vornehmer alter und neuer reiner Kirchen-Lehrer bestätiget/ Und Der so genannten Theosophiae Horbio-Spenerianae, Zur gründlichen verantwortung entgegen gesetzt* (Frankfurt [Main]: 1680).

68   Probably Wolfgang Dominicus Beer, *Zwölff Klagen über das ärgerliche unchristliche Christenthumb/ So von unterschiedlichen Evangelischen Lehrern in diesem siebenzehenden Seculo geführet worden sind / Auß ihren Schrifften zusammen getragen/ und/ den heutigen sichern Welt-Christen zur Nachricht und Warnung/ Von einem Bekenner der Warheit Ans Licht Gestellt. Sampt einer Vorrede D Philipp Jacob Speners* (Duisburg: 1684).

69   Breckling/Gifftheil, *Fridericus Resurgens* (s.l.: 1683).

70   Breckling, *Anticalovius* ([Wesel]: 1688).

71   Friedrich Petri resp. Friedrich Petersen (c.1633–1665). Deacon in Viöl. Breckling mentions in his "Catalogus Testium Veritatis", nr. 105 that Petri was his cousin.

them in his *Hardes, Prediger* to reflect upon. Mr M. Becker[72] and Picker[73] in Königsberg have done the same. The person who wants to collect and publish such witnesses and testimonies as Flacius,[74] Wolfius[75] and Lauterbach[76] have done, bears witness and does a really good job. Everybody can search for the persecuted and banned which are known to him in his place of residence and reveal them.

Like all righteous confessors from Adam, Christ and Luther onwards, we try to be a unity and to coincide in one belief and commitment to the truth. We do not want to unify with the contemporary, schismatic, self-seeking and self-heightening, sanctifying, false, worldly-shaped, carnal and pharisaic sects, priests, prophets, alarm sounding rebellious libertines and rascals and their new gospel, because they have comforted, discharged and praised the old Adam from the time of Cain up to now. I hate such false rational teachings, carnal theology, spiritless doctrine, human works and pharisaic hypocrisy and will destroy them, even from the grave. I will follow the example of Luther, Tarnovius[77] and many other pious teachers who have done this likewise and are still doing this today, which the writings of Holzhausen, especially *Beneplacito*

---

72   Melchior Becker (*d. c.*1693).
73   Johann Piker (*c.*1640–1693). Breckling mentions Johann Piker and Melchior Becker in his "Catalogus Testium Veritatis", nr. 121, though he does not say a word about a collection of witnesses of truth. A copy of a work with such a content could not be identified.
74   Matthias Flacius, *Catalogus testium Veritatis, Qui ante nostram aetatem reclamarunt Papae. Opus varia rerum, hoc praesertim tempore scitu dignißimarum, cognitione refertum, ac lectu cum primis utile atq; necessarium. Cum Praefatione Mathiae Flacii Illyrici* [...] (Basel: 1556).
75   Johann Wolff, *Lectionum memorabilium et reconditarum tomus secundus. Habet hic lector ecclesiae, Vatum, Politicorum, Philosophorum, Historicorum, aliorumq́; sapientum & eruditorum pia, grauia, mira, arcana, & stupenda; iucunda simul & utilia, dicta, scripta, atq; facta; Vaticinia item, vota, omina, mysteria, Hieroglyphica, miracula, visiones, antiquitates, monumenta, testimonia, exempla virtutū, vitiorum, abusuum; typos insuper, picturas, atq; imagines* [...] (Lauingen: 1600). The *Lectiones Memorabilis* were an extended version Flacius' *Catalogus testium veritatis*. See Sabine Schmolinsky "Positionen in den Lectiones memorabilis des Johann Wolff (1600)", in *Endzeiten. Eschatologie in den monotheistischen Weltreligionen*, ed. Wolfram Brandes and Felicitas Schmieder (Berlin: 2008), 369–417, here 384–386.
76   Matthias Flacius, *Catalogus Testium Veritatis. Historia der zeugen/ Bekenner und Märterer/ so Christum und die Evangelische warheit biß hieher/ auch etwa mitten im Reich der finsternus/ warhafftig erkennet/ Christlich und auffrichtig bekennet/ und dem Bäpstlichen vermeinten Primat/ irrthum/ ergerlichen leben und lastern/ erstlich widersprechen/ Auch mehrertheils über solchem Christlichen kampff/ unbillichem haß/ grewliche verfolgung/ harte gesencknus/ und den todt selber ritterlich außgestanden und erlidten haben.* [...]. Translated by Conrad Lautenbach (Frankfurt [Main]: 1573).
77   Probably Paul Tarnow (1562–1633), professor in theology in Rostock.

Stultiae Divinae[78] prove clearly. He who does not leave this Babylon and antichristian phariseedom and does not come to us, to Christ's truth, kingdom of the cross and spiritual church community on mount Zion should perish with the world, its sects and mendacious realm. He, who leaves the light, spirit and community of Christ and of His good members of the cross will be imprisoned by devilish hypocrisy, satanic evil, lies and darkness of the world, though he imagines himself to be seeing, rich, righteous, pious, full, to be something and everything. That person will go to waste and is doomed and damned like Quirin Kuhlman,[79] Eva Fröhlig,[80] Peter Maurits[81] and many other false sects, followers of Böhme, Lutherans, Quietists, Quakers, Separatists, libertines and rascals, with whom I absolutely do not have an alliance. Woe betide me if someone like that would praise me! The more they scold, despise and blaspheme me, the more it suits me and the more God's praise can be applied to us. Luke. 6.

Our Lutheran teachers believe that they are, like the old Jewish priests, sent and called by God before all other sects and that they teach God's word rightly. They believe that they are God's true servants and ministry, through which God wants to teach, convert and enlighten the people properly and that apart from their service and office no word and enlightenment of the spirit can be found.

---

78 Johann Christoph Holtzhausen, *Divinum Salvificae Stultitiae Beneplacitum, Das Göttliche Wolgefallen durch eine solche Predigt seelig zu machen/ Welche für aller Menschen Natürlicher Vernunft und Weltweißheit Thorheit ist. Dem verdamlichen Irrthum und falschem Fundament der Socinianischen Haupt-Ketzerey. Und aller Derer/ Die es in diesem Punct halßstarrig mit ihnen halten entgegen gesetzt* (s.l.: 1680). Cf. also Breckling, "Catalogus testium veritatis", nr. 113.

79 Quirinus Kuhlmann (1651–1689), German poet and prophet. From 1673, Kuhlmann lived in Leiden, where he changed his views radically under the influence of Boehme. Breckling and his wife visited him 1674 in Leiden, where Kuhlmann caused, at least in Breckling's opinion, confusion and aberration. Quirin Kuhlmann, *Widerlegte Breklingsworte aus zweien Brifen an Andreas Luppius gezogen. Hibei sind gefüget das 34 (49) und 35 (50) Kühl-Jubel aus dem Kühlsalomon* (Amsterdam: 1688), A1^r.

80 The prophet Eva Margaretha Frölich (d.1692), originally from Riga, was banished from Sweden in 1685 because she tried to convince King Charles XI to travel to the holy land to build the visible Jerusalem. She moved to Amsterdam afterwards. Johann Heinrich Feustking, *Gymnaeceum heretico fanaticum, Oder Historie und Beschreibung Der falschen Prophetinnen/ Quäckerinnen/ Schwärmerinnen/ und andern sectirischen und begeisterten Weibes-Personen/ Durch welche die Kirche Gottes verunruhiget worden; sambt einem Vorbericht und Anhang/ entgegen gesetzet denen Adeptis Godofredi Arnoldi* (Frankfurt [Main]/Leipzig: 1704), 299–304, here 300–301.

81 Peter Mauritius, also Peter Moritz (c.1670) was a salter and freethinker in Halle an der Saale in Germany. He was banished first from Halle and later from Dresden and lived subsequently as a chemist and doctor in the Dutch Republic. Gottfried Arnold, *Kirchen- und Ketzerhistorie*, vol. 3/4 (Frankfurt [Main]: 1729), 109–115.

They think that they know God's testimony on earth better than anyone else. They believe that they have the holy scripture on their side and are the only truly reformed and pure church from which nobody should separate himself. In their opinion, they alone possess the true, pure and apostolic teachings. They think that their teachings and teachers have no flaws, but that only life and the listeners have deficiencies. They are convinced that they have left Babel and the world completely and have gone to God in His Zion. These and other advantages they accredit to themselves with the old Jews still this very day. By this they turn, the Papists and every other sect, against God and His word, who also accredit themselves these advantages. I have continuously proved to them that this is wrong in every one of my writings and have showed as clear as the sun the contrary to be truly true as well. I will bear the debts of all humans, orally or in writing, if Christian authorities, teachers and listeners desire this and would like to be told and convinced very clearly of God's spirit and word. God has commanded me and them to believe His ancient prophets and apostles, to examine and accept their testimony, to convert to their truth and to defend God's ancient word and truth against these new Pharisees. | Fortunately, there are nowadays still some who hear, believe and follow Christ and His prophets more than the contemporary false teachers and apostles, because Christ and His testimony, spirit and word still lives, walks, speaks and testifies in His spiritual church body among them.

Even if we have found Joshua and His priests in the holy scripture, we still need to search and research God's testimony on earth today, to look for what God tells us and testifies of our teachers, churches, word and sects, because there is so much dispute and quarrel over that in the world and everybody justifies himself and wants to be the greatest and best and interpreter of God's word after His own meaning, spirit, opinion and head. Nobody shows the people, with the help of John the Baptist, the way to the light, to their salvation, truth, wisdom, leader, life, king, shepherd, teacher, high priest and bridegroom Christ and orders them to follow only Him. Almost nobody is saying "it is not me"; "I have to become smaller, in order that Christ can grow and become great, rich, wise and learned again". They all want to become, do, learn and develop without God and thus they deny God in everyone and respect Him for nothing and they say together with Babel "it is me" and actually mean that they are the best teacher, priest, false God of the pulpit and horse in the stable and do not have to listen to John, a truly great teacher, sent by God personally, who says, "it is not me" and to Daniel who is extremely humble, like Christ and Paul are too John 1, Gal. 6, 1 Tim. 1.

Because our Pharisees heighten themselves enormously and choose to sit next to the Antichrist in God's temple and believe that they alone possess the right to teach and that God should not have the power to use the talents of a simple shoemaker like Jacob Böhme to make apostles out of unlearned fishermen, to call a publican to the gospel, to appoint a cowherd as a prophet, to choose the foolish to disgrace the wise, to use the mouths of young children to praise himself in the temple, to ban the buyers from the temple with the help of his whip, to send His son and messenger to their vineyard and claim its fruits or to install a preacher and carpenter in His temple who does not belong to the pharisaic, academic party or to talk about what he likes, when and where he likes and to whom he likes by the mouth of a simple man, woman, child and fool. Our Lutheran teachers and high priests have even robbed God's godliness, power, honour, office, regiment and everything else and have placed themselves over God. Now they have to be, do, develop, teach and preach everything themselves and they want to do everything better than God. By doing so, they deny God and show in all of their actions that they think nothing of Him, after Psalm 14, 53, 73. They do not want to know God anymore, whose task is to lead them, reign over them and command them to free His captured people and sheep from their spiritual Egypt and Babylon. Luke 19. They think that God should have to say as little among them as under the rule the pharaoh in the Old Testament. If a converted Saul comes to their temple, he is immediately considered a rebel. Barabbas is esteemed more highly among them than Christ is. Why should God treat those Pharisees differently than the ancient ones? And how could they end better than the old Jerusalem?

God has punished them, not just with themselves, but also with blindness and darkness, with wrong appreciation and judgments, with false, spiritless teachings and opinions, with loads of impressive titles and books, with their own mind and discretion and with all kinds of spiritual sins and plagues, with which he has haunted ancient Egypt and Jerusalem like Johann Arndt has proven thoroughly about the ten plagues of Egypt.[82] They also do not consider those things that concern their peace, but are only looking after themselves and their old pharisaic nature and peace and try to hold on to them in the same preposterous way as the ancient Pharisees did. They neither listen to nor tolerate Christ and Paul in their midst, but worship their golden calf and phoney gods of the pulpit. For that reason, they should punish and condemn themselves

---

82   Johann Arndt, *Zehen Lehr- und Geist-reiche Predigten: Von den Zehen grausamen und schröcklichen Egyptischen Plagen: welche der Mann Gottes Moses für dem verstockten Könige Pharao in Egypten/ kurtz vor dem Außzug der Kinder Israel/ durch Gottes Würckung hat gethan: Was massen all solche Plagen geistlicher Weise vor dem Ende der Welt widerkommen/ und über das Menschliche Geschlecht/ insonderheit über die jetzt verstockte böse Christenheit/ ergehen und verhänget werden sollen* (Frankfurt [Main]: 1657).

and every one of their actions, judgments and undertakings, take the walk of shame and fail in everything that they undertake against God and His foolish servants of the cross. They should be treated as they treat us and others. | By condemning, blaspheming or persecuting us, they condemn themselves and work themselves into the ground. Retaliation is due for the way they leave us, cast us out and starve us. They look at us in their own peculiar way and scold us for that which they are in God's eyes. They think that we are separatists, but they are separatists themselves who isolate themselves from Christ, His church of the cross and us. They scold us for Enthusiasts and Quakers and follow their own spirit and Satan's plan with Judas. They call others syncretists, but have mixed and reconciled themselves with the flesh, the world, with Satan and hell. Everything they call us, they are themselves and we are not. Everything they plan together with Saul against us makes sinners out of them and will eventually destroy them. They have been examined and weighed a long time ago and have been found to be too light by Christ who still walks physically hidden among them, in order to test them.

We alone have the right and power to do in every church, consistory and academy whatever we want! What we do, is commonly valid! Who wants to master us? Who wants to convince us and prove that our teachings and actions are not right? We have the Holy Scripture on our side which is the Lord's temple! Here is Christ! We are in God's office and all our preaching and absolving is nothing, but the word and voice of God, because God has attached His word to His office. Who does not hear us, does not hear God! Who wants to claim that our calling is not godly? Or that we do not teach God's pure word or are His true church? Why should God ask about Jacob Böhme? Why should he pay attention to Breckling and others who we have hated, blasphemed, expelled and persecuted? Should God enhance and straighten such unimportant things? So proud and wrong are our Pharisees that they do not value God's word and judgment at all, until it strikes them for sure.

Who makes them so blind and stubborn, but Satan? Who makes them look at us bad-tempered, after the Book of Wisdom 2:5, but Satan? Who teaches them that the heart spares what belongs to you? They retire as soon as they have gotten hold of a lucrative office and rich marriage. In that moment, they think their soul is good, because now they have everything they have longed for and will have for many years, after Matt. 16, Luke 1, 2, 3. Who makes them so proud to judge and condemn Jacob Böhme and us this presumptuously, but Satan? Who drives them in the direction of Calovius to agree with him and with the rest of the crowd, but Satan? Who imagines them to masquerade as angels of light and preachers of justice, but Satan? Who has put them on top of the temple and before the highest altar to speak as presumptuous as the Pharisees before

God and to spit out such unspiritual and unsalted sermons, like Satan? Isa. 28, 29, Luke. 18. Who has taught them every false delight of the world that Christ, Paul and His other apostles despise? Who gives them a worthless payment for their loyal services and sermons, but Satan who they and the Antichrist serve to obtain worldly money? Matt. 4. Would you like to encounter fire and hammer, the iron sceptre and the double-edged sword of God's word? Will not all believers praise God to be overcome by His word and truth? Is not he who mistakes such false teachers for Christ's servants and regards their sermons as God's pure word very blind and does he not reveal that he was not sent and enlightened by God? He who mistakes such worldly crowds and their blind leaders for Christ's spiritual church body, does not know the true Church of Christ and the way in which it differs from the world.

If Jacob Böhme, I or another servant of the cross speak to them by the authority of the cross or write to them and make God's word and testimony known to them, they run off very fast and think by themselves "what does he have to write us about", "what should he talk about to us" or "why should he punish us or teach us what is righteous and good"? What is that, but total spiritual arrogance and pharisaic pride and impertinence? | What do you arrogant mules imagine yourselves to be? What are you, but blind persons and fools in the eye of the word and judgment of Christ? Matt. 23. You hypocrites and varnished grave diggers! Who has made you this arrogant? In what are you better than I, Jacob Böhme and others who try to serve and follow Christ under His banner with the cross without ever looking back at the world and its benefits? Should we practice usury with our talents to please you? Or should the devil alone have the power in the world to speak to the priests and should Christ and His members of the cross be silent? Who has picked you and raised you to the pulpit? God or humans and liars? Say goodbye to your fine outward appearance and abandon your stubborn courage or God will humiliate you very soon and speak with such derisive lips and serious anger to you that you will feel for sure there is a God in heaven who notices you and does not let such a plan succeed, after Psalm 2, 1 Sam. 2. Who has sent you? From where do you come? What are you looking for and what do you intend? For whom do you preach and who do you serve? Where have you learnt about God's word and from whom have you received it? For whom do you live? Who do you study and follow? What kind of spirit drives and moves you? Whose work drives you? Why do you learn and absolve? What do you have to say to those who have led you with their sermons into contemporary and future deterioration? What will be your reward in the end? You get the hell away from here, you accursed evildoers, after Matt. 7, 25!

Judge for yourselves, if one should attach the highest dishonour to the holy name of the holy God, because he sends such carnal, blind, wrong and incapable teachers and guardians to His church? Should God not first anoint them, enlighten them and instruct them with the help of His spirit, before He sends them to our Jerusalem? And how can they be recognised and accepted? After Matt. 22, 23. Do we nowadays speak and preach the word which God wants us to preach to these people? Does God himself teach them His word which has power in and through us?

Have we taught God's word and testimony with the help of His spirit and in such a way as God wants it to be taught today? Have we testified it properly and truthfully to everyone, without human favour, fear and respect of person? As God's word and testimony on earth? 1 Pet. 4. Or have we learnt it only from people through reason or have stolen it from the Bible and consequently talk about it and repeat it like unspiritual parrots do? Is our calling godly or human? Because it goes best without pursuing an agenda of our own! Do we hold God's or our own sermon? Do we search God or ourselves in there? Are our rational human teachings, theology, catechisms and their literal knowledge without deficiencies? Are our spirit- and powerless teachings, sermons and unspiritual priests actually faultless? Are not all spiritless and wrong actions among us caused by spiritless teachings and sinful priests? Do we know, hear and accept Christ's church body, members and servants among us or do we hate, persecute and banish them? Should we not have separated ourselves from people like that a long time ago as we have separated ourselves from the old Pharisees? What kind of difference is there between the church of Christ and the world? Are our contemporary churches, teachers and sects which we can recognise by the flesh the truthful and spiritual church and teachers of Christ or not? Because the flesh and carnal teacher are of no use and we do not recognise anybody after the flesh? After John 6, 2 Cor. 5, 6, 7. Are the contemporary wrong teachers not first and foremost guilty of every decay, hardship, punishment and wrongness, because they promote unspiritual sermons, rational teachings and wrong absolving among us? What do God and His word have to say to that? Do they want to be convinced of everything that is wrong and be corrected? Therefore, we offer to bear the debts of all human beings and to serve them through the spirit, out of love of Christ who leads in every truth. We want to make ourselves useful to everyone for the common benefit with the word and the talents which God has given us and still wants to hand to us and which He has taught us and will teach us with a thousand crosses and hardships until our 60th year.

They do neither want to regard nor recognise this but say together with the ancient Pharisees "how could this one teach what is righteous and good, we are the masters, everyone should listen to us and follow us", after Psalm 4, 73, Jer. 2, 5, 6, 7, 8. | and want to seduce everyone to go with them into the pit of destruction. Therefore, we are ordered by Christ to shake the dust off our feet onto your head and testify that on judgement day you should account for your household and for all souls that have been seduced. The great temptation, misery and judgment day will dawn on you and your Jerusalem. In God's eyes, you have no excuse anymore and neither can you accuse Him nor us that you did not know that God has testified to you about everything substantially through us and so many witnesses of truth. You have despised, persecuted and tried to extinguish God's testimony on earth. Your blood will be on your head, have we blazoned, after Isa. 58, Ezek. 3, 33. God will ask for your blood and downfall and will put an end to you and to all false shepherds. Amen. Ezek. 34. This has been announced to you!

Also all other sects, humans and free spirits would like to be brought from their blindness and roam to the only right path of Christ with the help of God's word and spirit which leads everyone to the truth. We are obliged to serve them after God's word like recipients of all humans and to convince them of the truth or to call their attention to the testimonies and writings of the true witnesses of God, through which they get excellent information about their decay and all disputable elements among them. If they notice this at all, they will have to search for God and call for Him.

The impartial writings of Jacob Böhme have served many up to now and will serve them in the future if they are used correctly and humbly and are not despised and rejected by the ungrateful world to heighten itself. Now, he who wants to be instructed by him about this will experience that there is no lack of God and that he has no reason to accuse God. He also does not have an excuse to claim that he did not know the truth and did not find it in anyone and anything. We are willing to be corrected by anyone who knows it better and who is like everybody else obliged to serve us with their talents. Judge for yourselves if there could be thought of a malicious deceit of Satan to impose on us the word of worldly humans instead of God's word, carnal sermons instead of spiritual ones, rational theology instead of God's wisdom, legalism instead of good deeds, letters instead of spirit, chaff instead of wheat, word instead of power and servants of dead letters instead of servants of the spirit? How can they posses God's word and be God's servants if they hate, banish and persecute Christ's word and His servants of the cross?

They do not know the true word of God! It is a folly to them! They blaspheme it in Christ and all of His members of the cross! How then can they preach it truly in the sense of the spirit if they condemn it in us? How can they love the spiritual word of the cross and search their own wisdom, honour, praise and fame at the same time? How can someone who is only interested in the honour of being a great doctor and in heightening himself above anyone else truly deny himself and profess, preach and heighten Christ by doing good deeds and by His imitation through faith? Judge for yourselves if Christ has not installed and renewed a godly animosity between Satan's worldly empire, teachings, desire, happiness and friendship and His spiritual empire of the cross in the world? Should not all enemies of Christ become also our enemies as soon as we cross over from the world and its Pharisees with the help of Paul to Christ into His church of the cross and military camp? Should we not have to fight with Christ that we also overcome, provided that we inherit everything from Him and do not want to be overcome by the world and ourselves and be deteriorated in eternity? Should we not regard all enemies of Christ and His cross as our enemies and declare them an eternal war, because they support Satan and the world and stand up against Christ and His followers? Judge for yourselves if these overambitious worldly priests hate and persecute the evil or the good in us? If they hate and persecute Belial or Christ with His truth? If they do not intend to smother God's kingdom, spirit, word of the cross and prophecy in us and in all single-hearted humans, enlightened and gifted by God and take their freedom from them? Why do they not research everything and hold fast the things that are good? | After 1 Thess. 5. Judge for yourselves if they do not recommend themselves and their followers to other people instead of Christ? If they not just attach, bind and advise absolution more than they attach, bind and advise Christ? If they do not point everyone away from Christ and His internal temple, bind them to their outward stone churches and false religion, want to imprison all blind people forever in their Babylon, fill their stomachs and convince them to worship their beastly images instead of Christ? Even though God has pronounced great anger and plagues Rev. 14!

Who wants to convince us to take these false apostles and servants of the flesh of Satan to be Christ's church of the cross and servants? Who wants to convince us that we should treat the enemies of Christ's cross as our friends and imitate them more than Christ himself? Who wants to convince us that we should consider birds of prey as doves, thistles as fig trees and wolves as sheep? Who wants to convince us that we should treat human spirit, human thoughts, words, reason and works of lies as God's spirit, word and faith or that we should even worship human beastly images and names in Christ? Who wants to be blind on purpose and walk next to the leader of the blind into ruin, should do so, but we do not anymore. We now walk away from the world towards the bridegroom and save our soul from the downfall of the world this way. Everything that has happened to you up to now and will happen to you in the future in the sects of this world, you should thank your false teachers for whom you have chosen yourselves. That is the reward of their false religion! These are the fruits of your false prophets! By that you can recognise them in the world!

Now, that they have preached you into unhappiness, you are stuck in that situation and will decay with your body and soul like the Jews and their kings in Jerusalem and Babylon. Jer. 22. And I should say together with Jeremiah: "where are now your prophets who foretold you that the king of Babylon would not come over you and over this country". Jer. 37:19. You should experience what kind of misery and pain it brings if you leave Christ in us to whom God has ordered us to listen and if you drift away with the heart from His easy life and leadership and follow blind humans and false gods of the pulpit who cannot give light and water of life. Also not everyone wants to fornicate spiritually with human creatures. If Christ is not your life, teacher and light in you, you are dead, blind and dark, without and outside Christ. Your teachers are also, even if they are very erudite, many and wise! Judge for yourselves if it is not a malicious deceit of Satan to keep all servants of the spirit and Christ in us away from the church, to banish them and to install in every pulpit lovers of the flesh and servants of dead letters. This way Satan tries to plant evil in the world, cover it with that and kill it entirely. Is our fall therefore not deeper than we can recognise at first sight? Should we not all change from godly folly and childish belief to human wisdom and outward temple affairs of the heathens and Jews? Do we not regard the word of the cross as a folly and flee from it like we flee from death and misery, because it does not accord with our worldly interpretation and crucifies and kills our own life?

On the contrary, do we not search, love and compliment human rational wisdom and mere learning of letters and its preachers, because this makes sense to us? Has, because of that, this last of the Reformation not become much worse than the first? After 2 Pet. 2. Have we left the world together with Paul and gone to Christ or did we go together with Judas from Christ to the Pharisees, because of money and the needs of our stomachs? Who has destroyed Christ and His spirit and word in and among us? Do we act nowadays better and are we better than the first world, Sodom, Egypt and Jerusalem during the times of Noah, Lot, Jeremiah and Christ? Should Christ and Jeremiah not find nowadays as many ears among us as they did among them? Should we not know Christ and His spiritual church body correctly after the spirit in and among us? Or should we throw them from the gates of our heart and construct a false Christ, word, spirit, servant and church after the flesh and make others also believe in them? Do we have the true word of the cross about the secret hidden wisdom of God among and in us or have we made up a new and false gospel with phoney apostles which promises to make us great, rich, wise and wonderful again with the old Adam? | Judge for yourselves if we can see or if we are blind? If we are wise or if we are fools? If we are something or if we are nothing? If we are Christ or if we are equal to the world? Are we a separated and chosen holy church community after the example of Israel or have we mingled with the world and with the heathens and adopted their ways until a new empire came into existence, in which worldly spirit, wealth and greatness rules? Has God not punished us therefore with false teachers and sects, because we have not been grateful for the possession of Christ, the crucified, and for God's word of the cross in which all fullness and treasures of wisdom were hidden? Have we not been weary of such heavenly manna and was not everyone craving for something new with the schismatic Israel? Was really nobody asking with the heathens and Jews for wisdom and signs, dreams and visions? Has Satan not found all of our doors open to seduce and bewitch us like he did with Eve with the help of his new prophets, false Christs and unsteady spirits? Can we not find the open doors to Lot's home? Do we not recognise our blindness and deterioration and look for the true Christ with His church of the cross and servants of truth, because we appreciate the new false prophets too much and believe only they talk unanimously about good things? Are we bound by God's word to believe, obey and follow such false apostles, prophets and teachers who enter like thieves and murderers to reign in the sheep shelter? Should Satan, who disguises himself in sheep's clothing to look like an angel of light and who conceals himself with the name of Christ, his false teachers and prophets do no harm anymore? Should we not avoid them much more than we avoid the obvious devils and wolves? Should Satan not be unable to mix his false and true teachers like poison and sugar under the pretext and name of Christ and His word, let them shine in the world and depict everything that comes from Christ as evil and wrong? Should bad people not be able to depict evil as good and good as evil, because this corresponds with their worldly interpretation? By doing so, do they not change honey into poison like spiders and make it unedible and thus preach and teach God's word in a completely wrong way? Can Satan really teach and present everything better than they are able to? Does God's word not warn us seriously of such a false light?

Hereupon, everyone should consider and judge themselves what should be and not be done today in the service and work of God. How and from what should we separate ourselves and go out together with Paul like God's word tells us to? How and from what should we not go out together with Judas? Should we not take all enemies of Christ to be our enemies and fight them until we die? Should we not love and save all friends of Christ until the end of our lives? Are Christ's people and kingdom not separated entirely from the world? If so, should they be mixed with the realm of the world? Should we not isolate ourselves from those who have commingled with Christ illegally? Or should we, on the contrary, mingle with those from whom Christ has isolated himself spiritually? Should we return from God to humans and their worldly Babylon or from the world and its priests to God? Should we leave the persecutors and defend and support the persecuted unanimously against their persecutors or not? Should we not suffer with those who suffer and choose the community of the church of the cross instead of the world, its sects and worldly priests like God's word tells us to do? Judge for yourselves if not most of your books are without spirit, light, salt, fire, life, power, attraction, beginning and ending, head and tail? And if you do not hate these, just because God wants to give something perfect to you? Judge for yourselves if there is a chance that you will be discarded like unsavoury salt? How can those who are without spirit, light and power in them deliver something good? And how can those who do not consider with Paul their best things to be damaging and filthy, become winners and find Christ? Should not all Jews in Jerusalem be destroyed together with their Pharisees, because they supported them more than they support Christ? What will happen to you, when Christ asks you, "my dear friend, how were you able to enter"? Will not Satan himself taunt you and ask you who you are? Acts 19. And what use has such unsavoury salt? But who listens to our sermons? If Christ himself does not find faith or hearing, how can we be able to find it? Luke 18, 19.

2 Catalogue of Heretics; A Present-Day History of Heretics (c.1697)

As long as all humans are liars and scholars write learned lies and do not deal just kindly with everything, but give wrong judgments about all things, they should be led by God's spirit towards the truth, be born again and renewed, and taught what is good and be governed by Him. Truly spiritual humans who are devoted to God and taught by Him should be able to apprehend with the guidance and enlightenment of the Holy Spirit, how everything is created in spirit before God after the internal ground. Therefore, they are able to write and judge correctly and cannot be judged and known by anyone who is not truly spiritual after the work of God. Cor. 1. 2. 3. 4. Joh. 3. As opposed to anyone else, they are in possession of the Holy Scripture and are sitting in the middle of God's temple, it is told after God's word and truth. The scribes tell vain lies, because what good can they learn, if they reject, demonise, cast out and ban the word of the Lord, even if it is used correctly and applied by a Jeremiah in spirit and truth? As long as they stay blind and wrong after the flesh and further teach all of us big and small humbug and false religion and try to heal the damage done to God's people by repairing the completely depraved and scorched hypocritical situation with false cloth and new patches, they just make the rip bigger instead. In contrast, those free and unsteady spirits who have left the large Babylonian sects and have erected and built a new Zion and Philadelphia[83] with the worst enemies of the cross of Christ, yes even with the hellish seed of evil before the old Babylon in and outside of us is destroyed, should because of that be disgraced and stumble upon each other, as truthfully as the word of God, Amen.

How high has the craving for success, books, gold and all kinds of cunning spiritual and worldly robbery in spiritual and worldly estates risen and how much has it increased! How much does everyone do his best to steal this all from God and humans, in order to become the highest, richest, best, wisest, oldest, most respectable and most powerful doctor, master, superintendent, provost, bishop and pope! How keen is everybody to heighten themselves and to acquire Christ's laws and power to occupy every pulpit and to usurp all open church offices, yes even to steal God's word from the Bible! Every wolf in sheep's clothing with the appearance and name of Christ wants to seduce us to come into the pit of eternal corruption where they try to persecute and destroy the wise prophets and scribes, which God has sent to me and which have

---

83 Brecklings use of the word "Philadelphia" for "New Jeruzalem" indicates that his manuscript was mainly directed against Jane Lead and the Philadelphians. Cf. Warren Johnston, "Jane Lead and English Apocalyptic Thought in the Late Seventeenth Century", in *Jane Lead and her Transnational Legacy*, ed. Ariel Hessayon (London: 2016), 119–142.

been recognised by me and which also have been sent to them, just as all Pharisees, murderers and thieves try too.

We think that the pope and the Jesuits show us quite clearly that they want to take possession of and absorb every soul and every property in the world. Our new popes and antichrists have been taught thoroughly by them, who are full of robbery and murder and whose throats are an open grave for the purpose to rob everything that belongs to God and which they will not stop to do until they are as highly risen as the pope, though eventually they will be pushed down with Lucifer into hell by God. If such people are heretics and belong like the papists and other sects in the catalogue of heretics, I will let the world judge. Because every sect and party among the sects of Babylon call themselves white and are only interested in justifying themselves and to brand others as heretics, every one of their books, devotional books, church histories and histories of heretics are as carnal, blind, partial and wrong as they are themselves and will be found before God's court of law. | You can neither build on their human books, testimonies and histories, nor rely on those who take night owls to be doves, birds of prey to be chickens, wolves to be sheep, disciples of Christ and fishermen to be hostile animals and heretics and who regard the good as bad and the bad as good and therefore judge everything wrong. Because of that all human actions, meaning, initiatives, preaching and absolving, devotional books and histories should be censored, distinguished and judged, in the sense of God's word with the help of His spirit, the way they are for God, in order that they be brought to the light without respect of persons and everything else which is hidden in the dark and all human knowledge and nature, actions, plans, intellectual flights and false Gods are thrown down and humiliated and that everything which humiliates itself is heightened instead, like David's men rose from the wilderness instead of Saul's.[84] It should be fulfilled what was initiated in the now expanding Davidic glorious war of Christ,[85] that not one self-chosen Saul or carnally minded doctor, master and priest will heighten his God, or will hold and possess Christ's office and church together with the pope.

---

84   Cf. 1 Sam. 24:1–22; 1 Sam. 26:1–25.
85   Cf. Jane Lead, *The Wars of David, and the Peaceable Reign of Solomon: Symbolizing the Times of Warfare and Refreshment of the Saints of the Most High God, to Whom a Priestly Kingdom is Shortly to be Given, After the Order of Melchisedeck. Set Forth in Two Treatises Written by J. Lead: and According to Divine Ordination Publish'd in this Present Year of Jubilee. For the Service of All the Children of the Captivity, Now Watching and Praying in Many Countries, for the Great Jubilee of the Lord to Begin, and Follow upon this very Speedily. Containing I. An Alarm to the Holy Warriours to Fight the Battels of the Lamb. II. The Glory of Sharon, in the Renovation of Nature, Introducing the Kingdom of Christ in his Sealed Virgins, Redeemed from the Earth* (London: 1700).

Therefore, all false glory of the sects will perish, but Christ will remain our only king, master, head, shepherd and high priest and everything in everything from now on until eternity amen, like it is said in the book of Revelation which gives Him all honour. Every church history and every other book from Constantine the Great, Gregory the Great and Charlemagne onwards, thus from the pope's rise and continuation until his fall and decline, should be revised, reformed and improved more and more, every register of heretics and expurgatory indexes should be purged and what Luther, Flacius, Wolfius[86] and others have begun should be continued until our times and completely according to God's word and in the way Moses, Samuel, the prophets and apostles have prescribed it in the Old and New Testament. The book of Judges and history of the Maccabees have gone ahead of us and also Amos Comenius who has summarised and improved the history of the Hussites,[87] but not in the way Eli, Abiathar, Absalom and Adonijah or the Pharisees and such apostles, rabbis and papists would write their histories and writings after their own mind.

The histories of the Quietists and Pietists should be purged of all evil, not in the sense of the anti-chiliastic opinion, but | according to the truth and the word of God, like doctor Spener[88] and others have begun, in the way also the best grapevine should be trimmed to keep them from sectarianism and lead them back to true Christian, Catholic and apostolic chiliasm. In this way they become shaped after Christ and so impartial that lovers of every aspect of truth among the Jews, Turks, heathens and Christians will be totally convinced to become members of one head and king, that is Christ, and the poults are being collected under the wings of our mother, after Christ's and his true Catholic and apostolic church, disciples and writings, rules and commandments, manner. All nuisance and partiality, offence and obstruction will be eradicated and removed from the church and Christ's kingdom and from the entire world, amen.

218

---

86 Johann Wolff, *Lectionum memorabilium et reconditarum centenarii XVI. Habet Hic Lector Doctorum Ecclesiæ, Vatum, Politicorum, Philosophorum, Historicorum, aliorum[que] sapientum & eruditorum pia, gravia, mira, arcane, & stupenda; jucunda simul & utila, dicta, scripta, atque facta; vaticinia item, vota, omnia, mysteria. Hieroglyphica, miracula, visions, antiquitates, monumenta, testimonia, exempla virtutum, vitiorum, abusuum; typos insuper, picturas, atque Imagines* [...] (Lauingae: 1600–1608).

87 Johann Amos Comenius, *Historia Persecutionum Ecclesiae Bohemicae, Iam inde a primordiis conversionis suae ad Christianismum, hoc est, Anno 894. ad Annum usque 1632. Ferdinando secundo Austriaco regnant. In Qua Inaudita hactenus Arcana Politica, consilia, artes, & iudicia horrenda exhibentur* (s.l.: 1648).

88 Philipp Jakob Spener (1635–1705). See my introduction, p. 135.

The holy scripture is arranged completely orderly and properly written by pious and impartial people with the help of God's inspiration, according to God's sense and will, without respect of persons or human favour, fear for the truth and for justice, like the way everything is in the eye of God and can according to human understanding only be understood in spirit and belief by the simple children of God. Because of that, they are able to regulate and judge all people and sects and should every human sect's teaching, life, book, writing, history and action be regulated, canonised, censored, reformed, brought to perfection and intensified, in order that the postscripts coincide with the prescripts. Because God does not begin anything, he does not continue to the end.

Because all humans and sects and also our Lutheran and Pietists' things, books, writings, teachings, lives, academies, schools, priests and students, pulpits, preaching and graduations, actions, church regiment, false church teachings and hearings, senses and beginnings about the holy scripture and Christ's thoughts, words, works, ways, dealings, belief, love, hope, life, example and rules | deviate too much to the left and to the right and do not reach at all the heights and depths in spirit and belief and therefore do not attain the goal toward which everyone should try to move and to head, to reach out and to fight for, according to Christ.

We should necessarily compensate God for everything which we, together with the world and its sects, have robbed from him from Adam onwards until this hour and reform and organise our entire being and existence according God's word and Christ's example, if we want to escape the severe judgment of God which will come upon the pagans, false Christians, sects and shepherds with certainty, as it did before upon the Jews, their synagogues and false churches. We should extirpate and destroy every plant which the heavenly father has not planted in his grapevine, which is Christ, with the help of a new birth of the spirit, as he has done before to many others. If we measure everything with precision in our hearts, houses and temples, sweep out the pharisaic and academic leaven[89] from the heart from which every evil comes, everything is purified and sanctified and God's heaven and temple in and among us is built correctly in spirit and truth and everything in front of our door is made justifiably beautiful and new, giving no one a cause or excuse why he should not enter with a good conscience into the true community of the saints. Because those who do not listen to, believe, obey and follow the holy Catholic and apostolic church, which is Christ's bride and spiritual mother on earth and which accords with Christ's spirit and word and His stations of the

---

89   Cf. p. 155, note 55.

cross, do not have a Father in heaven and Christ as a head and saviour. Math. 18. | According to that it is time that we preach and write, instruct and correct the papists, members of the reformed church, Baptists, Socinians, Quakers and every other sect, their enormities, exorbitances and errors in teaching and life and all of their other faults and excesses with humble hearts, mouths and hands, because the ones do too many and the others do not enough. By acting so, they deviate to the right and to the left, from God's canonical word, Christ's order and example and the true Catholic and apostolic concord and community erected in spirit among us. Especially if they coincide with the Antichrist will God's spirit and word emerge and will He rely on his royal rights and go upfront and be and do all of that, like nobody can do and arrange, begin, continue to the end without Christ's spirit in us and the church. As long as people want to be blessed, punished and corrected with the help of the spirit of God and our brotherly reprimand and give back everything which has been stolen from God and surrender to Him as obedient children, we should tolerate, forgive, overlook and improve all human weakness and afflictions in them, in the same way as God overlooks, tolerates and improves these things in us. He who does not want to be punished, persuaded and convinced by God's spirit and word, cannot be helped and should be isolated, shunned and forced out of our community. 1 Cor. 5, 2 Cor. 6. The rule, church and history should first of all be true, correct, perfect and universal, after which you can use them as a guideline and angular dimension to measure, regulate, slice off, demonstrate, cut off to bring the entire false, unjust, disorderly, unregulated being of the world and every one of its sects in an orderly fashion. | Such a canon, measurement, rule, norm and all-encompassing example in the world and in the church are Christ and God's word in the holy scripture, written down as a message for every human being. They should use this to judge all priests, teachings and human actions and to condemn and reject everything which does not accord with it or even contradicts it and which should thus be regarded by everyone as an unspiritual, factious and worldly shaped body and life, as sects and false teachers. The way Christ has saved, collected, unified and insured his disciples and apostolic church, we have to restore again such a perfect example for the sake of our churches, houses, schools, academies, teachers, writings, lives and histories and recognise, admit and reject every aberration and irregularity in teaching and in life with Ezra, Nehemiah, Moses, Joshua, David and Daniel.

It is time that we search for others and bring them to their true and only shepherd, king, master and head and, to begin with the last and most dangerous sects and explain first to the Quakers their terrible aberrations and abuses to their improvement and also to censor and improve their history after God's word and Christ's example, in the hope that they run out of arguments.

Taulerus, cap. 12 institutionem[90] and further, tries to correct many present-day sects and Luther, Jac. Böhme, Kromayer,[91] Valent. Alberti,[92] Puffendorf,[93] superintendent Majus,[94] Breithaupt,[95] Spener and others intend with Taulerus the truly Christian reunification of all sects which have been separated up to now and to restore the simple belief of his world and to search with so many for a pious revival and dissident alliance. For the sectarian teachers and communities, Quakers, Collegiants and all other free and unsteady spirits, who isolate themselves, do neither want to hear nor follow us, we warn our listeners and everyone else, because they are false prophets and apostles, dreamers and enthusiasts who come to them under the sheep's clothing of | Christ's name and who are as bold as brass to take control of, change or even reject God's word, appointments, regime, baptism and last supper, but which nobody can change at all without endangering his soul or who are as daring to add anything or to take anything away. Christ has warned us against them extensively Matt. 5, Rev. We should prevent that those who leave us, because of our disorderliness and abuses, change to the other side, lapse into the other extreme and fall into the trap of seven times more worse spirits, as it happened to us partly after we left the Roman Catholic Church. Therefore, we should enter sincerely with our spirits into God through the mediation of Christ, accept God's word with great gratitude, stick to it and prove our religious obedience to God and our neighbour and grace ourselves with worthy fruits of repentance.

Therefore, the same judgment awaits us like it awaited the Jews after the reformation of Josiah and Christ as certain as possible, as certain as God's word is. What should happen to the Quakers in the face of such confusion and mess which they have caused with their negligent behaviour, because all heretics who are responsible for the offence of the teaching which we have received from God, should be wiped out. Dum vitant stulti vitia, in contraria currunt, et sic incidit in Scyllam, qui vult vitare Charibbim Stultorum Stultiae sunt omnia.[96] Should we wipe out the terrible deviations of the Labadists,[97]

---

90 Johannes Tauler, *Insignis Theologi Sermones de festis, & solennitatibus Sanctorum. simúlque divinae Institutiones nuper inve[n]tae, cum Epistolis aliquot, quibus Deo uniri per spiritales exercitationes nemo non facile docetur [...]*. (Lugduni: 1558).
91 Hieronymus Kromayer (1610–1670).
92 Valentin Alberti (1635–1697).
93 Possibly Samuel Pufendorf (1632–1694).
94 Probably Johann Heinrich May senior (1653–1719), with whom Breckling corresponded.
95 Maybe Joachim Justus Breithaupt (1658–1732).
96 "While they whish to avoid the silly vice of the dangerous whirlpool Charybdis, they run in the opposite direction and fall into the Scylla of the fools, that way they are totally foolish."
97 Supporters of Jean de Labadie (1610–1694).

in order that they return to God in heaven and to their neighbour, which they do not know, and cast a light on how and in what way they have heightened themselves over God and over his word and truth, which they did in the same way the pope did, and have regarded themselves as the only and true chosen people? They have built on that their absolute decree | which they believed no one should reject and hold as infallible. Therefore, they think that all of their things, sermons and writings should be held as infallible without examination and that no one should judge words and deeds anymore. In contrast, they have even convicted everyone who was sympathising with them faithfully and was willing to agree with them as blindly as the Quakers, separated men and women from each other, interfered in God's royal rights and acted freely and unopposedly the way they wanted to like true popes. I will not speak about the hidden and secret things and opinions which the most prominent among them possess and of which some were described by Petrus Dittelbach.[98] This is why God will command to rob and shatter them.

We should reveal what aspects of a guideline are twisted and wrong and correct them. We should judge with the help of God's word and Christ's example if the papists, Calvinists, Mennonites, Socinians, Arminians and every other sect have done enough in teachings, life and actions, according to Christ's wishes, to uncover their darkness with the help of the light and to improve and correct their lies with the help of the truth, their false being with the help of the righteous being of Christ, in the same way as Cassander,[99] Ferus,[100] Vergerius,[101] Aventroth,[102] Marcus Anton de Dominis[103] Jacobus Faber Stapulensis[104] and others among the papists, Augustin Fuhrmann[105] among the Reformed, and Joachim Betkius,[106] Saubertus,[107] Meyfartus,[108] Meisnerus,[109] doctor Spener,

---

98   Petrus Dittelbach (c.1640–1703), pastor in Neudorf in East Frisia and a temporary member of the Labadists.
99   Maybe Georg Cassander (1513–1566).
100 Maybe Jiří Ferus, also Georg Ferus (c.1585–1665).
101 Maybe Pier Paolo Vergerio the younger (1498–1565).
102 Probably Johannes Bartholomeus Avontroot (also Juan Aventrot[e]) (c.1563–1632).
103 Marco Antonio de Dominis (1560–1624).
104 Jacques Lefèvre d'Étaples (c.1455–1536).
105 Augustin Fuhrmann (1591–1648), court chaplain at the court of the Calvinist duke Johann Christian von Brieg (1591–1631).
106 Joachim Betke (1601–1663), German theologian and spiritualist who was admired very much by Breckling.
107 Probably Johannes Saubertus senior (1592–1646).
108 Maybe Johann Matthäus Meyfart (1590–1642).
109 Balthasar Meisner the younger (1587–1626).

Vegel,[110] Kortholt,[111] doctor Henricus Müller,[112] Danhauer,[113] Anton Reisserus,[114] Hartmannus,[115] Glassius[116] and others have done and begun in their pious revival and Christian measurements, which have been continued by others and will not be completed without us.

At the same time we should heal, avoid and remove the principal causes of all evil among us, like they appear in schools, academies | and among false priests in Jerusalem and in the entire country. God's word warns us about that in old passages in the Old and New Testament. First, the causes of the disease should be removed and eliminated, by purification, before we can improve and heal the damaged wounds from scratch. Improve moral behaviour and eliminate bad pastors, if you want better sheep, it is said justly about everyone. If we do not participate, God will hold his tribunal over the false shepherds in Jerusalem and over their church, because as long as the salt is unsavoury and the light among us is turned off, with what should we enlighten them and others? Do not the blind leaders among the Jews, Turks, heathens and false Christians tear everyone with them into the pit of eternal doom? And what Satan cannot demonstrate to us with the help of his Babylonians and Pharisees in the large sects, he tries to achieve by creating the deceitful impression that his enthusiasts, dervishes and false apostles are acting in the name of Christ and are illusive angels of light. Further, he tries to seduce us to embrace external hypocritical things, sects and aberrations by diverting us from Christ's simple word, spirit, belief, love, kingdom and habitation in his temple in us with the help of our own spirit, reason, fantasy, carnal mind, human wisdom, false belief, our own life, meaning, love, lust and benefit, which are the most dangerous and most internal false gods and traitors in us. That way Satan blinds us so much that we believe that God's thoughts and ways, which are in the end much higher and deeper than we | can grasp ourselves, as our own thoughts are obstructing us. Isa. 55.

About the subject of God's plans and the devil's deceit and inscrutability Jac. Acontius' *Stratagematibus satanae*[117] and Jeremias Dyke's *Self-deception*[118] can

---

110   Maybe Elias Veiel (1635–1706).
111   Probably Christian Kortholt senior (1633–1694).
112   Heinrich Müller (1631–1675).
113   Probably Johann Konrad Dannhauer (1603–1666).
114   Maybe Anton Reiser (1628–1688).
115   Maybe Johann Ludwig Hartmann (1640–1680).
116   Maybe Salomon Glassius (Glaß) (1593–1656).
117   Jacopo Aconcio, *Stratagematum satanae. Accessit eruditissima Epistola, de ratione edendorum librorum, ad Ioannem Wolfium Tigurinum, eodem authore* (Basel: 1565).
118   Daniel Dyke, *The Mystery of Self-Deceiving. Or a Discourse and Discovery of the Deceit-*

be read with great advantage. In such a manner are these last and small sects who have been extracted and distilled from the Lutheran, Reformed, Catholic and other sects and who have heightened themselves above all previous sects and have promoted their sect masters as the best horse in the stable. They all try to crow the loudest that they mix up David, Daniel, Moses, Samuel, Paul and Christ with the sinners, try to change everyone into the greatest sinners, they even degrade everyone profoundly, help to carry every burden and pardon every sin and also die in their innocence like guilty heathens and could be counted among the evildoers.

Against this, they will protest most likely with Lucifer and all heretics, will say something and everything and will want to rise as high as the pope as they are able to, because their sectarian listeners follow them faithfully and everyone does his best anyway to be the first, wisest, richest, highest, best, most pious and holy unspiritual and worldly body and soul with the Antichrist. But Christ shines like the light in the darkness, intermingles like a bad habit among the seekers and sinners and teaches to those who believe that it is something suitable even for the greatest sinner that it is not.

Yes, God himself gives his fatherly love and mercy in Christ together with the entire heaven to the sinners and all humans, Jews, Turks and heathens, he enlightens and awakens them, and fills, feeds and refreshes their mouths and hearts with life and breath | and orders them to preach the gospel about the general mercy in Christ to all heathens on a daily basis and to educate them above others in the entire creation to become wise, to sound in their ears with Christ as long as is needed for the conversion, enlightenment and blessing of all sinners. For what it is we can do with God, we have no excuse and cannot say with God, "what should I do more, what have I not done yet for my neighbour", "what has God done for me and how?", "have I done to me what God wanted?" and "what do I think that God and all humans should do to me?", after Isa. 5, 6, 60 ff. I see every day, hear, smell and taste how good, friendly, loyal, truthful and merciful God treats all humans and covers them all with his heaven, enlightens them with his sun, refreshes them with his breath, supplies them with food, clothing and every need for the body and soul and fills their heart with life and mercy. All creatures try to imitate God by handing over everything they have and can produce for the sake of the service and the needs of all people and reach for the highest perfection as far as they can, in order that they go ahead of us and bring themselves to God and to every perfection.

226

---

fulnesse of Mans Heart. Written by the Late Faithfull Minister of Gods Word Daniell Dyke, Bachelour in Divinity. Published since his Death, by his Brother I.D. Minister of Gods word (London: 1615).

Do we want to work in the direction to serve God and all humans and to become everything to everyone, like Christ becomes to us every day? In the same way as the Labadists have risen with Lucifer among the reformed in spiritual pride and idiosyncrasy and were diffused in all directions, because of their perforated helmet,[119] has Antoinette Bourignon[120] risen from the Roman church, like a mother of all believers. How high she has ascended in spiritual pride and her own mind | in her own heaven, before she descended with Christ into nothing, hell and condemnation! And how they have declared themselves to be infallible and all of their words to be spoken by the Holy Spirit! They wanted to be believed without examination and all of their things to be accepted as godly fate. They also wanted to be consulted and heard as godly oracles and lively writings of the spirit and they even believed that they did not need to read the scripture and holy testament which God has written for us. They actually had the preposterous idea that they could recommend their own writings, which are built on Socinian foundations and constructed with Pelagianism from many old heresies, instead of scripture. This way they believed that they could build a new community of new believers.

This new community accepted Antoinette as a mother and its disciples consisted mostly of men who wanted to leave their wives, like Pierre Poiret[121] who left his pious wife for her and was accepted in her community, because he was able to comprehend her writings and to describe her life out of gratitude. In the case of the Labadists, it consisted of women who were willing to leave their husbands. Poiret was so blinded by false and selfish love that he could not see his and her spiritual destruction and could neither notice her cold-heartedness towards the poor, nor her injustice to lend her gold with usurious interest. Because of her distrust of people and children who, in her opinion, were all possessed and bewitched by Satan (although the spiritual love does not think of anything bad) and also because of her devilish advancement above all men and sects, who were not able to worship her entirely according to her spiritual measurement, she had to judge herself in everything in which she judged others, | until her judgement fell back on her. After P. Poiret found a new oracle and false god in Antoinette, he disposed of his pious wife and let her sink into misery and die, in order that he could rise with Antoinette much higher than with his wife,

---

119 In Ephesians 6:11–18, Paul warn believers to arm themselves against the powers of darkness by putting on the armour of God. The helmet of salvation is part of the armour of God. Breckling accuses the Labadists here of offering inadequate protection against the devil, which leads according to him to confusion and misconduct among them.
120 Antoinette Bourignon (1616–1680).
121 Pierre Poiret (1646–1719).

because he appreciated her as an extremely spiritual daughter of the whore of Babylon and treated everything she talked about as if it came directly from heaven. To become an heir of her gifts and of her large amount of money, he has committed himself solely to her discipline, leadership and obedience, and has learnt to interpret everything in the best tradition of the Roman church. For this reason, he advised the stressed and persecuted Huguenots in France in a public letter to join this Babylonic horror and whoredom, to participate in it and to worship everything that the papists demonstrate to them, in order to escape from the cross of Christ and the public testimony of truth. In a nutshell, this means to teach the denial of Christ to the people and to worship the image of the beast and to become part of the aberrations of papism.

Who, in the meantime, does not find large and capital faults in Antionette's many writings, is still blinded and understands as little of Christ and his supernatural kingdom, cross, word and religious life, hidden under godly foolishness as Antoinette and Pierre Poiret do. Poiret wanted to seduce the world with his hypocritical book *de Eruditione solida superficaria et falsa*[122] about the more heathen than Christ-shaped way to discipline children and lead her under the false appearance of the best religion away from the true childish innocence in Christ | towards a dishonest hypocrisy and subtle papism, like he has founded and hatched with this Antoinette. Her books he recommended so highly and distributed them with great effort. He promoted their translation in every language, although they deny Christ's satisfaction and denomination after the spirit of faith, like a gift to become blessed out of God's merciful love, which is donated to us for free. He thinks that everyone who does not accept and worship Antoinette's new Bible and moral teachings is enchanted. He and Antoinette want to replace Christ and God's word with their own beastly image in words and books.

Although such spirits and sects have some abilities to discover and destroy the exterior gifts, they cannot take away the permanent spiritual Babylon and root of all hypocrisy in themselves or in others. As long as they are too captivated and blinded by selfish love to embrace God against their subtle idiosyncrasy, they built a new Zion in Philadelphia, before the in- and outward Babylon in them has truly been destroyed and rooted out, except for the most interior spirit. Therefore, those who are lost in Christ are those whom the Holy Scrip-

---

122   Pierre Poiret, *De Eruditione Solida, Superficiaria, Et Falsa, Libri Tres. In quibus Ostensa Veritatum Solidarum via & origine, Cognitionum Scientiarumque Humanarum, & in specie Cartesianismi, Fundamenta, valor, defectus & errores deteguntur. Præmittitur Tractatus De Vera Methodo inveniendi verum, Confutationem Principiorum libri Belgici de Mundo fascinato in fine obiter exhibens. Subnectuntur nonnulla Apologetica* [...] (Amstelodami: 1692).

ture calls thieves and murderers. We should beware of them the more they shout "here is Christ" and let us believe that we can make a big start under the pretext of a false image. The good Horbius,[123] not noticing such abberations in Poiret's book about the correct education of youth, has suffered much from the publication of such a human writing and from | Poiret's arbitrariness. The count Dodo Kniphausen[124] has told me much about their hidden reasons which I want to keep quiet about as long as possible until God's honour and Christ's poverty require it to expose this, because everyone else wants to cover up human weakness with a cloak of love, just like God does to us. Poiret, like the false Christs and apostles, wants to enchant also the best and wants to win them over with great illusion of love, in order to blind and distract them with Antoinette's writings. He also wants to lead many, not with the body, but with love, back to papism. We should warn everyone of such false apostles and false Christs, after the example of Christ and Paul. Because the popularity of Johann Rothe[125] has come to an end, he does not attract anyone anymore, but tries to save his soul from this burning Sodom and Babylon by being quiet and expressing hope. For this reason, I have corresponded with him for over sixteen years, which made him accept the love of truth. We should thank God appropriately for such mercy and ask him in the name of all of his followers that He lead them further towards truth and protect them against every false spirit for eternity.

Quirinus Kuhlmannus,[126] bloated with the false praise and prophecies about him, rose high among the Lutherans in his own spirit and fantasy and has

---

123   Heinrich Horb (1645–1695).
124   Dodo Freiherr von Knyphausen (1641–1698).
125   Johannes Rothe (1628–1702).
126   Quirinus Kuhlmann (1651–1689). The poet Kuhlmann was a merchant's son in Breslau. He studied law in Jena from 1670–1673 and then in Leiden from 1673–1674. In Leiden, a radical intellectual change began. He became acquainted with religious dissenters in the Dutch Republic like Friedrich Breckling, Johann Georg Gichtel, Johannes Rothe and Tanneke Denys. In September 1674, he published his *Neubegeisterte Böhme* which was influenced by the German theosopher Jacob Boehme. Kuhlmann developed ideas about the coming of a fifth monarchy which he himself would initiate as a messiah. From 1675 onwards, Kuhlmann lived in Lübeck with his servant Magdalena von Lindaw and her three children. In March 1676, he travelled to England where he gained a small group of loyal followers. He moved into the house of John Bathurst (d.1694) in Bromley-by-Bow in 1677. Magdalena and her children joined him in England in the same year. In 1678, he travelled with his patchwork family to Constantinople to convert the sultan of the Ottoman Empire Mehmed IV, but he did not succeed. In 1679, Kuhlmann, Magdalena and her children moved to Amsterdam where he left them. He met Maria Gould [Maria Anglicana] (d.1686), a learned woman and a doctor of medicine in London, in 1683. Gould went with Kuhlmann to Amsterdam where they married in the following year. In that period, Kuhlmanns most important series of poetical works, the *Kühlpsalter*, was published. After

imagined himself not just becoming king of France and England, but also taking away the Roman empire from the emperor and splitting it up among the princes and potentates, | converting the sultan and being rewarded with the treasures of Egypt for his efforts. Moreover, he was convinced that he was Christ and the true Son of the Father *par excellence* and that he would sit between the Father and the Son and would engender a son himself who would bring like Solomon everything under his reign. There could be written entire books about his ample thoughts, plans, travels, deceits, imaginations and great pretentions. He further had three wives one after the other and he married his first wife to father his Solomon von Kayserstein.[127]

And while I have tried for many years and with great patience to bring him away from such high-flying ideas and fantasies towards humility, obedience and equanimity in Christ and to make public the manifold deceits of his soul and of many other false spirits who ascribe many lies to him, he became my worst enemy and did not just write against me, but he also threatened me with death. Because he and his superintendent Christoph Barthut[128] were burned in the fire in Moscow, his false catechism and writings also died. They should stay where they belong and we warn anyone for their own and for every other unstable spirit. Doctor Schott[129] saw that after his absolute rule only very few chosen are to be blessed, but understood from God's word that still a large crowd consisting of remaining heathens and Jews will enter God's Last Supper, quietness and honourable kingdom. He has therefore invented the fatherly incarnation and in this way enchanted many young students and human beings

231

     Goulds death, Kuhlmann met Esther Michaelis de Paew of Holland in 1686 who bore him a daughter, Salome. Kuhlmann travelled to Moscow in 1689 where he lived in the house of an adherent, Conrad Nordermann, and held millenarian sermons. Kuhlmann and Nordermann were denounced by the Lutheran pastor Joachim Meineke to the local authorities in Moscow and, after three months of imprisonement during which they were severy tortured, burned at the stake on 4 October 1689.

127 Salomon von Kaiserstein was also an alias Kuhlmann used. See Salomon von Kaiserstein [pseud., = Quirinus Kuhlmann], *Cosmopolita de monarchia jesuelitica ultimo ævo reservata ad politicos aulicosque orbis terrarium* (London: 1682). Breckling presumably meant the following three women—although it is unclear if Kuhlmann married them all or merely had relationships with them: Magdalena von Lindaw, Maria Gould [Maria Anglicana], Esther Michaelis de Paew [Marie Ackerlot].

128 Breckling inaccurately mentions the name of Christoph Barthut (d.1693) who was a disciple of Kuhlmann. The merchant Conrad Nordermann was burned with Kuhlmann in Moscow.

129 Maybe William Schott, the physician of the Duke of Zell. Cf. Ariel Hessayon, "Lead's Life and Times (Part Three): The Philadelphian Society", in *Jane Lead and her Transnational Legacy*, 71–90, here 81. See also Hessayon's chapter in volume 3 of this collection, pp. 50, 55, 59.

who lack true piety, and convinced them to leave Christ and his eternal gospel and to look out for the new incarnation of the Father. He has further denied that the remaining part of the people | should be redeemed and be ready to bring Christ into his honourable kingdom, like David made everything ready for Solomon and transferred it to him, which is the main focus of Schott's interpretation of the Book of Revelation from chapter 4 onwards.

Johann Heinrich Deichmann,[130] a student, has showed me several manuscripts written by others, in which I have not found anything correct or important, but just noticed a false application of an unfitting parable. For this reason, I have warned him against such a new and false gospel, but he has still proclaimed and disseminated it everywhere with great sincerity. Hereupon, Deichmann travelled to London to join Lead's community. This community consists of barons and others who have written and published her Acta Philadelphia[131] anew, which reveals her subtle seduction. Master [Magister] Krause Mark[132] has travelled there to research everything, but died shortly after in England and has therefore escaped from such subtle seduction which also jeopardises the chosen.

Franc. Mercurii Helmontii's[133] old and new pagan Jewish opinion about the metempsychosis, the teaching of how the soul can transmigrate into another body to achieve its blessedness in this world by Christ on the day of salvation, is so absurd that it should have died with him, but on the contrary it is resurrected again in someone who has found it apparently in Lead's writings about the destruction of the devil's blessedness and the devil's godless destruction by fire.[134] Those who believe and follow such unstable spirits are punished enough by their own faults.

I have known the new Philadelphian Society in London, which has emerged from Jacob Böhme, the writings of the Quakers and the followers of the Family of love of Henr. Niclas[135] in Emden | and which has come into existence anew in England, for more than 20 years from their fruits. Quirin Kuhlmann was inspired by their school and society to think that he is the son of God,

---

130 Johann Heinrich Deichmann, secretary of the Philadelphian Society in London until 1704.
131 See my introduction, p. 141.
132 Krausemark, whose first name remains unknown, was a religious refugee from the German lands in the Dutch Republic. Letter from Johann Overbeek to August Hermann Francke, (Kleve, 13 December 1695), AFSt/H C 153, fol. 5.
133 Franciscus Mercurius van Helmont (1614–1699).
134 Cf. Lucinda Martin: "God's Strange Providence. Jane Lead in the correspondence of Johann Georg Gichtel", in *Jane Lead*, 187–212, especially 196, 199.
135 The Family of Love or Familists were a sixteen-century religious sect, founded by Hendrik Niclas (*c*.1501–1580).

in which he was confirmed by many English prophecies. Through the devil's doctor Hollgraf's book about mountain trolls who are able to provide people with the philosopher's stone,[136] Kuhlmann was confirmed entirely in his arrogance. Kuhlmann travelled at great expenses from France to Smyrna and Constantinople, together with his first wife[137] and children whom he left behind in Smyrna. Sir Badhurst[138] lent him nearly 36,000 guilders to complete his travels, but regretted this very much. He complained to me about it and asked me to go with him to Kuhlmann to convince him of his huge ungratefulness and excesses. Hereafter doctor Hollgraff persuaded Sir Bathurst that Kuhlmann should impregnate Bathurst's daughter instead of Kuhlmann's first wife, with whom he wanted to father his Salomon who should inherit the philosopher's stone from the mountain trolls in the first place. This daughter was sent to Amsterdam, where she has borne a daughter who unfortunately died and was buried there.[139]

Later on, doctor Hollgraff promised the philosopher's stone to a baron in Germany and cheated him of 40,000 Gulden with the help of doctor Kortholt.[140] Hollgraf took this money to manufacture golden vessels, which were supposed to be of use to him to sacrifice to the mountain trolls, because otherwise they were not willing to hand the tincture over to him. Kortholt stabbed the son of doctor Hollgraf afterwards and had to flee the country. But while he was staying in Lübeck in great fear, he was built up by a daughter from Zwolle[141] who had experienced a lot of hardship in her life and whom he therefore took for his wife | to chase rainbows with her in his mercurial manner and inspired by a prophetical spirit. He took her to England, but when he

234

---

136 Dr Hollgraffen / Hoellgrafe / Holgraf (fl.1684); possibly of Amsterdam. Cf. Robert L. Beare, "Quirinus Kuhlmann: Where and When?", *Modern Lamguage Notes* 77 (1962), 379–397, here 395; Hessayon, "Lead's Life and Times (Part Two): The Woman in the Wilderness", in *Jane Lead*, 39–69, here 47; Idem, "Lead's Life (Part Three)", 81.

137 The name of Kuhlmann's first wife was Margaretha von Lindaw. See Hessayon, "Lead's Life and Times (Part Two)", 46.

138 John Bathurst (d. between November 1692 and March 1694), probably a merchant and property owner in Jamaica, who, according to Robert L. Beare, could have been a member of the gentry, without having a title, but who was certainly no member of nobility. Beare, "Quirinus Kuhlmann", 380–382. Breckling refers to him as "Ritter" (knight).

139 Apparently, this was not the daughter of Bathurst, but the daughter-in-law of his wife. She can probably be identified as Mary Gould [Maria Anglicana] or Esther Michealis de Paew. Hessayon, "Lead's Life (Part Two)", 47.

140 Doctor Kortholt's or Kartholt's first name could not be determined. He seems to have been inclined in fraudulent practices. Hessayon, "Lead's Life (Part Three)", 80–81. See Ariel Hessayon's chapter in volume 3 of this collection, pp. 46, 49, 51, 52, 55, 62, 64.

141 Catherina Barenz / Beerens (fl.1694–1697). See Hessayon's chapter in volume 3, pp. 45, 47, 50, 51, 64.

could not rise any higher, he left her and attached himself to a person who pretended to be a natural daughter of King Charles of England. This person said she had skills in chemistry and that she could produce the [philosopher's] stone. He married her straight away, so that the other one could not bother him any longer, and to be able to go with her to England or France or anywhere else.[142]

We should know about the actions and fate of these unstable spirits and become wise with the help of their example and harmful doing. This should prevent us from walking with unreliable enthusiasts and producers of false gold away from God's boundaries and calling towards our destruction, which causes sad parents sorrow. We should be aware not to ridicule marriage, like Kortholt, Kuhlmann, Nagel,[143] Peter Mauritz[144] and many others have done until their wings were burned and they punished themselves.

Bathurst's wife Jurien[145] and their daughter stayed after his death in the company of the Philadelphians who meet regularly every few weeks and tell each other the dreams, visions, inspirations and prophecies which everyone had individually, in order to awaken each other this way. They try to do this in the same way as the English church which pretends to be built on Christ with the help of God's word and preaching about Christ, until it finally lapsed into Arminianism, Socinianism, Pelaganism and Naturalism. And in the same way the Quakers build on their own spirit, light and ground in them, these Philadelphians build on their own inspirations, sentiments, enthusiasms, visions and prophecies which they call the true word of God. They accept everyone with loving | forgiveness in their Philadelphia, but those who disappoint them and do not accept everything they say as godly, they persecute with hatred and bitterness; indeed they ban them or flee their company.

As long as doctor Joh. Pordatsch[146] and Th. Bromley[147] still lived among them and were leaders in this Society, God's word was respected among them, but increasingly their own thoughts, opinions and dreams prevailed, as they

---

142 This woman, whose initials appear to have been A.M., claimed to be the eldest natural (i.e. illegitimate) daughter of Charles II of England. See Hessayon's chapter in volume 3, p. 50.
143 Probably Paul Nagel (c.1580–1624), German prophet, astrologer and critic of orthodox Lutheranism. See Leigh T.I. Penman, "Climbing Jacob's Ladder: Crisis, Chiliasm, and Transcendence in the Thought of Paul Nagel (†1624), a Lutheran Dissident during the Time of the Thirty Years' War", *Intellectual History Review* 20 (2010), 201–226.
144 See my introduction, p. 140 and *Paulus Redivivus* (source 1 above), p. 160.
145 Anne Bathurst, née Jurien or Jewrin was a leading light among the Philadelphians. She married Bathurst on 9 October 1681. Hessayon, "Lead's Life (Part Two)", 47.
146 John Pordage (1607–1681).
147 Thomas Bromley (1629–1691).

do in papism, and they excluded Joseph Sabbarthon,[148] because he neither wanted to agree with them in every aspect, nor wanted to worship their own human things as godly. Later on, Lead[149] was heard, consulted and followed in everything, so the female regime and preaching gained control in her community, like it once did among the Quakers, against God's word.

Because afterwards Heinrich von Schwinderen[150] and Tanneken Denys[151] travelled from here [the Dutch Republic] to England and saw such a state of disorder among them, that they have condemned and left them for that reason. They have told me much about them and also gave me their writings, which I passed down to others to read, through which they became known in Holland in the first place. Some people even fell in love with them and made false Gods out of them, after they read Jac. Böhme's and Hiel's[152] writings until they had enough of them. They have sought in Lead's writings the roads and things they selfishly wanted to choose and their spiritual self. In the same way, Lead has sought God selfishly in her own thing and has equated herself with God's gifts. If they are not abused for new idolatrousness, some of her writings can be appreciated as human writings, but they have been read too much and give us a too high and therefore an unreachable example. Moreover, they disdain God's word and rob us of time to read this, which is completely intolerable, | because anything which leads to a life of debauchery is wrong.

After Lead's writings gained much popularity in Germany and she was asked orally and in writing to publish more godly prophecies and answers from God and some important people started to support her, the publishing house of her books earned a lot of money. When Lead came with the eternal gospel of the devil and the blessing of Christ's worst enemy and her love of these hellish enemies of her God became too big in her, she denied her neighbourly love to everyone who offered resistance. A physician with good and consistent grounds who refuted her new gospel with the help of God's word, the natural light and Jac. Böhme's writings, caused Lead to publish a new writing which was directed against him and which has been equated in Germany with a new gospel.

In the meantime, some of the most important pillars of Lead's society have tumbled and also her Acta Philadelphia about the newborn Christ who is sup-

---

148 Hessayon, "Lead's Life (Part Two)", 42, 50; Idem, "Lead's Life (Part Three)", 78.
149 Jane Lead (1623–1704).
150 Hendrik van Swinderen (died after 1689).
151 Tanneke Denys (c.1637–1702?), married to Hendrik van Swinderen.
152 Pseudonym of Hendrik Janssen van Barrefelt (fl.1520–1594), member of the Family of Love.

posed to be born in their circles in Germany has caused great confusion among them.[153] For that reason, it is now more quiet among them, which hopefully gives them time to think and to perish voluntarily with John and to deny, lose and reject themselves, in order that Christ can rise in them and become everything in everyone and their secrets, with which they rebel against God and stand up against his authority, can be made public, to warn the many souls who have left the lively source which is Christ and who support and follow idolatrously the word and writings of humans more than God's. | The new sect of those who live alone of their faith, are not willing to work at all and do not want to harvest their field and garden, is so evidently against God's word and human-made rights, order and laws that they already should have been condemned in the first church and should eventually have fallen off itself, because those who have not sown anything and who do not carry the common burden, have nothing to say and should be abandoned by the community and not be supported, after Paul's reprimand: He who does not work, shall not eat, Thess. 3, 2, Ph. 3, 2, Cor. 8, 9.

How many want to be blessed by their heartless faith and push others away from Christ's faith and attract them towards their faithless love, through which they blind and seduce the entire world and bring them to love the things which God hates and forbids and which are after their own mind and will and to hate and neglect what God loves and commands. By acting in this manner, they fall into false love and false good works, back into the curse and condemnation of the law of Moses. Because he who relies on the works, stays under a curse. Gal. 3. The true love, which takes after Christ, stays as unknown in the world as Christ is. Therefore, Christ is treated like an outcast by the world, whereas someone who is shaped like the devil is respected by the world. The devil has no shape which pleases us. On the contrary, the devil nowadays wants to be regarded and respected as much as Christ. The false and worldly love of the flesh wants to be considered and praised as Christian love in every sect and church. On the other side, the Christian love and works of love are as despised by the world as Christ and his honest love were despised by the Pharisees. Therefore, those who have the name, do not have the deed and those who have the deed of love, do not have the name. In summary: for those who are wrong everything is wrong.

---

153   *Theosophical Transactions*, vol. 1, 46–52. Hessayon, "Lead's Life (Part Three)", 81–82; See also Hessayon's chapter in volume 3 of this collection.

CHAPTER 4

Huguenot Prophecies in Eighteenth-Century France

Lionel Laborie

Introduction[1]

The French eighteenth century was prophetic. It was no different in this respect from previous centuries, even though its historiography remains heavily dominated by the Enlightenment. Early modern France saw numerous outbursts of religious enthusiasm, supernatural claims and prophecies, especially in areas that had been torn by denominational tensions. In the 1630s, the city of Loudun, home to a large Protestant population, became notorious after possessed Ursuline nuns accused the priest Urbain Grandier (1590–1634) of signing a pact with the devil, for which he was publicly burned at the stake at Cardinal Richelieu's request.[2] A decade later, a mystical society worshipping medals appeared in Lorraine, while in Paris, Simon Morin's "Illuminés" prophesied into the 1650s and 1660s that the Reign of the Holy Spirit would begin at Louis XIV's death.[3] Around the same time, the Jesuit-turned-Jansenist-turned-Huguenot-turned-Pietist Jean de Labadie (1610–1674) roamed across France, believing himself to be divinely inspired and preaching millenarian doctrines along the way until he found refuge in the Dutch Republic.[4]

Contrary to the common perception of an age of rationalism and secularisation, these phenomena continued into the eighteenth century. Numerous

---

1 I am grateful to David van der Linden, Ariel Hessayon and William Mitchell for their comments and suggestions on earlier drafts of this chapter.
2 See Michel de Certeau, *La Possession de Loudun* (Paris: 1980). This notorious episode has also inspired works of popular fiction, for example Aldous Huxley's *The Devils of Loudun* (1952) and Ken Russell's *The Devils* (1971).
3 Sophie Houdard, "La Cabale des Médaillistes. Une affaire de spiritualité 'extraordinaire' à Nancy (1644–1648)", *Archivio italiano per la storia della pietà, Edizioni di storia e letteratura* (2018), 41–57; Bérengère Parmentier, "Radicalité et illégitimité", *Archives de sciences sociales des religions*, 150 (April–June 2010), 57–76. See more generally on this period, Sophie Houdard, *Les Invasions mystiques. Spiritualités, hétérodoxies et censures au début de l'époque moderne* (Paris: 2008).
4 See Pierre Antoine Fabre, Nicolas Fornerod, Sophie Houdard, Maria-Cristina Pitassi (eds), *Lire Jean de Labadie (1610–1674)—Fondation et affranchissement* (Paris: 2016).

prophets, mystics, and visionaries enlightened by the Holy Ghost emerged in France during the "Age of Reason". The death of the deacon François de Pâris in 1727 famously inspired the Convulsionaries of Saint-Médard, a Jansenist movement with thousands of followers making claims to prophecy, the gift of tongues and miraculous cures.[5] Although the original group was dissolved by the French authorities in 1732, satellite communities such as the Eliséens and the Pinelists survived in the provinces.[6] Lyon became the centre of convulsionary Jansenism until the French Revolution. Ecstatic nuns prophesied the near fall of the monarchy and the destruction of Paris, followed by massive bloodshed throughout the 1740s–1780s. One of these, sister Aile, predicted under inspiration in April 1787: "There shall be no escape from the Revolution … All I see is but ambushes and precipices, blood flowing all around me. I hear weapons clanking; the king's palace is destroyed, his crown taken back. I find myself trapped in this abyss, in the midst of so great a revolution."[7] Such was the confidence among the Jansenist revival that dramatic events would soon unfold that some sought to atone for the woes of their time with spectacular bodily performances. Still in 1787, a prophetess was thus voluntarily crucified by the movement inside the church of Fareins near Lyon as a symbol of death and rebirth announcing greater things to come.[8] The Convulsionaries became politically divided during the French Revolution, but remained active well into the nineteenth century.

Other parts of France saw similar phenomena in the latter half of the eighteenth century. In the 1770s and 1780s, the Swedenborg Rite and the Illuminati of Mount Tabor respectively founded a masonic lodge with the support of local aristocrats and Jacobite exiles in the Papal State of Avignon, based on the writings of the Swedish mystic Emanuel Swedenborg (1688–1772) and the German theosopher Jacob Boehme (1575–1624).[9] Around the same time, an

---

5   Catherine-Laurence Maire, *Les Convulsionnaires de Saint-Médard. Miracles, convulsions et prophéties à Paris au XVIIIe siècle* (Paris: 1985).

6   The priest Pierre Vaillant proclaimed himself to be the reincarnation of the prophet Elias and led his own sect of "Vaillantistes" or "Eliséens", while his contemporary the Oratorian Alexandre Darnaud pretended to be the prophet Enoch. The Pinelist movement was led by Michel Pinel (d.1775), who prophesied Elias's return on earth and the imminent conversion of the Jews. *La Bastille dévoilée, ou recueil des pieces authentiques pour server a son histoire* (Paris: 1789), 67–68, 89. Jean-Pierre Chantin, *Les Amis de l'œuvre de la verité. Jansénisme, miracles et fin du monde au XIXe siècle* (Lyon: 1998), 10–11.

7   Daniel Vidal, "Expériences de fin du monde: Un Jansénisme en convulsion, un calvinisme en prophétie", *Archives de sciences sociales des religions* 114 (2001), 26. All translations are mine, unless otherwise noted.

8   Vidal, "Expériences de fin du monde", 27.

9   Ariel Hessayon, "Jacob Boehme, Emanuel Swedenborg and Their Readers", *The Arms of Morpheus-Essays on Swedenborg and Mysticism* (2007), 33.

autochthonous Quaker community was emerging in the nearby Vaunage valley in Languedoc, while Moravian missionaries were traveling across southern France and established a community of United Brethren in Bordeaux.[10]

Paris was not spared by eschatological predictions in the late eighteenth century. The Elysée palace, today's official residence of French presidents, stood at the centre of this fascination for the occult. Its owner, Louise Marie Thérèse Bathilde d'Orléans (1750–1822), Duchess of Bourbon and Louis XVI's cousin, was a freemason and supporter of the Revolution despite her title of royal princess. Her regular guests and occasional residents included the Illuminists Louis-Claude de Saint-Martin (1743–1803)—aka le Philosophe inconnu—and Jacques Cazotte (1719–1792), the founding fathers of animal magnetism Franz-Anton Mesmer (1734–1815) and the Marquis de Puységur (1751–1825), and the constitutional bishops Claude Fauchet (1744–1793) and Pierre Pontard (1749–1832). The latter introduced the Duchess to the Périgord prophetess Suzette Labrousse (1747–1821), who had allegedly predicted the French Revolution. Labrousse became a guest resident of the Elysée palace, and Pontard founded Le Journal prophétique in 1791, financed by Bathilde d'Orléans herself, to publish his protégée's predictions of revolutionary millenarianism. Another prophetess soon joined the assemblies of the Elysée palace: Catherine Théot (1736–1801) ran her own temple on the rue de la Contrescarpe, and counted among her followers a certain Maximilien de Robespierre.[11]

It should come as no surprise in this context that hundreds of titles on prophets and prophecies and supernatural manifestations were published in eighteenth-century France. Many of these offered exegeses of biblical prophecies by theologians, but the predictions of famed early modern prophets and mystics like Guillaume Postel (1510–1581), Michel de Nostredame aka Nostradamus (1503–1566), Jacob Boehme, and Jan Amos Comenius (1592–1670) were also reprinted and translated in the last decades of the century. Many new ones also emerged around that time, inspired by a growing feeling of a universal regeneration. In many ways, the French Revolution marked a peak in the literary production of a prophetic century.

10   Lionel Laborie, "From English *Tremblours* to French *Inspirés*: A Transnational Perspective on the Origins of French Quakerism (1654–1789)", in *Radicalism and Dissent in the World of Protestant Reform*, ed. Anorthe Kremers and Bridget Heal (Gottingen: 2017), 225–244; Dieter Gembicki and Heidi Gembicki-Achtnich (eds), *Le Réveil des coeurs. Journal de voyage du Frère Morave Fries (1761–1762)* (Saintes: 2013).

11   Nicole Jacques-Levèvre, "1789: interprétations eschatologiques de la Révolution française", in *Révolutions du moderne, colloque interdisciplinaire, Université Paris X-Nanterre, 6–9 décembre 2000*, ed. Daniela Gallingani, Claude Leroy, André Magnan et Baldine Saint Girons (Paris-Méditerrannée: 2004), 271–281.

Chapter Focus

The present chapter focusses on the oral prophetic culture of the Protestants of Languedoc and Dauphiné in the "long" eighteenth century. Louis XIV's military campaigns in southern France—the *dragonnades*—had coerced French Protestants to abjure their faith in the early 1680s. The revocation of the Edict of Nantes in October 1685 ended nearly a century of tolerance, forcing most Huguenots to convert as "nouveaux catholiques", while some 200,000 fled their homeland to seek refuge abroad. Those refusing to abjure thereafter survived underground to avoid persecution until the French Revolution, a period of clandestinity known as the "Désert", in reference to the Jews fleeing Egypt.[12] In Languedoc and Dauphiné, where religious tensions had remained palpable throughout the seventeenth century, the Revocation sparked a new wave of revolts.

More importantly, the revocation of the Edict of Nantes gave birth to several generations of prophets animated by millenarian beliefs anticipating a future era of peace and justice. Charismatic lay preachers replaced exiled ministers and held clandestine assemblies in the remote mountains of Dauphiné and the Cévennes. Abandoned by their shepherds to lead them, the flocks were now left free to wander by themselves into new pasture. In a context of renewed persecution, the Protestants of the Cévennes and Dauphiné rapidly embraced an ethos of martyrdom as a divine trial of God's "true church".[13] Their resistance climaxed in the Camisards' revolt or War of the Cévennes, from which I present sources below. Between 1702 and 1710, peasant prophets allegedly inspired by the Holy Spirit waged a violent rebellion against state persecution and fought what is today reappraised as the last French war of religion.[14]

The death of Louis XIV in 1715 opened a new chapter in the history of French Protestantism. Between 1715 and 1760, the Huguenot minister Antoine Court (1695–1760) rebuilt and re-institutionalised the Reformed Church in Languedoc and Dauphiné as it existed before the revocation of the Edict of Nantes. Under Court's leadership, clandestine assemblies resumed in forests and at night during the Regency (1715–1723) and under Louis XV (r.1724–1774). The

---

12 Didier Boisson, "The Revocation of the Edict of Nantes and the Désert", in *A Companion to the Huguenots*, ed. Raymond Mentzer and Bertrand van Ruymbeke (Leiden: 2016), 221–245.
13 W. Gregory Monahan, *Let God Arise: The War and Rebellion of the Camisards* (Oxford: 2014), 21–35.
14 Monahan, *Let God Arise*.

reconstruction of the Church was a slow and risky process, as Huguenots continued to face waves of sporadic persecution, when ministers were executed, men sent to the galleys and women imprisoned. Court's restoration of Calvinist orthodoxy entailed the condemnation of violence, claims to prophecy and female preachers. It sought to quell the prophetic culture and violence of the post-Revocation period by advocating instead passive resistance as the sole response to ongoing persecution.[15]

Despite Court's efforts to restore Calvinist discipline and ministry, lay prophetic movements continued to emerge in Languedoc and Dauphiné, as the sources presented below illustrate. The cult of the Multipliants, founded in 1719 by a recanted Camisard, counted several hundred followers across the Vaunage valley by the time its leaders were caught in Montpellier in 1723. Their ecumenical movement practiced the gift of tongues, allowed women to prophesy and anticipated Christ's Second Coming later that year. More surprising still, and unlike the Camisards before them, the Multipliants appealed primarily to the literate, urban bourgeoisie of Lunel, Montpellier and Nîmes, and held clandestine assemblies away from the ongoing persecution of the Huguenots in the region.[16]

Official documents and correspondence attest to further regular prophetic outbreaks in the region in the following decades, for which no first-hand account appears to have survived. These often coincided with major geopolitical turmoil in Europe, which French authorities feared might fuel new rebellions like the Camisards' during the War of the Spanish Succession (1701–1714). In 1745, during the War of the Austrian Succession (1740–1748), for example, the prophet Maroger predicted under inspiration that his followers, the Couflaïres of Nages, would be carried by an angel to an English island, of which he would be crowned king.[17] And while some charismatic ministers continued to encourage a rebellion in the Cévennes during the Seven Years' War (1756–1763), a few hundred Huguenots fled to England and South Carolina with Jean-Louis Gibert by the time the conflict ended.[18]

---

15 Hubert Bost, "De la Secte à l'Église. La Quête de légitimité dans le protestantisme meridional au XVIIIe siècle", *Rives méditerranéennes* 10 (2002), 53–68; Pierre Rolland, *Dictionnaire du Désert huguenot: La Reconquête protestante (1715–1765)* (Paris: 2017).

16 Daniel Vidal, "La Secte contre le prophétisme: les Multipliants de Montpellier (1719–1723)", *Annales. Économies, Sociétés, Civilisations* 37/4 (1982), 801–825.

17 Montpellier, Archives départementales de l'Hérault (hereafter ADH), C 218 (liasse), fols 262–358, here fol. 264ᵛ.

18 Geoffrey Adams, *The Huguenots and French Opinion, 1685–1787: The Enlightenment Debate on Toleration* (Waterloo, Ont.: 1991), 46, note 22; London, Lambeth Palace Library (hereafter LPL), Ms 1122/3, fols 170–216.

By the 1760s, with a changing international context marked by the rise of Protestant powers and the spread of Enlightenment ideas in Europe, religious violence began to decline progressively in Languedoc and Dauphiné. France came out weakened and heavily indebted from the Seven Years' War; Louis XV began to distance himself from Rome and tacitly tolerate the Huguenots as he increasingly depended upon the support of Swiss bankers.[19] With the executions of François Rochette and Jean Calas, which Voltaire helped publicise together with the Sirven affair, the year 1763 marked the end of Huguenot persecution in France.[20] The last female prisoners detained in the so-called Tower of Constance in Aigues-Mortes were gradually released by the end of 1768.[21] Despite the Edict of Versailles in 1787,[22] which did not restore tolerance, but only gave the Huguenots a legal identity, episodes of religious violence resurfaced sporadically thereafter, as the "Bagarre de Nîmes", the massacres of Avignon, and the riots of Montauban and Uzès in 1790–1791 demonstrate.[23]

Selected Sources

Prophetic discourse and millenarian beliefs remained the backbone of the French Protestant resistance for most of the eighteenth century. But studying an oral prophetic culture implies by definition that printed sources are scarce. These prophecies typically emanated from illiterate teenage shepherds with no access to a printing press and who would have faced royal censorship anyway.

---

19   Adams, *The Huguenots and French Opinion*, 197–306.
20   François Rochette was the last Huguenot minister to be executed for preaching illegally, in 1762. Jean-Paul Sirven, a Protestant craftsman in Mazamet, was wrongfully sentenced to be burned at the stake for murdering his daughter the same year, allegedly to prevent her from converting to Catholicism. Sirven and his family had fled to Switzerland before the trial. The family was rehabilitated thanks to Voltaire's help in 1771. Adams, *The Huguenots and French Opinion*, 143, 151, 224–226.
21   Adams, *The Huguenots and French Opinion*, 204–205.
22   The Edict of Versailles is often wrongly presented as an edict of tolerance, even though the term "tolérance" does not appear in the text. Instead, the edict created a civil register of non-Catholics that allowed French Protestants to marry, baptise their children and inherit according to the law. Roman Catholicism was reasserted as France's official religion and Protestants remained excluded from positions in the public service, education and the military. They were granted freedom of conscience by the Declaration of the Rights of Man and of the Citizen in August 1789, but did not obtain freedom of worship until September 1791.
23   Céline Borello, "Les Sources d' une altérité religieuse en révolution: Rabaut Saint-Étienne ou la radicalisation des representations protestantes", *Annales historiques de la Révolution française* 378 (2014), 32–33.

None of the sources presented here were published in France at the time and very few survive in manuscript form today as a result. They did, however, make their way to Protestant territories as far as New England, where they were promoted as evidence of God's providential manifestation among his true believers. The support of prominent theologians like Pierre Jurieu (1637–1713), Cotton Mather (1663–1728) and August Hermann Francke (1663–1727) convinced many that supernatural manifestations signalled the triumph of Protestantism, leading to the fall of Rome and its Catholic allies, chief among whom was France.

Ironically, our understanding of this oral prophetic culture is largely obstructed by the Huguenots themselves. Indeed, orthodox Huguenots downplayed the prophetic claims of their co-religionists of Dauphiné and the Cévennes, and emphasised instead the political benefits of supporting a Protestant rebellion in France. Yet the clandestine assemblies of charismatic lay preachers that spread across southern France from the 1680s onwards also deserve our attention in that they prefigured the open field preaching of the Great Evangelical Awakening. Preachers like Claude Brousson (1647–1698) achieved international fame during their lifetime and maintained personal links with British evangelicals and German Pietists.[24]

Thus, the sources presented below aim to give back a voice to a silenced oral prophetic culture of resistance. They consist primarily of fragments of prophecies pronounced in Languedoc and Dauphiné between 1688 and 1755. Some, as shall be seen, were published abroad in the aftermath of the revocation of the Edict of Nantes as testimonies of Louis XIV's brutality against French Protestants. Others only survive in manuscript form and for that reason offer a rare insight into the oral prophetic culture of Southern France in the long eighteenth century.

1. Isabeau Vincent and the "Petits Prophètes" of Dauphiné
The first four texts concern the famous case of Isabeau Vincent and the "petits prophètes" of Dauphiné. Shortly after the Revocation, voices of inspired children allegedly began to be heard at night in the southern mountains of Béarn, Vivarais and the Cévennes. The most charismatic of these was Isabeau Vincent, a fifteen-year old shepherdess from nearby Crest in Dauphiné, who from February 1688 prophesied the imminent fall of Rome and the deliverance of God's

---

24 Alan C. Clifford, "Reformed Pastoral Theology Under the Cross: John Quick and Claude Brousson", *Western Reformed Seminary Journal*, vol. 5/1 (1998), 21–35. Gotha, Forschungsbibliothek (FB Gotha), Chart. A 306, fols 194–195. On Brousson's life, see Walter C. Utt and Brian Eugene Strayer, *The Bellicose Dove: Claude Brousson and Protestant Resistance to Louis XIV, 1647–1698* (Brighton: 2003).

true church. Most remarkably, Vincent prophesied in her sleep and in French instead of her native dialect. Her condition rapidly gained popularity across Dauphiné until she was imprisoned in Grenoble in June 1688 and disappeared in a convent shortly afterwards, after having inspired dozens of young prophets in the region.

The first account of her prophecies (1.1., p. 201 below) was published by Jacques Massard in Amsterdam in 1688 as *Abrégé de l'histoire de la bergère de Saou près de Crest en Daufiné*. Massard, a physician from Grenoble who turned mystic after he emigrated to Amsterdam around 1685, had evidently retained local contacts in Dauphiné that enabled him to first report on Vincent's case a few months before the famous Huguenot theologian Pierre Jurieu in Rotterdam.[25] The text is a transcription made by a lawyer named Gerlan, who witnessed Vincent's prophecies on 20 May 1688. It was subsequently reproduced in Jurieu's *Lettres pastorales*, a series of open letters addressed to the clandestine Protestant community of southern France.

The remaining three fragments (1.2.–1.4., pp. 202, 207 and 210 below) are reproduced from various English translations that circulated in 1689–1690. Vincent's prophecies rapidly took a particular resonance in England and the Dutch Republic as the Glorious Revolution seemed to fulfil her prediction for the autumn of 1688.[26] The *Abrégé* includes astrological predictions concerning England for October, November and December 1688 (pp. 17–21). These are also attributed to Vincent, but were in reality a French translation of John Partridge's astrological predictions.[27] For this reason, they have not been included in our selection below.

2. Daniel Raoux

The next section consists of a fragment of a sermon allegedly pronounced by the prophet Daniel Raoux around 1701 (p. 215 below). Little is known about this charismatic ploughman who was executed in 1701. The text is important for two reasons: First because Raoux is generally regarded as having introduced prophetism from Dauphiné into the Cévennes on the eve of the Camisards' revolt (1702–1710). Second because French Quakers, who also appeared in

---

25 On Massard, see Leslie Tuttle and Kristine Wirts's chapter in this volume.
26 *Lettre d'un gentilhomme de Dauphiné a un de ses amis a Geneve. Contenant ce qu'il a oüi dire d'Isabeau Vincent Bergere* (Amsterdam: 1688); *Pertinent verhaal van de propheet, die in Vrankryk is opgestaan* (Amsterdam: 1688); *Nader berricht, Aangaande een Herderin In't Dauphiné, daar God wonderlijke en bovennatuurlijke dingen tot een yders verwondering in uitwerkt* (s.n.: 1688).
27 *Mene Tekel, Being an Astrological Judgment on the Great and Wonderful Year 1688. Deduced From the True and Genuine Principles of That Art: Shewing the Approaching Catastrophe of Popery in England, &c.* (London: 1688), 14–15.

Languedoc in the eighteenth century, hold him as one of their forefathers.[28] Raoux may therefore be considered as the link between three charismatic traditions, namely Vincent and the infant prophets of Dauphiné; the Camisards in the Cévennes; and French Quakers in the Vaunage valley. His sermon was copied towards the end of the eighteenth century by the Quakers of Congénies. It was sent to the Society of Friends in England and probably translated by the former officer and physician Jean Louis Lecointe de Marcillac (1755–1818). Both the original transcript and the English translation reproduced below survive in the Friends House Library, London.[29]

3. The Camisards

Part three consists of two prophecies (3.1. and 3.2., pp. 217 and 221 below) delivered by the Camisards Durand Fage and Jean Cavalier upon their arrival in London in the summer 1706. The Camisards were a radical minority within the Huguenot community who revolted against Catholic persecution from 1702 in the Cévennes mountains. After an initial truce in 1704, the region was pacified the following year, but sporadic outbreaks of violence continued until 1710.[30] Throughout the war, the Camisards were driven by their own bellicose prophetic culture, justifying their guerrilla warfare with divine inspirations. As a result, few written accounts of the Camisards' prophetic culture survive; most come from their Catholic opponents and are by definition heavily biased.

Although both were pronounced in England, the two prophecies presented below were delivered shortly after their departure from the Cévennes and therefore offer a rare, first-hand insight into the Camisards' oral prophetic culture. Fage and Cavalier spoke in the presence of Huguenot refugees in London, including prominent diplomats like the Marquis de Miremont[31] and the Dutch ambassador Henri Saunière de l'Hermitage. Their prophecies were copied by scribes such as the Swiss mathematician Nicolas Fatio de Duillier,[32] the travel writer François-Maximilien Misson[33] and the lawyer Jean Daudé. Unlike Daniel

---

28 Laborie, "From English Trembleurs to French Inspirés", 229–230.
29 London, Library of the Society of Friends (hereafter LSF), Ms Vol. 314, nos 1–2; LSF, Ms Vol. 315, fols 13–15.
30 Monahan, Let God Arise, 212–252.
31 Lionel Laborie, "Bourbon, Armand de, marquis de Miremont (1655–1732)", Oxford Dictionary of National Biography (hereafter ODNB) online (http://www.oxforddnb.com/view/article/109568, accessed 27 May 2016).
32 Scott Mandelbrote, "Fatio, Nicolas, of Duillier (1664–1753)", ODNB (http://www.oxforddnb.com/view/article/9056, accessed 30 July 2007).
33 Craig Spence, "Misson, Francis Maximilian (c.1650–1722)", ODNB (http://www.oxforddnb.com/view/article/18821, accessed 14 March 2013).

Raoux's sermon, their prophecies appear defiantly bellicose in content; they compared the Camisards' resistance to the plight of the Jews in the Bible and aimed by their apocalyptic tone to raise a regiment of Huguenot exiles led by Miremont to rekindle the rebellion in the Cévennes.

Fage and Cavalier were joined in London by the more prominent prophet Elie Marion in September 1706.[34] The three Camisards and their Huguenot scribes formed the core of a new millenarian movement soon to be known in England as the "French Prophets".[35] Marion's apocalyptic prophecies were published in both French and English in April 1707 and attracted a wider audience of British millenarians, including Philadelphians, Quakers and Scottish Quietists.[36] Their charismatic movement spread across Britain, Protestant Europe and North America, and influenced Pietist revivals and the Evangelical Awakening along the way. Fage and Cavalier's prophecies therefore take us back to the very origins of the French Prophets in London, before Marion's arrival, with prophecies delivered as they were in the Cévennes. Both manuscripts are preserved today at Lambeth Palace Library in London and are published here for the first time.[37]

4. Isaac Elzière and the New Zionists

Part four reproduces a fragment delivered under inspiration by the prophet Isaac Elzière of Sauve around 1742. Elzière was the charismatic leader of the "sect of the New Zion", a non-violent millenarian community that was first reported in Quissac near the Cévennes in 1736. A Huguenot by birth, Elzière may have been a former Multipliant survivor after they were crushed by French authorities in the previous decade. He is also known to have travelled to Switzerland, Germany, the Low Countries and England in the early 1730s before founding his own millenarian community in Languedoc.[38]

In line with the revivalist movements of England and Germany, these New Zionists believed that because the reigns of the Father and of the Son were over,

---

34 Lionel Laborie, "Marion, Elie (1678–1713)", ODNB (http://www.oxforddnb.com/view/article/109569, accessed 19 Feb 2019).

35 Lionel Laborie "French Prophets", ODNB (https://doi.org/10.1093/odnb/9780198614128.013.109707, accessed 9 May 2018).

36 Lionel Laborie, *Enlightening Enthusiasm: Prophecy and Religious Experience in Early Eighteenth-Century England* (Manchester: 2015). On the Philadelphian Society and the Scottish Quietists, see respectively Ariel Hessayon and Michael B. Riordan's chapters in volume 3 of this collection.

37 LPL, Ms 932/10 and Ms 934/52.

38 Samuel Ribard, "Un Inspiré, Isaac Elzière, de Saint-Ambroix, d'après ses manuscrits." *Bulletin historique et littéraire* 40/1 (1891), 365–372.

the prophetic age of the Holy Spirit had now come.[39] Accordingly, they burnt the Old and New Testaments and read instead the French Prophets' works *Eclair de lumière descendant des Cieux* (1711), *Cri d'alarme en avertissement aux nations* (1712) and *Plan de la justice de Dieu sur la Terre* (1714).[40] All three titles were collections of prophecies pronounced by Elie Marion and Jean Allut during their missions across continental Europe.[41] The fact that they inspired the New Zionists indicates a French reception of the Camisards' writings a quarter of a century after their publications abroad.

The text presented here (p. 228 below) is entitled "Le Flambeau de Justice"—*The Torch of Justice*—and is the only known fragment surviving from the "sect of the New Zion". It circulated in the Cévennes in the nineteenth century and was published by Samuel Ribard in 1891, but the original now appears to have been lost. Its title and ecumenical tone suggest that Elzière may have been influenced by the French Prophets and other millenarian movements during his travels abroad. Because of his emphasis on non-violence, passive contemplation and charismatic preaching, Elzière is considered today as the first French Quaker theologian.[42]

5. Paul Rabaut

The final source (p. 232 below) is a sermon delivered in 1755 by the Huguenot minister Paul Rabaut (1718–1794). Rabaut was a leading figure of the clandestine church of the Désert alongside Antoine Court. From 1741, he was in charge of the church of Nîmes and dedicated his life to the defence of the rights of French Protestants and the relief of the female prisoners of the Tower of Constance.[43] His son, the minister Jean-Paul Rabaut Saint-Étienne (1743–1793), followed in his footsteps. The Marquis de Lafayette, encouraged by George Washington, visited the Rabauts in Nîmes during the summer of 1785. He reportedly heard them preach and exhorted Rabaut Saint-Etienne to meet secretary of state Malesherbes in Paris and help draft the Edict of Versailles of 1787, which granted

---

39 ADH, C 509, no. 158.
40 ADH, C 509, no. 174.
41 Lionel Laborie, "Spreading the Seed: Toward a French Millenarian Network in Pietist Germany?", In *Kriminelle-Freidenker-alchemisten. Räume Des Untergrunds in Der Frühen Neuzeit*, ed. Martin Mulsow and Michael Multhammer (Köln/Weimar/Wien: 2014), 99–117, esp. 103–108.
42 Jean-Paul Chabrol, "Mémoire et identité religieuse: la 'légende' des Couflaïres de la Vaunage", in *La Vaunage au XVIIIe siècle* (Nîmes: 2003), 5–7.
43 He is the author of *Très humble et très respectueuse requête des protestants de la province de Languedoc au roy* (1761). See https://www.museeprotestant.org/en/notice/paul-rabaut -1718-1794-2/, accessed 14 February 2019.

civil rights to French Protestants. Rabaut Saint-Etienne became a deputy for the Third Estate during the French Revolution. He was executed during the Terror in December 1793, while Rabaut was imprisoned in Nîmes until Robespierre's fall in July 1794 and died shortly after his release.[44]

Rabaut wrote numerous sermons throughout his long ministry in the Cévennes. None were printed during his lifetime and only a few have been published since the nineteenth century.[45] The one presented here remains in manuscript form. It is preserved at the Bibliothèque du Protestantisme français in Paris.[46] It was preached in the *Désert* on the eve of the Seven Years' War (1756–1763), which saw the rise of Protestant powers in Europe. Rabaut not only drew upon biblical prophecies, but also saw in this changing political landscape the impending deliverance of the clandestine Huguenot community in France. This sermon is all the more interesting as Huguenot ministers under Antoine Court's leadership had long condemned prophecies after the trauma of the Camisards' revolt. But Rabaut was not alone in anticipating the deliverance of his church based on Daniel's prophecy.[47] His sermon therefore illustrates the persisting importance of millenarian interpretations among the Huguenot community.

---

44 Adams, *The Huguenots and French Opinion*, 268–277; André Dupont, *Rabaut Saint-Etienne 1743–1793. Un Protestant défenseur de la liberté religieuse* (Genève: 1989).
45 Paul Rabaut, *La Livrée de l'Église chrétienne, sermon ... prêché au désert, le 23 avril 1750* (Paris: 1829); Albert Monod, *Les Sermons de Paul Rabaut, pasteur du Désert (1738–1785)* (Paris: 1911).
46 Paris, Bibliothèque du protestantisme français (hereafter BPF), MS 716/3, no. 28.
47 "The Gibert Brothers", (http://www.museeprotestant.org/en/notice/the-gibert-brothers/, accessed 18 Jun 2014).

1 Isabeau Vincent's Prophecies

∴

1.1. A LETTER From a Gentleman of DAUPHINE To one of his Friends at GENEVA, Containing what he heard said of ISABEL VINCENT THE SHEPERDESS. Printed first at Geneva, and Reprinted at Amsterdam, and now done into English from the French Copy.[48]

The Following Words were related to me by persons worthy of Credit, who heard them themselves.

There will be a Year in which the Sacks will be dearer than the Corn: The Second Year, will be followed with a Famin: And the Third, with a Pestilence that shall begin one the side of *Rome*, the *Friday* before *Easter day:* Since you cannot Communicate at *Easter*,[49] you would do well to fast: This was the Day on which *Jesus Christ* did Eat the *Paschal Lamb:* and if you cannot Communicate in publick, do it in private, and what you have done in secret, he shall repay you openly.

There is a little Root that shall encrease by little and little: Our deliverance also shall come by little and little, like this little Root.

If any come that are not of the Faithful, I shall catch them, for I will say nothing at all.

Have a care you come not hither out of Curiosity: God will not be well pleased if the Wicked come to make them sport: Better it were for them that hot Coals of Fire should pass through their Mouths, than that they should mock at the Word of God: They had better swallow a Serpent with all its Poyson: For a Serpent wounds but the Body: but *Satans* Poyson wounds both Body and Soul.

If all were observed that I shall say, it would contain as much as three Bibles of a Cubit Heighth.

---

48 Pierre Jurieu, *The Reflections of the Reverend and Learned Monsieur Jurieu, Upon the Strange and Miraculous Exstasies of Isabel Vincent, the Shepherdess of Saov in Dauphiné. To Which is Added a Letter of a Gentleman in Dauphiné* (London: 1689), 50–57. This passage is a contemporaneous English translation from *Abrégé de l'histoire de la bergère de Saou près de Crest en Daufiné* (Amsterdam: 1688) and the spelling has been preserved here. The letter in the original French copy is dated 14 June 1688.

49 All Protestant temples had been closed—and many demolished—with the revocation of the Edict of Nantes in October 1685. Protestants were no longer allowed to worship in public thereafter.

It is not I that speak, but the Spirit that is within me:[50] In the later Days your young People shall prophesy, and your Old Men shall dream Dreams.[51]

If you pray, you shall obtain Mercy: for a Servant cannot receive his Salary if he hath not Faithfully served: Do not you like the Foolish Virgins: Keep your Lamps ready:[52] Have a care lest the Measure being full, the Lot do not fall upon you, but that your Fervent Prayers may make it fall upon your Enemies. Our Lord hath given us Forty two Months of Persecution,[53] we have no longer time to suffer, and our deliverance shall be in the time of the Vintage.

The Day on which our Lord *Jesus Christ* was Crucified, which was upon *Fryday*, in the beginning of the said Month there shall be a great Persecution, but it will not last: He will yet have Mercy upon such as have turned, but not upon such as have taken Pensions.

57   Observe, that before she [Isabeau Vincent] went to her Bed, she desired that certain Children that were unknown to her might be put out of the Room: And it was believed, that it was that that gave the Spirit occasion to say, That such should go out, that were not capable to understand the Word.

∴

1.2. *A sincere and true Relation of what was spoken by the Mouth of* ISABEL VINCENT, *as she Slept on the 20th of* May *at Night, in the Year* 1688.[54]

57   After she had Sung the 42ᵈ Psalm, *Ainsi qu'on oit le cerf braire* (or, *As the Hart panteth*, &c)[55] unto the next pause, with a clear and Audible Voice, without

---

50   The prophets of Languedoc and Dauphiné always claimed to act as God's passive instruments. The Holy Spirit allegedly spoke through them while possessed, and they did not remember what had been said when they woke up from their inspirations.
51   Joel 2:28; Acts 2:17.
52   Matt. 25:1.
53   Reference to the three and a half years (1,260 days, or 42 months) ministry of the two witnesses of the Apocalypse (Rev. 11:3–14). At the end of this period, the two witnesses were killed by the beast; their bodies lay unburied for three and a half days before their resurrection and ascension to Heaven. The Huguenots of Dauphiné and the theologian Pierre Jurieu interpreted St John's vision as evidence that French Protestants would be liberated from persecution three and a half years after the Revocation, i.e. in 1689. See Leslie Tuttle and Kristine Wirts's chapter in this volume.
54   Jurieu, *The Reflections of the Reverend and Learned Monsieur Jurieu*, 57–64.
55   In October 1685, when the Edict of Nantes was revoked, the people of Orthez in Béarn reportedly heard angelic voices singing psalm 42 and others at night. Similar manifestations were observed in the Cévennes and Dauphiné at the same time. *A Wonderful Account From Orthez, in Bearne, and the Cevennes, of Voices Heard in the Air, Singing the Praises of*

missing one Musical Note, she then made a little stop, and then spoke of the necessity of hiding the Word of God: saying, that it ought not to be spoken to such as could not understand it: nay, that they ought to be bid go out of the Room. Then she presently fell upon the Persecutions, and Wrongs | that had been done to the Faithful, and said, that it was Sin that was the cause of them, and that we ought to avoid the occasions of Sin: saying if you knew the uglyness of Sin, you would be much more afraid of committing it, than you are. And notwithstanding the Evils inflicted upon you, you ought always to say, I will praise the Lord: for God chasteneth whom he loveth, but God will tame all the Wild Beasts that persecute you. She said also That we ought to prepare our selves for the Table of the Lord: saying, Let us go and tast [sic] of his Paschal Lamb: Take, eat this Body that hath been Crucified for you: and do not believe that Jesus Christ is there in Body and Soul, for he is in Heaven: It is by Faith that we are to penetrate into this Mystery. He should have a good many Bodies to be given to so many People at once: And continuing upon the Subject of the Persecutions made upon the Faithful, she Exhorted them to hold fast, and to Repent: and when God shall come, he will say to the Faithful, *Come*, &c. And continuing to speak of the Assurance we have in his Promises: she said, *The Heavens and the Earth shall pass away, but the Word of God shall continue.* The Wicked shall be mowed down like the Grass that is mowed: wherefore Christians hold fast, and let your Faith be always founded in Jesus Christ, who hath shed his Blood for our Sins. For he that shall persevere to the end, shall receive Eternal Life. We must suffer for his Word, | for he saith, He that will love me must bear my Cross. It is upon Jesus Christ that we must bestow our Love: It is he that hath said, *He that shall love another more than me, is not worthy of me*.[56] The Angels and the Saints groan when they see you in Persecutions. But Christians, have a good Courage, and repent you of your Sins: search his Word, and you will find it by Repentance: obey the Commandments of God and not those of Men: For he that will follow the Commandments of Men, shall dye the death. Be ye assured Christians, that if he loved not his People, he would not Chastize them The People of Israel was always persecuted: but he that shall persevere to the end, shall obtain Eternal life.

    God, in the Words and Tunes of the Psalms; Used By Those of the Reformed Religion: At the Time of Their Cruel and Inhumane Persecution. By the French King: Credliby [Sic] Attested. (London: 1706), 8. See also Hubert Bost, "L'Apocalypse et les Psaumes dans l'arsenal des Pastorales de Jurieu", in *Ces Messieurs de la R.P.R.: Histoires et écritures de huguenots, XVIIe–XVIIIe siècles*, ed. Hubert Bost (Paris: 2001), 175–213.

56   Matt. 10:37.

Here was a Silence of about half an Hour, and then she resuming her Discourse said:

Be not ye surprized, my Brethren, if you have felt the Anger of God: for we have trampled upon his Word, and put it under our Feet: but Repent and Seek God, and he will be in the midst of you. The Wicked shall perish: They shall have Courage enough to harm you now: but they will have no power at the Hour of Death. Have pity upon us O God! We are poor scattered Sheep, thou hast gathered us, according to thy good pleasure, have pity upon us.

Here she stopped for the space of about two hours, and after that she sung about two or three Verses of the Commandments of God in | Rhime;[57] and continuing the Threatnings against the Wicked, that persecute the Faithful, she said, their Efforts and Malice was like the Stones flung against Trees, and like Feathers cast against the Wind. The Wicked shall perish with their Wickednesses, and shall be mowed down like the Grass of the Fields, which is withered. And therefore, Christians, let us refer our selves to God, and then God will refer himself to us, for his Mercy is not yet exhausted. O Lord, marvellous are thy Works: the Wicked shall make a loud enough Cry, but God will no more hear them: he will exterminate them under his hand: But as for the Good, he will say to them, *Come ye Blessed of my Father, posseß ye my Inheritance, the Kingdom that was prepared for you before the Foundation of the World.* Let us go then to search the Word of God, and we shall find it: and persevere ye unto the End, and ye shall obtain Eternal Life: For when we search his Word, we search God himself. It is Earthly Goods that have occasioned our Purgatory, and our Destruction: but let us not rely thereon any more, and cease not to bewail your Sins. Look you, there are but two ways in all, that of Hell and that of Paradise: The former of these is a large and spacious way, by which the Wicked go in great Numbers: but the Way of Paradise is strait, they that are laden with Sins cannot pass by it because it is uneven and crooked. They must pass by Persecutions to come thither: But to you, Faithful Ones, he will one day say, | *Come ye Blessed of my Father*. As to the Wicked, he will say to them: *Go to the Eternal Fire which is prepared for the Devil and his Angels.* The Wicked have persecuted you: but, O Faithful Soul! thou oughtest to be assured of this, That thô thou diest, thou shalt yet live. Repent you, and Sin no more: for a day will come when you must appear before God. We ought then to fear offending of him, and not to follow

---

57 On the Huguenots' love of music and dancing, see Angela McShane, "A Resounding Silence? Huguenots and the Broadside Ballad in the Seventeenth Century", *Proceedings of the Huguenot Society of Great Britain and Ireland* 28:5 (Summer 2007), 604–625, here 605.

the course of the Ungodly: for they shall perish. Let us search his Word, and hide it in our Hearts, and God by his Grace will make his Glory shine upon us. And hereby the Wicked shall be disabled from hurting us, their Arrows shall be broken. Let the Word of God be your Fortress, and then God will bless you, and preserve you from all the Evils that they can do you. He is always the same God, his Arm is not shortned, he has always the same Power. You may assure your selves, that if the Wicked had the same power over God, that they have over you, they would do the very same to him: But God will pronounce the Sentence of Malediction upon them, and will say unto the Wicked, *Go thou into Eternal Fire, prepared for the Devil and his Angels:* for thou hast persecuted my Children and me. The Wicked cry to God continually, but God doth not hear them, because they have no Repentance: But thou, O Faithful Soul, bless the Eternal God, and say unto him: As long as I shall have a being, I will sing a Psalm unto thee. As for thee, O Wicked Man, thou | hast persecuted God, thy Sins are the cause of thy Damnation: And as for you, Faithful Souls, your Sins are the cause of your Persecution: but be not at all amazed at it, we have not suffered so much as Jesus Christ, who is our Master, and could have saved himself: He sees you, he considers you: he is afflicted when he sees the Wicked persecute you.

Here she stopped for some moments, and putting her Nose under the Sheet, she gave three Laughs with a Female Voice, crying, Hé, Hé, Hé.

And presently she sung the *Pater Noster*, as at high Mass, from the beginning to the end, very agreeably: and afterwards said, Do you understand this? This is very like some Profane Songs, and therefore the Wicked have put it into another Language: But when our Lord taught it to his Disciples, he said to them, say thus, *Our Father* &c. and so she repeated it to the end:[58] Pray then to your Father. Have a care of Worshipping the Saints, and pollute not your selves: for we are the Temple of God, and these Hearts are his Temples. We beseech thee, O God! that thou wouldst pity these poor scattered Sheep. We hope, that of thy Goodness thou wilt gather again thy Flock by thy great Mercy: and if we are at present in Captivity, that thou wilt bring us out of it. After which she again repeated *Our Father* &c. *I believe,* &c. and some little of the *Commandments*, and then said, They observe not him that said, *Thou shalt not Covet:* and, *Thou shalt not commit Adultery,* | because they keep many Concubines.[59] And as for their *Confession,*

---

58   Reference to the Huguenots worshipping in the vernacular, as opposed to the Latin of the Catholic Mass.
59   Another attack on Catholic mores, specifically against monks and priests violating their vow of celibacy.

she said, *The* Devil *and* Judas *were the first that made Confession.* And as for the Sacrifice of the *Maß*, she said, It was an Abominable Sacrifice, and that God would say to them one day: You sell my Word, but I did not give it you to sell: But what do I say? It is none of my Word. Thou hast sold Execrable Words: for they sell a *Maß* for Five pence, two for Ten pence, four for Twenty pence and Eight for Forty pence.[60] Do not go to the Mass, for it is a great Sin, and a mortal Sin: for you abuse the Talents that God hath given you. Those Truckers for Souls, that sell them like Meat in the Shambles, shall be severely dealt with: because they do not sin through Ignorance. Let us pray to God, Good Christians, that he would pardon our Sins: and let us say to him, *Not unto us Lord, not unto us; but to thy Name be the Glory and Honour.* Have mercy therefore upon thy Children, O Lord! and let not the Wicked say, *Where is their God?* Remember that you ought to search, and observe his Word, that it may be said unto you one day, *Come ye Blessed of my Father,* &c. And after this she said, Let us Pray: and so she followed her Ordinary Form of Prayer that she had learned some time since, and then said, *Our Father,* and *I believe in God*: and so closed all with, *The Blessing of God be upon us.*

64 Her Father, who had changed his Religion before the Revocation of the Edict of *Nantes*, for Lucre of a little Mony, and Misused her very often to make her go to Mass: which she did some few times, but not of late. Almost in all her Discourses she Talks of the Violence her Father offered her: and yet while she much Condemns him, she doth not omit to pray God to Pardon him.

She made an Exhortation to Patience in the Presence of *Monsieur Monjoux*,[61] saying, *That the Wicked held but by one little Root, but that it shall be plucked up, and shall dry like the Mowen Hay: and, That the Faithful shall be delivered, and shall flourish at the time she had pointed at.*[62]

---

60   With the revocation of the Edict of Nantes in 1685, Huguenots ceased to exist legally. They were referred to as "new converts"—*nouveaux convertis*—and were forced to attend Mass on Sundays.

61   Possibly Charles Rigot, Count of Montjoux, nearby Saou, where Vincent prophesied. Rigot was married to Ennemonde de Rochegude de Barjac, aunt of the famous Huguenot diplomat Jacques Barjac, Marquis de Rochegude (c.1654–1718), who had just fled to Switzerland in 1688. Emile Jaccard, "Le Marquis Jaques de Rochegude et les protestants sur les galères", *Revue de théologie et de philosophie et compte-rendu des principals publications scientifiques* 31 (1878), 35–73, esp. 36–37.

62   The original source in French, *Abrégé de l'histoire de la bergère de Saou près de Crest en Daufiné* (Amsterdam: 1688), includes astrological predictions concerning England for October, November and December 1688 (pp. 17–21). These are also attributed to Vincent, but were in reality a French translation of John Partridge's predictions. For this reason, they have not been included here.

1.3. A Relation of several hundreds of children and others that prophesie and preach in their sleep, &c. First examined and admired by several ingenious men, Ministers and Professors at *Geneva*, and sent from thence in two letters to *Rotterdam* (London: 1689)[63]

These are Articles or several interrupted pieces of the Sermon, being only some sentences of it taken here and there.[64]   20

Rejoice, Brethren, that God has sent you a little Candle to light you, make use of it, repent ye, and take heed lest the Rod of sin turn against you. Pray to God with all your Hearts, and mend your Lives. God says in his Scriptures, I will pour out my Spirit upon all Flesh,[65] *and the rest of the Passage.* Jacob's Ladder[66] was neither of Wood nor of Stone, but of Prayer and Supplication; God has taken away his Candlestick from you, *Seek and you shall find, knock and it shall be opened unto you.*[67]

Some of our Doctors found something extraordinary and very strong in this Article. I pass over some to be short, and mention only those that are precisely to the purpose, though all the rest is equally good, whether it be when he speaks of the cause of the destruction of our Churches, or whether it be when he promises us the re-establishment of them in case we repent.

Brethren, is it not a strange thing that you, who have promised to follow Jesus Christ, should have renounced him for the sake of a little spot of Ground? (He speaks no more to Country Folks) He who shed the last drop of his Blood for you? Don't trouble your selves in heaping up earthly riches but lay up Treasures where the Moth and Rust do not corrupt.

The Scripture tells you, Be not surprised when you see your selves under Persecution for my name's sake: Pray God heartily, the Devil is about to be shut up in the midst of Hell.

---

63   *A Relation of several hundreds of children and others that prophesie and preach in their sleep, &c. First examined and admired by several ingenious men, Ministers and Professors at Geneva, and sent from thence in two letters to* Rotterdam (London: 1689), 20–22.
64   Collected by an anonymous observer, who visited the prophets of Dauphiné. The fragments were presumably addressed to Jurieu in Rotterdam.
65   Joel 2:28; Acts 2:17.
66   Gen. 28:10–19.
67   Matt. 7:7; Luke 11:9.

I must speak freely to you, I have not the Wit to say all these things, but 'tis God that speaks by me: since your riches have ruined, it must be by your Prayers that you must redeem your selves: and what are ye afraid of for a little wealth? Be afraid of nothing though you were to die: *Happy are they that die in the Lord, for they rest from their Labours.*[68] Hardn'd, Stubborn, Blind Men that we are! We harken not to the Voice of God, and we put no confidence in his promise: Read the 68. Psalm, *Let God arise,* &c.[69]

21　The way of Paradise is a streight way, it is no larger than a Hair, and as fine: the faithful only can walk therein, there is no entering into it for those that are loaden with sins: But the way to Hell is large and spacious, there is a high Road thither.

One of our Doctors, because one of the company wonder'd at that comparison, satisfied him with that of the Camel passing through the eye of a Needle,[70] *and brought on the same or the like occasion.*

It has been told us, That in the last times many shall fall away from the Faith, and we see it now but too much, and above all when we see those base souls, who after having been gone and partaken of the Blood of the Lamb, afterwards come back and plunge themselves into the Abyss of Corruption and Filthiness.

't is a long time since you, who are here present, have been at Mass, but I am afraid the first persecution will make you return thither again: but be sure not to do it, suffer your selves rather to be cut in pieces, suffer your selves rather to be brought to the Block, then return thither again: Lord have pity on these poor sinners, O Eternal strengthen them by thy Grace.

Jesus Christ has poured out all his blood for us, and we can't endure the prick of a pin: fear not men, who can only kill the body, but fear God and that can destroy both soul and body (and concerning that, says the Relation,) He cited the 1. and 2. Verses of the 146. Psalm,[71] and continued to the beginning of the 3. Verse: Brethren, Princes have no power over your Souls, &c. and he spoke a great deal thereon.

68　Rev. 14:13.
69　The Huguenots of the south were known to be powerful psalm singers and the Camisards generally sang the sixty-eighth psalm before battle. Monahan, *Let God Arise*, 10.
70　Matt. 19:24.
71　"Praise ye the Lord. Praise thou the Lord, O my soul. / I will praise the Lord during my life: as long as I have any being, I will sing unto my God."

Speaking of those that had sold that Children for Mony, he saith, They have sold their Children and made an Offering unto Idols, as the 106. Psalm mentions.[72] But God shall redeem the Children, and their Fathers shall perish.

I believe, Sir, here is enough to shew what effect of these Shepherds have produced not only amongst the common People, but amongst all sorts of Men, even the most understanding, there being no one that has ever written or spoken any thing contrary to what I have here mentioned: which I desire our small Assembly to take notice of. Whereupon some of those that hadn't had what Mr. ... had said, reported that 'twas really impossible to see a Man more touched or perswaded of the | thing than he was, being to that degree, that speaking to our chiefest Doctors here, he told them: You may say, Gentlemen, what you please, but if you heard those Children, you would be just as those that have heard them, there is no possibility of resisting. I know what you say concerning the belief we had of the Miracle before hand, concerning our sad condition in *France*, concerning the novelty of the matter of Fact: all this might cause an admiration and astonishment, but there is more than that: For, to tell you the truth, you must know that for an hour and a half, we wept every one of us like so many Children.

[...]

The Prophecies which are that which the Reader will, without doubt, look most after, or perhaps that which he ought to mind least: because we are not certain that the Collections have been well made. The Word, nay the Letter, oftentimes changes the whole Sense of a Discourse. What is not to be questioned in that great number of matters of Fact, is that People fall, that they are in an Ecstasie, that they discourse in their sleep, and others awake, and speak things that have not been suggested to them, and that they themselves knew not.[73] No other Prophecies are to be looked upon as well reported, but only those that have had their Accomplishment. 1. The Deliverance that was to begin in the Month of *September*, as it did really begin by the business of *England*, and by the Declaration of War.[74] 2. The new Prophets which the Shepherdess had Prophesied

---

72 Psalm 106.36–37.
73 On the nature of the prophets' inspirations, see Daniel Vidal, *Le Malheur et son prophète: inspires et sectaires en Languedoc calviniste (1685–1725)* (Paris: 1983).
74 Isabeau Vincent had predicted the deliverance of the Huguenots for September 1688, which coincided with the Glorious Revolution in England, when the Dutch Stadtholder, Prince William of Orange, overthrew the Catholic King James II, as well as with the subsequent outbreak of the Nine Years' War (1688–1697).

of. 3. The King of *England* driven out by the Prince of *Orange*.⁷⁵ 4. The Assemblies that were to be made in several Places. 5. And the cruel Persecution which is now in the Provinces greater than ever, since there has been a Massacre of 400. persons, without reckoning those that have been Executed, according as 'tis reported. These matters of Fact, and several others, so precisely happening, as they had been foretold, shews that if anything does not happen, 'tis because the Prediction was not well taken nor understood: For one and the same spirit cannot be False and True.

∴

1.4. A Postscript. Endeavouring the Satisfaction of them that are Inquisitive after the late Stupendous Extasies and Prophesies in France.⁷⁶

[57] THe *Words* of God are *True*, in the Notice which they have given us, *That the Works of God are Great:* and certainly no Age did ever afford Instances of *Greater* than those which are *Now* the matters of Discourse and Wonder throughout the World.

Among the *Marvellous Things* which at this Day strike the minds of Men with a just Astonishment, there are not many more considerable, than those of *the late Extasies in France.* Concerning which we have undoubted Information:

That about the beginning of the Year 1688: a young Shepardess in the Province of *Dauphine*,⁷⁷ fell into unaccountable *Trances*, wherein tho' the standers by, pull'd her, struck her, cut her and burnt her, yet it was impossible to awaken her. In this condition, her custome was to utter many Divine things: | [58] and though she could neither write nor read, nor could speak any *Language* but that of her Countrey, which has nothing of pure *French* in it, yet she now *Pray'd* and *Preach'd* at a most prodigious rate, and Sang Psalms after the manner of the *French* Protestant Congregations: and when Auditors that could thereby be edified, were present, she expressed herself, not only in *French* of a Dialect most Exact and Correct, but also having occasion to speak *Latin*, in the Refutation of the *Romish Superstitions*, she did it with a distinctness that fill'd all the

---

75 Another reference to the Glorious Revolution (see previous footnote).

76 Cotton Mather, *The Wonderful Works of God Commemorated Praises Bespoke for the God of Heaven in a Thanksgiving Sermon Delivered on Decemb. 19, 1689: Containing Reflections Upon the Excellent Things Done By the Great God.: To Which is Added a Sermon Preached Unto a Convention of the Massachuset-Colony in New-England* (Boston: 1690), 57–62.

77 Isabeau Vincent.

Hearers with Admiration—And though when she came out of her sleep, she remembred not what had befallen her;[78] yet she had her wits thereby made more Sparkling and Refined.

Those new *French* Apostles, the *Dragoons*,[79] quickly did their utmost, for the suppression of this *Rare Thing:* but behold the event! It was not long before other persons fell into the like *Trances*, with *Symptoms* not unlike to those which had attended her: and the Number encreased unto several Hundreds of these *Prophets*,[80] if I may call them so? whereof even the Kings own Guards afforded *One*. And at length some that were *Awake* were carried forth unto Rapturous Exercises with an *Eloquence* and *Energy* equal to that of those that were *Asleep*.

They are People of all Ages and Sexes; but the greatest part of them are *Boyes* and *Girles*, from six or seven to five and twenty years of age; and persons very old;[81] all of them the meaner sort of People: but of Families Exemplary for their good living; the whole affair being indeed so prodigious, that the most obstinate *Sadducees* in the Kingdom confess it, *A natural Distemper directed by Providence to procure the Repentance of a sinful World*.

The Ministry of these *Extraordinary People*, does chiefly consist of two things.

One part of it is, the *Admonition* of those unhappy persons that have provoked God by many notorious Miscarriages, but especially by *Apostasie* under the late Persecution. They deride the Follies of the *Mass*, with a surprizing ingenuity: and in a vast Assembly of perhaps two thousand People come together to hear these *Preachers*, if there be any that have abjured the *Protestant Religion*, they will call them before them, and address them in such powerful Terms, as usually make not not [sic] only the whole Congregation shed floods of Tears, but the *Apostates* themselves to become *Penitents:* and there comes not one away, who does not positively declare, *That he had rather be torn to pieces with wild Horses than ever go to Mass again*. No | man is able to resist their Words! And they make the *Penitents* now and then confess other particular sins, which they convince them of, though the Transgressors had imagined

---

78 See my introduction on Vincent's alleged gift of tongues (pp. 195–196).
79 In the 1680s, Louis XIV quartered soldiers on Huguenot families and allowed them to use violence to convert them to Catholicism. These military campaigns leading to the revocation of the Edict of Nantes in 1685 were known as "dragonnades".
80 A contemporary source estimated their number at about 200–300 by the end of 1688. The best known of these young prophets were Bonpar, Mazet and Pascalin, three shepherds respectively aged 8, 26 and 15. *Lettre de Geneve contenant une relation exacte au sujet des petits prophetes de Dauphiné, le 13. Fevrier 1689* (Rotterdam: 1689), 1–2.
81 Joel 2:28.

these Faults impossible to be discovered. A whole Council assembled could not manage any matter with more Authority than *They* do the Conviction of those, who have gone to *Mass*, that they may shun the Severities of the *French Dragoons*.

It may not be unprofitable to recite a few of the Sentences, which fell from the mouths of these *Extaticks*.

Have a care (said one of them) *that you come not hither out of Curiosity. Better it were for the Wicked that hot Coals of Fire should pass through their mouths, than that they should mock at the Word of God: they had better swallow a Serpent with all its Poison.*[82]

If the Wicked (said one of them) *had the same power over God, that they have over you, they would do the same to Him that they do to you: but God will pronounce the Sentence of Malediction on them, and will say,* Go into Eternal Fire.[83]

Brethren, (said another of them) *Pray hard; and then though we should meet an Army of Enemies at the Door, God will place a million of Angels for your Guard.*

Brethren, (said another of them) *We | have always apprehended more the Threats of Men than those of God, else what happened to us, would not have happened.*

One of them said, *Your Riches have ruined you, and your Prayers must Relieve you.*[84]

One of them said, *I am afraid the first Persecution will make you return to Mass again: but O suffer your selves rather to be first cut in pieces. Alas! Jesus Christ has poured out all his Blood for us, and we can't endure the prick of a pin for Him.*[85]

To the *Apostates*, they generally so conclude their Warnings: *You have sinned against the Father, you have sinned against the Son, take heed of sinning against the Holy Ghost, for God will then pardon you no more.*

And when the Children are told, *They shall be Hang'd*, they are not at all afraid, but answer, *That is but a little harm for a greater, good.*

But the other part of their Ministry is, The *Prediction* of Things quickly to come to pass. They do indeed foretell many Things of a more private concern; they foretell a thousand Things that must happen to themselves and their Friends: and the issue confirms the Prophesie. One of them being thrown into

---

82   These are the words of Isabeau Vincent. See *A LETTER From a Gentleman of DAUPHINE To one of his Friends at GENEVA*, reproduced above (source 1.1. p. 201).

83   Also attributed to Vincent in the same source. See source 1.2. above, p. 205.

84   See *A Relation of Several Hundreds of Children and Others that Prophesie and Preach in Their Sleep*, reproduced above (source 1.3., p 207). Cotton Mather's compilation provides evidence that several accounts of the *petits prophètes* of Dauphiné were circulating in New England as early as 1689.

85   Idem, p. 208.

a Dungeon, said, *The man who sent her thither should within eight Dayes fetch her out*, and it strangely was accomplished.[86]

But the Things of a more publick Concern, are chiefly those which they fore- [60][87] tel. The Gentlemen, who give us the History, tell us, that they judge it not yet convenient to publish a large part of the Authentick and sufficient Collections which they have made of these Prophecies. However, they have given us a Taste. In general, The Subjects of this *Enthusiasm*[88] all agree in foretelling, *A Speedy Deliverance to the Church of God:* and they declare, *The Late Revolutions in England, to be the Beginning of that Deliverance.*[89]

Tho' all *France* was fill'd with a Rumour, That the Late K. *James*[90] had Defeated the (then) Prince of *Orange*,[91] both by Land and Sea, *these* then said, *The Authors of these Reports commit a great sin, for the Prince of Orange has Chas'd, and shall Chase the King out of England: and that is the Beginning of the Deliverance of the Church.*

They foretold a fresh Assault of Persecution in *France*, and it had a very dreadful fulfilment: for after it Ensued a Terrible Storm of Outrage upon the Relicks of Protestantism in the Desolate Kingdom: in one Article of which, there was a Massacre, of about four hundred people: but they foretold within how many Days the Persecution should be over: and they give hopes of a *Protestant | King*, very quickly to be seen in *France*. They proclaim, *The Divel is going* [61] *to be shut up in the midst of Hell!* They say, *The Accomplishment of the Prophetical Months and Dayes is at Hand:*[92] *but it must be accompanied with very Terrible Wars and Plagues.*

The whole is a Thing very unaccountable: and when I consider the Fate of the famous *German Prophets*,[93] which made such a Noise in the World: or, when I consider, that while the *Jews* were under their Infatuations about their false Messiah, *Sabatai Saevi*,[94] some Hundreds of people fell into *Extasies* (as 'tis

---

[86] Presumably Isabeau Vincent again, who was incarcerated in Grenoble in July 1688. *Lettre de Geneve*, 1.

[87] Erroneous pagination: this should read p. 62.

[88] Enthusiasm is understood in the early modern sense of the term here, i.e. a charismatic form of religious fanaticism. See Lionel Laborie, "Enthusiasm, Early Modern Philosophy, and Religion", in *Encyclopedia of Early Modern Philosophy and the Sciences*, ed. D. Jalobeanu and C.T. Wolfe (Springer, Cham: 2020), online (https://doi.org/10.1007/978-3-319-20791-9_376-1)

[89] I.e., the Glorious Revolution (1688–1689).

[90] King James II (r.1685–1688).

[91] William, Prince of Orange and future King of England (r.1689–1702).

[92] On the prophets' eschatological timeline, see notes 53 and 74 above.

[93] Presumably Jan van Leyden and the Anabaptist kingdom of Münster.

[94] Sabbatai Zevi (1626–1676). See Cengiz Sisman, *The Burden of Silence: Sabbatai Sevi and the Evolution of the Ottoman-Turkish Donmes* (Oxford: 2015).

Reported) wherein they Prophesied, the speedy Deliverance of the Jews by that Impostor, and *Little Children* that could not stammer a word, yet repeated and pronounced the *Name* of this Deceiver, with Happy Omens of Him; but consider on the other side, That *not to Regard the Works of the Lord, is a Destroying evil:* I dare not make any Reflections on it. I dare not say, what *Authority*, or what *Original* is to be assigned unto these *Inspirations:* but this I know, the *Comfort* and *Counsil* of the Church is without such things *now* sufficiently provided for: and our Lord Jesus having foretold the State of the Church until He come again, hath so concluded His Predictions, *If any man shall add unto these things, God shall add Plagues unto | Him.*[95] Nevertheless, This also *I* shall, take for granted, That the Great God intends hereby to *Awaken* us unto a Consideration of what is before us: *That* is a proper use of *Miracles:* and when we are once Awakened, there is provided for our Entertainment *A more Sure Word of Prophecy:* which O that our God may help us to *Give Heed* unto. *Amen.*

∴

---

95 Rev. 22:18.

2 Fragments of a Sermon Preached by Daniel Raoul [Raoux], c.1701[96]

.... as the Dove is a clianly [cleanly] & pure bird, so must our Church be pure, true & free from all filthiness: but this cannot be said of the Church of Rome, nor of that of Calvin:[97] which are incessantly contaminated with all kinds of vice impurity & murder. They have honey in their mouths & gall in their hearts & their savage hands are always ready to shed innocent blood.

As the Dove is mild & peaceable bird so must the Church of Christ also be, which is being enlivened by the spirit of God is endowed with mildness & gentleness. My Friends, let us follow the example of her divine Spouse who said "learn of me for I am meek and low in heart"[98] & "blessed are the peacemakers".[99] But it is not thus with the Church of Rome. She is obdurate & unmerciful, composed of crual persons who oppress their brethren & tyrannise over them with every species of persecution & torment, who plunder the true & faithful disciples of Jesus Christ of their temporal possessions, drive them from their habitations, & drag them into dungeons in order to convey them afterwards to the galleys, to the gallows, or the scaffold. Let us lament their cruel tyranny, my dear Friends, the Lord will ship the veil from their souls & will bring their works to nought and whilst they are tormented with remorse even to death, our souls having become meek & peaceable will enjoy for ever a tranquil felicity.

Thus in our grievous calamity we ought to lift up our eyes towards heaven & to put our trust in God & not in men. Let us bravely arm ourselves with the sword of the word, the helmet of Truth and the shield of Faith: remembering the Glory & happiness in store for them who suffer for the Gospel: but let us never take those cruel arms which destroy the works of the Creator and drench the house with human blood ...

The voice to which Jesus will hearken is that of our grief when we repent for our sins, the cry of our sense of our misery, our sighs, our prayers, & our continual tears & in short, our thanksgivings for all the benefits which our heavenly Father bestows on us day by day ...

---

96 LSF, Ms Vol. 315, fols 13–15. The original in French is found at LSF, Ms Vol. 314, no. 1.

97 As stated in my introduction, Daniel Raoux is generally regarded as the first French Quaker prophet. He was active around the time of the outbreak of the Camisards rebellion in 1702; he and his followers did not identify as Calvinists and therefore claimed to be separate from the Huguenot community. They condemned the use of violence, both by Catholic oppressors and by the Camisards, and advocated passive resistance and martyrdom instead. Laborie, "From English *Trembleurs* to French *Inspirés*", 225–244.

98 Matt. 11:29.

99 Matt. 5:9.

Are those that Dove of Jesus Christ who within these two years have defiled themselves with abominable idolatry, with innumerable murders & horrible persecutions contrary to the exhortation & command of Christ "Love your enemies" & "do good to them who despitefully use you".[100] Have not these forsaken the holy communion of Jesus in persisting in their rebellion & apostasy? Let us then imitate the piety of the apostles who chose rather to suffer affliction with the people of God, than to enjoy the fruits of sin ...

Yes my dear Friends, let us imitate our divine Saviour who foretold that we should suffer much affliction for his name's sake: who commanded us to forgive our enemies, to love them, to pray for them, to do all manner of good to those who persecute us, & | to manifest to them, by our resignation, our patients and our good Works, that we, and not these murderous persecutors are the true children of Jesus Christ. Let us bless the hand that strikes us, & let us beseech the God of Mercy to open the eyes of their understandings by purifying their souls from such complicated murders & iniquity.[101]

∴

---

100   Matt. 5:44.
101   French Quakers condemned the use of violence, both by Catholic oppressors and by the Camisards, in the aftermath of the revocation of the Edict of Nantes. They advocated passive resistance and martyrdom instead, which is why this sermon his regarded as the earliest evidence of a Quaker community in France. See note 97 above.

3 Camisard Prophecies

3.1. A Precis of the discourse of Mr Durand Fage of Aubaye,[102] pronounced under the operation of the Spirit, in London on 30 August 1706, at 8 or 9 o'clock in the morning. O.S.[103]

Prayer

Lord, do not let me ... &c.

I tell you, in truth, my Child,[104] great Events are soon to come. I assure you, my Child, that you will see amazing things. I want to send my Graces in abundance. Rejoice yourself, for I am soon to come; and sooner than the World expects. Many will want to see it, but they will not. They have rejected by their Incredulity &c. Confess my Word openly. I am going to show that this is not what they think: but it is my powerful arm that comes over my followers. Do not be surprised. You shall soon see these things. Lord, thy will be done. I tell you openly, I assure you, that the Beast will soon be defeated. Do not mutter against the effects of my Graces. Be assured that I do not deceive you. I shall soon revisit you, and I shall announce to you the things that shall come to pass; but at least, beware, and make sure to announce my truth.

A Precis of the discourse of Mr Jean Cavalier of Sauve,[105] pronounced under the Operation of the Spirit, shortly after the preceding one

---

102 Durand Fage (1681–c.1750), a silk weaver by trade, used to carry weapons for Louis XIV's dragoons until he deserted to join the Camisards. Little is known about his activities during the rebellion. He left the Cévennes in 1705 and was the first of three Camisards to arrive in London in June 1706. Together they inspired the millenarian movement of the "French Prophets". See Laborie, "French Prophets", ODNB.

103 LPL, Ms 932/10 [my translation]. These prophecies were transcribed jointly by the lawyer Jean Daudé (1651–c.1730), the merchant and secretary Charles Portalès (1676–1763) and the Swiss mathematician Nicolas Fatio de Duillier (1664–1753). Laborie, Enlightening Enthusiasm, 31–32; Mandelbrote, "Fatio, Nicolas, of Duillier (1664–1753)", ODNB.

104 In a typical Camisard fashion, Fage begins vocalising the Holy Spirit while under inspiration and expresses himself in the first person. Therefore "I" refers to God here, and "my Child" to the prophet himself.

105 Jean Cavalier of Sauve (1686–c.1740), was educated by the Jesuits during his childhood and allegedly began prophesying around 1701. He was imprisoned in Perpignan during most of the War of the Cévennes and was the second Camisard to arrive in London, in August 1706.

Prayer

O God, I commit myself into your arms, my Father of Graces; and I come at this moment, o God, to give you thanks for so many Blessings, that I receive, despite being a Sinner. May it please you, O my Father, | to numb the Spirit of the Flesh in me; and reawaken your Holy Spirit in me. And take possession of my Limbs. And may my Tongue remain stuck to my Palate, until your Spirit moves it. Do not let me speak out of Zeal to please men; nor out of Zeal to announce your wonders: and do not let me force your Spirit, but I commit myself into your hands.

I come, my Child,[106] to revisit you at this moment, and to declare you the Truth. Be assured of my Promise. I come now to reveal great things to you. Muster your Courage. Here I come to demonstrate the strength of my Arm on Earth: for every Nation shall recognise me as their God and their Father. Here are the Events [that have been predicted]: The Time has passed. The term has expired. You shall see wonderful things, in a few Days. I come to strike twisted and perverse Nations. I come to disperse whatever is not in Union with my Church. I come to destroy men's Buildings from the Earth. I come to save my followers from the Blindness and Errors, in which they have fallen. Nations ****[107] shall recognise me in part. I shall make my Voice heard to all Nations *** I come to enlighten part of the Nations that are not in the Light. *** I shall show great things. Floods, Earthquakes, Plagues and Famines shall be seen. You have never seen anything like this *** Be assured of my Promises. My Judgements are just. My Promises shall be fulfilled in a little time. I shall gather you in a corner of the Earth, that I have saved. I shall gather my Children in a few Days. Write down these Words, and the day; and their Accomplishment shall soon be. Here come | the Accomplishment of the Revelation of St John *** The Destruction of the wicked is near. I come, for my followers, armed with peace; yet with an iron Sceptre for my Enemies. Soon there shall only be one Law, and one Faith.[108] I shall destroy the Beast. Rejoice, and you shall fight again. The Lamb shall yet give a terrifying Fight. He shall be victorious. I have crushed the Head of the old Serpent, who is Satan. You shall see these things, despite Satan and his Companions. I come to repeat what I have already told you [several

---

106 Cavalier's inspiration begins here. "I" now refers to God and "my Child" to the prophet himself.
107 Asterisks are included in the manuscript by the scribe(s) writing down these prophecies, presumably to indicate missing word(s).
108 The original ("qu'une Loi, et qu'une Foi") rhymes in French and echoes the French absolutist motto "un Roi, une Loi, une Foi": "One King, one Law, one Faith".

times]: the six shall be raised to the seven; and the seven to the eight, and the eight to the nine; Peace, general Peace. Zion shall no longer be tormented. Take Courage; I am coming, my coming is near. You shall not see me with your Eyes. You shall recognise my Coming, by the Blessings that you shall receive; but the wicked shall recognise it even more, by &c. I shall defeat Satan; he shall not rise again. The Beast shall be destroyed. There shall be no other God than me. No Nation shall worship false Gods any longer. They shall have no Cities. It will come soon. Be prayerful and vigilant, for fear of being surprised in your Sins. I shall reveal Signs and Miracles, great things on Earth. Woe to he who will doubt and be frightened. I shall strike him, and let him fall in Satan's Trap. Reassure yourselves by your Prayers. I am the Almighty; I shall not retract. The Oath I have made shall be fulfilled. Those of the earthly Kings &c. I shall demonstrate my Power. I am the | God of Truth; I shall be recognised as such. Take Courage, these Events shall come. A cruel partition shall take place on Earth, but determine yourselves to serve me. There is no more Prolongation, no more Delay nor Capitulation for the wicked. This Judgement, more just than dreadful, is near. They shall be judged fairly. I come to call you, to invite you, to dwell with you. Be ready to receive me. I come to reject the defilement that is in you, to clothe you with a Dress of glory and magnificence. I have abridged the Time of your Deliverance. Your Wishes shall be accomplished. Your Prayers, albeit weak, are fulfilled. I shall deliver you from the second Pharaoh,[109] who shall be destroyed. You shall see these things, and those who hear them. You shall declare its Truthfulness, and be its Witnesses. If I have chastised you, it is because I love you. I come to give you a Legacy, and to write to you, in my Book of Life, in a Golden Letter. Your Name shall be inscribed in it, and shall not be erased, if you are faithful to me.

You shall see the Events of all these things that you are hearing. You shall see greater and (more) amazing ones. The Olive tree and its greenery is unlike the greenery (that) my Church (will have). They shall be smitten to death. Peace to my followers, and to my Church, in a little time. Some shall cry, Lord, but I shall not listen to them. Coward Servants; You shall take no part in &c. If you have been cowardly, resume my Work. What is written in the Revelation of St John, She[110] [shall be?] Queen ** She shall be Queen, but only in the Abyss. You shall lead her, and chase her away, by the singing of my | followers. You shall

---

109 Presumably Louis XIV, who continued to persecute French Protestants after the revocation of the Edict of Nantes. It is worth emphasising that, although a temporary truce to the War of the Cévennes was agreed in May 1704, the conflict resumed shortly afterwards and continued until 1710.
110 The beast. Rev. 11:7.

no longer drink from leaking Cisterns, from those corrupt Fountains; but ****. Extend your hand and I will extend mine to you. To those afflicted comes Consolation. Zion's Joy shall be greater &c. Such things were bound to occur ***. You have yet to a small Storm, a harsh Tempest. It shall be harsher than it has been so far, but it shall be dispersed in a little time, like Smoke by the Wind, and shall only pass by. Fight with your Prayers, and not with your earthly Weapons. You shall fight, and I shall conquer. Do not fear men. I come to strike by the power of my Arm the Nations who &c. The laurel has never been so green &c.

Peace to my followers. I hold these seven Vials,[111] to pour them on sinful Nations. They shall see the power of my Arm. I shall receive them in part. I shall reject them in part. Take Courage. Rejoice.

I tell thee that You are like a soiled Flag. I shall purify you from your stains. I come to assure you of everything that I have marked in my Writings. These Events are near. Pray. Heed. Strike violently. Don't be a double-edged Sword, a Body cut in half. For you cannot serve two Masters.[112] Choose the path of Life; Your Works are bad. Pray. Again and again. Leave Evil; do Good. You shall still receive greater News of Victory over the Pharaoh. Your Joy be through Prayer. I shall act, and work. I make use of men. I shall tear down the Walls of Babylon.

6   The time | is near. I come, by grace, to liberate you. In a little time the general Assembly shall rise. Many shall enter, only to be chased away, like those who enter the Feast with the Robe of Defilement. Several shall see the Deliverance and its open Pastures, who shall not taste them. He who loves the World, my Love is not in him. The World and its Greed shall pass in a little time. My Sheep shall no longer be encamped with Rams.

The six shall be raised to the seven; and the seven to the eight, and the eight to the nine (and all shall be completed ^perfected).[113]

I leave you now. I shall return soon.

You will be called in a little time before the Greats of this City.[114] They are worldly, so I shall talk to them about this World, the Armies &c. Leave the Goods of this World, for it shall pass. Leave the Darkness, and come toward the Light. Leave Evil. Pray again and again.

Lord, I commit myself into your Will. I await your Advent.

---

111   Rev. 15–16.
112   Presumably a reference to the Huguenots' desire to worship God according to their faith and their loyalty to Louis XIV. Although the Camisards always insisted they remained loyal to the Sun King and that they only took up arms to end their persecution, this passage argues otherwise. See Monahan, *Let God Arise*, 15.
113   Written in superscript in the original manuscript, presumably as an alternative transcription.
114   The Camisards rapidly established diplomatic contacts in London and expected to build on their support to plead their cause in England.

The Original was signed by Messieurs.¹¹⁵

***   *** NB
***   ***
***
***

who all witnessed and were present during these Discourses.

∵

3.2. A Precis of the Discourse of Mr Durand Fage of Aubaye, pronounced under the Operation of the Spirit, in London on 3rd Sept. 1706, at 8 or 9 o'clock in the morning. O.S.¹¹⁶

Prayer

Lord my God, my Father, I commit myself into your good Will. Thy Will be done. However, if thou want Me to speak the Truth, I commit myself into your Power and Authority. Numb the Spirit of the Flesh so that I can speak no Word but by your Spirit &c. My Tongue be stuck to my Palate rather than speaking one Word which comes not from your Will.

My Child, you may speak openly. You have to openly voice my Wonders. Do not worry about the things that &c. I shall support you, in every thing. I tell you, you shall soon see things that one cannot fathom. I do not explain it to you now. Have Courage. Let nothing sadden you. Soon your *** great Events *** Soon I shall demonstrate to you the effects of Graces. Courage. Here comes the time. Here is the progress of the things that shall happen. Muster up your Courage. Pray me in faith. I shall soon set Zion at Liberty. All those who make Efforts, on Earth, shall be confused, in a little time *** Some shall suffer Martyrdom in my Name. Here comes soon the Unfolding of things that shall be accomplished. I shall inform you of what takes place *** soon in the Cévennes.¹¹⁷ Farewell, my

---

115 Besides the three aforementioned scribes—Fatio, Daudé and Portalès (see note 103)—the Presbyterian minister Thomas Cotton (1653–1730), the Irish Baronet Sir Richard Bulkeley (1660–1710) and the Marquis de Miremont (1656–1732) are known to have attended and hosted early Camisard assemblies in the summer 1706. Warren Johnston, "Bulkeley, Sir Richard, second baronet (1660–1710)", ODNB (http://www.oxforddnb.com/view/article/3898, accessed 30 July 2007); Laborie, "Bourbon, Armand de, marquis de Miremont (1655–1732)", ODNB.
116 LPL, Ms 934/52 [my translation].
117 Further evidence that the Camisards maintained ties with the Cévennes and planned to revive the rebellion from London.

Child. Have faith in my Promise; it is certain and true. I shall in no way defend *** the Plans ** I shall disperse them like the Wind disperses the Smoke. To those who shall be faithful to me, I | promise eternal Felicity; and the Pasture of Life, that had been stolen from them. I shall inform you of what you will need to do. Some, among you, are doubting, and others have received my Graces.

A Precis of the Discourse of Mr Jean Cavalier of Sauve,
pronounced under the Operation of the Spirit,
shortly after the previous Speech.

Prayer.

O God, I commit myself, in this moment, into your arms, as you come, Lord, to revisit me. O God, I am ready to receive any thing from you, even though I am a Sinner; if it is your Will to make me feel the effects of your Graces, I await the power of your Spirit. Thy Will ^{truth} be pronounced by it. May the Spirit of the World, and of my Members, the Carnal Spirit be dissipated from my body. May I not speak to be seen by men, (nor) for the World to glorify you. If thou have Trials and Chastisements to send me, I am unworthy of receiving your Graces. I ought instead to receive a Rod to hit me. Let me not force thy Spirit; but let me await the Advent of thy Spirit in me.

My Child, I tell you in Truth that I am coming, at this time, to reveal to you the Effects of my Graces. I come to enlighten you with the pure Truth. Be assured of the Strength of my Arm. I come to give you strength and courage. For I declare it, in Truth, that I am going to show the Strength of my Arm. Lean on the Strength of my protecting Arm. I am going to completely crush and shake up the yoke of the Antichrist. Behold the Sentence of the Wicked; I shall vomit them out of my mouth. I shall reject them; and chase them out of me. | I swore in my Wrath, that they shall never enter my Rest. I shall put aside my Sheep. I shall brand them. You shall carry my Sign. I come in a little time. I hold this iron Sceptre. I come to strike the Nations of the Earth, those marked with the sign of the Beast. It will be in a few Days. Here comes the Destruction of the Beast. Rejoice. Prepare thyself to receive, in a little time, to receive the Heritage from the Heavens. I shall make all my faithful part of it. You are too impatient *** You would like to see, in an Instant, &c like the break of Day &c but beware that it does not come too early for you. *** Day of Peace, of Cries, and of Separation. Cruel Partition. *** The wicked shall not mix any longer. I shall destroy them and smite them with the Strength of my Arm. *** I could well destroy them without giving them Torment: But I wanted them to suffer Torment ** But their greatest Torment shall be in the Abyss *** V *** Death at your feet shall surprise you ** But here is the Healing at your feet. The sick shall be healed. The weak shall receive strength; and the afflicted Consolation. You have fallen into your Sins, but here comes the Healing at your feet. This is Consolation for my Followers. ᙾWork diligently by your Prayers. Renounce the Goods of this World, that have caused the ruin of my Followers.ᙾ[118] How many lost Souls, to work for these Goods *** Time is short, it is approaching. Think of the Master you have to serve. For you cannot serve me and the World ᴰᵉᵛⁱˡ. Choose one side or the other. The Time is near, I assure you. I come to make you feel it today. Be assured that you will soon see its effects and that you will bear Witness to it. Now the weak shall be strong, the small great, the poor rich; | and the dead shall receive Life. Although you have called upon the Doctors of this World,[119] You are in a Hospital of Stench and Corruption. You entered it. You defiled yourselves again. You entered it. Pray. You shall receive my Healing in little time, by your Prayers. Work for eternal Life. Prepare thyself. Behold a scaffold raised in a little time, and I as its Judge. Never was a scaffold to Man's eyes alike. I shall send Flames of Fire on Earth to repress the wicked. The Fall of your Enemies is near. And you, o Rome, your Fall is near. You shall no longer wallow in your Decadence. You shall no longer invite my followers into thy Decadence. Take courage *** It is I who shall accomplish my Work, I who hold this double-edged Sword; Armed with Peace and Wrath, I come to destroy *** Cruel Separation; cruel Partition! Terrible Pain! Torment! Never was prison nor Captivity comparable to that of the wicked. Heaven is closed to the wicked, and open to the virtuous. Prepare yourselves. You shall soon embark on a journey. You shall all be gathered in a little time. Peace, general peace. Peace, I say, in a little time.**** For although I have told you many times, ** that the six shall be raised to the seven, and the seven to the eight, and the eight to the nine, and that all shall be perfected, You shall receive signs of it sooner. In a little time ** Relief before the nine. Once raised to the nine, there shall be no more Corruption. I shall overthrow the walls of Babylon; and I shall destroy this twisted and perverse Race that cheers the Beast. Woe upon those who shall have defiled themselves | with the Beast. My Children were ravished from me by their Cowardice. They who did it out of Cowardice shall receive more Torments. O cowardly Servants! Useless servants! You shall be rewarded with fire, not with eternal felicity. You shall be clothed in a Burning Robe, instead of a Robe of Magnificence; a Robe of iniquity ** Instead of entering with your head up, with Song of Glory and Triumph,

---

118   This sentence was added in the margin preceded by the symbol ᙾ.
119   Huguenot theologians understood the persecution of their coreligionists in France as a divine trial and were almost unanimously opposed to an armed rebellion against a lawful monarch like Louis XIV as a result.

you shall go to the sentences that are awaiting you. ** This Partition shall come ** Make your peace *** Enter my Council, and my Parliament. Behold, I am sending you Ambassadors. Hear the Revelations, and the Warnings that I send you: and you shall receive Relief. Decide for yourselves. Send me an answer to the Letter ** I tell you, in truth, that I am going to demonstrate the Effects of my Graces; wonderful things; miraculous things. It will be in little time, in a few days. Do not bore yourselves. You are no sooner ill than you would like to be healed. But do not bore yourselves. A short time to me is a long one to you. A moment to me is very long to you. You shall receive it soon. The time is short. Your Prayers have not shortened it, but my Graces, and the Charity and Compassion I have for you: Take courage. Take Courage my Child. [120] Yes I say to you, I come again to shew you truthfully, and as the very Truth myself, that the six shall be raised to the seven, and the seven to the eight, and the eight to the nine, all shall be perfected. No more strength shall the wicked have, despite the Devil, his Rage and his Companions. He shall be chained. He shall do no more Ravages. Remember that if he has entered, and has ravished some of you, it is because I wanted to put you to the Trial. Have I not warned you, that I would try you like gold. I will recognise you as my faithful. I said persevere to the end. By these Words You were to understand that you would have Crosses and Tribulations. That is, whatever Whirlpools and Storms that blow, hold on to me. You are on dry land, not on ice, nor on man's Arms. It is my Arm that supports you. | The Trial is won. You have made your peace with me. Purify yourselves. Do not fall into Sin again, into the things of the World. If you are my faithful, act as if You were already in Heaven. Rejoice, Zion, and declare their Joy to your Children. Your pains shall pass. Since we are two opposites; I shall break the Head of the Old Serpent. He who loves me cannot love the world. Decide for yourselves. The time is near. Pray ceaselessly. Forsake evil; do good. Answer the many Couriers, Expresses (Messengers) Ambassadors, whom I send you. It is a Treaty of Eternal Peace. I do not mean fleeting peaces *** The Devil and the Beast will be destroyed. The Lamb is the Victor. Victory is yours. Be assured in my Promises. They are certain. My Judgements are righteous ** You have been captives and you are still. But, he who led in Captivity will be led into Captivity, into a Place where there are Barriers of Fire, and Barriers of Iron, and Satan for Sentinel. Nations of Sinners! Nations that were not in my knowledge! You who have persevered in the train of men, of Satan and of his Companions! I have sworn in my Ire that they shall not enter into my rest. You who have stood firm, who have

---

120 This space in the original manuscript presumably indicates that the scribe may have missed a sentence when writing down Cavalier's words or perhaps to indicate the beginning of a new paragraph.

kept the Shield of Faith &c this Crown of Glory * this Robe of Glory and Magnificence will be given to you. You are inscribed in my Book with a Golden Letter. *. You will be reunited, O You, driven out of Israel, in a corner of the earth, in a place that I have prepared. I will sprinkle you with Dew (a) gentle Rain; not a Rain like that which is for the Trees of the Earth. ** Your Prayers must join the Prayers of those in Captivity. I talk to you as much as to your Brothers. You are one Body. I shall give you the same Rewards. All my children will receive the same Salary. You will be equal, poor and rich. You hear my Voice. If You see me with your Eyes. ***. My Word is not like my Face, which would knock you to the ground. You would not be able to see the Crowns, that I have prepared for you. My Face *** Whatever Storms and Persecutions that | come, do not stumble into Satan's Slavery. It will not be when this Assembly will be formed, it will not be a Partition, like that of the Goods of this World. In that time there will be neither Doctor, nor Lawyer, nor Prosecutor, who will take your Cause in his hands. I am your lawyer. It will be I, who will judge You, according to Your merits. Come treat this Peace, this Covenant, which you have broken. By which means should you attach yourself to me? By your Prayers. Be cautious like the Snake, and simple like the Dove. Like the Serpent sheds its Skin, you will be stripped of impure clothes and Filth. But a Robe of Glory and of Magnificence shall be given to you. ** the ** Clothes of Heaven, this Glory, which belongs to you, Take heed that it be not taken from you. My Coming is near. You will not see me. ~~It will be in a little time and soon my Child, I repeat to you that his pain~~ It is not the Coming that the Jews expect. You will recognise it by   [121] and strength **. You will see relief. The Man of the Earth will no longer afflict you. In a little time, in a few days, extraordinary and amazing things will be seen. For I assure you, my Child, that the Flames of Fire are red: and Pharao will be consumed by them. It will be the second Red Sea. It will be in a little time and soon, my Child, I repeat to you that his Pain will be great, and so will his Torment. The Afflictions of your Enemies the Scare and Fear will seize from all sides. He is about to make his greatest Effort, all at once. But all this will be nothing. Who can resist me, slay me, or defeat me! His words his Efforts, his Undertakings are but in vain. Courage. You will see great things. He will not die. Once he has cast his venom, he will want to shake the Beast's Yoke. Many will cry out to me, Lord, Lord; but I will give no answer. Rejoice. And know | that I will use a handful of my <u>Faithful to fight still</u>: but I will be victorious for them. Prepare yourself.

---

121 Space left for a missing word in the original manuscript.

I want you to know in truth that my work will be completed soon. My Servants do not have much longer to fight.[122] The Fruit is near. What you have asked and wished for, your desires, will be given to you. Rejoice. Do not be surprised. Courage. Be prayerful and vigilant. My Coming is near. Satan again will enter Prison soon, ** will take, will dissipate some ˢᵉᵛᵉʳᵃˡ. But do not be surprised. No more Delay, Prolongation &c Peace, General Peace. A Blessed Day for my Faithful; but some will curse it: some will receive it in Tribulation. How many times have I told that you were but Passengers. You have trampled upon my Words, like the Mule tramples upon the Grain. This Judgment more righteous than terrible *** You will be judged justly: But to you, who have been warned, your Judgment will not be terrible; since you deserved it. The Beast will be Queen in the Abyss.[123] She will reign an Eternity; as the Revelation of St. John says, I am Queen, and will see no mourning. You will be Queen, Empress, in Hell. Your burial is coming. You must help accompany her to her Burial. You will accompany her to her Tomb, to the Gates of the Abyss. They will speak to you, and ask for your grace. They will want to apologise to you. But it is neither to you nor to me, because there is no time left. Their Condemnation has come. Its Walls shall become Dust. His Revelation &c soon. Prepare yourselves to receive these Goods from Heaven, this Heritage; and to attend my Throne. I am Alpha and Omega,[124] be assured. | Real promises! Just judgment! Never has the Tree of the Earth been in a higher flower than my Church will be *** Candelabra *** There shall be no more Darkness. The Earth will bear Seed and Fruit: but no one will reap. Several will sow, and will not reap. Several will plant a vine, and will not eat its Fruit. I am going to part with you now. I warn you not to be afraid. Do not fear men. Fear me. I part with you as for the Word. **** You will speak to the Greats of this City:[125] but you will tell them that you are doing my Will.

Lord I thank you for the so many blessings, that you have given me in this *** I will take the Cup of Deliverance. I will invoke your Holy Name†. I commit myself into your hands. I await your Advent.

---

122 The Camisards were still fighting in the Cévennes at the time this prophecy was delivered.
123 Rev. 11:7.
124 Rev. 1:8, 21:6; 22:13.
125 London.

The original was signed by Messrs

    ***
    ***
***   ***
    ***
    ***
    ***

who were all present during these Discourses.

NB As Mr Cavalier began, one of the men, who were present, fainted.

Before starting, Mr Cavalier had raised his right arm up high for some time, and stiffened it very hard. His Face then resembled that of a man dying of a pestilent and terrible death. And his eye, having opened, looked excessively severe, all [...] and a little inflamed, and of a yellow Colour very different from its Natural one.

† Thy Will be done. Thy Will be done, and not mine; as we pray in the Everyday Prayer.

The raised Arm was a Sign of the Wrath of Heaven, threatening of some Judgments: at least judging by what one had previously heard from the mouths of Messrs Portalés[126] and Fage. The Fist was closed; and the Arm turned in a manner which, when Mr Cavalier brought it down, little by little, on the Table, looked like he was imitating the movement of a man who, having grabbed a phial, by the neck, was going to pour it in front of him on the ground.

At the place marked ~~~~~~~ the Movements of Mr. Cavalier's head were violent, beyond what could be conceived. Which usually happens to him when he touches upon such Subjects.

∴

---

126 Charles Portalès (1676–1763). See note 103.

4   Isaac Elzière and the New Zionists (1742)[127]

366   This book[128] shall be called *the torch of justice*,[129] the book of clear interpretations, the awakening of spirits fallen asleep by their sins, the cream of the Holy Scriptures, the sword of the spirit, the weapons of the faithful believers, the joy and consolation of Zion of afflicted souls, the treasure of the spiritual lights that the Holy Spirit comes to develop by the enlightenment it gives us of its Holy Scriptures in these last days. For the Holy Spirit is the architect of the heavens; that has deployed the treasures of its lights and of its spiritual knowledge in order to build this work, this edifice by the hand of Isaac Elzière, native of in Saint-Amboix, in Languedoc. […]

367   I saw in a vision through the eyes of the spirit a flock of doves, of white pigeons who came to rest on my head, so much so that my head was all covered and surrounded. And then I saw three characters in front of me. These three characters appeared to me as the divinity of the Father, the Son and the Holy Spirit. And one of them was carrying a paper roll in his right hand, which was written half way with passages from the Holy Scriptures that are in that book. He told me to take a quill in my hand and to prepare myself to write clear interpretations of these passages. But one of these three characters was standing before me and was preventing me from seeing and knowing this spiritual light that I would have wished to see and know in order to be enlightened by it. And so the other two told him: "Make room for this man and move aside from my eyes, so that he can see", and he came next to me. But before he moved aside, I saw a ray of light penetrating my body, and this light was so penetrating that it clothed me all over. So this character gave me this paper roll that he was holding in his right hand, and he told me to take the quill and write. So I began writing this book that I name *the torch of justice* because I saw a torch lit to enlighten me before as I was writing it before dawn.[130] And at first I was

---

127   Ribard, "Un Inspiré, Isaac Elzière", 365–372 [my translation].
128   Isaac Elzière had allegedly written a book of prophecies. To the best of our knowledge, it was never published and the manuscript appears to be lost.
129   Jean-Paul Chabrol has suggested that this title strongly echoed several of the French Prophets' works a few decades earlier. Jean-Paul Chabrol, "Mémoire et identité religieuse: la « légende » des Couflaïres de la Vaunage", in *La Vaunage au xviiie siècle* 2 (Nîmes: 2003), 5–6. Local archives provide evidence that the New Zionists read *Éclair de Lumière descendant des Cieux* (1711), *Cri d'alarme en avertissement aux Nations, qu'ils sortent de Babylone, des Ténèbres, pour entrer dans le repos du Christ* (1712), and *Plan de la justice de Dieu sur la Terre dans ces derniers jours, et du Relèvement de la chute de l'homme par son péché* (1714). ADH, C 509, no. 174.
130   Similar to Elzière's vision, the Camisard prophet Elie Marion was once depicted in an

negligent and was not paying attention to this work, so my fleshy eyes closed all at once, and I saw from the spirit's eyes a character coming to snuff this torch that was enlightening me and talking to me. I was very sad and afflicted to see that this light had withdrawn from my presence as a result of my negligence, and so I gave up my work until it returned. But having returned to enlighten me, I took my quill this time with more diligence, lest the Lord might take his wrath at me even more. And when I had neglected to write a passage that was to be put in writing in this book, I could hear a voice telling me to read in such a chapter of the Holy Scriptures, and when I found the said passage, I wrote it down where it was to be placed. And one day, as I was writing at three o'clock after noon, my fleshy eyes closed all of a sudden, but the spirit's eyes opened to me instead, and I saw in a vision of the spirit's eyes, that I was following a path drenched in a glorious sunlight, but that outside of that path all I could see was darkness and obscurity. Yet soon afterwards, I saw that this | sun(light) was spreading farther over the wilds of the earth, and I heard a voice that said that this sun was the sun of justice, the divine light of the Holy Spirit that is to spread over all flesh in these last days to enlighten its elected people[131] with its light and knowledge.

368

But, as I walked along that pleasant path, I saw a Lord who was walking to my right, but I could not see his face. And he said to me, twice: "The book you are writing shall be contradicted by the enemies of your Lord, by the unbelievers, for some time, but thereafter, I assure you that it will have a great impact on several."

Then I saw again in two visions of the spirit's eyes that I was lying on the waters of a sea, and over this sea was a great sun shining, and I was not sinking at all, and the water of that sea was very calm and marvellously clear, and I rested there with my hands joined on my stomach, and my face, my eyes raised towards the sky looking at this wonderful sun shining over this sea and over my body. And the brightness of that sun was so penetrating that I could see the bottom of this sea in several places. But I saw an infinite number of human philosophers, who had dived into this sea with their different stubborn minds, but they drowned because of their misery, and that sea was called: the Holy Scripture. [...]

---

engraving having a vision of an angel holding a paper roll that read "I come to light you". S. Conneand, *New Prophets: Their Historical and True Picture* (London: 1708).

131   Although Elzière was almost certainly influenced by the French Prophets, it is worth noting that they rejected the Calvinist doctrine of predestination and prophesied universal salvation instead. Laborie, *Enlightening Enthusiasm*, 89–90.

My name is Isaac Elzière, and I confess before God and before men that I am neither of the Papist law, nor of the Lutheran law, nor the Calvinist law,[132] nor of any other of those different sects, which are | invented and fabricated by the philosophy of men of this kind. But I am of the religion of Jesus-Christ and of his prophets and apostles, and of all those who have been invested with the Holy Spirit, by faith or by prophecy, as were the prophets and apostles and the faithful believers of the past. [...]

At the time when I was blind of the spirit's eyes, I had as false guides of my mind in my childhood the ecclesiastics of the pope's sect, being forced to it by their persecution;[133] and later, as I travelled from one land to another, in abundance of ecclesiastics of Calvin's sect and also of the Anglican sect.[134] [...]

The Holy Spirit is the divine light that guides me, the pastor who instructs me, who grazes me, who enlightens me, who teaches me. [...] although I believe in the true prophets of the present time, I do not venerate them, because I believe that they are not infallible, no more than the ancient prophets, because we have not yet reached the era of perfection, to be perfected, but I have faith in the prophetical Holy Spirit that speaks from time to time through their mouth, because I do not worship the tree that brings the fruit, nor do I prostrate myself before it, but I love he who make it produce. [...]

It is true that the false guides of Calvin's sect tell all their followers and listeners that the pope is the only antichrist; but St John teaches us in the IInd chapter of his first epistle that there are several antichrists,[135] before there was a pope: all these guides who, like the pope and his disciples, oppose the light and the reign of Christ, are antichrists who have grafted all sorts of different doctrines and sects of perdition on the teaching of J.-C.: the lie of human traditions, the fantasies of their hearts, their own thoughts, their imaginations, that they put down in writing in their different books and sermons to feed souls ... the waste, the wood and the stubble. [...]

They[136] make him [God] known through their doctrine that they teach differently from one another because they have not received the gift of the Holy-Spirit, nor any commandment from God that appointed them with this responsibility. For, if God had sent them, they would not need to train as

---

132 Like Daniel Raoux (see section 2 above), Elzière clearly did not identify as a Huguenot.
133 After the revocation of the Edict of Nantes, Protestants were forced to attend Mass. They were referred to as "nouveaux catholiques".
134 This suggests that Elzière travelled to England via Switzerland and the Dutch Republic in his youth.
135 1John 2:18.
136 Ministers and theologians.

apprentices to study mass or sermons, artificially composed by human wisdom to gain a good pension and vain glory from the people who listen to them. But they would remain subjects at the service of their master, and they would not pronounce anything else in their ministry than what the Holy Spirit would place in their mouth, like the apostles | of ancient times did. But it seems rather that they have succeeded the scribes and the Pharisees.

5   Paul Rabaut[137]

Sermon on Daniel's prayer[138]

My beloved brethren in our Lord Jesus Christ,

Among so many reproaches that the Lord makes to the Jewish people through his prophet Isaiah, those that we read in the 22nd chapter of his revelations[139] deserve all the more serious attention because, as we find ourselves in more or less the same circumstances, we commit the same faults, except even more criminal, and therefore more punishable in our case than in theirs. Surrounded by an army of Assyrians threatening to invade Judea; about to face the brutality of the soldier, all the horrors of war, and an awful captivity in idolatrous countries; what are they doing to prevent such great evils? In truth, they do not neglect the means that human prudence may suggest on such occasions. They race to arms; they count the inhabitants able to defend the capital; they demolish their houses to fortify their ramparts; they stock large supplies of water: But in taking all these precautions they neglect the most important one, which is to turn to the Lord, to trust in His promises, to implore His help and protection, to beseech His clemency by their repentance. What imprudence! What recklessness! They want to defend Jerusalem, and yet they do not look to He who created and shaped it from a long time, and without whose help all their efforts are entirely useless.

That is not all yet. Instead of humbling themselves before the Lord, of being alarmed in a salutary manner at the sight of this flood of evils threatening them, and of giving external and public marks of a contrite and repentant heart, as if they did not care to perish and wanted to brave divine justice, in this time of affliction and alarm, they surrender themselves to the most indecent and least moderate joy. Hear what the prophet and the Almighty Lord of hosts said to them, when he called you in those days to weeping

---

137   BPF, MS 716/3, no. 28 [my translation]. A marginal note, possibly by Rabaut Saint-Etienne, reads: "This sermon is one of the most beautiful ones on the resemblances between the plight of the Jews under Darius and the plight of the [French] Reformed. The whole introduction is of the highest eloquence. A few longueurs towards the end. I recommend it for publication." ("Ce sermon est un des plus beaux sur le rapport entre les malheurs des Juifs sous Darius et les malheurs des Réformés. Tout l'exorde est de la plus haute éloquence. Quelques longueurs vers la fin. Je le propose pour l'impression.").
138   Dan. 9:1–19.
139   Isa. 22:8–14.

and mourning, to pulling out your hair and wearing sackcloth;[140] and [...] there is joy and gladness: oxen are killed, sheep are slaughtered, flesh is eaten and wine is drunk; and they say: let us eat and drink for we shall die tomorrow. Yet, added Isaiah, the Lord of hosts said unto me, if this iniquity be ever forgiven to you, you shall not die from it, said the Almighty Lord of hosts.[141]

This, my dear brethren, is a picture in which we can easily recognise the situation we are in and our conduct. Exposed as we are to a more cruel and desolate | persecution than the deadliest war; oppressed in every way, not by strangers, but by our own fellow citizens who attack not only our property, our freedom, our reputation, our lives, but also our souls and those of our children; in this terrible state therefore, what have we done to end our plight? We shall say nothing about human means; there are few that we can put to use. But can we not be blamed, like the Jews, for lacking confidence in God? For many people, who even want to pass for the most intelligent and wise, it seems that our deliverance is impossible, that God would face too many obstacles to overcome, as if his arm were shortened and his strength diminished. Consequently to these ideas one is content to lament of one's condition, instead of turning to God, and to try to beseech Him with fervent prayers, and full confidence in his paternal care. But what is even more shocking, and which only makes it worse, is that instead of feeling penetrated by the desolations of the church, of afflicting our souls before the Lord, of humiliating ourselves under his powerful hand, of wearing sackcloth and ashes, we behave just as if we had no subject of affliction. Although the ways of Zion are mourning, that our virgins and our sinful people are held in captivity, that prisons and galleys are full of confessors, that our pastors are being beaten,[142] and the sheep are scattered from the flock, that souls are dying of starvation from not hearing the words of the Almighty; despite all of this there is almost no sign of affliction to be seen. Everywhere, on the contrary, joy and gladness burst. There are only parties of pleasure, games, dances and sumptuous meals in which the rules of sobriety are often hardly observed. O LORD, you have struck them, and they have

2ᵛ

---

140   Isa. 22:12.
141   Isa. 22:13–14.
142   Huguenot ministers faced execution if they were caught preaching in France after the revocation of the Edict of Nantes. The period 1715–1760 was marked by ongoing persecution, during which dozens of ministers were executed and celebrated as martyrs by their coreligionists. "Pasteurs et prédicants martyrs", (http://www.museedudesert.com/article5918.html, accessed 8 August 2016).

not felt any pain, you have consumed them, and they have refused to receive instruction. They have hardened their faces like a rock, they have refused to be converted.

We assume, my dear brethren, that in coming here today to humiliate yourselves before God so extraordinarily, you have taken on very different feelings from those we have just depicted and that you intend to hold an entirely opposite conduct. That is why we are going to propose the example of the prophet Daniel as your model, well worthy of our imitation. Blessed and so animated by the beautiful feelings that he expresses in the prayer that we have just read, we fast as this day requires, so that our voice may be heard from the Heavens. Follow us, my dear brethren, in the reflections we are about to make. It is to the heart that we want to speak rather than to the spirit; obey the voice of God; let the passions be silent, let the conscience speak; but speak to us, Lord, directly through your holy spirit. Let Him break our hearts, let Him change them so that we may truly become your people and may you show yourself to be our God. Amen.

3^r Let us first pay attention, my dear brethren, to the circumstances in which the prophet Daniel found himself; and which are in so much conformity with those in which we find ourselves. A member of the Jewish Church and a prophet of the Almighty, his love for God, his zeal for religion, and his strong attachment to his brethren, did not allow him to look with indifference at the desolations of this people who were infinitely dear to him. What a sad spectacle indeed for a soul like his, than the devastating catastrophes of which he had been the witness and the victim: Jerusalem, the centre of religion, reduced to a pile of ruins; this august temple where God gave the most perceptible marks of his presence, and which contained so many precious monuments, consumed by the flames; the sacrificing priests and the prophets of the living God, some put to death, others taken into captivity; a great part of the people consumed by the sword or by famine, and almost all the rest transplanted into a foreign land. These were some of the gloomy objects which the prophet had before his eyes, and which pierced his heart with the most bitter pain. He saw in these tragic events the execution of the threats that God had made through his servant Moses and which can be read in the chapter 28th of Deuteronomy. He therefore saw that the Jewish people had brought corruption to its height, exhausted the treasures of God's mercy and patience, who resolves to punish only as a last resort. All of this afflicted him at the highest level, and in order to relieve his pain, to give impetus to his zeal, and to contribute with all his power to the recovery of the Jewish church, he humbles himself extraordinarily before God by fasting, wearing sackcloth and ashes, he pours his worries into the bosom of this merciful God who in his anger remembers his compassion; he confesses his sins to him, as well as those of the people, and begs him as fervently as he can to exercise his mercy towards this desolate nation and to restore it to his homeland.[143]

But here is a new reason that increases the prophet's hope, that greatly excites his zeal and animates his devotion; it is that he had read in the book of the prophet Jeremiah that the captivity of the Jews in Babylon was to last for seventy years, and that he saw that this term was about to end. Here is indeed how Jeremiah expresses himself in the 29th ch. of his revelations: Thus, saith the LORD, when the seventy years are fulfilled in Babylon, I shall visit you, and execute my promise upon you to return you to this place. For I know that the thoughts | I have upon you, saith the LORD, are thoughts of peace, not of adversity, to give you the outcome you expect, then shall you call upon me in order to depart; and you shall pray to me and I shall answer you; you shall seek me and you shall find me, after seeking me with all your heart.[144] It is that promise that filled Daniel with the sweet hope that his humiliation would be effective, and that his prayers would rise before God's throne like a sweet fragrance. The Eternal is no man to lie, nor a son of man to repent; he hath spoken, and why would he not do it? What joy for this prophet to see the seventy years about to end! What encouragement for him to beg God for mercy on his people!

As we have already suggested, my dear brethren, the circumstances in which we find ourselves are the same as those in which Daniel found himself. The state which our churches have long been in is no less sad than that of the Jewish church then. Is it necessary to redraw here a picture of our long and overwhelming miseries, but what brush could represent all of these atrocities? The Jews only lost one temple, we lost nearly a thousand. These holy houses where truth was proclaimed in all its purity and where God was worshipped as he requires of his true followers, were razed to the ground. Not only were the ambassadors of Jesus Christ silenced so that they would no longer announce good news to come, but they were also chased away from their homeland, to make it easier for the wolves to devour the sheep in the absence of their shepherds. And if some of these messengers of the Almighty had the courage to risk their lives for their sheep, to feed them with spiritual pasture through the perils that threatened them, hardly a few died peacefully; so that we witnessed in them what is said in the psalm 79. The dead bodies of your servants were given for meat to the birds of heaven, and the flesh of your beloved to the beasts of the earth; their blood was shed like water around Jerusalem.

---

143   Dan. 9:3–6.
144   Jer. 21:10–13.

What gloomy objects stand before my eyes! Here I see a multitude of believers tormented into renouncing their Saviour, into betraying the lights of their conscience, but who remain faithful to their duty; and who become confessors for some and martyrs for the others. There I see a much greater number of them becoming apostates, and who, in order to protect themselves from the persecutions of men, expose themselves to the devouring remorse of their conscience, and to the dreadful vengeance of the Almighty. Here I see troops of fugitives who, unable to find rest in their homeland, seek asylums in foreign climates;[145] there I see others reduced to hide in the caves and caverns of the earth, and who find more compassion in ferocious beasts than in men. Here I see | husbands who are separated from their wives, wives who are taken from their husbands; there, children who are torn from the arms of those who gave them birth, to make them suckle the venom of error and idolatry. Have we only seen these objects from a distance, my dear brothers? Alas they are still before our eyes! We do not need to go far back to see the sad marks of the Lord's wrath. So many of our brothers and sisters groaning under the weight of an oar, the others in the darkness of a prison. Our Pastors persecuted and put to death, our religious assemblies proscribed, the Lord's table overthrown, our virgins confined in convents; the famine that the Lord sent upon our land, not the famine of bread, nor the thirst for water, but the famine of hearing the words of the Lord: how much more is needed to convince us that our situation is no less miserable than that of the Jews in Babylon? How could we not see such a lamentable state where the wrath of the Almighty is marked in such large print!

Even though we will have armed the vengeful arm of this righteous judge, we will have violated his most respectable laws; we shall see his now-raised arm strike us; we will have dismissed his most precious blessings, attracted his most dreadful scourges and we will not be in anguish. Out of here these ungodly who in these unfortunate times dare to indulge in the joy and amusements of the century. It is clear that they have no fear of God, no apprehension of his judgments, no zeal for his glory, no sensitivity to the misfortunes of the Church. Let us abhor such feelings, my dear brethren, and let us clothe ourselves in a state of suffering and humiliation in which we are struck by the long captivity under which the Church groans, afflicted to be ourselves its cause by the sins into which we have had the misfortune to fall. Following Daniel's example, let us strive to supplicate the Lord with fasting, sackcloth and ashes.

---

145 Reference to the Huguenot diaspora towards Protestant countries. See Susanne Lachenicht, "Diasporic Networks and Immigration Policies", in *A Companion to the Huguenots*, ed. Raymond Mentzer and Bertrand van Ruymbeke (Leiden: 2016), 249–272.

We have seen that what excited Daniel's zeal, what animated his devotion, was that he knew that the 70 years that the captivity was to last for was about to expire. If we do not have the same certitude as Daniel, as we must concede, we nevertheless have strong reasons to hope that after 70 years of captivity[146] God in his great compassions will allow the restoration of our dear churches, provided that we turn to him with all our heart. We know that God does not delight in seeing his people in a state of suffering, and that he does not resort to making his judgments fall upon them until all the other means of conversion that he has employed have proven useless. He chastises only to correct, hence it is not doubtful that when one has renounced the disorders which had made him take the rod, he withdraws it and stops striking. That is what he proclaims in many places of his word. Turn to me | and I will turn to you, said the Lord of hosts. Come closer to God and he will come closer to you. There is an infinite number of other similar statements. The natural consequence of this is that if we renounce our vices God will put an end to our calamities. What could possibly stop him, is there any obstacle he cannot easily overcome? The hand of the Lord is not shortened that he could not deliver; his ear is not become heavy that he could not hear; but your iniquities have separated you from your God, and your sins have caused him to hide his face from you, so that he should not hear you. When God takes pleasure in man's voices, he appeases his enemies towards himself.

But beyond this general reason, there are particular ones that give us hope that God will soon visit us in his love. Saint Paul tells us that what happened to the Jews happened to them in images. The captivity of the Jewish Church in Babylon thus served to represent the captivity of some Christian Church, but which Churches have better fulfilled this image than ours? Not a single one will be found whose desolations conform so closely to the captivity of the Jewish people, whether in relation to the greatness of their afflictions or in relation to their duration. Besides we find in the first chapter of the revelations of the prophet Zechariah an oracle which seems to have us in sight rather than the Jews. The Lord promises that after 70 years there will be compassion in Jerusalem and the cities of Judea.[147] Yet in those days the Jews had been re-established in their homeland for many years, from where it follows that this oracle does not refer to the literal Jerusalem and Judea; it must therefore be applied to the mystical Jerusalem and Judea. And to whom, I pray you, could this application be better made than to the Reformed churches of this

---

146　Rabaut preached this sermon in March 1755, i.e. 69 years and five months after the revocation of the Edict of Nantes, which marked the beginning of the Huguenots' clandestinity.

147　Zech. 1:12–17.

kingdom? We therefore have reason to hope that God will restore our flocks, for the year we now live in is precisely the 70th year of our captivity. Add to that that we cannot be far from the end of the reign of the Antichrist. He was given 1260 years to make war against the saints and to defeat them.[148] But while we do not want to set the precise beginning of this period, it is certain that the end of the 1260 years cannot be far away. The imperial dignity which hindered the manifestation of the sinful man according to St Paul's prediction was abolished in the West in the fifth century, and consequently if the 1260 years have not expired since then, they cannot be long to do so.[149] Now the reign of the Antichrist, once abolished, no more persecutions. Finally, we see clearly that the spirits are becoming enlightened. The rights of conscience are better known than ever, and persecution is now deemed unjust and harmful.[150] Based on all these reasons, we believe we are | justified in believing that the end of our misfortunes is near and that God will soon put our beloved Zion in a flourishing and renowned state on earth. What a powerful motive, what encouragement this must be for us, my dear brethren, to turn to the lord, the sovereign master of events, to humble ourselves before him, seeking like Daniel to make request and supplication with fasting, sackcloth and ashes. Do you think that a criminal sentenced to death, who would have strong reasons to hope that he would be pardoned, would not hasten to beg for it? Ah, he wouldn't need strong reasons. The slightest glimmer of hope would suffice to make him throw himself at the feet of his judge, and surely he would try to bend him by his prayers, by his tears, by his protestations of amendment. My brethren, we can tell you along with a prophet, that the Eternal is waiting to give you grace. Everything indicates that if we look for him properly, we will find him. Perhaps he is only waiting for the celebration of this fast to break our chains and set us free. But not all sorts of fasts are effective, there are some that he hates and that irritate him sorely from appeasing him; such are the hypocritical fasts where one merely shows appearances of penance, without truly feeling it. The true fast that unerringly disarms the Lord's arm is one where one tears one' s heart rather than one's clothes. It is a matter for fasting well to seek our ways, to probe them and to return to the eternal our God. This is how Daniel fasted. Let us examine what feelings he expresses and try to imitate them.

Our prophet does not satisfy himself with being a spectator of the evils of the Church, and groaning inwardly about it. He goes straight to the source of deliv-

---

148   Dan. 7:25; Rev. 11:3.
149   On early modern eschatological calculations, see Johnston, *Revelation Restored*, 53–58.
150   On the French Enlightenment and changing attitudes towards religious toleration, see Adams, *The Huguenots and French Opinion*, 42–43 and part 2.

erance; he asks God with all the ardour he is capable of to deign to appease his people. That is how God's children use it when they desire deliverance either from their own evils or from those of the Church. They know very well that this supreme judge of events directs them as he pleases, and thus that one cannot count on the success of the means that they use and that as much as his blessing accompanies them. They even know that God can operate without means, and that nothing is difficult for him, that it is he who elevates and lowers, who impoverishes and enriches, who creates light and darkness, who makes peace and truth. For this reason prayer is their refuge, especially in the days of calamity. God is, they say, our retreat and strength and help in times of distress; very easy to find. Yes, God stands near the desolate hearts, he stands by those who ask for him in sincerity and truth. Let us therefore pray, my dear brethren, especially in these times of affliction. It is the key that opens the heavens; it is a ladder that reaches to the throne of God. It is a weapon that this great God cannot resist, the sure way to overcome. How and to whom Jacob overcame God, weeping and asking him for his mercy; he would not let him go until he had blessed him. Hence this exhortation of an apostle; is anyone in the affliction that they pray.

Daniel adds fasting to prayer, and it is indeed a very suitable accompaniment, especially in extraordinary devotions. Everything must indicate the deep pain in the heart, the strong feeling that he has of his unworthiness and his misery, the ardent desire that drives him to retain the graces that he is going to ask of the master of the world. In great afflictions one does not hasten to consume food, one is disgusted by it, one finds it insipid; the soul is occupied only with its pain. Would it not be easy to abstain from it when, concentrated in pious meditations, one feels how abhorrent sin is to the divinity, harmful to individuals and to the public, and how terrible it is to fall into the hands of the living god when he is irritated. When it comes to bending the Almighty one cannot humiliate oneself enough in His presence. By abstaining from the food that is necessary for the maintenance of our lives, we testify that we recognise ourselves unworthy of living, and that we have deserved death. Lastly, fasting helps devotion considerably. The body being not laden with food, the soul rises with more freedom and facility towards its God. It has more activity, more attention, more fervour. Among the Jews it was customary on fasting days to cover oneself with a sackcloth and to lie on ashes, in order to express in a more sensitive way the contusion and pain with which one was penetrated.

But this is not essential to fasting, the most important thing is to examine one's conduct, to confess one's sins to God with the most profound compunction and humility; to implore his mercy with ardour; to stop doing wrong, and to learn to do well.

So today we must confess our sins to God, which we cannot do unless we know them. Let us therefore silence our self-esteem. We are before the lord who probes hearts and kidneys, what good would it do us to try to hide from him what is wrong with our feelings and our behaviour? It would only add hypocrisy to godlessness. Let us therefore bear in mind that everything is naked and entirely discovered in the eyes of him to whom we are accountable. Let us not disguise anything in his presence. He who omits his transgressions shall not prosper, but he who confesses and forsakes them shall obtain mercy. Let us say with Daniel: Alas! Lord, the mighty god, the great the fearsome, who keeps the covenant and gratuity to those who love you and who keep your commandments.

This preface is well suited to humiliate sinners, to slay them in the dust, but at the same time it offers them reasons for hope and amendment. The god before whom we are here assembled is infinitely powerful. One act of his will sufficed to create the world, one act of that same will would suffice to annihilate it. Who would not fear this sovereign might? This great god is an infinite | majesty in front of whom we are but powder and ash that would only be wiped out in his presence. He is a dreadful god whose justice demands that crime be punished, and before whom the wicked cannot subsist [...] fear and alarm. But at the same time he is a merciful and pitiful God; by virtue of his covenant of grace, he shows mercy to those who love him sincerely and strive to do his will. This must raise our hopes, encourage us to approach with confidence the throne of grace to obtain mercy, and to be relieved in times of need; but we must also aspire to reform our lives, for he only forgives to be feared.

Let us therefore say to God with the prophet Daniel: we have sinned. But let us not say it with our mouths alone, may our hearts feel it and be bitterly afflicted by it. We have sinned, yes we have sinned in every possible way against God, against our fellows, against ourselves. We have sinned by our thoughts, by our words and by our actions. So many sins against God! Instead of this sovereign love that we owe him and because of his kind perfections, and consequently of the equally numerous and excellent blessings that we derive from his pure liberality, especially the invaluable gift that he bestowed onto us with his dear son, what coldness, what indifference do we not have to blame ourselves for! How lukewarm our acts of devotion, our reading of the word of God, our participation in the sacraments, our prayers, whether public or particular. What respect have we for the Lord? Is it respect to pronounce his name all the time, without consideration, without necessity; unfortunate custom that has become only too general. Ah if we considered carefully what the name of God signifies, if we were well penetrated by the greatness of this immense majesty before which the seraphim themselves cover their wings, we would undoubtedly be more reserved to pronounce this unspeakable name. And what shall we say about those infamous mouths that blaspheme him? Why was the commendable custom of piercing their tongues with a burning iron, still too sweet a torture for such an enormous crime, abolished? What fear do we have of the Lord? If we truly feared him, would we so easily indulge in sin? Would we not fear to suffer the effect of the threats he makes to the offenders of his laws, and would not the terror of his threats balance out the fatal delights of crime? If we feared God, would we fear men so much, and would we not rather expose ourselves to all their fury than displease this great Being who can cast the body and soul into the Gehenna of fire?[151] God is infinitely | more loving than terrible and he has spared no effort to convince men of his tender love for them in order to encourage them to confide in him, to rely on the paternal care of his good and wise providence. But in spite of all this we are full of worry and disquiet whenever events do not unfold according to our desires. We are agitated, we are tormented, we fear lacking everything, as if God did not intervene in human affairs. With regard to the obedience that is due to this great God, we have so many reproaches to blame ourselves for. We believe we have done our duty well when we have performed some external works, but what good is it if the heart is not submitted to the Lord, if these movements are not subordinated to His will? We are willing to obey in things that do not hinder greed, but when it comes to taming the passions, to sacrificing the inclinations of the heart, we shake the yoke, and we follow our own will rather than that of God. We have therefore too many reasons to write with Daniel: we have sinned.

It is not only with regard to our duties towards God that we have to blame ourselves, we have hardly been more attentive to our duties towards our fellows. One would have to love them sincerely and take an interest in their happiness from the bottom of one's heart, but one only loves oneself and is all ice for others. Hence the ease with which we tend to judge their intentions and approaches so recklessly here. Hence the little sensitivity one has for their reputation, which is torn to pieces. Hence the tardiness with which one goes to the help of the needy. And how could one fulfil the duties of charity when we fail even those of justice, when we do not trouble ourselves with causing harm, with withholding the property of others and dying without returning it. With regard to our fellows, therefore, we again have reason to say with Daniel, we have sinned.

We have no less reason to say this in relation to our duties toward ourselves. Are we always happy with our condition, and do we never [...] against the Lord?

---

151   Jer. 19:2–6.

Do we care more about our souls than our bodies? Do we never fall into the excesses of greed and drunkenness? Have we not too much fondness for earthly goods, too much eagerness to acquire them? Let us not form too many great ideas of ourselves, and let us not think ourselves beyond what is needed | each one of us should question his heart; let us not delude ourselves and we shall have no trouble to say: we have sinned. We have committed iniquity, we have been rebellious, and we have turned away from your commandments and your ordinances.

The ideas of iniquity, rebellion and the like contained in Daniel's prayer must remind us of the aggravating circumstances that have accompanied our sins. Who knows not that those sins that are committed knowingly are far more atrocious, more abhorrent to the Lord, and therefore more punishable than those in which one falls out of ignorance? And how many sins of this sort have we not committed, knowingly and willingly, despite the warnings and pangs of our conscience? Who does not know that when one sins deliberately one is much more criminal than when one sins by surprise, and how many times have we not offended God after carefully pondering it, after having had considerable time to consider the consequences of our actions? And what can I say about the sins of habit that are absolutely incompatible with regeneration and the state of grace. Far from being considered from this point of view, many people allege this in order to make their apology, which makes them completely inexcusable. Whenever we want to rebuke those who have taken the unfortunate custom of taking God's name in vain or uttering other evil words, they hope to absolve themselves by telling us it is a habit we have taken. That is to say that you have fallen back so often into the same error that it is now difficult for you to correct yourselves, but that is what makes you more guilty and therefore more worthy of punishment.

Let us pay attention to another circumstance that Daniel did not forget, it is the disobedience to the exhortations of the prophets. Many places in the Old Testament show indeed that the Jews took little heed of the salutary warnings given to them by the Lord's messengers, which was one of the main causes of the terrible punishments he inflicted upon them. The ministers of the Gospel are the prophets of the New Testament; and how many times, my dear brethren, have they not made the voice of their Divine Master resound in our ears? How many times have they not warned us of our duties and urged us to fulfil them? How many times have they not censored our disorders by exhorting us with the strongest reasons to turn back toward the Lord's testimonies? How many times have they not foretold us that God would deprive us of the ministry of the word that we so disregarded. However, what fruit did their speech produce? What sinners have changed their ways? What reformation has there been among us?

It can be said without exaggerating that depravity has been increasing in recent years. What licentiousness do we not see in the discourses, what disruption in the actions, which marks a great corruption of the hearts. | Our predictions are 7ᵛ
therefore only too verified. The word of God has become rare in Israel, because we have despised it.

The prophet Daniel confesses to the Lord that all the orders of the Church and the State had become corrupt. We only have too many reasons to even confess. From the sole of the foot to the top of the head, there is nothing whole in us. Those who were to lead others, did not always know how to lead themselves. [We?] ministers of the Lord, have not always fulfilled exactly the duties imposed upon us by the glorious but arduous work with which we are entrusted. What negligence and lukewarmness in the exercise of our functions; we have so many reproaches to blame ourselves for! Yes Lord, to you is justice, and to us is the shame and confusion of the face. The flocks have also essentially failed in what they owed their Pastors, what attention has been given to their conservation; here I cannot say all I can, whoever has ears to hear it hears! I would be too long if I wanted to go into the other orders of persons of which society is composed in detail. What a sad picture would not present to you the various shortcomings of the great and the small, the rich and the poor, the merchants and the craftsmen, the husbands and the wives, the fathers and the children, the masters and the servants.

What shall we say after all these things, my dear brethren? Will we not agree that the Lord is just in his punishments, will we complain that he treats us too severely? Our situation is sad, that is true, but it would be so much sadder still, if God had not tempered by his mercy the terrible blows of his justice. We must therefore understand that this mercy is our only refuge; we must be aware of our need for it; and we must hate our disorders; we must be frightened in a salutary manner at the sight of such a dark ingratitude and such a voluntary, universal and inexcusable rebellion. May our hearts melt with anguish, but at the same time, let us, contrite and humiliated, resort to the throne of grace. We have sinned, but we have a [...] towards the Father namely J.C. the righteous who propitiated for our sins. He is the mediator in us from whom Daniel prays to God and hopes to be heard, praying the love of the Lord, says he, makes your face shine on your desolate sanctuary.

But, my brothers, what good would it do us to confess our sins if we wanted to persevere in them? You have heard already what the Scripture says. He who conceals his transgressions shall not prosper, but he who confesses and forsakes them shall obtain mercy. You see, therefore, that it is not enough to confess them and that they must necessarily be abandoned, or else there is no grace to await. What use would our prayers to the Lord be if they were not accompanied by making amends? Solomon tells us: the sacrifice of the wicked is an abomination to the Eternal, but the prayer of the righteous pleases him.[152] | How effective would our fast be if, while we are happy to mortify our body for a few hours, we did not want to mortify our passions, to sacrifice them to the Lord. The fast that God has chosen is not one of afflicting one's soul for [...] day, of putting on sackcloth and ashes, it consists mainly in renouncing sin and practicing virtue.

Let us fast in this way, my dear brethren, and we shall soon experience the effectiveness of our humiliation. God will yield to our prayers and tears. He will cast away our sins as far as the East is removed from the West. He will cause our august monarch[153] to allow our exiles and captives to return to their homeland like another Cyrus, and together we shall rebuild the house of the Lord. Then our flocks shall graze under the guidance of their legitimate shepherds, who shall lead them into grassy pastures and along clear and calm waters. Then no more desolation in our homeland nor damage in our lands. You have seen, my dear brethren, the strong reasons we have to believe that this happy time is not far away. Let us hasten it by our vows and especially by the reformation of our lives [...] and man iniquitous his thoughts that he returns to the Eternal and he shall have mercy upon him and upon our God for he forgives again and again: Lord convert us and we shall be truly converted and renew our days as they were formerly. Lord hear, Lord forgive, Lord be attentive and be diligent, do not delay because of yourself [...] God, for your name has been called upon your city and your people. Amen.

This 7th of March 1755.

---

152   Prov. 15:8.
153   King Louis XV (r.1715–1774).

Bibliography

Manuscripts

Berlin, Staatsbibliothek (StaBi Berlin), Francke-Nachlass, 7/7:32, Friedrich Breckling to August Hermann Francke, The Hague, March 1703.

Berlin, Staatsbibliothek (StaBi Berlin), Francke-Nachlass, 7/7:40, Friedrich Breckling to August Hermann Francke, [The Hague?], [after March 1702].

Cambridge, Corpus Christi College, MS 484: Bible.

Gotha, Forschungsbibliothek (FB Gotha), Chart A 297, fols 283–335, Friedrich Breckling MSS (without title).

Gotha, Forschungsbibliothek (FB Gotha), Chart. A 306, fols 194–195, Friedrich Breckling, *Catalogus Theodidactorum et Testium Veritatis*, entry on Claude Brousson.

Gotha, Forschungsbibliothek (FB Gotha), Chart. A 306, fols 215–237, Friedrich Breckling, *Catalogus Haereticorum Ketzer-Historia dieser Zeiten* (c.1697–1703).

Halle, Archiv der Franckeschen Stiftungen (AFSt), H C 153, Johann Overbeek to August Hermann Francke, Cleve, 13.12.1695.

Halle, Archiv der Franckeschen Stiftungen (AFSt), H D 93, fols 62–64, Friedrich Breckling to August Hermann Francke, [The Hague?], c.07.01.1698–26.09.1698.

London, Lambeth Palace Library (LPL), Ms 1122/3, fols 170–216, Papers relating to the emigration from France in 1763 of a large group of Protestants led by Jean Louis Gibert (1722–1773).

London, Lambeth Palace Library (LPL), Ms 932/10, "Preciz du Discours de Mr Durand Fage d'Aubaye, prononcé sous l'operation de l'Esprit, à Londres le 30 Aoust 1706".

London, Lambeth Palace Library (LPL), Ms 934/52, "Preciz du Discours de Mr Durand Fage d'Aubaye, prononcé sous l'Operation de l'Esprit; A Londres, le 3e 7bre 1706".

London, Library of the Society of Friends (LSF), Ms Vol. 314, nos 1–2, Fragments d'une prédication de Daniel Raoul le laboureur.

London, Library of the Society of Friends (LSF), Ms Vol. 315, fols 13–15, Fragments of a Sermon preached by Daniel Raoul.

Montpellier, Archives départementales de l'Hérault (ADH), C 509, no. 158, M. Comte, priest of Quissac to Cardinal de Fleury (10 Aug. 1736).

Montpellier, Archives départementales de l'Hérault (ADH), C 509, no. 174, M. Comte, priest of Quissac to Cardinal de Fleury (15 May 1736).

Montpellier, Archives départementales de l'Hérault (ADH), C 218 (liasse), fols 262–358, papers relating to the prophet Maroger and the Couflaïres of Nages (1745).

Paris, Bibliothèque du Protestantisme Français (BPF), MS 716/3, no. 28, Paul Rabaut, Sermon sur la prière de Daniel (1755).

Prague, National Library of the Czech Republic, XI D 5, 168^r–179^r, Jacobellus de Misa (Jakoubek of Stříbro), "Posicio de Anticristo".

Printed Primary Sources

Aconcio, Jacopo, *Stratage-matum satanae. Accessit eruditissima Epistola, de ratione edendorum librorum, ad Ioannem Wolfium Tigurinum, eodem authore* (Basel: 1565).

Ammersbach, Heinrich, *Rettung der reinen Lehre Dd. Lutheri, Meisneri, Speneri, und andrer/ welche lehren: Daß aus einem Christen und Christo gleich als eine Person wärde/ daher ein gläubiger Christ wol sagen könne: Ich bin Christus/ Gott zu Ehren und frommen Christen zum Trost/ Satan aber zum Trotz/ und sonderlich dem so genandten Balthasar Rebhan, als einem Erz-Lästrer das Maul zustopffen/ Und dann nicht weniger Hn. Johann Conrad Schneidern/ Predigern im Dom zu Halberstadt/ Seine hiebevor von diesem Punct heraußgegebne Theses zu examiniren / Auffgesetzet und in den Druck gegeben Von Henrico Hansen/ M. I. U. D.* (Frankfurt/Main: [1678]).

Amyraut, Moïse *Discours sur les songes divins* (Saumur: 1659).

Anon. [Massard, Jacques?], *Abrégé de l'histoire de la bergère de Saou près de Crest en Daufiné* (Amsterdam: 1688).

Anon., *A Relation of Several Hundreds of Children and Others that Prophesie and Preach in their Sleep, &c. First Examined and Admired By Several Ingenious Men, Ministers and Professors at Geneva, and Sent from Thence in Two Letters to Rotterdam* (London: 1689).

Anon., *A Wonderful Account from Orthez, in Bearne, and the Cevennes, of Voices Heard in the Air, Singing the Praises of God, in the Words and Tunes of the Psalms; Used By Those of the Reformed Religion: At the Time of Their Cruel and Inhumane Persecution. By the French King: Credliby [Sic] Attested* (London: 1706).

Anon., *La Bastille dévoilée, ou recueil des pieces authentiques pour server a son histoire* (Paris: 1789).

Anon., *Lettre d'un Bourgeois de Cologne, a un ami, sur la prise de Bude, et sur les autres affaires presentes* ([Cologne]: 1686).

Anon., *Lettre d'un gentilhomme de Dauphiné a un de ses amis a Geneve. Contenant ce qu'il a oüi dire d'Isabeau Vincent Bergere* (Amsterdam: 1688)

Anon., *Lettre de Geneve contenant une relation exacte au sujet des petits prophetes de Dauphiné, le 13. Fevrier 1689* (Rotterdam: 1689)

Anon., *Mene Tekel, Being an Astrological Judgment on the Great and Wonderful Year 1688. Deduced From the True and Genuine Principles of That Art: Shewing the Approaching Catastrophe of Popery in England, &c.* (London: 1688).

Anon., *Nader berricht, Aangaande een Herderin In't Dauphiné, daar God wonderlijke en bovennatuurlijke dingen tot een yders verwondering in uitwerkt* (s.l.: 1688).

Anon., *Pertinent verhaal van de propheet, die in Vrankryk is opgestaan* (Amsterdam: 1688).

Anon., *Réponse de M. ***, Ministre, à une lettre écrite par un Catholique Romain, sur le sujet de P. Prophetes du Dauphiné et du Vivarets. De Hollande le 30 May 1689* (S.l.: 1689).

Arcularius, Johann Daniel, *Das Zeugnüß Gottes auff Erden. Wie solchs nach Anweisung Göttl. Worts auf Erden zu finden/ und heylsam zu gebrauchen stehet. Sam[m]t kurtzen Anmerckungen über des so genanten Bartholomaei Sclei, Theosophische Schrifften/ Die Er nennet: Allgemeine und geheime/ doch einfältige Teutsche Theologie, gegründet in dem dreyfachen Göttlichen Offenbahrungs-Buch/ der H. Schrifft/ der grossen und kleinen Welt. Deren Grund und Warheit hiessigen Christlichen Gemeinde/ und allen rechtglaubigen Christen zum Unterricht und Warnung kürtzlich auff die Prob gestellet* (Frankfurt/Main: 1688).

Arndt, Johann, *Zehen Lehr- und Geist-reiche Predigten: Von den Zehen grausamen und schröcklichen Egyptischen Plagen: welche der Mann Gottes Moses für dem verstockten Könige Pharao in Egypten/ kurtz vor dem Außzug der Kinder Israel/ durch Gottes Würckung hat gethan: Was massen all solche Plagen geistlicher Weise vor dem Ende der Welt widerkommen/ und über das Menschliche Geschlecht/ insonderheit über die jetzt verstockte böse Christenheit/ ergehen und verhänget werden sollen* (Frankfurt/Main: 1657).

Beer, Wolfgang Dominicus, *Zwölff Klagen über das ärgerliche unchristliche Christenthumb/ So von unterschiedlichen Evangelischen Lehrern in diesem siebenzehenden Seculo geführet worden sind / Auß ihren Schrifften zusammen getragen/ und/ den heutigen sichern Welt-Christen zur Nachricht und Warnung/ Von einem Bekenner der Warheit Ans Licht Gestellt. Sampt einer Vorrede D Philipp Jacob Speners* (Duisburg: 1684).

Betke, Joachim, *Excidium Germaniæ. h.e. Gründlicher und warhafftiger Bericht/ wer daran Ursach/ daß zur Zeit des Alten Testaments/ das Judenthumb/ und zur Zeit des Newen Testaments/ Deutschland/ zum zehenfachen Sodom worden/ und Gott deßwegen mit Schwerdt/ Krieg/ Hunger und Pest/ als seines Zorns-Plagen/ dasselbe verderben/ außbrennen/ schleiffen/ zur Wüsten machen/ und Menschen und Vieh darin ohne Barmhertzigkeit außrotten lassen; und vollends wie das Alte Israel/ nach der Drewung Pauli, Rom. 11. v. 20. von seinem Angesicht verstossen muß. Sampt einer kurtzen Delineation des Decreti Stultiæ, oder dem Geheimnüß der Göttlichen Thorheit. Durch Joachim Betkium, Weyland trewen Zeugen und Dienern Jesu Christi, des Königs über alle Könige/ zu Linumb verfertiget/ und nun durch Christliche Hertzen zum Druck befordert; mit einer Vorrede des Editoris von dem Inhalt und Zweck dieses Buchs* (Amsterdam: 1666).

Böhme, Jakob, *Morgenröte im Aufgang/ Das ist: Die Wurtzel oder Mutter Der Philosophiæ, Astrologiæ und Theologiæ, Aus rechtem Grunde. Oder Beschreibung der Natur/ wie alles gewesen* […] (Amsterdam: 1682).

Breckling, Friedrich, "Catalogus einiger Tractaten, welche noch bey mir theils entworffen/theils außgearbeitet zum Gemeinen Nutzen und Dienst der Christenheit/ ob Gott dazu Verlag geben/ oder Verleger erwecken wolle", in Friedrich Breckling, *Compendium Apocalypseos Reseratæ* (S.l.: 1678), 8–16.

Breckling, Friedrich, "Catalogus Testium Veritatis post Lutherum continuatus huc usque", in Gottfried Arnold, *Unparteyische Kirchen- und Ketzer-Historie: vom Anfang des Neuen Testaments biß auff das Jahr 1688*, vol. 3/4 (Frankfurt/Main: 1729), 1008–1110.

Breckling, Friedrich, "Letzter Abschied und Außgang. Von allen heutigen Phariseern/ Secten/ falschen Propheten und Aposteln mit allen ihren eigen-gemeinschafften/ falschen Gottesdienst/ Babelkirchen/ zusammen-rottungen/ und äusserlichen Tempel-wesen/ darinnen sie wie die Fleder-mäuse [...] in und ausser ihren Stein-Kirchen/ um ihre güldene Kälber/ und thierische Menschen-bilder herumb lauffen [...] und mit ihren Cantzel-götzen/ Menschen und Creaturen [...] lauter abgötterey treiben: Dafür daß sie mit den klugen Jungfrauen/ von der welt und ihrem Babelwesen/ ausgehen/ und mit dem Bräutigam durch recht Christliche absonderung zu seiner ruhe eingehen sollten [...] ja auch keinen falschen Geistern/ Lehrern/ Seelen und Propheten mehr glauben zustellen [...]", in Gottfried Arnold, *Unparteyische Kirchen-und Ketzer-Historie*, vol. 3/4 (Frankfurt/Main: 1729), 1116–1127 (= *Paulus Redivivus*: 1688).

Breckling, Friedrich, "Zustand und Beschreibung der Kirchen", in Gottfried Arnold, *Unparteyische Kirchen- und Ketzer-Historie*, vol. 3/4 (Frankfurt/Main: 1729), 1110–1115.

Breckling, Friedrich, *Anticalovius sive Calovius cum Asseclis suis prostratus et Jacob Bôhmium Cum aliis testibus veritatis defensus. Darin gelehret wird was von D. Abraham Calovii, Pomarii Francisci und anderer falschgelehrten Büchern/ Apologien und Schriften wider Jac. Böhmen/ Hermannum Jungium, I.C. Charias M. Henricum Amerßbach/ mich und andere Zeugen der Wahrheit zu halten sey. Und ob ein recht christlicher Lehrer oder Zuhörer Darin mit D. Calovio, Pomarius und andern Feinden der Warheit übereinstimmen. Und des Iacob Böhmens/ Jungii/ Seidenbechers/ Grosgebawers unserer und anderer Zeugen der Warheit Personen und Schrifften ohne verletzung seines gewissens und übertretung des Wortes Gottes also richten und verdammen könne wie D. Calov, Pomarius, Artus, Francisci der unverständige gerrard Antognossius und andere so unGöttlich gethan haben [...]. Dabey zugleich des sel. J. Böhmen und vieler anderer Zeugen der Warheit Unschuld gerettet und verthädiget wird/ und angewiesen/ was doch von Jacob Böhmen Person und Schrifften nach dem Grunde der Warheit zu halten seye/ und wie solche mißbrauchet/ theils recht gebrauchet werden können? Und Ob ein rechter Christ mit gutem Gewissen in solcher falschen Lehrer Richter und Verfolger Kirchen oder Gemeinschafft sich begeben bleiben und beharren könne/ welche also die Warheit und dessen Zeugen von sich außstossen lästern und verfolgen?* [...] ([Wesel]: 1688).

Breckling, Friedrich, *Paulus Redivivus Cum suo Vale Mundo, sive Separatismus Verus â falso Syncretismo ac Mixtura Pharisæorum & Pseudo apostolorum cum Satana carne & mundo vindicatus, ut nos â communione amicatia & interitu hujus Mundi ejusque Sectarum educat, & ad unionem cum Deo ac Sabbathismum Christi reducat:*

atque sic causam Dei ejusque Ecclesiæ & verbi contra tot homicidas ac infanticidas Gentium & animarum defendat ad solius Die ejusque Christi Ecclesiae & Regni triumphantis gloriosam exaltationem, Babelis & omnium Mundi Sectarum perpetuam Confusionem, & Universalis Gratiae ac Theosophiæ ac Divinæ æternam prædicationem. Letzter Abschied und Außgang. Von allen heutigen Phariseern Secten/ falschen Propheten und Aposteln mit allen ihren eigen Gemeinschafften/ falschen Gottesdienst/ Babelkirchen/ zusam[m]enrottungen und eusserlichen tempelwesen/ darinnen sie wie die Fledermäuse/ Nacheulen/ Kirchenteuffel/ Irrwische/ Poltergeister/ Gespenster und Nachtthiere in und ausser ihren Stein-Kirchen umb ihre Guldene Kälber und Thierische Menschen Bilder herumb lauffen/ heulen/ singen/ tantzen/ und mit ihren Cantzelgötzen Menschen und Creaturen/ denen sie mehr als Gott selbst nachlauffen/ lauter Abgötterey treiben/ dafür daß sie mit dem klugen Jungfrauen von der Welt und ihrem Babelwesen außgehen/ und mit dem Brautigamb durch recht Christliche absonderung zu seiner Ruhe eingehen sollten; ja auch keinen falschen Geistern Lehrern Secten und Propheten mehr Glauben zustellen/ all sagten sie auch hier oder dar ist Christus selbst/ weil uns der rechter Christus einmahl so hoch für solche gewarnet/ und auch die klugen Jungfrauen mit Daniel das alles von sich bekennen und sich dessen alles schuldig geben/ was Gottes Wort an sie straffet/ ja daß sie noch dazu eingeschlaffen sind/ da nun im Finstern alle Katzen und Brodtratzen nach Gold und Brodt/ Geld und Welt herumb laufen und viele gutmeinende Seelen mit ihrem falschen Engelschein und vorgewandten Glaubens leben verführen und betriegen. Der Welt zum Zeugniß Bezeuget durch Fridrich Breckling, unwürdigen Diener Christi (Amsterdam: 1688).

Breckling, Friedrich, *Religio libera Persecutio relegata, Tyrannis Exul & Justitia Redux. Hochnötige Erinnerung an die hohe Obrigkeiten in Deutschland/ Engeland/ Dennemarck/ Schweden/ und andern Fürstenthümern/ Ländern und Statten Europæ über einige Gewissens Fragen Von der Gewissens Freyheit/ und andern hochnötigen Sachen der Obrigkeit Ampt und Persohn anbelangend: Daß sie sich nicht durch ihre Phariseer/ Hoffteufel und Bauchdiener zur Verfolgung und Außrottung deß Unkrauts/ vielweniger der rechten Nachfolger Christi anreitzen lassen: sondern in Religions Sachen einem jeden seine Gewissens-Freyheit/ nach Gottes Wort/ lassen/ wenn sie nur in eusserlichen Dingen der Obrigkeit gehorsam seyn/ damit sich die Obrigkeit nicht weiter versündige/ und Gottes Gericht über sich und ihre Unterthanen bringe. Zur Rettung derer bißher unter dem Nahmen des Unkrauts unschuldig verfolgeten Kinder Gottes/ an die hohe Origkeiten in Europa geschrieben und bezeuget/ durch Fridericum Breckling, aus Holstein/ Evangelischer Prediger in Zwoll.* Freystat ([Amsterdam]: 1663).

Breckling, Friedrich, *Speculum Seu Lapis Lydius Pastorum: Darinnen alle Prediger und Lehrer dieser letzten Welt sich beschawen/ und nach dem Gewissen/ als für Gottes alles sehenden und richtenden Augen/ ohne Heucheley ihrer selbst/ ernstlich prüfen und examiniren sollen/ Ob sie rechte/ von Gott erkandte und gesandte Prediger/ Lehrer/ Bisschöffe und Superintendenten seyn/ oder nicht; Ob sie den rechten oder falschen*

Propheten gleich; Ob sie Christi oder deß Antichrists Bild an sich haben; Ob sie mit der rechten oder falschen Apostel Ken[n]zeichen und Eigenschaften bezeichnet. Denen Frommen/ und die sich von dem Geist Gottes lehren und straffen lassen/ zu Christbrüderlicher Erinnerung/ Aufweckung/ Prüfung und Besserung; den Gottlosen/ Heuchlern/ Halßstarrigen und Wiedersprechern aber zum Zeugniß auffgesetzet/ und auff ihr Gewissen/ nach der Regel deß Wortes Gottes/ vor Augen gestellet/ durch M. Fridericum Brecklingium, Pastorem zu Handewitt/ in dem verwüsteten Holstein (Amsterdam: 1660).

Breckling, Friedrich, *Verbum abbreviatum ad victoriam verbi & Regni Divini, interitum verbi humani & excidium mundi Diabolici.* (S.l.: [c.1682]).

Breckling, Friedrich; Ludwig Friedrich Gifftheil, *Fridericus Resurgens. Anfang und Aufgang des Wortes und Zeugnissen* GOTTES/ *Welches der tewrer in Gott ruhender Mysteriarch/ Zeuge/ Knecht und Kriegsman Gottes Ludwig Friderich Gifftheil/ im Geist und Glauben/ Davids/ Josua/ Elias und der Alten Propheten dieser gegenwertigen Welt und allen ihren Secten/ Königreichen/ Fürstenthumern/ Regenten/ Priestern/ Ländern und Städten in gantz Europa und Deutschland bey 40. Jahr lang an allen Ortern biß in den Todt bezeuget hat. Wie solches alles heut in der That anbrennet und erfüllet wird/ und an dem Heiligthumb oder Hause Gottes und dessen falschen Lehrern und Priestern den Anfang nehmen muß. Samt einem Bann und Fluch/ damit Er die Erde geschlagen/ und die Ungehorsame und Ungläubige Welt-Menschen nach Gottes Wort verfluchet. Dabey ein Extract und Abschrifft der Wunderbahren Vision Käysers Sigismundi von dem Priester Friderico Langenaugio. Und wie viel andere Zeugen mit der Wahrheit des Wortes Gottes von diesen letzten Zeiten übereinstimmen. Durch ein Mitt-Glied der Jesus-Liebenden Früchtbringenden Apostolischen Gesellschaft von dem Orden des gecreutzigten/ einen Königlichen Priester und Frey-Herrn in Christo/ den Brechenden. Auff daß durch das Geistliche Schwerd und Hammer des Wortes Gottes alle Gewalt/ Heucheley/ Lügen/ Abgötterey/ Thorheit und Eigenheit der Gottlosen Phariseer und falschen Apostel in der Welt zu erst zerbrochen und außgerottet/ und also Gottes Nahmen/ Ehre/ Gewalt/ Wort/ Reich/ Ampt und Kinder wieder erhöhet werden in Gerechtigkeit.* Amen/ Halleluja (S.l.: 1683).

Březová, Vavřinec of, *Husitská kronika; Píseň o vítězství u Domažlic*, trans. František Heřmanský and Jan Blahoslav Čapek (Prague: 1979).

Comenius, Jan Amos, Christoph Kotter, Krystyna Poniatowska, and Nicolaus Drabicius, *Lux in tenebris; hoc est prophetiæ donum* (Amsterdam: 1657).

Comenius, Jan Amos, *Historia Persecutionum Ecclesiae Bohemicae, Iam inde a primordiis conversionis suae ad Christianismum, hoc est, Anno 894. ad Annum usque 1632. Ferdinando secundo Austriaco regnant. In Qua Inaudita hactenus Arcana Politica, consilia, artes, & iudicia horrenda exhibentur* (S.l.: 1648).

Commines, Philippe de, *Les memoires de messire Philippe de Commines, sieur d'Argenton* (Paris: 1661).

Conneand S., *New Prophets: Their Historical and True Picture* (London: 1708).

Derschau, Reinhold von, *Hodosophia Viatoris Christiani. Das ist: Die Christliche Wanderschafft Des Christlichen Wandersmanns/ auff dem Wege deß Lebens/ denselben zu finden und zu gehen; hingegen den Weg des Verderbens/ zu fliehen und zu meyden. In einer Tafel Bildnüßweise vorgestellet/ und mit heylsamer Erklärung außgeleget. Darin unser gantzes Christenthumb practice gezeiget/ auch eines jeden Menschen/ insonderheit Christen/ Ursprung und Anfang/ Leben und Wandel/ Mittel und Ende/ mit lebendigen Farben abgemahlet wird. Zuförderst aus Heil. Göttl. Schrifft/ hernach aus vieler vortrefflicher Theologen und anderer vornehmer und berühmten Männer Schrifften/ methodicè zusammen getragen/ mit lieblichen Rosen und Lilien/ Christlicher Freundlichkeit und Bescheidenheit/ auch bittern durchdringenden/ doch heilsamen Wermuth der nöthigen Redlichkeit und Warheit angefüllet/ und zur treuen Nachfolge und Warnung/ und vätterlicher Schuldigkeit/ Kindern und Kindes-Kindern hinterlassen* (Frankfurt/Main: 1675).

Du Moulin, Pierre. *De l'Accomplissement des propheties* (Geneva: 1612).

Dyke, Daniel, *The Mystery of Self-Deceiving. Or A Discourse and Discovery of the Deceitfulnesse of Mans Heart. Written by the Late Faithfull Minister of Gods Word Daniell Dyke, Bachelour in Divinity. Published Since his Death, by his Brother I.D. minister of Gods Word* (London: 1615).

Emler, Josef, Jan Gebauer, and Jaroslav Goll (eds), *Fontes Rerum Bohemicarum* 5 (Prague: 1893).

Engelbrecht, Jean, *Divine Vision et révélation des trois états, l'ecclesiastique, le politique, et l'oeconomique* (Amsterdam: 1680).

Feustking, Johann Heinrich, *Gymnaeceum heretico fanaticum, Oder Historie und Beschreibung Der falschen Prophetinnen/ Quäckerinnen/ Schwärmerinnen/ und andern sectirischen und begeisterten Weibes-Personen/ Durch welche die Kirche Gottes verunruhiget worden; sambt einem Vorbericht und Anhang/ entgegen gesetzet denen Adeptis Godofredi Arnoldi* (Frankfurt/Main, Leipzig: 1704).

Flacius, Matthias, *Catalogus testium Veritatis, Qui ante nostram aetatem reclamarunt Papae. Opus varia rerum, hoc praesertim tempore scitu dignißimarum, cognitione refertum, ac lectu cum primis utile atq; necessarium. Cum Praefatione Mathiae Flacii Illyrici* [...] (Basel: 1556).

Flacius, Matthias; Conrad Lautenbach (translator), *Catalogus Testium Veritatis. Historia der zeugen/ Bekenner und Märterer/ so Christum und die Evangelische warheit biß hieher/ auch etwa mitten im Reich der finsternus/ warhafftig erkennet/ Christlich und auffrichtig bekennet/ und dem Bäpstlichen vermeinten Primat/ irrthum/ ergerlichen leben und lastern/ erstlich widersprechen/ Auch mehrertheils über solchem Christlichen kampff/ unbillichem haß/ grewliche verfolgung/ harte gesencknus/ und den todt selber ritterlich außgestanden und erlidten haben.* [...] (Frankfurt/Main: 1573).

Gottfried, Arnold, "Von Peter Moritzen zu Halle/ Kozak, Regero, und andern Adeptis", in idem, *Kirchen- und Ketzerhistorie*, vol. 3/4 (Frankfurt/ Main: 1729), 109–115.

Holtzhausen, Johann Christoph, *Divinum Salvificae Stultitiae Beneplacitum, Das Göttliche Wolgefallen durch eine solche Predigt seelig zu machen/ Welche für aller Menschen Natürlicher Vernunft und Weltweißheit Thorheit ist. Dem verdamlichen Irrthum und falschem Fundament der Socinianischen Haupt-Ketzerey. Und aller Derer/ Die es in diesem Punct halßstarrig mit ihnen halten entgegen gesetzt* (S.l.: 1680).

Holwell, John, *Catastrophe mundi, or, Europe's Many Mutations until the Year 1701 ...* (London: 1682).

Jurieu, Pierre, *L'Accomplissement des prophéties ou la délivrance prochaine de l'Eglise* (Rotterdam: 1686).

Jurieu, Pierre, *Lettres Pastorales addressées aux fidèles de France qui gémissent sous la captivité de Babylon* (Rotterdam: 1686–1694).

Jurieu, Pierre, *The Reflections of the Reverend and Learned Monsieur Jurieu, Upon the Strange and Miraculous Exstasies of Isabel Vincent, the Shepherdess of Saov in Dauphiné. To Which is Added a Letter of a Gentleman in Dauphiné* (London: 1689).

Kaiserstein, Salomon von [= Quirinus Kuhlmann], *Cosmopolita de monarchia jesuelitica ultimo ævo reservata ad politicos aulicosque orbis terrarium* (London: 1682).

Kotter, Christoph, Krystyna Poniatowska, Nicolaus Drabicius, and Jan Amos Comenius. *Lux e tenebris: novis radiis aucta, hoc est, Solemnissimæ divinæ revelationes in usum seculi nostri factæ* (Amsterdam: 1665).

Krofta, Kamil, "Zur Geschichte der husitischen Bewegung: Drei Bullen Papst Johannis XIII aus dem Jahre 1414", *in Mittheilungen des Instituts für Oesterreichische Geschichtforschung* 23 (Innsbruck: 1902), 598–610.

Kuhlmann, Quirin, *Widerlegte Breklingsworte aus zweien Brifen an Andreas Luppius gezogen. Hibei sind gefüget das 34 (49) und 35 (50) Kühl-Jubel aus dem Kühlsalomon* (Amsterdam: 1688).

Le Mercure Galant (Paris: 1672–1710).

Lead, Jane, *The Wars of David, and the Peaceable Reign of Solomon: Symbolizing the Times of Warfare and Refreshment of the Saints of the Most High God, to Whom a Priestly Kingdom is Shortly to be Given, after the Order of Melchisedeck. Set Forth in Two Treatises Written by J. Lead: and According to Divine Ordination Publish'd in This Present Year of Jubilee. For the Service of All the Children of the Captivity, Now Watching and Praying in Many Countries, for the Great Jubilee of the Lord to Begin, and Follow upon this Very Speedily. Containing I. An Alarm to the Holy Warriours to Fight the Battels of the Lamb. II. The Glory of Sharon, in the Renovation of Nature, Introducing the Kingdom of Christ in his Sealed Virgins, Redeemed from the Earth* (London: 1700).

[Lee, Francis & Roach, Richard (eds)], *Theosophical transactions by the Philadelphian Society, consisting of Memoirs, Conferences, Letters, Dissertations, Inquiries, &c. For the Advancement of Piety and Divine Philosophy* (London: 1697).

Loserth, Johann, "Beiträge zur Geschichte der Husitischen Bewegung", in *Archiv für Oesterreichische Geschichte* 82 (Vienna: 1895), 326–419.

Ludewig, Johann Peter von (ed.), *Reliquiae Manuscriptorum Omnis Aevi Diplomatum ac Monumentorum*, vol. 6 (Frankfurt: 1724).

Luther, Martin, *Hundert und zwanzig Propheceyunge/ oder Weissagung/ des Ehrwirdigen Vaters Herrn Doctoris Martini Luthers/ von allerley straffen/ so nach seinem tod vber Deutschland von wegen desselbigen grossen/ und vielfaltigen Sünden kommen solten. Aus seinen Büchern zusammen gezogen/ und welche Lateinisch geschrieben verdeutscht Durch M. Petrum Glaser/ Kirchendiener zu Dresden* (Eisleben: 1557).

Massard, Jacques, *Explication de quelques songes prophetiques et theologiques qu'il a plu à Dieu d'envoier à quelques dames refugiées pour nôtre instruction, & pour nôtre consolation dans ces tems de deuil, d'iniquité et d'ignorance ...* (Amsterdam: 1691).

Massard, Jacques, *Explication d'un songe divin de Louis XIV, et de deux autres songes divins d'une personne de qualité et de mérite de La Haye: avec sept révélations de la Dem[oiselle] réfugiée à Amsterdam, qui éclaircissent le songe du Roi, et prouvent l'esprit de prophétie* (Amsterdam: 1690).

Massard, Jacques, *Harmonie des Propheties anciennes avec les modernes, sur la durée de l'Antechrist et les souffrances de l'Eglise*, 5 vols ([Cologne]: 1686–1688).

Massard, Jacques, *Panacée, ou Discours sur les effets singuliers d'un Remede experimenté, & commode pour la guerison de la pluspart des longues maladies ...* (Grenoble: 1679).

Massard, Jacques, *Recueil des prophéties et songes prophetiques concernans les temps presens & servant pour un eclaircissement de les Propheties de Nostradamus* (Amsterdam: 1691).

Massard, Jacques, *Relation exacte et curieuse des malheurs extremes et prochains tant de Louis XIV que de toute la France prédits par Nostradamus* (Amsterdam: 1693).

Mather, Cotton, *The Wonderful Works of God Commemorated Praises Bespoke for the God of Heaven in a Thanksgiving Sermon Delivered on Decemb. 19, 1689: Containing Reflections Upon the Excellent Things Done By the Great God.: To Which is Added a Sermon Preached Unto a Convention of the Massachuset-Colony in New-England* (Boston: 1690).

Mézeray, François Eudes de, *Abrégé chronologique de l'histoire de France* (Paris: 1667).

Micraelius, Johannes, *Historia Ecclesiastica, Qua Ab Adamo Judaicae, & à Salvatore nostro Christianae Ecclesiae, ritus, persecutiones, Concilia, Doctores, Haereses & Schismata proponuntur, edita cura Danielis Hartnacci, Pomerani.* (Leipzig, Frankfurt/Main: 1699).

Müller, Heinrich, *Himmlischer Liebes-Kuß/ Oder Ubung deß wahren Christenthumbs/ fliessend auß der Erfahrung Göttlicher Liebe / Vorgestellet von M. Henrico Müllern/ Predigern der Gemeind zu S. Marien in Rostock.* (Frankfurt/Main, Rostock: 1659).

Nostradamus, *The True Prophecies or Prognostications of Michael Nostradamus, Physician to Henry II, Francis II, and Charles IX, Kings of France and One of the Best Astronomers That Ever Were*, trans. Theophilus Garencières (London: 1685).

Nouvelles de la République des Lettres (Amsterdam: 1684–1718).

Pez, Bernard (ed.), *Thesaurus anecdotorum novissimus* IV, ii (Augsburg: 1723).

Poiret, Pierre, *De Eruditione Solida, Superficiaria, Et Falsa, Libri Tres. In quibus Ostensa Veritatum Solidarum via & origine, Cognitionum Scientiarumque Humanarum, & in specie Cartesianismi, Fundamenta, valor, defectus & errores deteguntur. Præmittitur Tractatus De Vera Methodo inveniendi verum, Confutationem Principiorum libri Belgici de Mundo fascinato in fine obiter exhibens. Subnectuntur nonnulla Apologetica* [...] (Amsterdam: 1692).

Potinius, Conrad, *Deß Ehrwürdigen hochbegabten Herren Conradi Potinii Pastoris zu Wittmund/ Sehr heylsahme Erinnerung/ Von der letzten grossen Trübsal/ Welche der gerechte Gott/ über den gantzen Erdenkräyß* [...] *Fürnehmblich über Teutschlandt/ und gantz Europam, zwar Zur Läuterung und Reinigung der Frommen und Bußfertigen/ Aber gäntzlicher vertilgung und schändlichem untergang der Gottlosen in kurtzem ergehen lassen wird. Zwar ohn vorwissen deß Authoris, doch auß guter Wolmeinung/ und vielen irrigen Sündern zur warnung/ und Rettung Ihrer Seelen/ kürtzlich ans Liecht gegeben/ Von Christophero Roselio, Predigern zu Schwarne* (Bremen: 1636).

Praetorius, Elias [= Christian Hoburg], *Apologia Praetoriana. Das ist: Spiegels derer Mißbräuche beym heutigen Predig-ampt/ Gründliche Verthedigung: Wider die Lutherische Prediger in Lübeck/ Hamburg und Lüneburg. Darinnen Dero gedruckte Warnung von Wort zu Wort ordentlich und gründlich wiederleget/ auch dero Crimina falsi, in verfälschung der Allegaten, zerstümelung und verkehrung der Worte/ fein deutsch vor augen gestellet werden. Ihnen Zur nottürfftigen Uberweisung ihrer Verführung/ Heucheley und Falschheit/ auch zu besserer Prüffung/ und da es beliebet zur redlichen Beantwortung/ fein deutsch vorgehalten. Vor dem nunmehr hereinbrechenden grossen Gerichtstage des Herrn/ Herrn Zebaoth* (S.l.: 1653).

Příbram, Jan, *Život kněží táborských*, ed. Jaroslav Boubín (Příbram: 2000).

Rabaut, Paul, *La Livrée de l'Église chrétienne, sermon ... prêché au désert, le 23 avril 1750* (Paris: 1829).

Sclei (Scleus), Bartolomaeus, *Pater Noster. Das ist Eine geheime allgemeine Außlegung Des Heiligen Unsers/ Darinnen gehandelt wird/ Was Bethen seye? Was man Anbeten solle? Neben einem Anhange etlicher Notwändiger Puncten zum Verstande des Wahren Christenthumbs gehörig* (S.l.: 1639).

Sclei (Scleus), Bartolomaeus, *Theosophische Schrifften: Oder Eine Allgemeine und Geheime/ jedoch Einfältige und Teutsche Theologia; Anweisend/ wie ein jeder Mensch durch das Geheimnuß Jesu Christi in uns/ zu dem wahren und lebendigen Glauben und Erkäntnuß des Drey-Einigen Gottes/ seiner selbst und aller Creaturen wesent-*

lich gelangen/ und also das Reich Gottes in der Seele wieder finden/ eröffnen/ und im rechten Gebrauch aller Dinge/ empfindlich geniessen solle. Gegründet und angewiesen In dem Dreyfachen Göttlichen Offenbahrungs-Buche/ Der H. Schrifft/ der grossen und kleinen Welt. Geschrieben aus Göttlichem Liecht und Liebe zur Warheit vor alle Menschen Anno 1556 in Klein-Pohlen, Anjetzo aber wegen seiner Vortrefflichkeit und hohen Nutzen in dieser Zeit/ zum gemeinen Besten ans Liecht befördert/ und mit einem Register versehen (S.l.: 1686).

Spener, Philipp Jakob, *Die allgemeine Gottesgelehrtheit aller glaubigen Christen und rechtschaffenen Theologen. Auß Gottes wort erwiesen/ mit den zeugnüssen vornehmer alter und neuer reiner Kirchen-Lehrer bestätiget/ Und Der so genannten Theosophiae Horbio-Spenerianae, Zur gründlichen verantwortung entgegen gesetzt* (Frankfurt/Main: 1680).

Stříbro, Jakoubek of, *Výklad na Zjevenie Sv. Jana* 1, ed. František Šimek (Prague: 1932).

Tauler, Johannes, *Insignis Theologi Sermones de festis, & solennitatibus Sanctorum. simúlque divinae Institutiones nuper inve[n]tae, cum Epistolis aliquot, quibus Deo uniri per spiritales exercitationes nemo non facile docetur […]* (Leiden: 1558).

Thomson, S. Harrison (ed.), *Mistra Jana Husi Tractatus Responsivus* (Prague: 1927).

Trigault, Nicolas, *Vita Gasparis Barzaei Belgae Societate Iesu, B. Xaverii in India socii.* (Antwerp: 1610).

Ussher, James, *Strange and Remarkable Prophesies and Predictions of the Holy, Learned, and Excellent James Usher, Late L. Arch-Bishop of Armagh …* (London: 1678).

Welz, Justinian Ernst von, *Ein kurtzer Bericht/ Wie eine Newe Gesellschafft auffzurichten wäre/ unter den rechtglaubigen Christen der Augspurgischen Confession. Mit einer Christlichen Vermahnung an die Herren Reformirte, nur mit wenigen Zeilen angezeiget/ und in Druck verfertiget* (S.l.: [c.1665]).

Welz, Justinian Ernst von, *Eine Christliche und treuhertzige Vermahnung An alle rechtgläubige Christen/ der Augspurgischen Confession. Betreffend eine sonderbahre Gesellschafft/ Durch welche/ nechst Göttlicher Hülffe/ unsere Evangelische Religion möchte außgebreitet werden* (S.l.: 1664).

Welz, Justinian Ernst von, *Einladungs-Trieb zum heran-nahenden Grossen Abendmahl und Vorschlag zu einer Christ-erbaulichen Jesus-Gesellschaft. Behandlend die Besserung des Christentums und Bekehrung des Heidentums* (Nuremberg: 1664).

Wolff, Johann, *Lectionum memorabilium et reconditarum tomus secundus. Habet hic lector ecclesiae, Vatum, Politicorum, Philosophorum, Historicorum, aliorumq́; sapientum & eruditorum pia, grauia, mira, arcana, & stupenda; iucunda simul & utilia, dicta, scripta, atq; facta; Vaticinia item, vota, omina, mysteria, Hieroglyphica, miracula, visiones, antiquitates, monumenta, testimonia, exempla virtutū, vitiorum, abusuum; typos insuper, picturas, atq; imagines […]* (Lauingen: 1600).

Zesen, Philipp von, *Beschreibung der Stadt Amsterdam: Darinnen von Derselben ersten ursprunge bis auf gegenwärrtigen zustand/ ihr unterschiedlicher anwachs/ herliche*

Vorrechte/ und in mehr als 70 Kupfer-stükken entworfene führnehmste Gebeue/ zusamt ihrem Stahts-wesen/ Kauf-handel/ und ansehlicher macht zur see/ wie auch was sich in und mit Derselben märkwürdiges zugetragen/ vor augen gestellet werden (Amsterdam: 1664).

Secondary Sources

Adams, Geoffrey, *The Huguenots and French Opinion, 1685–1787: The Enlightenment Debate on Toleration* (Waterloo, Ont.: 1991).

Baar, Mirjam de, "Denijs, Tanneke", in *Digitaal Vrouwenlexicon van Nederland*, online (http://resources.huygens.knaw.nl/vrouwenlexicon/lemmata/data/Denijs, accessed 13 January 2020).

Bailey, Margaret Lewis, *Milton and Jakob Boehme. A study of German Mysticism in Seventeenth-century England* (New York: 1964).

Bartoš, František M., "Do čtyř pražských artykulů: Z myšlenkových i ústavních zápasů let 1415–1420", *Sborník příspěvků k dějinám města Prahy* 5 (1932), 481–591.

Bartoš, František M., "Španělský biskup proti Táboru a Praze", *Jihočeský sborník historický* 11 (1938), 67–70.

Bautz, Friedrich Wilhelm, "Breckling, Friedrich", in *Biographisch-Bibliographisches Kirchenlexikon*, vol. 1. ed. idem, (Herzberg: 1990 [= Hamm 1975]), 736–737.

Beare, Robert L., "Quirinus Kuhlmann: Where and when?", *MLN* 77/4 (Oct. 1962), 379–397.

Ben Massaoud, Samy, "Bayle et Christine de Suède", *Bulletin de la Société de l'Histoire du Protestantisme Français* 155 (2009), 626–655.

Blaufuß, Dietrich, "Breckling, Friedrich", in *Theologische Realenzyklopädie*, ed. G. Krause and G. Müller, vol. 7 (Berlin; New York: 1993), 150–153.

Boisson, Didier, "The Revocation of the Edict of Nantes and the Désert", in *A Companion to the Huguenots*, ed. Raymond Mentzer and Bertrand Van Ruymbeke (Leiden: 2016), 221–245.

Borello, Céline, "Les Sources d'une altérité religieuse en révolution: Rabaut Saint-Étienne ou la radicalisation des representations protestantes", *Annales historiques de la Révolution française* 378 (2014), 32–33.

Bosc, Henri, *La Guerre des Cévennes*, vol. 1 (Montpellier: 1985).

Bost, Hubert, "L'Apocalypse et les Psaumes dans l'arsenal des Pastorales de Jurieu", in *Ces Messieurs de la R.P.R.: Histoires et écritures de huguenots, XVIIe–XVIIIe siècles*, ed. Hubert Bost (Paris: 2001), 175–213.

Bost, Hubert, "De la Secte à l'Église. La Quête de légitimité dans le protestantisme meridional au XVIIIe siècle", *Rives méditerranéennes* 10 (2002), 53–68.

Bruckner, John, "Breckling, Friedrich", in *Biographisches Lexikon für Schleswig-Holstein und Lübeck*, ed. on behalf of the "Gesellschaft für Schleswig-Holsteinische Geschichte und des Vereins für Lübeckische Geschichte und Altertumskunde", vol. 7 (Neumünster: 1985), 33–38.

Carbonnier-Burkard, Marianne, "Le Prédicant et le songe du roi", *Etudes théologiques et religieuses* 62:1 (1987), 19–40.

Carbonnier-Burkard, Marianne, "Propagande et prophéties protestantes autour d'un rêve de Louis XIV", *Bulletin de l'Association Suisse pour l'histoire du Refuge huguenot* 27 (2006), 2–15.

Cermanová, Pavlína, "The Apocalyptic background of Hussite radicalism", in *A Companion to the Hussites* (Leiden: 2020), 187–218.

Cermanová, Pavlína, *Čechy na Konci Věků: Apokalyptické Myšlení a Vize Husitské Doby* (Prague: 2013).

Certeau, Michel de, *La Possession de Loudun* (Paris: 1980).

Chabrol, Jean-Paul, "Mémoire et identité religieuse: la 'légende' des Couflaïres de la Vaunage", in *La Vaunage au XVIIIe siècle* (Nîmes: 2003), 5–7.

Chantin, Jean-Pierre, *Les Amis de l'œuvre de la verité. Jansénisme, miracles et fin du monde au XIXe siècle* (Lyon: 1998), 10–11.

Charbonneau, Jason, "Huguenot Prophetism, Clerical Authority, and the Disenchantment of the World", M.A. thesis (Carleton University: 2012).

Chopelin, Caroline, *L'Obscurantisme et les Lumières: Itinéraire de l'abbé Grégoire, évêque révolutionnaire* (Paris: 2013).

Clifford, Alan C., "Reformed Pastoral Theology Under the Cross: John Quick and Claude Brousson", *Western Reformed Seminary Journal* 5/1 (1998), 21–35.

Čornej, Petr, "Potíže s Adamity", *Marginalia historica* 2 (1997), 33–63.

Čornej, Petr, *Velké Dějiny Zemí Koruny České*, vol. 5 (Prague: 2000).

Coufal, Dušan, "Key issues in Hussite theology", in *A Companion to the Hussites* (Leiden: 2020), 261–296.

Coufal, Dušan, "*Sub utraque specie*: Die Theologie des Laienkelchs bei Jacobell von Mies (†1429) und den frühen Utraquisten", *Archa Verbi* 14 (2017), 157–201.

De Vooght, Paul, *Jacobellus de Stříbro (†1429) premier théologien du hussitisme* (Louvain: 1972).

Debus, Allen, *The French Paracelsians: The Chemical Challenge to Medical and Scientific Tradition in Early Modern France* (Cambridge: 2002).

Delumeau, Jean, *La Peur en Occident (XIVe–XVIIIe siècles): Une cité assiegée* (Paris: 1978).

Dolejšová, Ivana, "Eschatological Elements in Hus's Understanding of Orthopraxis", *Bohemian Reformation and Religious Practice* 4 (2002), 127–141.

Döllinger, Ignaz von (ed.), *Beiträge zur Sektengeschichte des Mittelalters* 2 (Munich: 1890).

Dupont, André, *Rabaut Saint-Etienne 1743–1793. Un protestant défenseur de la liberté religieuse* (Geneva: 1989).

Eeghen, Isabella Henriette van, *De Amsterdamse boekhandel 1680–1725*, vol. V[1] (Amsterdam: 1978).

Fabre, Pierre Antoine, Nicolas Fornerod, Sophie Houdard and Maria-Cristina Pitassi (eds), *Lire Jean de Labadie (1610–1674)—Fondation et affranchissement* (Paris: 2016).

Flajšhans, Václav (ed.), *Mistra Jana Husi Sebrané spisy: Spisy latinské* (Prague: 1904).

Fudge, Thomas A. (ed.), *The Crusades against Heretics in Bohemia, 1418–1437* (Aldershot: 2002).

Fudge, Thomas A., *The Magnificent Ride: The First Reformation in Hussite Bohemia* (Aldershot: 1998).

Gembicki, Dieter and Heidi Gembicki-Achtnich (eds), *Le Réveil des coeurs. Journal de voyage du Frère Morave Fries (1761–1762)* (Saintes: 2013).

Gerson, Stéphane, *Nostradamus: How an Obscure Renaissance Astrologer Became the Modern Prophet of Doom* (New York: 2012).

"The Gibert Brothers", online (http://www.museeprotestant.org/en/notice/the-gibert-brothers, accessed 18 Jun 2014).

Grosse, Sven, "Thomas Aquinas, Bonaventure, and the critiques of Joachimist Topics from the Fourth Lateran Council to Dante", in *A Companion to Joachim of Fiore*, ed. Matthias Riedl (Leiden: 2018), 144–189.

Herold, Vilém, "The Spiritual Background of the Czech Reformation: Precursors of Jan Hus", in *A Companion to Jan Hus*, ed. František Šmahel and Ota Pavlíček (Leiden: 2015), 69–95.

Hessayon, Ariel, "Jacob Boehme, Emanuel Swedenborg and Their Readers", *The Arms of Morpheus-Essays on Swedenborg and Mysticism* (2007), 33.

Hessayon, Ariel, "Lead's Life and Times (Part Two): The Woman in the Wilderness", in *Jane Lead and her Transnational Legacy*, ed. Ariel Hessayon (London: 2016), 39–69.

Hessayon, Ariel, "Lead's Life and Times (Part Three): The Philadelphian Society", in *Jane Lead and her Transnational Legacy*, ed. Ariel Hessayon (London: 2016), 71–90.

Heyd, Michael, *"Be Sober and Reasonable": The Critique of Enthusiasm in the Seventeenth and Eighteenth Centuries* (Leiden: 1995).

Holeton, David R., "Revelation and Revolution in Late Medieval Bohemia", *Communio Viatorum* 36 (1994), 29–45.

Houdard, Sophie, "La Cabale des Médaillistes. Une affaire de spiritualité 'extraordinaire' à Nancy (1644–1648)", *Archivio italiano per la storia della pietà, Edizioni di storia e letteratura* (2018), 41–57.

Houdard, Sophie, *Les Invasions mystiques. Spiritualités, hétérodoxies et censures au début de l'époque moderne* (Paris: 2008).

Jaccard, Emile, "Le Marquis Jaques de Rochegude et les protestants sur les galères", *Revue de théologie et de philosophie et compte-rendu des principals publications scientifiques* 31 (1878), 35–73.

Jacob, Margaret C., "Millenarianism and Science in the Late Seventeenth Century," *Journal of the History of Ideas* 37/2 (April–June 1976), 335–341.

Jacques-Levèvre, Nicole, "1789: interprétations eschatologiques de la Révolution française", in *Révolutions du moderne, colloque interdisciplinaire, Université Paris X-Nanterre, 6–9 décembre 2000*, ed. Daniela Gallingani, Claude Leroy, André Magnan et Baldine Saint Girons (Paris-Méditerrannée: 2004), 271–281.

Johnston, Warren, "Bulkeley, Sir Richard, second baronet (1660–1710)", ODNB (http://www.oxforddnb.com/view/article/3898, accessed 30 July 2007).

Johnston, Warren, "Jane Lead and the English Apocalytic Thought in the Late Seventheenth Century", in *Jane Lead and her Transnational Legacy*, ed. Ariel Hessayon (London: 2016), 119–142.

Jukl, Jakub Jiří, *Adamité: Historie a vyhubení husitských naháčů* (Prague: 2014).

Kaminsky, Howard, "Chiliasm and the Hussite Revolution", *Church History* 26/1 (March 1957), 43–71.

Kaminsky, Howard, "The Free Spirit in the Hussite Revolution", in *Millennial Dreams in Action*, ed. Sylvia L. Thrupp (New York: 1970), 166–186.

Kaminsky, Howard, *A History of the Hussite Revolution* (Berkeley: 1967).

Kaminsky, Howard, "Nicholas of Pelhřimov's Tábor: an Adventure into the Eschaton", in *Eschatologie und Hussitismus*, 139–167.

Kaminsky, Howard, "The Prague Insurrection of 30 July 1419", *Medievalia et Humanistica* 17 (1966), 106–126.

Kybal, Vlastimil, "M. Matěj z Janova a M. Jakoubek ze Stříbra: Srovnávací kapitola o Antikristu", *Český Časopis Historický* 11 (1905), 22–37.

Laborie, Lionel, "Bourbon, Armand de, marquis de Miremont (1655–1732)", ODNB (http://www.oxforddnb.com/view/article/109568, accessed 27 May 2016).

Laborie, Lionel, *Enlightening Enthusiasm: Prophecy and Religious Experience in Early Eighteenth-Century England* (Manchester: 2015).

Laborie, Lionel, "Enthusiasm, Early Modern Philosophy, and Religion", in *Encyclopedia of Early Modern Philosophy and the Sciences*, ed. D. Jalobeanu and C.T. Wolfe (Springer, Cham: 2020), online (https://doi.org/10.1007/978-3-319-20791-9_375-1).

Laborie, Lionel, "French Prophets", ODNB (https://doi.org/10.1093/odnb/9780198614128.013.109707, accessed 9 May 2018).

Laborie, Lionel, "From English *Trembleurs* to French *Inspirés*: A Transnational Perspective on the Origins of French Quakerism (1654–1789)", in *Radicalism and Dissent in the World of Protestant Reform*, ed. Anorthe Kremers and Bridget Heal (Gottingen: 2017), 225–244.

Laborie, Lionel, "Marion, Elie (1678–1713)", ODNB (http://www.oxforddnb.com/view/article/109569, accessed 19 Feb 2019).

Laborie, Lionel, "Philadelphia Resurrected: Celebrating the Union Act (1707) from Irenic to Scatological Eschatology", in *Jane Lead and her Transnational Legacy*, ed. Ariel Hessayon (London: 2016), 213–239.

Laborie, Lionel, "Spreading the Seed: Toward a French Millenarian Network in Pietist Germany?", in *Kriminelle-Freidenker-alchemisten. Räume Des Untergrunds in Der Frühen Neuzeit*, ed. Martin Mulsow and Michael Multhammer (Köln/Weimar/Wien: 2014), 99–117.

Lachenicht, Susanne, "Diasporic Networks and Immigration Policies", in *A Companion to the Huguenots*, ed. Raymond Mentzer and Bertrand Van Ruymbeke (Leiden: 2016), 249–272.

Lerner, Robert E., "Medieval Millenarianism and Violence", in *Pace e Guerra nel Basso Medioevo* (Spoleto: 2004), 37–52.

Lerner, Robert E., "Refreshment of the Saints: the time after the Antichrist as a station for Earthly progress in Medieval Thought", *Traditio* 32 (1976), 97–144.

Lotz-Heumann, Ute, "'The Spirit of Prophecy has not Wholly Left the World': The Stylisation of Archbishop James Ussher as a Prophet", in *Religion and superstition in Reformation Europe*, ed. Helen Parish and William G. Naphy (Manchester: 2002), 119–132.

Macek, Josef, "K počátkům táborství v Písku", *Jihočeský Sborník Historický* 22/4 (1953), 113–128.

Macek, Josef, "Táborské Chiliastické Články", *Historický Sborník* 1 (1953), 53–64.

Macek, Josef, *Tábor v Husitském Revolučním Hnutí* I (Prague: 1952).

Maire, Catherine-Laurence, *Les Convulsionnaires de Saint-Médard. Miracles, convulsions et prophéties à Paris au XVIIIe siècle* (Paris: 1985).

Malcom, Noel, *Aspects of Hobbes* (Oxford: 2002).

Mandelbrote, Scott, "Fatio, Nicolas, of Duillier (1664–1753)", *ODNB* (http://www.oxforddnb.com/view/article/9056, accessed 30 July 2007).

Martin, Lucinda, "God's Strange Providence. Jane Lead in the correspondence of Johann Georg Gichtel", in *Jane Lead and her Transnational Legacy*, ed. Ariel Hessayon (London: 2016), 187–212.

Mazalová, Lucie, *Eschatologie v díle Jana Husa* (Brno: 2015).

McGinn, Bernard, *Antichrist: Two Thousand Years of the Human Fascination with Evil* (San Francisco: 1994).

McGinn, Bernard, *Visions of the End: Apocalyptic Traditions in the Middle Ages* (New York: 1979).

McShane, Angela, "A Resounding Silence? Huguenots and the Broadside Ballad in the Seventeenth Century", *Proceedings of the Huguenot Society of Great Britain and Ireland* 28/5 (Summer 2007), 604–625.

Meinhold, Peter, "Breckling, Friedrich", in *Neue Deutsche Biographie*, ed. on behalf of the "Historische Kommission bei der Bayerischen Akademie der Wissenschaften", vol. 2 (Berlin: 1971 [= Berlin: 1955]), 566.

Monahan, W. Gregory, *Let God Arise: The War and Rebellion of the Camisards* (Oxford: 2014).

Monod, Albert, *Les Sermons de Paul Rabaut, pasteur du Désert (1738–1785)* (Paris: 1911).
Moran, Bruce T., *Distilling Knowledge: Alchemy, Chemistry, and the Scientific Revolution* (Cambridge, MA: 2015).
Mutlová, Petra, "Major Hussite Theologians before the Compactata", in *A Companion to the Hussites* (Leiden: 2020), 101–140.
Nejedlý, Zdeněk, *Dějiny husitského zpěvu* 4, 6 (Prague: 1955–1956).
Nielsen, Friedrich, "Breckling, Friedrich", in *Realencyklopädie für protestantische Theologie und Kirche*, vol. 3, ed. Albert Hauck, 3rd ed. (Leipzig: 1897), 367–369.
Novotný, Václav, *M. Jan Hus: Život a Učení* 1/2 (Prague: 1921)
Palacký, František (ed.), *Archiv Česky Čili, Staré Písemné Památky České i Morawske* 3, 6 (Prague: 1844, 1872).
Palacký, František (ed.), *Documenta Mag. Joannis Hus* (Prague: 1869).
Palacký, František (ed.), *Scriptorum Rerum Bohemicarum* 3 (Prague: 1829).
Parmentier, Bérengère, "Radicalité et illégitimité", *Archives de sciences sociales des religions* 150 (April–June 2010), 57–76.
"Pasteurs et prédicants martyrs", (http://www.museedudesert.com/article5918.html, accessed 8 August 2016).
Patschovsky, Alexander, "Der taboritische Chiliasmus: Seine Idee, sein Bild bei den Zeitgenossen und die Interpretation der Geschichtswissenschaft", in *Häresie und vorzeitige Reformation im Spätmittelalter*, ed. Franti̇sek Šmahel (Munich: 1998), 169–195.
Patschovsky, Alexander, and František Šmahel (eds), *Eschatologie und Hussitismus* (Prague: 1996).
Pavlíček, Ota, "The Chronology of the Life and Work of Jan Hus", in *A Companion to Jan Hus*, ed. František Šmahel and Ota Pavlíček (Leiden: 2015), 9–68.
Penman, Leigh T.I., "Climbing Jacob's Ladder: Crisis, Chiliasm, and Transcendence in the Thought of Paul Nagel (†1624), a Lutheran Dissident during the Time of the Thirty Years' War", *Intellectual History Review* 20/2 (2010), 201–226.
Pjecha, Martin, "Spreading Faith and Vengeance: Human Agency and the 'Offensive Shift' in the Hussite Discourses on Warfare", *The Bohemian Reformation and Religious Practice* 10 (2015), 158–184.
Pjecha, Martin, "Táborite Revolutionary Apocalypticism: Mapping Influences and Divergences", in *Apocalypse now!*, ed. Damien Tricoire (Routledge: forthcoming).
Pohlig, Matthias, "Konfessionskulturelle Deutungsmuster internationaler Konflikte um 1600—Kreuzzug, Antichrist, Tausendjähriges Reich", *Archiv für Reformationsgeschichte*, 93 (2002), 278–316.
Popkin, Jeremy D. and Richard H. Popkin (eds), *The Abbé Grégoire and His World* (Dordrecht: 2000).
Popkin, Richard H., "Predicting, Prophecying, Divining and Foretelling from Nostradamus to Hume", *History of European Ideas* 5/2 (1984), 117–135.

Ransdorf, Miloslav, *Kapitoly z geneze husitské ideologie* (Prague: 1983).
Ribard, Samuel, "Un Inspiré, Isaac Elzière, de Saint-Ambroix, d'après ses manuscrits." *Bulletin historique et littéraire* 40/1 (1891), 365–372.
Riedl, Matthias (ed.), *A Companion to Joachim of Fiore* (Leiden: 2018).
Riedl, Matthias, "Eschatology", in *New Dictionary of the History of Ideas*, vol. 2, ed. Maryanne Cline Horowitz (New York: 2005), 708–710.
Rolland, Pierre, *Dictionnaire du Désert huguenot: La Reconquête protestante (1715–1765)* (Paris: 2017).
Rose, Jacqueline, *Godly Kingship in Restauration England: The Politics of Royal Supremacy, 1660–1688* (Cambridge: 2011).
Schicketanz, Peter (ed.), *Der Briefwechsel Carl Hildebrand von Cansteins mit August Hermann Francke.* (Berlin; New York: 1972).
Schmolinsky, Sabine, "Positionen in den Lectiones memorabilis des Johann Wolff (1600)", in *Endzeiten. Eschatologie in den monotheistischen Weltreligionen*, ed. Wolfram Brandes and Felicitas Schmieder (Berlin: 2008), 369–417.
Sedláčková, Jitka, "Jakoubek ze Stříbra a jeho kvestie o Antikristu", PhD thesis (Masaryk University: 2001).
Sedlák, Jan, *M. Jan Hus* (Prague: 1915).
Seibt, Ferdinand, *Hussitica: Zur Struktur einer Revolution* (Cologne: 1990).
Sisman, Cengiz *The Burden of Silence: Sabbatai Sevi and the Evolution of the Ottoman-Turkish Donmes* (Oxford: 2015).
Šmahel, František and Ota Pavlíček (eds), *A Companion to Jan Hus* (Leiden: 2015).
Šmahel, František, *Dějiny Tábora* I (České Budějovice: 1988)
Šmahel, František, *Die Hussitische Revolution*, vols. 1–3 (Hannover: 2002).
Šmahel, František, "The National Idea, Secular Power and Social Issues in the Political Theology of Jan Hus", in *A Companion to Jan Hus*, ed. František Šmahel and Ota Pavlíček (Leiden: 2015), 214–253.
Solé, Jacques, *Les Origines intellectuelles de la Revocation de l'Edit de Nantes* (Saint-Etienne: 1997).
Soukup, Pavel, "The Masters and the End of the World: Exegesis in the Polemics with Chiliasm", *Bohemian Reformation and Religious Practice* 7 (2009), 91–114.
Soukup, Pavel, *Jan Hus: The Life and Death of a Preacher* (West Lafayette: 2019).
Soukup, Pavel, *Reformní kazatelství a Jakoubek ze Stříbra* (Prague: 2011).
Spence, Craig, "Misson, Francis Maximilian (c.1650–1722)", ODNB (http://www.oxforddnb.com/view/article/18821, accessed 14 March 2013).
Spinka, Matthew, *John Hus: A Biography* (Princeton: 1968).
Spunar, Pavel, *Repertorium auctorum Bohemorum provectum idearum post Universitatem Pragensem conditam illustrans* 2 vols. (Warsaw: 1985–1995).
Spurr, John, *The Restauration Church in England, 1646–1689* (New Haven: 1991).
Tomek, Václav Vladivoj, *Dějepis města Prahy*, IV, 2nd ed. (Prague: 1899).

Tricoire, Damien, "What Was the Catholic Reformation? Marian Piety and the Universalization of Divine love", The Catholic Historical Review 103 (2017), 20–49.

Utt, Walter C. and Brian Eugene Strayer, *The Bellicose Dove: Claude Brousson and Protestant Resistance to Louis XIV, 1647–1698* (Brighton: 2003).

Van Dussen, Michael and Pavel Soukup (eds), *A Companion to the Hussites* (Leiden: 2020).

Vidal, Daniel, "Expériences de fin du monde: Un Jansénisme en convulsion, un calvinisme en prophétie", *Archives de sciences sociales des religions* 114 (2001), 21–37.

Vidal, Daniel, *Le Malheur et son prophète: inspires et sectaires en Languedoc calviniste (1685–1725)* (Paris: 1983).

Vidal, Daniel, "La Secte contre le prophétisme: les Multipliants de Montpellier (1719–1723)", *Annales. Économies, Sociétés, Civilisations* 37/4 (1982), 801–825.

Vonka, R.-J., "Les évangéliques tchèques et les protestants français au XVIe et XVIIe siècles", *Bulletin de la Société de l'Histoire du Protestantisme Français* 76/4 (Oct.–Dec. 1927), 484–490.

Wall, Ernestine van der, "'Antichrist Stormed': The Glorious Revolution and the Dutch Prophetic Tradition", in *The Worlds of William and Mary*, ed. Dale Hoak and Mordechai Feingold (Stanford, CA: 1996), 152–164.

Webster, Charles, *From Paracelsus to Newton: Magic and the Making of Modern Science* (Cambridge; New York: 1982).

Webster, Charles, *Paracelsus: Medicine, Magic and Mission at the End of Time* (New Haven and London: 2008).

Whalen, Brett Edward, "Joachim the Theorist of History and Society", in *A Companion to Joachim of Fiore*, ed. Matthias Riedl (Leiden: 2018), 88–108.

Zachová, Jana and Jaroslav Boubín, "Příbramova Excerpta z Táborských Traktátů z Kapitulního Sborníku D 49", *Mediaevalia Historica Bohemica* 8 (2001), 139–167.

Index

Ackerlot, Marie, *see* Paew, Esther Michaelis de
Aconcio, Jacopo   178n117
Alberti, Valentin   176n92
alchemy   87, 99–100n49, 123n87, *see also* iatrochemistry
Americas   146n42, 198
Ammersbach, Heinrich   139, 140n26, 157n59
Amsterdam   84, 86, 119, 134, 137, 143n35, 151n47, 160n80, 182n126, 185, 196, 201
Amyraut, Moïse   128
Anglicana, Maria, *see* Gould, Maria
Anabaptists   9, 10, 213n93
Anna Sophie of Denmark, Elector of Saxony   135
Antichrist   1–13, 16, 19, 20, 25, 27–29, 35–40, 46, 60, 62, 85, 89, 93–95, 97, 98, 99, 100, 103, 106, 107, 108, 111, 114, 115, 116, 119, 125, 149, 154, 155, 157n61, 160, 161, 164, 172, 175, 179, 222, 230, 238
Antwerp   146n43
Apocalypse   3, 20, 26, 29, 30, 32, 43, 46, 48, 73, 84–86, 89, 90, 91, 92, 96, 100, 126, 143, 145, 147, 148, 149, 150, 160, 168, 169, 171, 172, 181, 198, 202n53
Arcularius, Johann Daniel   156n56
Arminians / Arminianism   177, 186
Arndt, Johann   162n82
Arnhem   134
Arnold, Gottfried   136n11, 137, 138n15, 141, 160n80
Artus, Gottfried   140n26
Asia   146
astrology   20, 87, 88, 96, 109, 186, 196, 206n62
Augustine of Hippo, Saint   36, 69
Avontroot / Aventrot(e), Johannes Bartholomeus (Juan)   177n102

Babylon   8, 12, 13, 62, 65, 78, 79, 89, 94, 102, 115, 116, 117, 143, 145, 147–150, 160, 162, 167, 168, 169, 171, 172, 178, 181, 182, 220, 223, 235–237
Baptists   175
Barenz / Beerens, Catherina   185n141
Barrefelt, Hendrik Janssen van   187n152

Barthut, Christoph   183n128
Barzaeus, Caspar   146n43
Baumgart, Samuel, *see* Pomarius, Samuel
Bathilde d'Orléans, Louise Marie Thérèse   191
Bathurst, Anne   186n145
Bathurst, John   182n126, 185n138&139, 186n145
Becker, Melchior   159n72
Beer, Wolfgang Dominicus   158n68
Berlin   14, 135
Betke, Joachim   137, 139, 157n62, 177n106
Boehme / Böhme, Jacob   137, 139, 140n26, 144n36, 145, 146, 151n47, 152, 155, 156, 160n79, 162–164, 166, 176, 182n126, 184, 187, 190, 191
Bourignon, Antoinette   134, 140, 141, 180n120, 181
Breckling, Friedrich   14, 18, 20, 133, 135n6–8, 136n9–11, 137n14, 138n15–17, 139, 140n26&27, 141n30–32, 142, 151n47&48, 152n49&50, 157n61, 158n64&69–71, 159n73, 160n78&79, 171n83, 177n106, 180n119, 182n126, 183n127, 185n138
Breithaupt, Joachim Justus   176n95
Breslau   182n126
Brieg, Johann Christian von   177n105
Bromley-by-Bow   182n126
Bromley, Thomas   186n147
Brousson, Claude   195
Burrough, Edward   137

Calas, Jean   194
Calov, Abraham   140, 145n40, 155n54, 163
Calvin, Jean   5, 6, 8, 215
Calvinists / Calvinism   20, 21, 84, 85, 86, 134, 151, 175, 177, 179, 180, 193, 215, 229n131, 230
Camisards   104, 106, 118, 192–193, 196, 197–198, 199, 200, 208n69, 215n97, 216n101, 217–227, 228n130
Canstein, Carl Hildebrand von   135
Capernaum   147n44
Cassander, Georg   177n99
Catherine of Siena   87, 89, 97, 99

INDEX   265

Catholics / Catholic Church   11, 12, 13, 24,
    25, 28, 87, 88, 98, 93–94, 101, 108, 134,
    176, 179, 192, 194, 195, 197, 205, 211n79,
    230n133
Cavalier of Sauve, Jean   197–198, 217–227
Cazotte, Jacques   191
censorship   88, 172, 174, 175, 194
cessationism   88, see also miracles
Cévennes   99, 192–200, 202n55, 221, 226n122
Charias, Johann Caspar   140n26
Charlemagne   173
Charles II, King of England, Scotland, and
    Ireland   186n142
Charles XI, King of Sweden   160n80
chiliasm   25, 32, 58, 173
Christian August, Count Palatine of Pfalz-
    Sulzbach   134
Christian love   188
Church history   141, 172, 173
Collegiants   133, 135, 176
Comenius, Jan Amos   89, 95n30&31,
    97n39, 99, 100, 115, 134n3, 137, 173n87,
    191
Constantine I (Constantine the Great / Saint
    Constantine), Roman emperor   173
Constantinople   182n126, 185
conversion   3–4, 133, 136, 147n45, 149, 150,
    153, 183, 190n6, 192, 206n60
Convulsionaries of Saint-Médard   190, see
    also Jansenists
Couflaïres   193
Court, Antoine   192, 199, 200
Cunradus, Christoffel   134, 137n13, 143n35

Daniel, biblical prophet   48, 50, 57, 65, 66,
    94, 96, 115, 118, 119, 123, 153, 156, 161, 175,
    179, 232–243
Dannhauer, Johann Konrad   178n113
Daudé, Jean   197, 217, 221
Dauphiné   90, 98, 103, 127, 192–197, 201, 202,
    210, 212
deceit   37, 38, 39, 44, 55, 58, 81, 143, 166, 168,
    178, 181–182, 183, 184, 185, 186, see also
    False church
Deichmann, Johann Heinrich   184n130
Delft   134
Denys, Tanneke   137, 142, 182n126, 187n151
Derschau, Reinhold von   158n66
Deventer   134

Devil   81, 82, 94, 110, 122, 164, 169, 178, 180,
    184–185, 189, 204–207, 224, see also
    Satan
Dieren   134
discord among Christians   144, 151–152
dissenters   14, 15, 133, 137, 140, 182n126
Dittelbach, Petrus   177n98
Dominis, Marco Antonio de   177n103
Drábik / Drabicius, Mikuláš   89, 97, 100, 102,
    108, 113, 115, 116, 118
dragonnades   98, 103, 109, 192, 211, 212
dreams, divine or prophetic   87, 90–92,
    120–121, 126, 128–129, 131–132, 186,
    202
Dresden   160n81
Düsseldorf   134
Dutch Republic, see Netherlands
Dyke, Daniel   178–179n118

East Frisia   177n98
Egypt   46, 53, 58–60, 62, 114, 162, 183,
    192
Elzière, Isaac   198–199, 228–231
Emden   184
England   12–13, 15, 18–19, 98, 108, 110, 120n85,
    125n89, 141, 142, 182n126, 184, 185, 186,
    187, 193, 196, 197, 198, 209–210, 213,
    220n114, see also London
Enlightenment   21, 22, 189, 194, 238n150
    spiritual   43, 124, 130–131, 139, 144, 145,
    153, 160, 164, 165, 167, 171, 179, 218, 222,
    228–230
enthusiasm   15, 17, 18, 20, 91, 163, 176, 186,
    189, 213n88

Fabricius, Johann Jakob   134
Fage, Durand   197–198, 217, 221–222, 227
false church   28, 36, 45, 93–93, 140, 143, 148–
    149, 156, 159–162, 167, 171, 173–174, see
    also deceit
Family of Love / Familists   184n135,
    187n152
Fatio de Duillier, Nicolas   197, 217n103,
    221n115
Felgenhauer, Paul   137
Ferus, Jiří (George)   177n100
Feustking, Johann Heinrich   160n80
Flacius, Matthias   159n74–76, 173
Flensburg   133

Fox, George   137
France   20–21, 86, 98, 100–111, 113, 116–118, 124–125, 181, 185, 186, 189–244
Francke, August Hermann   14, 15, 20, 135, 184n132, 195
Francisci, Erasmus   140n26
Frankfurt/Main   156n56
freedom of conscience   16, 105, 109n65, 139, 194n22, 238
freedom of the press   138, 194–195, see also censorship
Freemasonry   191
French Prophets   198, 199, 217n102, 229n131, see also Camisards
French Protestantism, see Huguenots
French Revolution   190, 191, 192, 200
Frölich, Eva Margaretha   140, 160n80
Fuhrmann, Augustin   177n105
Furly, Benjamin   137

George William, Duke of Zell (Celle)   183n129
Germany   2, 6, 8, 9, 15, 101, 160n81, 184n132, 185, 187–188, 198
Gichtel, Johann Georg   151n47, 182n126, 184n134
Gießen   133
Gifftheil, Ludwig Friedrich   139, 152n49&50
Glaserius, Petrus   157n58
Glassius (Glaß), Salomon   178n116
Goa   146n43
Gould, Maria [Maria Anglicana]   182–183n126, 183n127, 185n139
Gregory the Great   173
Grenoble   84, 86, 196, 213n86
Großgebauer, Theophil   140n26
Guyana   147n45

Halle/Saale   9, 14, 16, 18, 135, 160n81
Hamburg   133, 145
Handewitt   133, 157n61
Hartmann, Johann Ludwig   178n115
heathens   14, 20, 38, 40, 139, 143–147, 150, 151, 153, 173, 179, 183
Helmont, Franciscus Mercurius van   184n133
Helmstedt   133
heretics   24, 34, 37, 38, 51, 73, 140–141, 171–172

Hiel, see Hendrik Janssen van Barrefelt
Hoburg, Christian   137, 158n65
Hollgraffen (Hoellgrafe, Holgraf)   185n136
Holstein   138n16, 157n61, 158
Holtzhausen, Johann Christoph   159, 160n78
Honselerdijk   134
Horb, Heinrich   182n123
Hormuz Island   146n43
Huguenots   12, 20–21, 84–85, 89–91, 92, 93n24, 109–112, 117–118, 124, 132, 181, 189, 192–200, 202n53, 204n57, 205n58, 206n60, 208n69, 210, 211n79, 219n109, 220n112, 223n119, 233n142, 236n145
Hus, Jan   23, 24, 28, 29, 76

iatrochemistry   84, see also alchemy
Idolatry   43, 62, 78, 96, 99, 102, 143, 153, 156, 162, 180, 187–188, 209, 216, 236
Illuminati of Avignon   190
Isaiah, biblical prophet   41, 43, 46, 49–56, 62, 63, 64, 66, 70, 75, 77, 78, 79, 99, 116, 232, 233
Israel   3, 10, 53, 58, 67, 99, 114, 145, 148, 169, 203, 225, 243

Jacobites   190
Jakoubek of Stříbro   24, 26, 27, 28, 29, 30, 44
Jamaica   185n138
James II, King of England, Scotland and Ireland   91, 120n83, 125, 209n74, 210, 213
Jansenism   14, 190, see also Convulsionaries of Saint-Médard
Jean de Roquetaillade (John of Rupescissa)   4, 87, 99
Jena   182n126
Jeremiah, biblical prophet   16, 18, 44, 49, 50, 52, 53–55, 62, 65, 68, 79, 154, 156, 168, 235
Jerusalem   52, 53, 66, 116, 145, 148n46, 234, 237
Jesu, Thomas à   146n42
Jesuits   13, 88, 98, 111, 139, 146, 172
Jesus Christ   25, 26, 30, 32, 35–46, 48–54, 56, 58, 60–68, 70–78, 80–82, 86, 93, 94, 106n58, 115, 116, 119, 147n44, 202, 203, see also Second Coming of Christ

Jews   3–4, 14, 37, 46, 95, 99, 111, 116, 117, 134, 139, 143–148, 150, 151, 153, 156, 173, 179, 192, 213–214, 225, 233–237, 239, 242
Jurien / Jewrin, *see* Bathurst, Anne
Jurieu, Pierre   20, 84–85, 86n5, 89–90, 92, 95n29, 127–130, 195, 196, 202n53, 207n64

Kaiserstein, Salomon von, *see* Kuhlmann, Quirinus
Kampen   134
Katwijk   134
Knyphausen, Dodo Freiherr von   182n124
Königsberg   133, 159
Kortholt / Karthold, Dr [*pseud.*]   185n140
Kortholt (senior), Christian   157, 178n111
Kotter / Kotterus, Christoph   89, 92, 95–96, 100n52, 113, 115, 118
Krausemark   184n132
Kromayer, Hieronymus   176n91
Kuhlmann, Quirinus   140, 141, 160n79, 182–183n126, 183n127&128, 184, 185n137, 186

Labadie, Jean de   134, 176n97, 189
Labadists   140, 141, 177n98, 180n119
Labrousse, Suzette   191
Lafayette, marquis de   199
Languedoc   98, 127, 191, 192–195, 197–198
Lautenbach, Conrad   159n76
Lead, Jane   141n29, 142n33, 171n83, 172n85, 184, 187n149
League of Augsburg   106
Lefèvre d'Étaples, Jacques   177n104
Leiden   160n79, 182n126
Leipzig   133
Lesser Poland   151n48
Lindaw, Magdalena von   182n126, 183n127, 185n137
London   14, 135, 182n126, 184, 197, 198, 217, 220n114, 221n117, 226n125, *see also* England
Loosduinen   134
Loudun, possessed nuns of   189
Louis XIV, King of France   20, 85, 89, 91, 95, 100n52, 101–102, 108, 110, 112n69, 113n71, 125n89, 189, 192, 195, 211n79, 219n109
Lübeck   145n39, 182n126, 185
Luppius, Andreas   160n79

Luther, Martin   6, 8, 9, 11, 14, 16–18, 139, 154, 155, 156, 157n58&59, 173, 176
Lutherans / Lutheran church   19, 20, 133–134, 139, 140, 144, 145n39&40, 146, 151, 155, 156, 160, 179, 182, 186n143

Malesherbes, Guillaume-Chrétien de Lamoignon de   199
Marcillac, Jean Louis Lecointe de   197
Marion, Elie   198, 199, 228n130
Maroger (leader of the Couflaïres)   193
marriage   45, 71, 74, 76, 186, 194n22
martyrdom   30, 85, 97, 118, 192, 215n97, 216n101, 221, 233n142
Mary II, Queen of England, Scotland, and Ireland   135
Massard, Jacques   20, 84–92, 103n54, 127n95, 129n100, 131–132, 196
Mather, Cotton   195, 212n84
May (senior), Johann Heinrich   176n94
Mehmed IV, Sultan of the Ottoman Empire   95n32, 182n126
Meineke, Joachim   183n126
Meisner (the younger), Balthasar   157n59, 177n109
Mennonites   134, 135, 177
Mesmer, Franz-Anton   191
Meyfahrt / Meyfart, Johann Matthäus   157, 177n107
Micraelius, Johannes   156n57
millenarianism   1, 5, 7–10, 14, 19, 20, 26n17, 84, 95n33, 183n126, 189, 191, 192, 194, 198–200, 217n102
millennium   3, 5, 8, 11, 21
miracles   45, 88, 125–131, 195–196, 214, 219, 224, *see also* cessationism
Miremont, Armand de Bourbon-Malause, marquis de   197, 198, 221n115
Missions / missionary works   14, 20, 139, 143, 144, 145, 146n42&43, 147n45, 150, 151, 199
Misson, François-Maximilien   197
Monster (village of)   134
Moravians   24, 73, 191
Moritz (Mauritius), Peter   140, 160n81, 186
Moscow   183n126&128
Moulin, Pierre du   85
Müller, Heinrich   157n60, 178n112
Multipliants   193, 198

Nagel, Paul 186n143
Nantes, Edict of (1598) 118, *see also* tolerance / toleration
  revocation of (1685) 20, 84, 85, 92, 104, 108n63, 109n65, 111–112, 118, 124–125, 127n95, 192, 195, 201n49, 202n55, 206, 230n133, 233n142
Natural philosophy 86–88, 186
Netherlands / Dutch Republic 14, 15, 85, 86, 112n70, 113, 133, 142, 152n49, 160n81, 184n132
Neudorf 177n98
New Jerusalem 10, 11, 160n80, 171n83, *see also* Revelation, Book of
New Zionists 198–199, 288–231
Niclas, Hendrik 184n135
Nordermann, Conrad 183n126&128
Nostradamus 87–90, 92, 96, 97–98, 100–114, 117, 118, 124–125, 191

Olivi, Pierre de Jean (Peter John) 4, 5
Overbeek, Johann 184n132

Paew, Esther Michaelis de 183n126–127, 185n139
Papacy / Pope 5, 23, 27, 28, 37, 93–108, 113, 123, 124, 172, 230
Paracelsus / Paracelsianism 84, 86
Pelagianism 180, 186
Pella 148n46
Penn, William 137
persecution 2, 6, 20, 29, 30, 34, 37, 43n109, 46, 51, 69, 75, 84, 85, 95n30, 138, 141, 145, 148, 150, 153, 156, 159, 163, 166, 171, 181, 186, 192–194, 197, 203–205, 210, 219n109, 223n119, 233n142, 236, 238
Petri (Petersen), Friedrich 158n71
Philadelphia (church of) 171n83
Philadelphians / Philadelphian Society 140, 141, 142, 171n83, 184, 186–187, 198
Pietists / Pietism 14, 16, 133–135, 173, 174, 195
Pikart 26n16, 81, 83n467
Piker, Johann 159n73
Pinel, Michel 190
Poiret, Pierre 141, 180n121, 181, 182
Pomarius [Baumgart], Samuel 140n26, 145n39, 155n54
Poniatowska / Poniatovie, Krystyna / Christine 89, 100n52, 113, 115, 118

Pontard, Pierre 191
Pordage, John 186n146
Potinius, Conrad 157n63
Praetorius, Elias, *see* Hoburg, Christian
Prague 24–27, 28, 30, 31–33, 44, 45, 51, 58, 65, 72, 73, 81
predestination 5, 229n131
Příbram, Jan 33, 77
primitive Church 25, 40, 52, 55, 75, 149
Pufendorf, Samuel 176n93

Quakers 134, 139–140, 145, 146, 160, 163, 175–177, 184, 186, 187, 191, 196–197, 198, 199, 215n97, 216n101
Quietists 140, 145, 160, 173, 198n36

Rabaut, Paul 21, 199–200, 232, 237n146
Rabaut Saint-Etienne, Jean-Paul 199–200, 232n137
Raoux, Daniel 196–197, 215n97
Rathmann, Hermann 157, 158n64
Reformation 1–19, 21, 62, 85, 88, 95, 97–101, 133, 168
refugees, religious 84, 112, 119, 123, 184n132, 197
Reiser, Anton 178n114
religious nonconformists, *see* dissenters
Revelation, Book of 3, 5, 7, 8, 9, 10, 43, 48, 53, 56, 67, 75, 76, 78, 82, 84, 85, 87, 88, 93–95, 173, 184, 218
  beasts 60, 85, 94, 96, 217, 219n110, 224, 226
  eternal damnation 78, 98
  fall of Babylon 78, 115
  new Jerusalem 67, 75, 76
  seven churches prophecy 150
  seven seals prophecy 50n171, 115, 126, 150
  seven trumpets prophecy 48, 95, 109, 114, 150
  seven vials / bowls prophecy 82, 150, 220
  time periods mentioned in 56, 62, 65, 89, 93–94, 202n53
  two witnesses prophecy 85, 90, 94, 95n29, 96, 97, 103, 111, 114, 118, 202n53
  whore of Babylon 43, 181
Richelieu, cardinal Armand Jean du Plessis 109n65, 111, 189

INDEX

Riga   160n80
Robespierre, Maximilien de   191, 200
Rochegude, marquis de   206n61
Rochette, François   194
Rostock   133, 159n77
Rothe, Johannes   134, 182n125&126
Rotterdam   134, 196

Sabbarthon, Joseph   187
Saint Bartholomew's Day Massacre (1572)   90, 106, 117–118, 125
Saint-Martin, Louis-Claude de   191
Salvation   29, 38, 39, 47, 60, 70, 139, 144, 146n42, 149, 150, 153, 161, 180, 184, *see also* predestination
Satan   11, 37, 38, 147, 148, 154, 157n59, 163–168, 170, 178, 180, 201, 218, 219, 224–226, *see also* Devil
Saubertus (senior), Johannes   157, 177n107
Schott, William   183n129, 184
Sclei (Scleus), Bartholomäus   139, 151n48, 156n56
Second Coming of Christ   5, 8, 10, 13, 75, 85n3, 193
sectarianism   143, 147, 173, 176, 179
sects   58n264, 134, 136n9, 137n14, 139, 140, 143–152, 154, 159, 160n80, 161, 165–181, 188, 190n6, 193, 198–199, 230
Seidenbecher, Georg Lorenz   140n26
Sigismund of Luxembourg, King of Hungary and Holy Roman Emperor   25n111, 45n122
Smyrna   185
Socinians / Socinianism   134, 175, 177, 180, 186
Spener, Philipp Jakob   135, 139, 157n59, 158n67&68, 173n88, 176, 177
Spitzel   157
Sulzbach   134
Surinam   147n45
Sweden   160n80
Swedenborg, Emanuel   190
Swinderen, Hendrik van   187n150

Tábor   25, 26, 30, 32, 73, 74, 81
Tarnow, Paul   159n77

Tauler, Johannes   176n90
The Hague   126, 134, 135n6&8
Théot, Catherine   191
tolerance / toleration   15, 133, 192, 194, 238, *see also* dissenters
tongues, gift of   190, 193, 211n78, *see also* miracles
Trigault, Nicolas   146n43
true church   5, 6, 20, 133, 136, 139, 141, 143, 144, 148, 151, 163, 164, 173–175, 192, 196, *see also* Primitive Church
Turks   16, 101, 107, 139, 143, 144, 145, 150, 151, 153, 173, 178, 179
two witnesses of the Apocalypse, *see* Revelation, Book of

universal apostolic church   149, 161, 173, 174, 175
utraquism   24, 25, 29, 41n96
Utrecht   134

Vaillant, Pierre   190n6
Veiel, Elias   178n110
Vergerio (the younger), Pier Paolo   177n101
Versailles, Edict of (1787)   194, 199
Vincent, Isabeau   90, 103n54, 127n95, 195–196, 201, 202, 209n74, 210n77, 213n86
Viöl   158n71

Welz, Justianian Ernst von   139, 147n45
William III, King of England, Scotland, and Ireland   111, 112n69, 113n71, 135, 209n74, 210, 213n91
Winckler   157
Wittenberg   145n40
Woerden   134
Wolff, Johann   159n75, 173n86
Wyclif / Wycliffe, John   5, 6, 16, 23

Zesen, Philipp von   137n12
Zevi, Sabbatai   213n94
Zion   46, 52, 53, 60, 63, 64, 67, 79, 150, 160, 161, 171, 181, 219–221, 224, 228, 233, 238
Žižka, Jan   26, 27, 34, 81
Zwolle   134, 137, 138n16, 185